Editorial project:
2020 © **booq** publishing, S.L.
c/ Domènech, 7-9, 2º 1ª
08012 Barcelona, Spain
T: +34 93 268 80 88
www.booqpublishing.com

ISBN 978-84-9936-711-8

monsa
publications

© 2020 Instituto Monsa de ediciones, S.L.
c/ Gravina, 43
08930 Sant Adrià de Besós, Barcelona, Spain
T: +34 93 381 00 50
www.monsa.com
monsa@monsa.com

ISBN 978-84-17557-2429

Editorial coordinator:
Claudia Martínez Alonso

Art director:
Mireia Casanovas Soley

Editor:
Cayetano Cardelús Vidal

Layout:
Cristina Simó Perales

Printing in Spain

At the time of writing this introduction, our society is facing a pandemic unprecedented in modern history that is changing the living habits of millions of people and is likely to do so for years to come. Within this exceptional situation, the educational field is being especially punished by the closure of schools and universities, which has forced students from all over the world to continue their studies from their homes in a telematic way.

However, it is not so obvious that this educational system can replace the multiple factors that influence the education of children during their first years of life and the fundamental socialization processes that they acquire by attending schools and kindergartens. Learning at these stages is not primarily academic, but represents a process of discovery determined by the stimuli received from the environment and assimilated through the five senses. For this reason, architecture and design are fundamental in the construction of friendly and welcoming contexts that stimulate creativity and in which children can relate and develop their personality.

The projects brought together in this volume are great examples of how architecture approaches the design of educational spaces dedicated to the youngest children and reflects their needs with great sensitivity at a decisive stage in their development, adapting to new pedagogical systems that replace traditional models and introducing into their programmes the new realities of today's world, such as the advance of new technologies or concern for the environment and sustainability.

Zum Zeitpunkt des Verfassens dieser Einleitung steht unsere Gesellschaft vor einer in der modernen Geschichte beispiellosen Pandemie, die die Lebensgewohnheiten von Millionen von Menschen verändert und wahrscheinlich noch für Jahre verändern wird. Innerhalb dieser Ausnahmesituation wird der Bildungsbereich besonders durch die Schließung von Schulen und Universitäten bestraft, was Studenten aus aller Welt dazu zwingt, ihre Studien von zu Hause aus auf telematischem Wege fortzusetzen.

Es ist jedoch nicht so offensichtlich, dass dieses Bildungssystem die vielfältigen Faktoren ersetzen kann, die die Bildung der Kinder in den ersten Lebensjahren und die grundlegenden Sozialisationsprozesse, die sie durch den Besuch von Schulen und Kindergärten erwerben, beeinflussen. Das Lernen in diesen Phasen ist nicht in erster Linie akademisch, sondern stellt einen Entdeckungsprozess dar, der durch die von der Umwelt erhaltenen und über die fünf Sinne aufgenommenen Reize bestimmt wird. Aus diesem Grund sind Architektur und Design von grundlegender Bedeutung für den Aufbau freundlicher und einladender Kontexte, die die Kreativität anregen und in denen Kinder sich aufeinander beziehen und ihre Persönlichkeit entwickeln können.

Die in diesem Band versammelten Projekte sind großartige Beispiele dafür, wie die Architektur an die Gestaltung von Bildungsräumen für die Kleinsten herangeht und ihre Bedürfnisse in einer entscheidenden Phase ihrer Entwicklung mit großer Sensibilität widerspiegelt, indem sie sich an neue pädagogische Systeme anpasst, die traditionelle Modelle ersetzen, und in ihre Programme die neuen Realitäten der heutigen Welt einführt, wie etwa den Vormarsch neuer Technologien oder die Sorge um Umwelt und Nachhaltigkeit.

Au moment où nous rédigeons cette introduction, notre société est confrontée à une pandémie sans précédent dans l'histoire moderne qui modifie les habitudes de vie de millions de personnes et qui risque de le faire pendant des années. Dans cette situation exceptionnelle, le domaine de l'éducation est particulièrement pénalisé par la fermeture d'écoles et d'universités, ce qui a obligé des étudiants du monde entier à poursuivre leurs études depuis leur domicile de manière télématique.

Cependant, il n'est pas si évident que ce système éducatif puisse remplacer les multiples facteurs qui influencent l'éducation des enfants durant leurs premières années de vie et les processus fondamentaux de socialisation qu'ils acquièrent en fréquentant les écoles et les jardins d'enfants. L'apprentissage à ces stades n'est pas principalement académique, mais représente un processus de découverte déterminé par les stimuli reçus de l'environnement et assimilés par les cinq sens. C'est pourquoi l'architecture et le design sont fondamentaux dans la construction de contextes conviviaux et accueillants qui stimulent la créativité et dans lesquels les enfants peuvent s'identifier et développer leur personnalité.

Les projets rassemblés dans ce volume sont de bons exemples de la manière dont l'architecture aborde la conception d'espaces éducatifs dédiés aux plus jeunes et reflète leurs besoins avec une grande sensibilité à un stade décisif de leur développement, en s'adaptant aux nouveaux systèmes pédagogiques qui remplacent les modèles traditionnels et en introduisant dans leurs programmes les nouvelles réalités du monde actuel, comme le progrès des nouvelles technologies ou le souci de l'environnement et de la durabilité.

En el momento en que se redacta esta introducción, nuestra sociedad afronta una pandemia sin precedentes en la historia moderna que está modificando los hábitos de vida de millones de personas y que, con toda probabilidad, los modificará durante años. Dentro de esta excepcional situación, el ámbito educativo está siendo especialmente castigado con un cierre de colegios y universidades que ha obligado a alumnos de todo el mundo a proseguir sus estudios desde sus casas de forma telemática.

Sin embargo, no resulta tan evidente que este sistema de enseñanza pueda suplir los múltiples factores que influyen en la educación de los niños durante sus primeros años de vida y los fundamentales procesos de socialización que adquieren al acudir a escuelas y jardines de infancia. El aprendizaje en estas etapas no se nutre principalmente de enseñanzas académicas, sino que representa un proceso de descubrimiento determinado por los estímulos recibidos del entorno y asimilado a través de los cinco los sentidos. Por este motivo, la arquitectura y el diseño resultan fundamentales en la construcción de contextos amables y acogedores que estimulen la creatividad y en los que los niños puedan relacionarse y desarrollar su personalidad.

Los proyectos reunidos en este volumen son grandes ejemplos de cómo la arquitectura aborda el diseño de los espacios educativos dedicados a los más pequeños y refleja con gran sensibilidad sus necesidades en una etapa decisiva para su desarrollo, adaptándose a nuevos sistemas pedagógicos que sustituyen a los modelos tradicionales e introduciendo en sus programas las nuevas realidades del mundo actual, como son el avance de las nuevas tecnologías o la preocupación por el medio ambiente y la sostenibilidad.

1+1>2 Architects
Hoang Thuc Hao

// PROJECTS //

1. SENTIA SCHOOL
2. JUNGLE FLOWER
3. DA HOP SCHOOL

http://hoangthuchao.vn/duanchitiet/38/sentia-shool.htm
http://hoangthuchao.vn/duanchitiet/35/jungle-flower.htm
http://hoangthuchao.vn/duanchitiet/1065/da-hop-school-.htm

1+1>2 Architects
Hoang Thuc Hao

1.

2.

3.

Globalization has brought the world together, however it has also brought the disadvantaged groups away from the majority. My approach is to aggregate different resources: architects, NGOs, social groups, local communities, university and institutions, to help build projects together for disadvantage communities.
In my design, modern technologies combine with local construction method and material to bring a contemporary look for vernacular architecture. And, on top of all, it needs to be self-sustained, livable, as at the end it will be used by the locals.
Practicing in community architecture has helped me reveal the beauty of local values; and give me the happiness of the ability to connect people and support them. It also shows me the unlimited ability of architecture to raise happiness, for the architects, for the users, and for the building itself. This is the core value of our firm and myself: architecture is not merely buildings and space. It is happiness.

La mondialisation a rapproché le monde, mais elle a aussi éloigné les groupes défavorisés de la majorité. Mon approche consiste à regrouper différentes ressources : architectes, ONG, groupes sociaux, communautés locales, universités et institutions, pour aider à construire ensemble des projets en faveur des communautés défavorisées.
Dans ma conception, les technologies modernes se combinent avec les méthodes et les matériaux de construction locaux pour donner un aspect contemporain à l'architecture vernaculaire. Et, par-dessus tout, elle doit être autonome, vivable, car à la fin elle sera utilisée par les locaux.
La pratique de l'architecture communautaire m'a aidé à révéler la beauté des valeurs locales ; et m'a donné le bonheur de pouvoir relier les gens et les soutenir. Cela me montre également la capacité illimitée de l'architecture à susciter le bonheur, pour les architectes, pour les utilisateurs et pour le bâtiment lui-même. C'est la valeur fondamentale de notre cabinet et de moi-même : l'architecture n'est pas seulement un bâtiment et un espace. C'est le bonheur.

Die Globalisierung hat die Welt zusammengebracht, aber sie hat auch die benachteiligten Gruppen von der Mehrheit entfernt. Mein Ansatz besteht darin, verschiedene Ressourcen zusammenzuführen: Architekten, NGOs, soziale Gruppen, lokale Gemeinschaften, Universitäten und Institutionen, um gemeinsam Projekte für benachteiligte Gemeinschaften zu bauen.
In meinem Entwurf verbinden sich moderne Technologien mit lokalen Baumethoden und Materialien, um einen zeitgemäßen Look für volkstümliche Architektur zu schaffen. Und zu allem Überfluss muss es selbstversorgend und bewohnbar sein, da es am Ende von den Einheimischen genutzt wird.
Die Praxis der Gemeinschaftsarchitektur hat mir geholfen, die Schönheit der lokalen Werte zu enthüllen und mir das Glück zu geben, Menschen miteinander zu verbinden und sie zu unterstützen. Es zeigt mir auch die unbegrenzte Fähigkeit der Architektur, das Glück zu wecken, für die Architekten, für die Nutzer und für das Gebäude selbst. Dies ist der Kernwert unseres Unternehmens und meiner Person: Architektur ist nicht nur Gebäude und Raum. Sie ist Glück.

La globalización ha unido al mundo, pero también ha alejado a los grupos desfavorecidos de la mayoría. Mi enfoque consiste en agregar diferentes recursos: arquitectos, ONG, grupos sociales, comunidades locales, universidades e instituciones, para ayudar a construir juntos proyectos para las comunidades desfavorecidas.
En mi diseño, las tecnologías modernas se combinan con el método y material de construcción local para dar un aspecto contemporáneo a la arquitectura vernácula. Y, por encima de todo, necesita ser auto-sostenible, habitable, ya que al final será utilizado por los locales.
Practicar en la arquitectura comunitaria me ha ayudado a revelar la belleza de los valores locales; y me da la felicidad de la capacidad de conectar a la gente y apoyarla. También me muestra la capacidad ilimitada de la arquitectura para elevar la felicidad, para los arquitectos, para los usuarios y para el edificio mismo. Este es el valor central de nuestra empresa y de mí mismo: la arquitectura no es solo edificios y espacio, es la felicidad.

SENTIA SCHOOL

LOCATION: **TRUNG VAN COMMUNE, TU LIEM DISTRICT, HANOI CITY, VIETNAM**
PHOTOS: **© SON VU**

The school is structured in three blocks differentiated by their program and arranged in a zigzag to adapt to an asymmetrical site. This organization generates a series of playgrounds and gardens that provide natural light and ventilation and reduce the noise level. The roof of the building is developed on an inclined plane and houses a garden organised in a playful manner that promotes the interest of the students in agriculture and biology. Together with the gardens on the lower level, it also becomes a green lung for the tall buildings surrounding the school. The design of the façades contains a fun set of windows with different positions and sizes. The solar protection elements and the vertical slats of the volume that houses the canteen and the multifunctional space provide a cheerful note of colour that stands out from the predominant white and brown.

L'école est structurée en trois blocs différenciés par leur programme et disposés en zigzag pour s'adapter à un site asymétrique. Cette organisation génère une série de terrains de jeux et de jardins qui fournissent une lumière et une ventilation naturelles et réduisent le niveau de bruit. Le toit du bâtiment est développé sur un plan incliné et abrite un jardin organisé de manière ludique qui favorise l'intérêt des étudiants pour l'agriculture et la biologie. Avec les jardins du niveau inférieur, il devient également un poumon vert pour les grands bâtiments qui entourent l'école. La conception des façades contient un ensemble amusant de fenêtres de différentes positions et tailles. Les éléments de protection solaire et les lattes verticales du volume qui abrite la cantine et l'espace multifonctionnel apportent une note de couleur joyeuse qui se démarque du blanc et du marron prédominants.

Die Schule ist in drei Blöcke gegliedert, die sich durch ihr Programm unterscheiden und in einem Zickzack angeordnet sind, um sich an einen asymmetrischen Standort anzupassen. Diese Organisation erzeugt eine Reihe von Spielplätzen und Gärten, die für natürliches Licht und Belüftung sorgen und den Lärmpegel reduzieren. Das Dach des Gebäudes ist auf einer schiefen Ebene entwickelt und beherbergt einen spielerisch angelegten Garten, der das Interesse der Studierenden an Landwirtschaft und Biologie fördert. Zusammen mit den Gärten auf der unteren Ebene wird es auch zu einer grünen Lunge für die hohen Gebäude, die die Schule umgeben. Die Gestaltung der Fassaden enthält eine lustige Reihe von Fenstern mit verschiedenen Positionen und Größen. Die Sonnenschutzelemente und die vertikalen Lamellen des Volumens, das die Kantine und den Multifunktionsraum beherbergt, sorgen für eine fröhliche Farbigkeit, die sich von dem vorherrschenden Weiß und Braun abhebt.

La escuela se estructura en tres bloques diferenciados por su programa y dispuestos en zigzag para adaptarse a un solar asimétrico. Esta organización genera una serie de patios de juego y jardines que aportan luz y ventilación natural y reducen el nivel de ruido. La cubierta del edificio se desarrolla en un plano inclinado y alberga un jardín organizado de forma lúdica, que promueve el interés de los alumnos por la agricultura y la biología. Junto a los jardines del nivel inferior, se convierte también en un pulmón verde para los edificios altos que rodean la escuela. El diseño de las fachadas contiene un divertido juego de ventanas con diferentes posiciones y tamaños. Sus elementos de protección solar y las lamas verticales del volumen que alberga la cantina y el espacio multifuncional aportan una alegre nota de color que destaca sobre el blanco y el marrón predominantes.

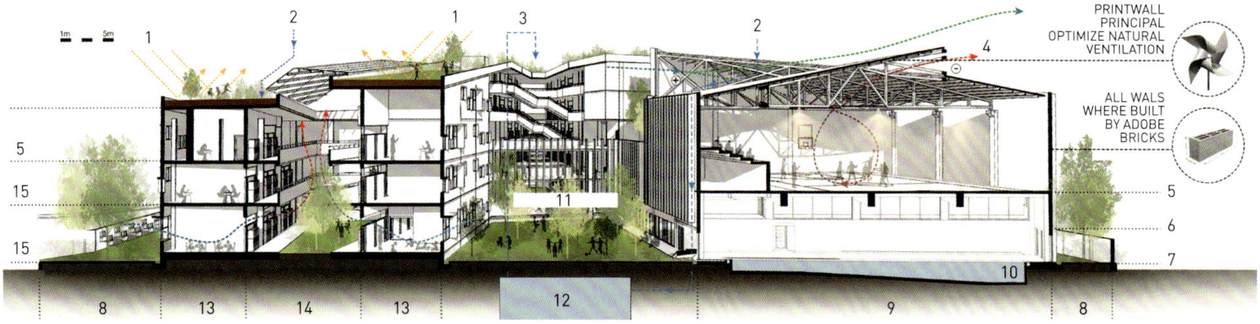

Section

1. Solar radiation
2. Rainwater collection
3. Irrigation
4. Natural ventilation promoted by pressure difference
5. Gym
6. Canteen
7. Kitchen
8. Greenery
9. Multi-purpose sport hall
10. Swimming pool
11. Central playground
12. Rainwater storage for irrigation and fire-fighting
13. Classroom
14. Playground
15. Primary
16. Roof top garden

JUNGLE FLOWER

LOCATION: **LUNG LUONG VILLAGE, THUONG NUNG COMMUNE, VO NHAI DISTRICT, THAI NGUYEN PROVINCE, VIETNAM**
PHOTOS: **© SON VU**

Located in a poor, hard-to-reach village in the mountains of northern Vietnam, the new Lung Luong Primary School appears like a fresh jungle flower, in bright colours and with a modern visual language. The aim of the project is to improve the living conditions of the village children, most of whom belong to the Mong ethnic group, by creating a comfortable school that fights against a harsh natural environment and ensures standards of lighting, ventilation and sound insulation. The building is located on a steep peak and is developed in different units that sit on the ground respecting the topography, connected by a winding corridor that becomes a mountain road. Recycled earth bricks from the excavation were used in the construction, which reduce costs and bring balance to the interior temperature.

In einem armen, schwer zugänglichen Dorf in den Bergen Nordvietnams gelegen, erscheint die neue Lung-Luong-Grundschule wie eine frische Dschungelblume, in leuchtenden Farben und mit einer modernen Bildsprache. Ziel des Projekts ist es, die Lebensbedingungen der Dorfkinder, die meist der ethnischen Gruppe der Mong angehören, zu verbessern, indem eine komfortable Schule geschaffen wird, die gegen eine raue natürliche Umgebung ankämpft und Standards bei Beleuchtung, Belüftung und Schalldämmung gewährleistet. Das Gebäude liegt auf einem steilen Gipfel und wird in verschiedenen Einheiten entwickelt, die unter Berücksichtigung der Topographie auf dem Boden stehen und durch einen gewundenen Korridor verbunden sind, der zu einer Bergstraße wird. Für den Bau wurden recycelte Erdsteine aus dem Aushub verwendet, was die Kosten senkt und die Innentemperatur ins Gleichgewicht bringt.

Située dans un village pauvre et difficile d'accès dans les montagnes du nord du Vietnam, la nouvelle école primaire Lung Luong apparaît comme une fleur de jungle fraîche, dans des couleurs vives et avec un langage visuel moderne. L'objectif du projet est d'améliorer les conditions de vie des enfants du village, dont la plupart appartiennent à l'ethnie mongo, en créant une école confortable qui lutte contre un environnement naturel difficile et assure des normes d'éclairage, de ventilation et d'isolation acoustique. Le bâtiment est situé sur un pic escarpé et se développe en différentes unités qui s'assoient sur le sol en respectant la topographie, reliées par un couloir sinueux qui devient une route de montagne. Des briques de terre recyclée provenant de l'excavation ont été utilisées dans la construction, ce qui réduit les coûts et équilibre la température intérieure.

Situada en una aldea pobre y de difícil acceso de las montañas del norte de Vietnam, la nueva escuela primaria Lung Luong aparece como una flor fresca de la jungla, en colores vivos y con un lenguaje visual moderno. El objetivo del proyecto es mejorar las condiciones de vida de los niños de la aldea, pertenecientes en su mayoría a la etnia mong, creando una escuela confortable que luche contra un entorno natural duro y garantice unos estándares de iluminación, ventilación y aislamiento acústico. El edificio se ubica en un pico escarpado y se desarrolla en diferentes unidades que se asientan en el terreno respetando la topografía, conectados mediante un corredor sinuoso que se transforma en un camino de montaña. En la construcción se utilizaron ladrillos de tierra reciclada procedente de la excavación, que rebajan los costos y aportan equilibrio a la temperatura interior.

1. Kindergarten
2. Multifunction hall
3. Administration
4. Stage
5. Primary playground
6. Primary
7. Entrance
8. Playground
9. Kitchen for kindergarten
10. Water tank
11. WC
12. Kitchen & dining room
13. Experimental garden
14. Teacher room
15. Studens hostel

Ground floor plan

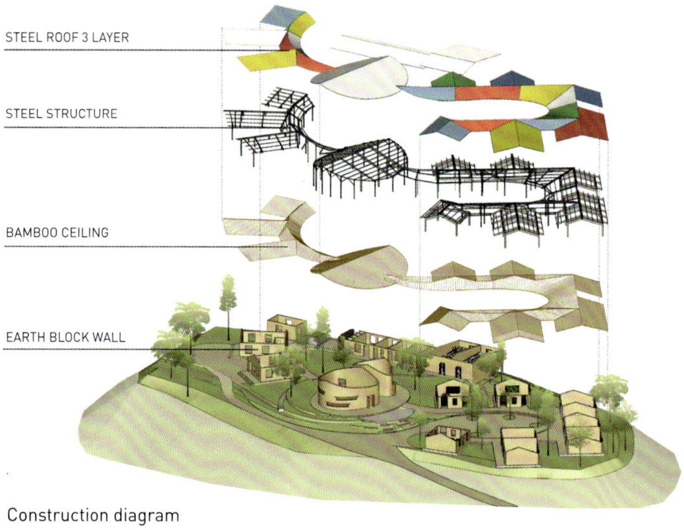

Construction diagram

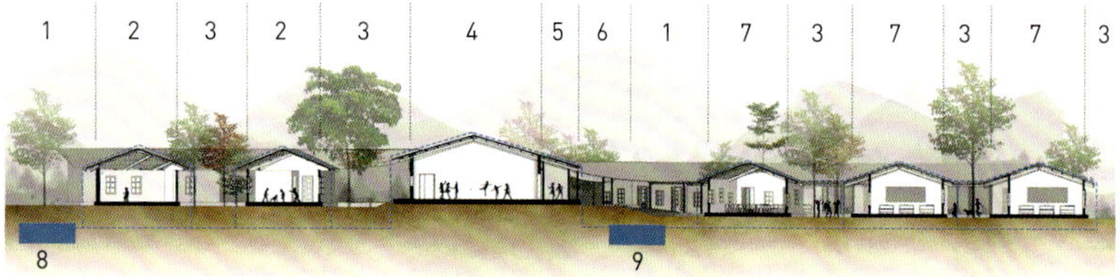

1. Playground
2. Kindergarten
3. Garden
4. Community house
5. Lobby
6. Stage
7. Primary
8. Water tank for kindergarten
9. Water tank for primary

Section

A SCHOOL BEING A MOUNTAIN BEING A SCHOOL, THE SPACES BETWEEN THE CLASSES ARE SLOTS MAKING AN ARCHITECTURAL IMAGE PASTED ON THE TERRAIN.

1. Steel roof 3 player
2. Wood door
3. Earth block
4. Aluminium window

Elevation

DA HOP SCHOOL

LOCATION: **ZEN VILLAGE, HUU NGHI WARD, HOA BINH CITY, VIETNAM**
PHOTOS: © **OKI PHOTOGRAPH**

The concept of this lively school is inspired by friendship, harmony with culture, nature and people. Through a variety of versatile spaces, children develop and learn in a familiar and welcoming context, while playing, experimenting and exploring freely. Its design is based on movement, interlacing several buildings linked by exterior corridors and located under a crinkled roof that evokes the surrounding mountains, and whose shape is inspired by the movement of children during traditional play. The organisation of the building on a north-south axis optimises ventilation and natural lighting. A colourful roof, inspired by the fabric patterns of the region's ethnic groups, provides ecological insulation, protects against noise and channels rainwater collection for later use.

Das Konzept dieser lebendigen Schule ist inspiriert von Freundschaft, Harmonie mit Kultur, Natur und Menschen. In einer Vielzahl von vielseitigen Räumen entwickeln und lernen Kinder in einem vertrauten und einladenden Kontext, während sie spielen, experimentieren und frei erforschen. Sein Entwurf basiert auf Bewegung, indem mehrere Gebäude, die durch äußere Korridore miteinander verbunden sind und sich unter einem Zickzackdach befinden, das an die umliegenden Berge erinnert und dessen Form von der Bewegung der Kinder beim traditionellen Spiel inspiriert ist, miteinander verflochten werden. Die Organisation des Gebäudes auf einer Nord-Süd-Achse optimiert die Belüftung und die natürliche Beleuchtung. Ein farbenfrohes Dach, das von den Stoffmustern der ethnischen Gruppen der Region inspiriert ist, sorgt für ökologische Isolierung, schützt vor Lärm und leitet das Regenwasser zur späteren Verwendung.

Le concept de cette école vivante est inspiré par l'amitié, l'harmonie avec la culture, la nature et les gens. Grâce à une variété d'espaces polyvalents, les enfants se développent et apprennent dans un contexte familier et accueillant, tout en jouant, en expérimentant et en explorant librement. Sa conception est basée sur le mouvement, entrelaçant plusieurs bâtiments reliés par des couloirs extérieurs et situés sous un toit en zigzag qui évoque les montagnes environnantes, et dont la forme est inspirée par le mouvement des enfants pendant les jeux traditionnels. L'organisation du bâtiment sur un axe nord-sud optimise la ventilation et l'éclairage naturel. Un toit coloré, inspiré par les motifs des tissus des groupes ethniques de la région, assure une isolation écologique, protège du bruit et canalise la collecte des eaux de pluie pour un usage ultérieur.

El concepto de esta animada escuela se inspira en la amistad, la armonía con la cultura, la naturaleza y las personas. A través de una gran diversidad de espacios versátiles, los niños se desarrollan y aprenden en un contexto familiar y acogedor, mientras juegan, experimentan y exploran libremente. Su diseño se basa en el movimiento, entrelazando varios edificios unidos por pasillos exteriores y situados bajo una cubierta en zigzag que evoca las montañas circundantes, y cuya forma se inspira en el movimiento de los niños durante un juego tradicional. La organización del edificio sobre un eje norte-sur optimiza la ventilación y la iluminación natural. Una colorida cubierta, inspirada en patrones de tejidos de grupos étnicos de la región, constituye un aislamiento ecológico que además protege del ruido y canaliza la recogida de agua de lluvia para su posterior aprovechamiento.

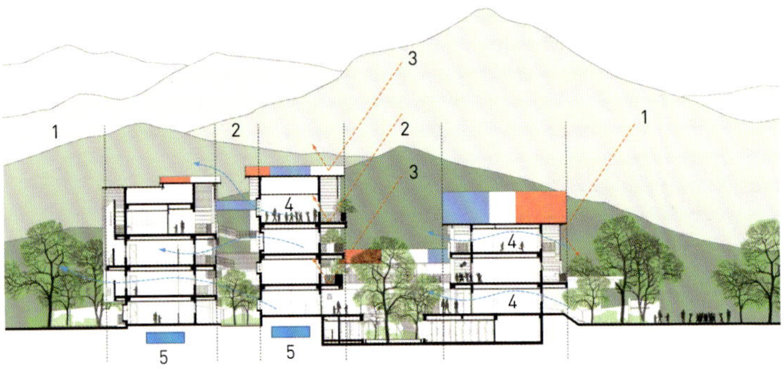

Section 1

1. Vegetation zone
2. Common yard
3. Natural lighting
4. Natural ventilation
5. Water tank

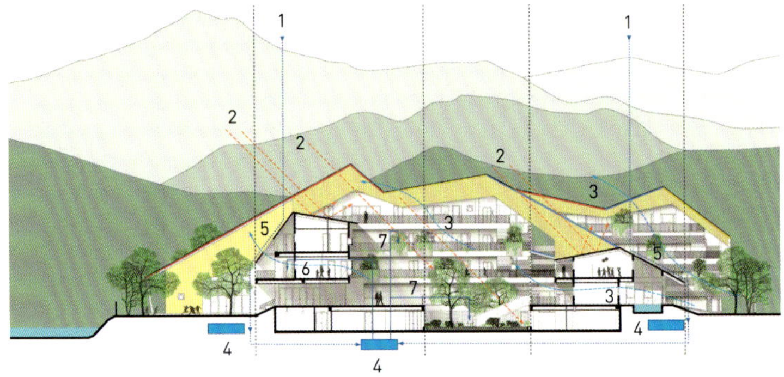

Section 2

1. Rain water
2. Natural lighting
3. Natural ventilation
4. Water tank
5. Collecting rainwater
6. Water toilet
7. Water for irrigation

Fourth floor plan

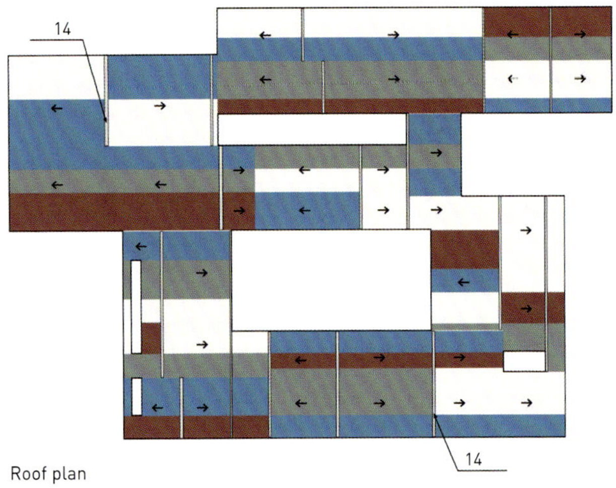

Roof plan

Second floor plan

Third floor plan

1. Class room
2. Multifunctional room
3. Play space
4. Canopy
5. WC
6. Void
7. Roof
8. Fine art room
9. Musical room
10. Administrative
11. Manager board
12. Meeting room
13. Teacher room
14. Gutter

abau | Antonio Blanco
architecture and urban planning

// PROJECTS //

1. KINDERGARTEN IN LA PAÑOLETA

www.abau.es
www.khayabau.co.za

abau | Antonio Blanco
architecture and urban planning

1.

ABAU is a small architecture practice based in Seville, Spain. Founded by architect Antonio Blanco Montero in 2001. By working on all scales, from furniture to urban planning, the office considers every project as a unique opportunity to explore the potential contained in the confluence of different elements at the same time and place. The aim of the practice is to bring solutions beyond the boundaries defined by the cultural, social and technological context, without denying that reality though. The fact of being small gives the opportunity to collaborate in every project with different professionals, and to put together a bespoke team. In the last years abau have expanded to Durban, South Africa, where is part of KHAYA + abau, an architecture practice focused on projects with high social impact.

ABAU est un petit cabinet d'architecture basé à Séville, en Espagne. Il a été fondé par l'architecte Antonio Blanco Montero en 2001. En travaillant à toutes les échelles, du mobilier à l'urbanisme, le bureau considère chaque projet comme une occasion unique d'explorer le potentiel contenu dans la confluence de différents éléments au même moment et au même endroit. L'objectif de la pratique est d'apporter des solutions au-delà des limites définies par le contexte culturel, social et technologique, sans pour autant nier cette réalité. Le fait d'être petit donne l'opportunité de collaborer dans chaque projet avec différents professionnels, et de constituer une équipe sur mesure. Au cours des dernières années, abau s'est développé à Durban, en Afrique du Sud, où il fait partie de KHAYA + abau, un cabinet d'architecture qui se concentre sur des projets à fort impact social.

ABAU ist ein kleines Architekturbüro mit sitz in Sevilla, Spanien, das 2001 vom Architekten Antonio Blanco Montero gegründet wurde. Das Büro arbeitet auf allen Ebenen, von Möbeln bis hin zur Stadtplanung, und betrachtet jedes Projekt als eine einzigartige Gelegenheit, das Potenzial zu erkunden, das im Zusammenwirken verschiedener Elemente zur gleichen Zeit und am gleichen Ort steckt. Ziel der Studie ist es, Lösungen jenseits der durch den kulturellen, sozialen und technologischen Kontext definierten Grenzen anzubieten, ohne diese Realität zu leugnen. Die Tatsache, dass wir klein sind, gibt uns die Möglichkeit, bei jedem Projekt mit verschiedenen Fachleuten durch ein maßgeschneidertes Team zusammenzuarbeiten. In den letzten Jahren expandierte Abau nach Durban (Südafrika), wo es Teil von KHAYA + abau ist, einem Architekturbüro, das sich auf Projekte mit hoher sozialer Wirkung konzentriert.

ABAU es un pequeño estudio de arquitectura con sede en Sevilla, España, fundado por el arquitecto Antonio Blanco Montero en 2001. Trabajando en todas las escalas, desde el mobiliario hasta la planificación urbana, el despacho considera cada proyecto como una oportunidad única para explorar el potencial contenido en la confluencia de diferentes elementos al mismo tiempo y en el mismo lugar. El objetivo del estudio es aportar soluciones más allá de los límites definidos por el contexto cultural, social y tecnológico, sin por ello negar esa realidad. El hecho de ser pequeño da la oportunidad de colaborar en cada proyecto con diferentes profesionales, a través de un equipo a medida. En los últimos años, Abau se ha expandido a Durban (Sudáfrica), donde forma parte de KHAYA + abau, un estudio de arquitectura centrado en proyectos de gran impacto social.

KINDERGARTEN IN LA PAÑOLETA

LOCATION: **CAMAS, SEVILLA, SPAIN**
PHOTOS: © **FERNANDO ALDA**

The location of this nursery in a development area close to a marginal zone where social housing and high-cost housing coexist, generated a series of tensions during the gestation of the project that resulted in a certain introverted character of the building. The configuration of the program, which also contemplates the use as a center for neighborhood meetings, and the elongated rectangular shape of the building cause the appearance of a series of patios that articulate the interior. A continuous roof rises in a controlled manner over certain areas to generate skylights that illuminate the distribution areas and provide indirect lighting for the classrooms. The chromatic composition of the building distances it from the clichés associated with design for children but at the same time confers a singularity that emanates good vibrations in such a peripheral environment.

L'implantation de cette pépinière dans une zone de développement proche d'une zone marginale où coexistent des logements sociaux et des logements à coût élevé, a généré une série de tensions pendant la gestation du projet qui ont abouti à un certain caractère introverti du bâtiment. La configuration du programme, qui prévoit également l'utilisation comme centre de réunions de quartier, et la forme rectangulaire allongée du bâtiment provoquent l'apparition d'une série de patios qui articulent l'intérieur. Un toit continu s'élève de manière contrôlée au-dessus de certaines zones pour générer des puits de lumière qui éclairent les zones de distribution et fournissent un éclairage indirect aux salles de classe. La composition chromatique de l'édifice l'éloigne des clichés associés au design pour enfants mais lui confère en même temps une singularité qui dégage de bonnes vibrations dans un environnement aussi marginal.

Die Lage dieser Kinderkrippe in einem Entwicklungsgebiet in der Nähe einer Randzone, in der Sozialwohnungen und teurer Wohnraum nebeneinander bestehen, führte während der Bauphase zu einer Reihe von Spannungen, die zu einem gewissen introvertierten Charakter des Gebäudes führten. Die Konfiguration des Programms, das auch die Nutzung als Zentrum für Nachbarschaftstreffen vorsieht, und die langgestreckte rechteckige Form des Gebäudes lassen eine Reihe von Innenhöfen entstehen, die das Innere artikulieren. Ein durchgehendes Dach erhebt sich kontrolliert über bestimmte Bereiche, um Oberlichter zu erzeugen, die die Verteilungsbereiche beleuchten und eine indirekte Beleuchtung für die Klassenräume bieten. Die chromatische Komposition des Gebäudes distanziert es von den Klischees, die mit Design für Kinder verbunden sind, verleiht ihm aber gleichzeitig eine Einzigartigkeit, die in einer solch marginalen Umgebung gute Schwingungen ausstrahlt.

La ubicación de esta guardería en un área de desarrollo próxima a una zona marginal donde conviven viviendas sociales y viviendas de elevado costo, generó una serie de tensiones durante la gestación del proyecto que dieron como resultado un cierto carácter introvertido del edificio. La configuración del programa, que contempla también el uso como centro de reuniones vecinales, y la alargada forma rectangular del edificio provocan la aparición de una serie de patios que articulan el interior. Una cubierta continua se eleva de manera controlada sobre determinadas áreas para generar unos lucernarios que iluminan las zonas de distribución y confieren iluminación indirecta a las aulas. La composición cromática del edificio lo aleja de los clichés relacionados con el diseño para niños pero a su vez confiere una singularidad que emana buenas vibraciones en un entorno tan marginal.

Sections

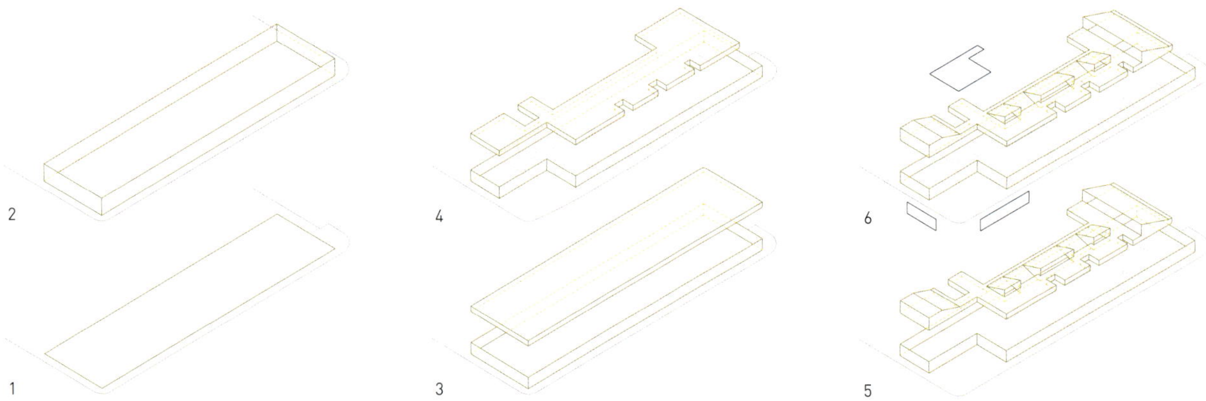

Construction diagrams

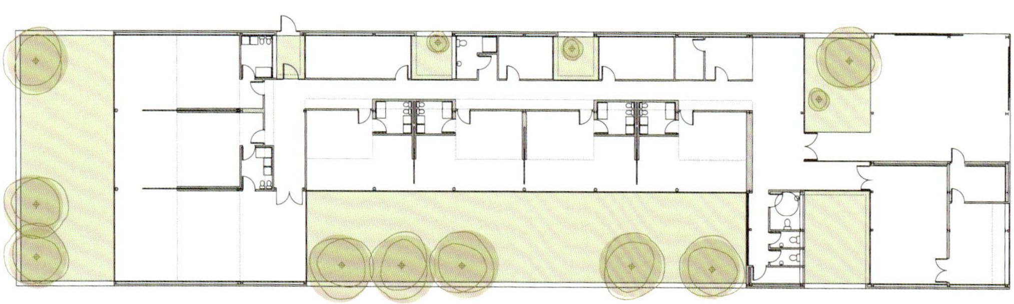

Floor plan

A2

ARCHIKON Architects

// PROJECTS //

1. VIZAFOGÓ KINDERGARTEN
2. FAIRYTALE KINDERGARTEN

www.archikon.hu

1.

2.

Founded in 1989 Archikon Architects in Budapest is responsible for the design of social, commercial, educational, residential, health care and mixed use projects. New build and reconstructions dedicated to communities, and innovative, sustainable solutions represent the majority of their portfolio, including the first 100 passive house apartment condominiums in Hungary. Along with realizing the transformation of monumental historic buildings, Archikon specialises in designing unique, high value real estates in the hotel and commercial investment sector. As a result of its innovative solutions, many of Archikon Architect's projects have been recognised by professional awards such as the Budapest Architecture Award of Excellence and the Hungarian Media's Architectural Prize, as well as the Hungarian nomination of the EUMiesaward and has been shortlisted for the Piranesi Award.

Das 1989 gegründete Architekturbüro Archikon Architects in Budapest entwirft Projekte in den Bereichen Soziales, Handel, Bildung, Wohnen, Gesundheitsfürsorge und gemischte Nutzung. Neubauten und Rekonstruktionen, die den Gemeinschaften und innovativen und nachhaltigen Lösungen gewidmet sind, machen den Großteil ihres Portfolios aus, darunter die ersten 100 Passivhaus-Wohnanlagen in Ungarn. Neben dem Umbau denkmalgeschützer historischer Gebäude ist Archikon auf die Gestaltung einzigartiger und hochwertiger Immobilien im Hotel- und gewerblichen Investitionsbereich spezialisiert. Aufgrund ihrer innovativen Lösungen wurden viele ihrer Projekte mit Fachpreisen wie dem Budapest Architecture Excellence Award und dem Hungarian Media Architecture Award sowie der ungarischen Nominierung für den EUMiesaward ausgezeichnet und für den Piranesi-Preis in die engere Wahl gezogen.

Fondé en 1989, Archikon Architects à Budapest est responsable de la conception de projets sociaux, commerciaux, éducatifs, résidentiels, de soins de santé et à usage mixte. Les nouvelles constructions et les reconstructions dédiées aux communautés, ainsi que les solutions innovantes et durables représentent la majorité de leur portefeuille, y compris les 100 premiers appartements en copropriété de maisons passives en Hongrie. Parallèlement à la réalisation de la transformation de bâtiments historiques monumentaux, Archikon se spécialise dans la conception de biens immobiliers uniques et de grande valeur dans le secteur de l'investissement hôtelier et commercial. Grâce à ses solutions innovantes, de nombreux projets d'Archikon Architect ont été reconnus par des prix professionnels tels que le Prix d'excellence de l'architecture de Budapest et le Prix d'architecture des médias hongrois, ainsi que par la nomination hongroise du EUMiesaward et ont été présélectionnés pour le Prix Piranesi.

Fundada en 1989, Archikon Architects en Budapest se encarga del diseño de proyectos sociales, comerciales, educativos, residenciales, de atención de la salud y de uso mixto. Las nuevas construcciones y reconstrucciones dedicadas a las comunidades y las soluciones innovadoras y sostenibles representan la mayor parte de su cartera, incluidos los primeros 100 conjuntos de apartamentos de casas pasivas en Hungría. Además de realizar la transformación de edificios históricos monumentales, Archikon se especializa en el diseño de bienes inmuebles únicos y de alto valor en el sector de la inversión hotelera y comercial. Como resultado de sus soluciones innovadoras, muchos de sus proyectos han sido reconocidos por premios profesionales como el Premio de Excelencia de Arquitectura de Budapest y el Premio de Arquitectura de los Medios de Comunicación Húngaros, así como la nominación húngara del EUmiesaward y ha sido preseleccionado para el Premio Piranesi.

VIZAFOGÓ KINDERGARTEN

LOCATION: **DISTRICT XIII, BUDAPEST, HUNGARY**
PHOTOS: **© TAMÁS BUJNOVSZKY**

The original prefabricated concrete kindergarten was built in a housing estate of the 1980s, as part of the socialist panel program near the Danube in Hungary, north of Budapest. During the modernization of the two-story, eight-room building, the narrow accessways and tight changing rooms were extended towards the classrooms, and the group rooms towards the courtyard. In front of the classrooms, a two-level, transitional, covered, open-air, wooden playground was created. With the redesign of the entrance hall and the passageway system, the building was organized around an inner atrium. The new extensions of the building mass have been covered with wood paneling, which turns into an open lamella in front of the covered terraces. Preserving and modernizing the existing building, the expansion has created a whole new, changed, but unified character.

Le jardin d'enfants original en béton préfabriqué a été construit dans un lotissement des années 1980, dans le cadre du programme de panneaux socialistes près du Danube en Hongrie, au nord de Budapest. Lors de la modernisation du bâtiment de deux étages et de huit pièces, les accès étroits et les vestiaires étroits ont été prolongés vers les salles de classe, et les salles de groupe vers la cour. Devant les salles de classe, un terrain de jeu en bois à deux niveaux, de transition, couvert et en plein air, a été créé. Avec le réaménagement du hall d'entrée et du système de passage, le bâtiment s'est organisé autour d'un atrium intérieur. Les nouvelles extensions de la masse du bâtiment ont été recouvertes de lambris en bois, qui se transforment en lamelle ouverte devant les terrasses couvertes. En préservant et en modernisant le bâtiment existant, l'extension a créé un tout nouveau caractère, changé mais unifié.

Die ursprüngliche Kindertagesstätte aus Betonfertigteilen wurde in den 1980er Jahren im Rahmen des sozialistischen Panelprogramms nördlich von Budapest in einer Wohnsiedlung gebaut. Bei der Modernisierung des zweigeschossigen, acht Gruppen umfassenden ...wurden die schmalen Eingänge Richtung Gruppenräume und diese wiederum richtung Hof erweitert. Vor den Klassenzimmern ..wurde im Aussenbereich als Übergangszone, ein zweistöckiger, überdachter Holzspielplatz angelegt. Mit der Neugestaltung der Eingangshalle und des Flursystems wurde das Gebäude um ein inneres Atrium herum organisiert. Die neuen Erweiterungen der Gebäudemasse wurden mit Holzpaneelen verkleidet, die vor den überdachten Terrassen Die Erweiterung des Gebäudemasse wurde mit Holzpaneelen verkleidet, welche vor den überdachten Terrassen in eine offene Lamellenfassade übergehen. Durch die Erhaltung und Modernisierung des bestehenden Gebäudes hat die Erweiterung einen völlig neuen, veränderten, aber einheitlichen Charakter geschaffen.

La guardería original de hormigón prefabricado fue construida en una urbanización de la década de 1980, como parte del programa de paneles socialistas al norte de Budapest. Durante la modernización del edificio de dos pisos y ocho habitaciones, los estrechos accesos y los estrechos vestuarios se ampliaron hacia las aulas, y las salas de grupo hacia el patio. Frente a las aulas se creó un patio de recreo de madera de dos niveles, transitorio y cubierto, al aire libre. Con el rediseño del vestíbulo de entrada y el sistema de pasillos, el edificio se organizó en torno a un atrio interior. Las nuevas extensiones de la masa de construcción se han cubierto con paneles de madera, que se convierten en una lámina abierta frente a las terrazas cubiertas. Preservando y modernizando el edificio existente, la ampliación ha creado un carácter totalmente nuevo, cambiado, pero unificado.

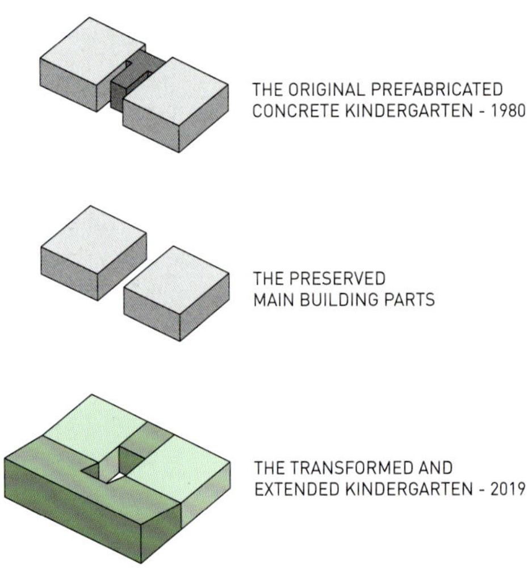

Concept figure

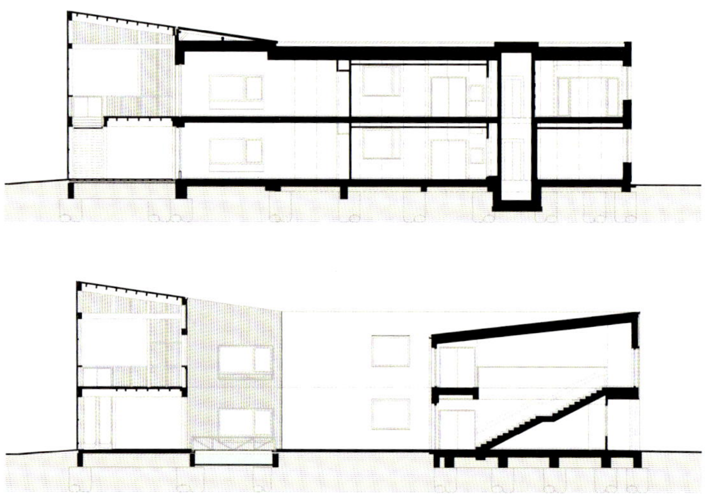

Sections

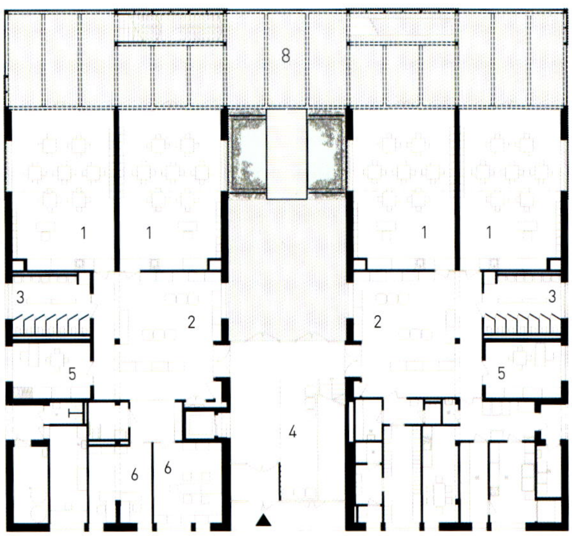

Ground floor plan

1. Classroom
2. Corridor / changing
3. Restroom
4. Foyer
5. Therapy room
6. Office / meeting
7. Gym
8. Wooden terrace - covered playground

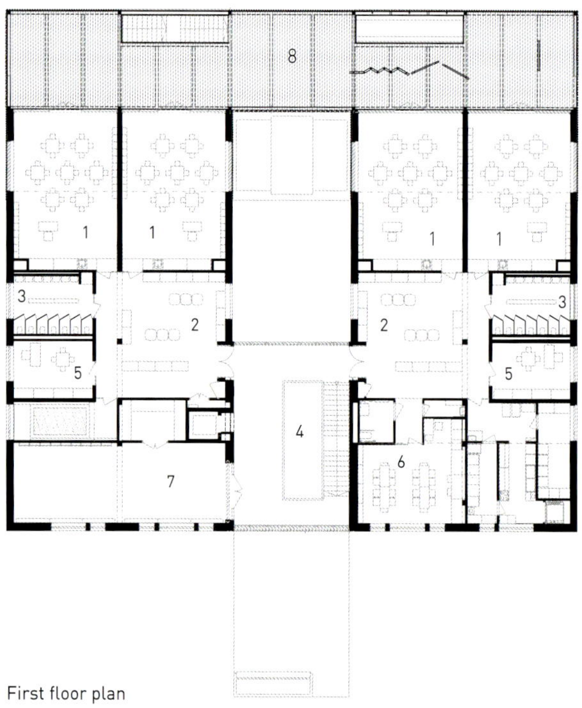

First floor plan

FAIRYTALE KINDERGARTEN

LOCATION: **DISTRICT XIII, BUDAPEST, HUNGARY**
PHOTOS: © **TAMÁS BUJNOVSZKY, BÁLINT JAKSA**

The Fairytale Kindergarten is the first passive house certified childcare institution in Hungary. The new building, which replaced the existing 8 classroom kindergarten, features 8-8 classrooms on the ground floor and first floor respectively. The custom-designed roof play garden acts as the fifth façade of the building in the urban setting, where children can play in a protected, shaded environment. The circular, square and triangular shapes of the roof terrace create a vertical connection with the interior changing rooms and accessways, through light wells. These unique design solutions help children feel at home, and well oriented. Unique, funny and lovely figures on the floors, walls, doors and glass are an integral part of the building. Walls with magnetic paint can be used to organize an exhibition of children's art in a moment.

Die Märchenkindergarten ist die erste als Passivhaus zertifizierte Kinderbetreuungseinrichtung in Ungarn, das den zuvor 8 gruppigen Kindergarten erstetzt hat, verfügt nun mit jeweils 8 Gruppenräumen im Erd- sowie im Obergeschoss. Ein speziell entworfener Spielplatz auf dem Dach fungiert als fünfte Fassade des Gebäudes in der städtischen Umgebung, wo Kinder in einer geschützten und schattigen Umgebung spielen können. Die runden, quadratischen und dreieckigen Formen der Dachterrasse schaffen durch Lichtschächte eine vertikale Verbindung zu den inneren Umkleideräumen und Zugängen. Diese Designlösung hilft den Kindern zur besseren Oreintierung und Wohlgefühl im Haus. Einzigartige, lustige und charmante Figuren auf den Böden, Wänden, Türen und Gläsern sind ein integraler Bestandteil des Gebäudes. Wandflächen mit magnetischem Farbenanstrich dienen als Organisations- und Ausstellungsfläche der Kinder.

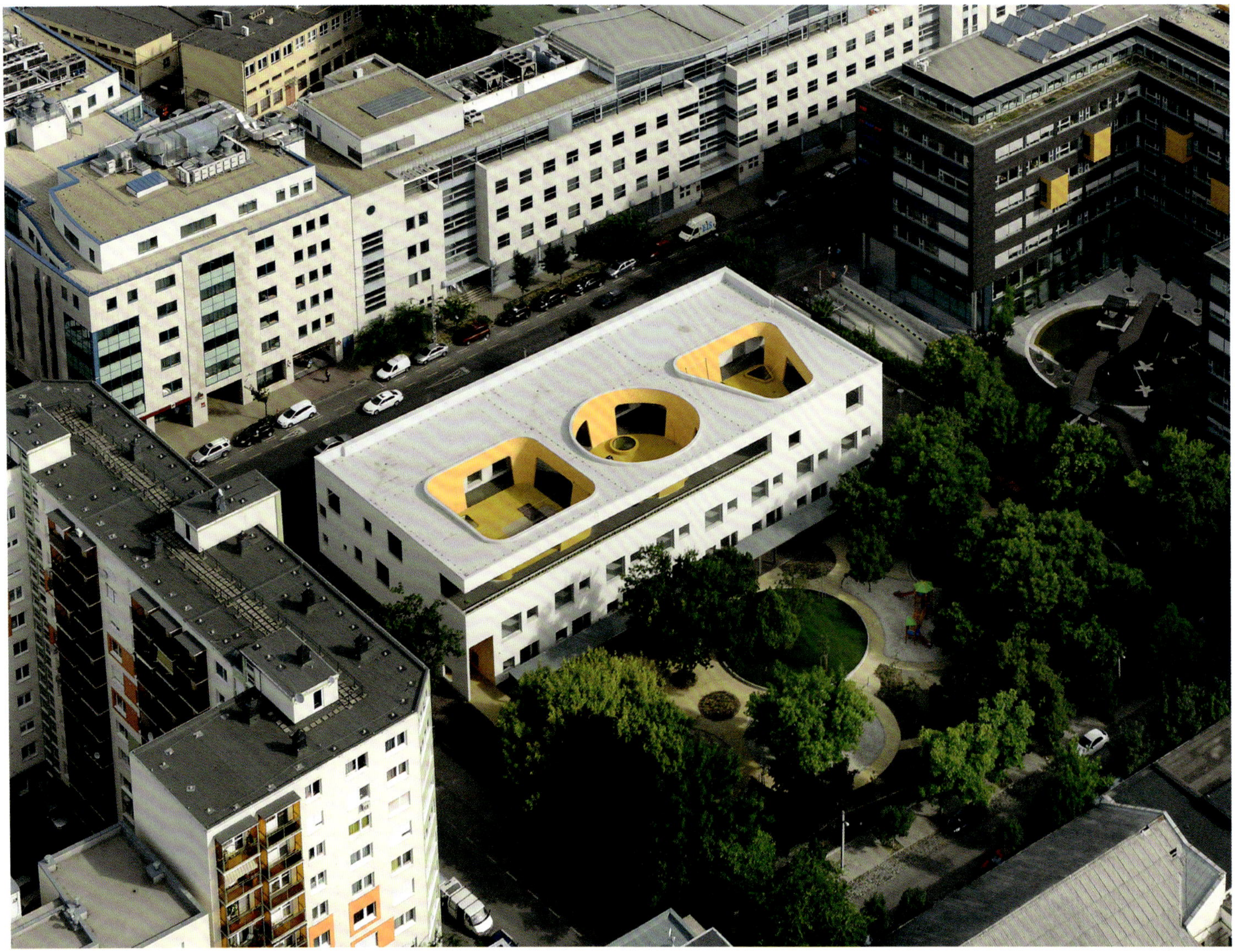

Le jardin d'enfants Fairytale est la première institution de garde d'enfants certifiée par la maison passive en Hongrie. Le nouveau bâtiment, qui a remplacé l'actuel jardin d'enfants de 8 classes, comprend 8 à 8 salles de classe au rez-de-chaussée et au premier étage respectivement. Le jardin d'enfants sur le toit, conçu sur mesure, constitue la cinquième façade du bâtiment dans le cadre urbain, où les enfants peuvent jouer dans un environnement protégé et ombragé. Les formes circulaires, carrées et triangulaires de la terrasse sur le toit créent une connexion verticale avec les vestiaires intérieurs et les accès, grâce à des puits de lumière. Ces solutions de conception uniques aident les enfants à se sentir chez eux et bien orientés. Des figures uniques, drôles et adorables sur les sols, les murs, les portes et les vitres font partie intégrante du bâtiment. Les murs avec peinture magnétique peuvent être utilisés pour organiser une exposition d'art pour enfants en un instant.

La Fairytale Kindergarten es la primera institución de cuidado de niños certificada como casa pasiva en Hungría. El nuevo edificio, que reemplazó al actual jardín de infancia de ocho aulas, cuenta con ocho aulas en la planta baja y ocho en el primer piso. Una zona de juegos ajardinada en el techo, diseñada a medida, actúa como la quinta fachada del edificio en el entorno urbano, donde los niños pueden jugar en un entorno protegido y sombreado. Las formas circulares, cuadradas y triangulares de la terraza del tejado crean una conexión vertical con los vestuarios interiores y los accesos, a través de pozos de luz. Estas soluciones de diseño ayudan a los niños a sentirse en casa, y bien orientados. Figuras únicas, divertidas y encantadoras en los suelos, paredes, puertas y cristales son una parte integral del edificio. Las paredes con pintura magnética pueden ser utilizadas para organizar exposiciones de arte infantil.

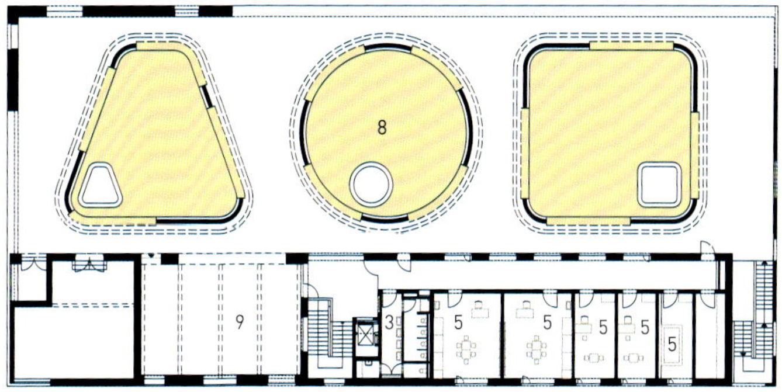

Second floor plan

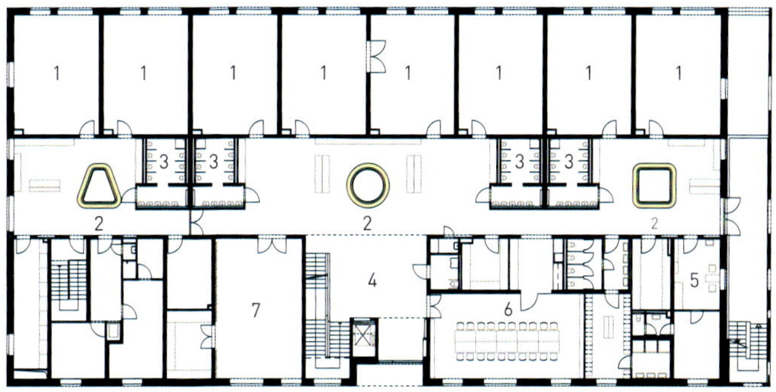

First floor plan

Ground floor plan

1. Classroom
2. Corridor / changing
3. Restroom
4. Foyer
5. Therapy room
6. Office / meeting
7. Gym
8. Roof terrace - covered playground
9. Roof terrace - open air theatre

Section

Architekten + Partner Dannien Roller

// PROJECTS //

1. DAY CARE CENTER MAX-PLANCK-CAMPUS TÜBINGEN

www.dannien-roller-architekten-partner.de

Architekten + Partner
Dannien Roller

1.

Architecture is not objective, but influenced by processes, requirements, budgets and cultural-spatial conditions. Our early cooperation with the client, already during the development of the task, creates a qualitative coherence between construction project, urban integration, space, form and material. This not only creates an unmistakable building culture, but also a high level of acceptance.
Our focus is on the workplace: the place where we spend most of our waking life. Although we live in a world that is becoming more and more mobile from day to day, administration, production, research, teaching, knowledge, information gathering and work are connected to physical places. This topos requires material, but also emotional criteria, which we respond with creativity, innovation and with outstanding design quality.

Architektur ist nicht objektiv, sondern beeinflusst durch Prozesse, Anforderungen, Budgets und kulturell-räumliche Gegebenheiten. Unsere frühe Zusammenarbeit mit dem Bauherrn bereits bei der Aufgabenentwicklung schafft eine qualitative Kohärenz zwischen Bauprojekt, städtebaulicher Einbindung, Raum, Form und Material. So entsteht nicht nur unverwechselbare Baukultur, sondern auch eine hohe Akzeptanz.
Unser Schwerpunkt liegt in der Beschäftigung mit dem Arbeitsplatz: dem Ort, an dem wir die meiste Zeit des wachen Lebens verbringen. Obwohl wir in einer Welt leben, die von Tag zu Tag mobiler wird, sind doch Verwaltung, Produktion, Forschung, Lehre, Wissen, Informationsbeschaffung und Arbeit mit physischen Orten verbunden. Dieser Topos bedingt materielle, aber auch emotionale Kriterien, die von uns kreativ, innovativ und mit herausragender Gestaltqualität beantwortet werden.

Architecture n'est pas objective, mais elle est influencée par les processus, les exigences, les budgets et les conditions culturelles et spatiales. Notre coopération précoce avec le client, déjà pendant le développement de la tâche, crée une cohérence qualitative entre le projet de construction, l'intégration urbaine, l'espace, la forme et le matériau. Cela crée non seulement une culture de construction sans équivoque, mais aussi un niveau d'acceptation élevé.
Nous nous concentrons sur le lieu de travail : l'endroit où nous passons la majeure partie de notre vie éveillée. Bien que nous vivions dans un monde qui devient de plus en plus mobile au quotidien, l'administration, la production, la recherche, l'enseignement, la connaissance, la collecte d'informations et le travail sont liés à des lieux physiques. Ce topos exige des critères matériels, mais aussi émotionnels, auxquels nous répondons de manière créative, innovante et avec une qualité de conception exceptionnelle.

La arquitectura no es objetiva, sino que está influenciada por procesos, requisitos, presupuestos y condiciones culturales y espaciales. Nuestra temprana cooperación con el cliente, ya durante el desarrollo de la tarea, crea una coherencia cualitativa entre el proyecto de construcción, la integración urbana, el espacio, la forma y el material. Esto no sólo crea una inconfundible cultura de la construcción, sino también un alto nivel de aceptación.
Nos centramos en el lugar de trabajo: el lugar donde pasamos la mayor parte de nuestra vida despiertos. Aunque vivimos en un mundo que se está volviendo cada vez más móvil día a día, la administración, la producción, la investigación, la enseñanza, el conocimiento, la recopilación de información y el trabajo están conectados a lugares físicos. Este topos requiere criterios materiales, pero también emocionales, a los que respondemos de forma creativa, innovadora y con una calidad de diseño excepcional.

DAY CARE CENTER MAX-PLANCK-CAMPUS TÜBINGEN

LOCATION: **TÜBINGEN, GERMANY**
PHOTOS: © **DIETMAR STRAUSS**

The converted existing building is wrapped around by a U-shape single-story-annex. The façade cladding of sand-coloured fibre cement panels covers the building with a uniform skin of old and new.
The outstanding element is the roofscape that is folded in motion: it functions as a fifth façade by presenting itself to the viewer like a second landscape. At the same time, it takes over the function of allocating different room heights to different functional areas in order to create individual room qualities.
Another special feature is the materiality of the ceiling: noise-absorbing wood-wool acoustic panels optimise the room acoustics and reduce the reverberation time many times over. The deliberately striking pink coating of the ceiling cladding reinforces the architectural significance of the roofscape right down to the interior colour concept.

Das umgebaute Bestandsgebäude wird von einem U-förmigen Holzrahmenanbau umschlungen. Die Fassadenverkleidung aus sandfarbenen Faserzementtafeln überzieht den Bau mit einer einheitlichen Haut von Alt und Neu.
Herausragendes Element ist die bewegt gefaltete Dachlandschaft: Sie fungiert als fünfte Fassade, indem sie sich dem Betrachter wie eine zweite Landschaft präsentiert. Gleichzeitig übernimmt sie innenräumlich die Funktion, unterschiedlichen Funktionsbereichen differenzierte Raumhöhe zuzuordnen um individuelle Raumqualitäten zu schaffen.
Weitere Besonderheit ist die Materialität der Decke: Lärm absorbierende Holzwolle-Akustikplatten optimieren die Raumakustik und reduzieren die Nachhallzeit um ein Vielfaches. Die bewusst auffällig rosa Beschichtung der Deckenverkleidung kräftigt die architektonische Bedeutung der Dachlandschaft bis in das innere Farbkonzept.

Le bâtiment existant est entouré d'une annexe d'un étage en forme de U. Le revêtement de la façade en panneaux de fibrociment de couleur sable recouvre le bâtiment d'une peau uniforme d'ancien et de nouveau.
L'élément remarquable est le toit qui est plié en mouvement : il fonctionne comme une cinquième façade en se présentant au spectateur comme un second paysage. En même temps, il prend en charge la fonction d'attribution de différentes hauteurs de pièces à différents domaines fonctionnels afin de créer des qualités de pièces individuelles.
Une autre particularité est la matérialité du plafond : des panneaux acoustiques en laine de bois absorbant le bruit optimisent l'acoustique de la pièce et réduisent plusieurs fois le temps de réverbération. Le revêtement rose du plafond renforce l'importance architecturale du paysage de toit jusqu'au concept de couleur intérieure.

El edificio está rodeado por una extensión de estructura de madera en forma de U. El revestimiento de la fachada de paneles de fibrocemento de color arena cubre el edificio con una piel uniforme de viejo y nuevo.
El elemento más destacado es la cubierta que se pliega en movimiento y funciona como una quinta fachada, presentándose al espectador como un segundo paisaje. Al mismo tiempo, asume la función de asignar diferentes alturas interiores a diferentes áreas funcionales para crear cualidades individuales en las estancias.
Otra característica especial es la materialidad del techo: paneles acústicos de lana de madera que absorben el ruido, optimizan la acústica de la habitación y reducen el tiempo de reverberación. El deliberadamente llamativo revestimiento rosa del techo refuerza el significado arquitectónico del paisaje del techo hasta el concepto de color interior.

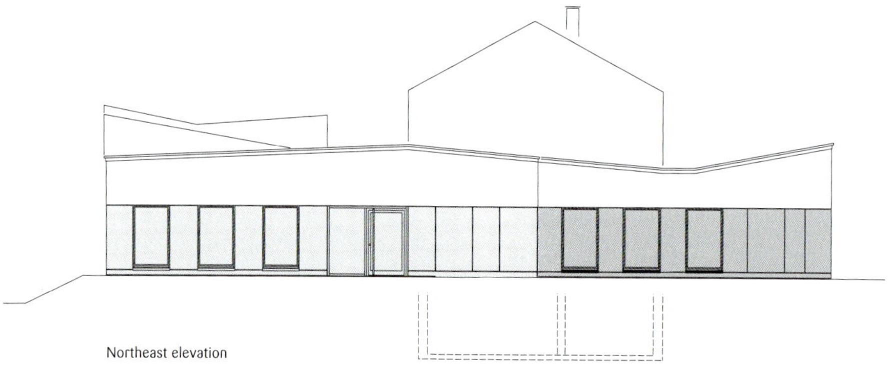

Northeast elevation

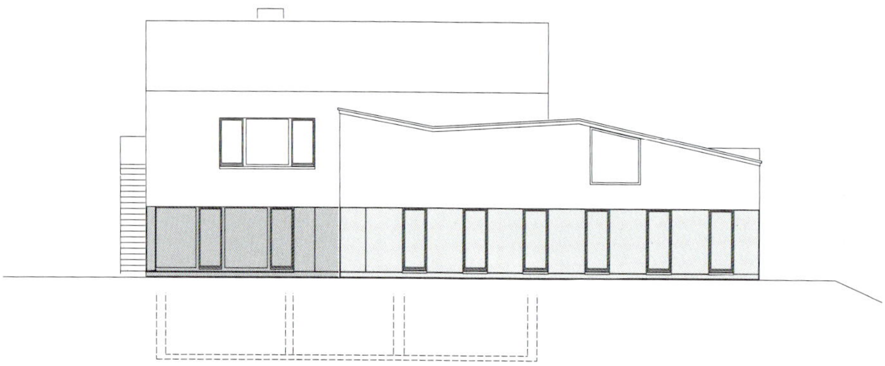

Southeast elevation

ATELIER 56S

// PROJECTS //

1. RECREATIONAL CENTER AND SCHOOL IN ELVEN
2. PRIMARY SCHOOL IN LA COUYÈRE

www.atelier56s.com

1.

2.

Atelier 56S was founded by Fanny Landeau and José Prieto in 2013. Our projects are mainly located in Brittany in municipalities between 500 and 5000 inhabitants, on various programs. The genesis of each project is based on the observation and questioning of pre-existing elements: urban context, landscape, site, materials, in order to confront them with the particular program of each commission. From this meeting are born urban, functional and formal strategies specific to each situation.
This approach allows us to use and reveal the assets of a site to qualify and anchor the architecture that will be created there in order to respond as accurately as possible to a particular physical and cultural context.
Structure, material and light materialize the intentions in the project by qualifying the space. We assert a sober and sensorial architecture, where constructive processes create a visual experience with the users.

L'agence Atelier 56S a été fondée par Fanny Landeau et José Prieto en 2013. Nos projets sont majoritairement situés en Bretagne dans des communes entre 500 et 5000 habitants, sur des programmes variés. La genèse de chaque projet se base sur l'observation et le questionnement des éléments préexistants: contexte urbain, paysage, site, matériaux pour les confronter au programme particulier de chaque commande. De cette rencontre naissent des stratégies urbaines, fonctionnelles et formelles spécifiques à chaque situation.
Cette approche nous permet d'utiliser et révéler les atouts d'un site pour qualifier et ancrer l'architecture qui y sera créée afin de répondre de la façon la plus juste à un contexte physique et culturel particulier.
Structure, matière et lumière matérialisent les intentions dans le projet en qualifiant l'espace vécu par l'homme. Nous affirmons une architecture sobre et sensorielle, où les procédés constructifs s'affirment pour créer une expérience haptique et visuelle avec les usagers.

Atelier 56S wurde 2013 von Fanny Landeau und José Prieto gegründet. Unsere Projekte sind hauptsächlich in der Bretagne in Gemeinden zwischen 500 und 5000 Einwohnern angesiedelt, die an verschiedenen Programmen teilnehmen. Die Genese jedes Projekts beruht auf der Beobachtung und Befragung bereits vorhandener Elemente: städtischer Kontext, Landschaft, Ort, Materialien, um sie mit dem jeweiligen Programm der Kommission zu konfrontieren. Aus diesem Treffen entstehen städtische, funktionale und formale Strategien, die für jede Situation spezifisch sind.
Dieser Ansatz ermöglicht es uns, die Vorzüge einer Stätte zu nutzen und offenzulegen, um die Architektur, die dort entstehen wird, zu qualifizieren und zu verankern, um so genau wie möglich auf einen bestimmten physischen und kulturellen Kontext zu reagieren.
Struktur, Material und Licht materialisieren die Intentionen im Projekt, indem sie den vom Menschen bewohnten Raum qualifizieren. Wir setzen eine nüchterne und sinnliche Architektur durch, in der sich konstruktive Prozesse durchsetzen, um ein haptisches und visuelles Erlebnis mit den Nutzern zu schaffen.

Atelier 56S fue fundada por Fanny Landeau y José Prieto en 2013. Nuestros proyectos se ubican principalmente en Bretaña en municipios entre 500 y 5000 habitantes, en varios programas. La génesis de cada proyecto se basa en la observación y el cuestionamiento de los elementos preexistentes: contexto urbano, paisaje, terreno, materiales, para confrontarlos con el programa particular de cada encargo. De esta reunión nacen estrategias urbanas, funcionales y formales específicas para cada situación.
Este enfoque nos permite utilizar y revelar los activos de un terreno para calificar y anclar la arquitectura que se creará allí a fin de responder con la mayor precisión posible a un contexto físico y cultural particular.
La estructura, la materia y la luz materializan las intenciones del proyecto al calificar el espacio vivido. Afirmamos una arquitectura sobria y sensorial, donde los procesos constructivos se afirman para crear una experiencia visual con los usuarios.

RECREATIONAL CENTER AND SCHOOL IN ELVEN

LOCATION: **ELVEN, FRANCE**
PHOTOS: **© JEREMIAS GONZALEZ**

Located within the boundaries of the existing school, the project is divided following the natural topography of the site : in the lower part, the recreational center directly connected to the public space benefits from an underexploited courtyard. On the upper level the new classrooms are oriented towards the current school courtyard. The complex takes advantage of an East-West exposure and quietly fits into its surroundings.
The materiality chosen for the recreational center is in continuity with the existing school in concrete. A mineral and monolithic shape emerges from the existing topography. The interior spaces surprise by their brightness and transparency brought by the patios and the warm atmosphere of the wood cladding. The upper part, which houses three classrooms is built in a mixed concrete and wood structure.

Das Projekt befindet sich innerhalb der Grenzen der bestehenden Schule und ist entsprechend der natürlichen Topographie des Geländes gegliedert: Im unteren Teil profitiert das direkt an den öffentlichen Raum angeschlossene Freizeitzentrum von einem wenig genutzten Innenhof. Auf der oberen Ebene orientieren sich die neuen Klassenräume zum heutigen Schulhof. Der Komplex profitiert von einer Ost-West-Ausrichtung und fügt sich ruhig in seine Umgebung ein.
Die für das Freizeitzentrum gewählte Materialität steht in Kontinuität mit der bestehenden Schule in Beton. Aus der bestehenden Topographie ergibt sich eine mineralische und monolithische Form. Die Innenräume überraschen durch ihre Helligkeit und Transparenz, die von den Innenhöfen und der warmen Atmosphäre der Holzverkleidung herrührt. Der obere Teil, der drei Klassenzimmer beherbergt, ist in einer gemischten Struktur aus Beton und Holz gebaut.

Situé dans les limites de l'école existante, le projet est divisé en fonction de la topographie naturelle du site : dans la partie inférieure, le centre de loisirs directement relié à l'espace public bénéficie d'une cour sous-exploitée. Au niveau supérieur, les nouvelles salles de classe sont orientées vers la cour de l'école actuelle. Le complexe bénéficie d'une exposition Est-Ouest et s'intègre tranquillement dans son environnement.
La matérialité choisie pour le centre de loisirs s'inscrit dans la continuité de l'école existante en béton. Une forme minérale et monolithique émerge de la topographie existante. Les espaces intérieurs surprennent par leur luminosité et leur transparence apportées par les patios et l'atmosphère chaleureuse du bardage en bois. La partie supérieure, qui abrite trois salles de classe, est construite dans une structure mixte en béton et en bois.

Situado dentro de los límites de la escuela existente, el proyecto se divide siguiendo la topografía natural del lugar: en la parte baja, el centro recreativo directamente conectado al espacio público aprovecha un patio poco utilizado. En la parte superior, las nuevas aulas están orientadas hacia el actual patio de la escuela. El complejo aprovecha una orientación este-oeste , adaptándose tranquilamente a su entorno.
Los materiales escogidos continúan el hormigón escogido para la construcción de la escuela. Una forma mineral y monolítica emerge de la topografía existente. Los espacios interiores sorprenden por el brillo y la transparencia que aportan los patios y el cálido ambiente que otorga el revestimiento de madera. La parte superior, que alberga tres aulas, está construida en una estructura mixta de hormigón y madera.

Site plan

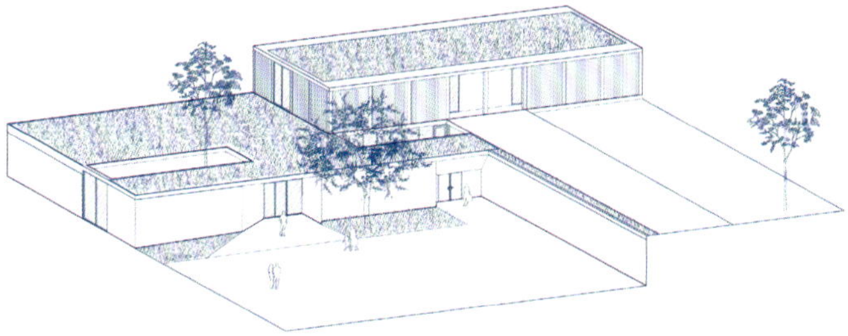

Axonometry

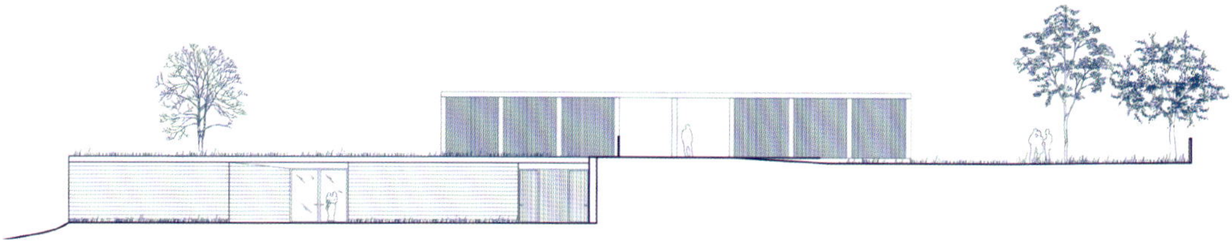

West elevation

North elevation

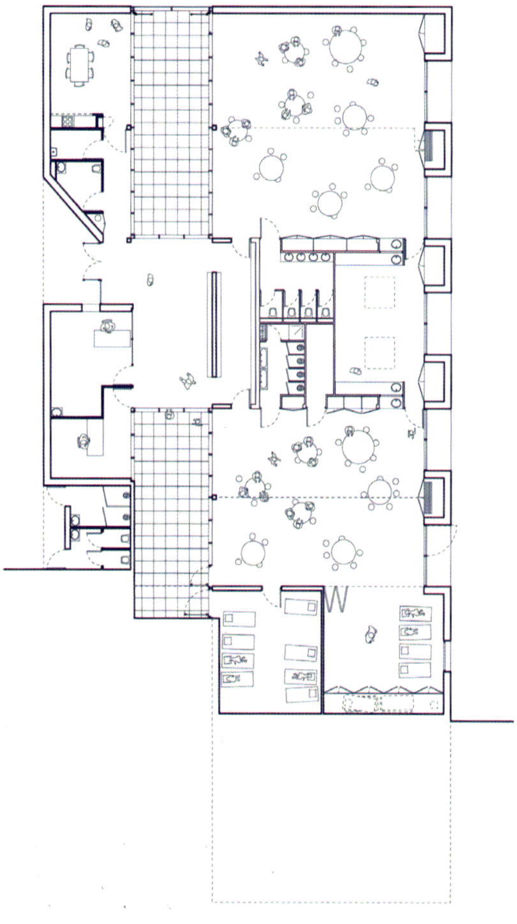

First level plan

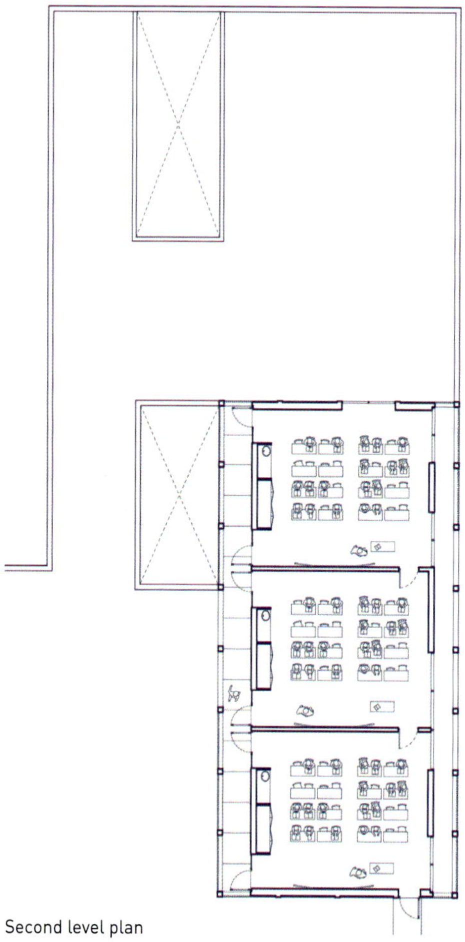

Second level plan

PRIMARY SCHOOL IN LA COUYÈRE

LOCATION: LA COUYÈRE, FRANCE
PHOTOS: © JEREMIAS GONZALEZ

The project reorganizes different urban facilities along a pedestrian path where the new school is located, and is inspired by elements of its immediate surroundings, such as the materials, the abundant vegetation or the low stone walls. The building is composed of a simple, compact and energy-efficient central teaching nucleus surrounded by spaces destined for diverse uses and delimited by traditional hand-molded brick walls, which represent a continuation of the existing stone walls. The project makes abundant use of natural materials and has a green roof throughout the building. The aim of the school is to create spaces of concentration for the collective classes, but also to generate more informal areas that encourage individual learning.

Das Projekt ordnet verschiedene städtische Einrichtungen entlang eines Fußgängerwegs, auf dem sich die neue Schule befindet, neu und lässt sich von Elementen der unmittelbaren Umgebung inspirieren, wie z.B. den Materialien, der üppigen Vegetation oder den niedrigen Steinmauern. Das Gebäude besteht aus einem einfachen, kompakten und energieeffizienten zentralen Lehrkern, der von Räumen umgeben ist, die für verschiedene Nutzungen bestimmt sind und von traditionellen, handgeformten Ziegelmauern begrenzt werden, die eine Fortsetzung der bestehenden Steinmauern darstellen. Das Projekt verwendet in seinen Bauelementen reichlich natürliche Materialien und verfügt über ein begrüntes Dach im gesamten Gebäude. Das Ziel der Schule ist es, Konzentrationsräume für die kollektiven Klassen zu schaffen, aber auch informellere Räume zu schaffen, die das individuelle Lernen fördern.

Le projet réorganise différents équipements urbains le long d'un chemin piétonnier où se trouve la nouvelle école, et s'inspire des éléments de son environnement immédiat, tels que les matériaux, la végétation abondante ou les murets de pierre. Le bâtiment est composé d'un noyau central d'enseignement simple, compact et économe en énergie, entouré d'espaces destinés à des usages divers et délimités par des murs traditionnels en briques moulées à la main, qui représentent une continuation des murs en pierre existants. Le projet fait un usage abondant de matériaux naturels dans ses éléments de construction et dispose d'un toit vert dans tout le bâtiment. L'objectif de l'école est de créer des espaces de concentration pour les classes collectives, mais aussi de générer des espaces plus informels qui encouragent l'apprentissage individuel.

El proyecto reorganiza diferentes equipamientos urbanos a lo largo de un camino peatonal en el que se ubica la nueva escuela y se inspira en elementos de su entorno inmediato, como los materiales, la abundante vegetación o los muros bajos de piedra. El edificio se compone de un sencillo núcleo central de enseñanza, compacto y de alto rendimiento energético, rodeado de espacios destinados a usos diversos y delimitados por muros de ladrillo tradicional moldeado a mano, que representan una continuación de los muros de piedra existentes. El proyecto hace un uso abundante de materiales naturales en sus elementos constructivos y dispone una cubierta vegetal a lo largo de todo el edificio. El objetivo de la escuela es crear espacios de concentración para las clases colectivas, pero también generar espacios más informales que fomenten el aprendizaje de forma individual.

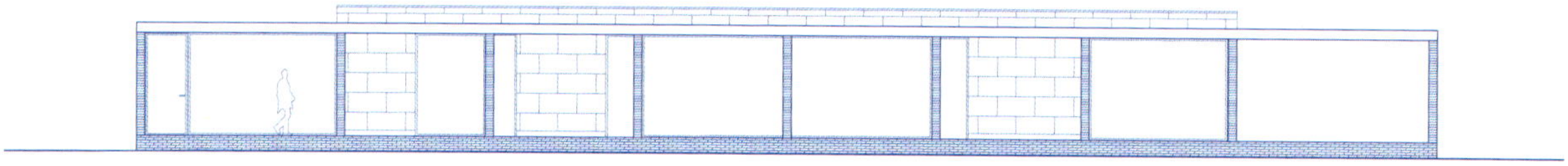

South elevation

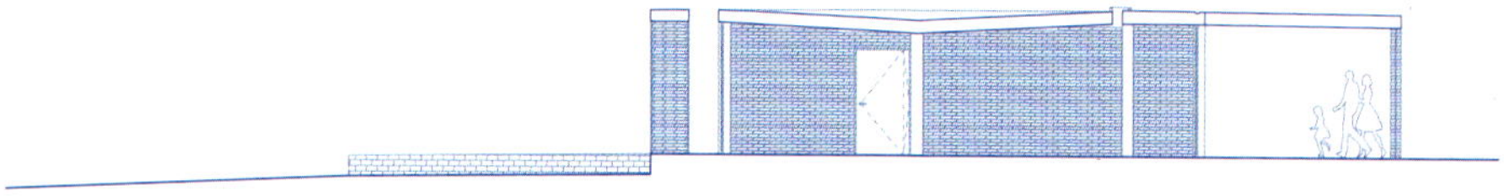

East elevation

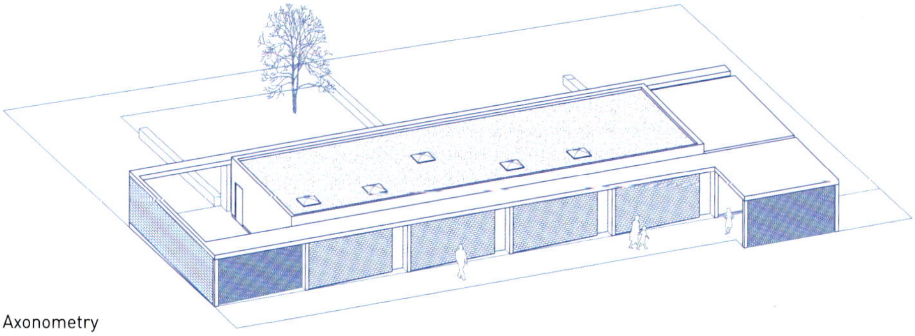

Axonometry

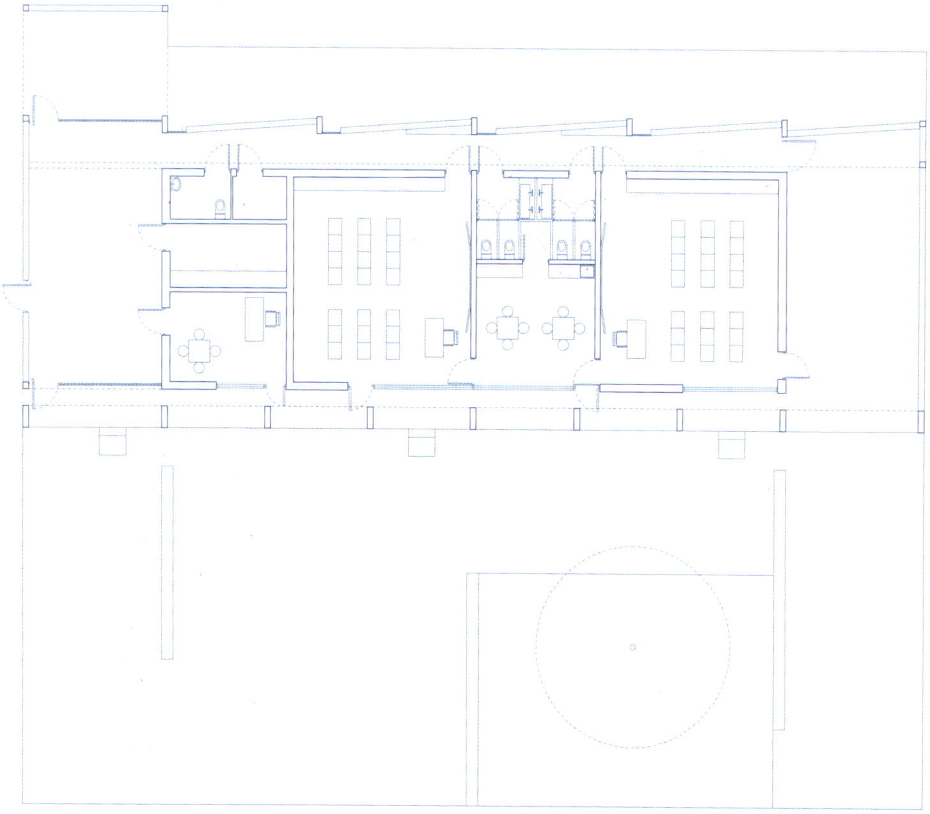

Floor plan

Atelier BNK

// PROJECTS //

1. YUNI NURSERY SCHOOL
2. ITOI ELEMENTARY SCHOOL
3. NUMATA ELEMENTARY SCHOOL

www.atelier-bnk.co.jp

Atelier BNK

1.

2.

3.

Atelier BNK, based in Sapporo (Hokkaido, Japan), has been involved in the design of many public buildings since its start in 1970. In the subarctic regions of Hokkaido, the time spent indoors tends to be longer due to the effects of snow and cold. For this reason, we have enhanced our design methods to create a bright and open space by securing sufficient natural lighting while reducing the energy needed for heating by adopting a compact form with a small outer wall area. All of our works have received a great deal of praise. We have received Annual Architectural Design Commendations of AIJ (one of the most prestigious awards in Japan) for four projects, and many works have been introduced both in Japan and abroad through media and magazines.

L'Atelier BNK, basé à Sapporo (Hokkaido, Japon), a participé à la conception de nombreux bâtiments publics depuis ses débuts en 1970. Dans les régions subarctiques d'Hokkaido, le temps passé à l'intérieur tend à être plus long en raison des effets de la neige et du froid. C'est pourquoi nous avons amélioré nos méthodes de conception afin de créer un espace lumineux et ouvert en garantissant un éclairage naturel suffisant tout en réduisant l'énergie nécessaire au chauffage en adoptant une forme compacte avec une petite surface de mur extérieur. Tous nos travaux ont reçu de nombreux éloges. Nous avons reçu la mention d'honneur annuelle de l'AIJ (l'un des prix les plus prestigieux au Japon) pour quatre projets, et de nombreuses œuvres ont été présentées au Japon et à l'étranger par les médias et les magazines.

Atelier BNK, mit Sitz in Sapporo (Hokkaido, Japan), war seit seiner Gründung im Jahr 1970 an der Gestaltung vieler öffentlicher Gebäude beteiligt. In den subarktischen Regionen von Hokkaido ist die Verweildauer in geschlossenen Räumen aufgrund der Auswirkungen von Schnee und Kälte tendenziell länger. Aus diesem Grund haben wir unsere Entwurfsmethoden verbessert, um einen offenen und hellen Raum zu schaffen, indem wir für eine ausreichende natürliche Beleuchtung sorgen und gleichzeitig die für die Heizung benötigte Energie reduzieren, indem wir eine kompakte Form mit einer kleinen Außenwandfläche wählen. Unsere gesamte Arbeit ist hoch gelobt worden. Wir haben die jährlichen Architekturdesignpreise der AIJ (eine der renommiertesten Auszeichnungen Japans) für vier Projekte erhalten, und viele Arbeiten wurden sowohl in Japan als auch im Ausland durch die Medien und Zeitschriften präsentiert.

El Atelier BNK, con sede en Sapporo (Hokkaido, Japón), ha participado en el diseño de muchos edificios públicos desde su inicio en 1970. En las regiones subárticas de Hokkaido, el tiempo de permanencia en el interior tiende a ser más largo debido a los efectos de la nieve y el frío. Por esta razón, hemos mejorado nuestros métodos de diseño para crear un espacio abierto y luminoso asegurando suficiente iluminación natural y reduciendo al mismo tiempo la energía necesaria para la calefacción, adoptando una forma compacta con una pequeña área de pared exterior. Todos nuestros trabajos han recibido encendidos elogios. Hemos recibido las Menciones Anuales de Diseño Arquitectónico de la AIJ (uno de los premios más prestigiosos de Japón) por cuatro proyectos, y muchos trabajos han sido presentados tanto en Japón como en el extranjero a través de medios de comunicación y revistas.

YUNI NURSERY SCHOOL

LOCATION: **YUNI, HOKKAIDO, JAPAN**
PHOTOS: **© SHINKENCHIKU-SHA**

The design of this municipal nursery gives special importance to the relationship between the interior spaces and the leafy exterior courtyard. For this reason, the collective playroom is located on the ground floor as a continuation of this courtyard. The first floor houses the kindergarten classrooms, whose distribution can be adjusted to the different activities thanks to the design of its furniture, and a terrace with a garden. The nursery and play rooms are connected by an atrium that serves as a dining room and encourages cross ventilation in the interior. Glass block walls facing south and north generate a diffuse and homogeneous light that bathes the classrooms and the atrium. The design of the structure with multidirectional verandas and hollow-core slabs contributes to the thermal comfort of the interior thanks to their properties as heat and cold accumulators.

Bei der Gestaltung dieser städtischen Kindertagesstätte wird der Beziehung zwischen den Innenräumen und dem begrünten Außenhof besondere Bedeutung beigemessen. Aus diesem Grund befindet sich das kollektive Spielzimmer im Erdgeschoss als Fortsetzung dieses Hofes. Im ersten Stock befinden sich die Klassenzimmer des Kindergartens, dessen Verteilung dank der Gestaltung seiner Möbel an die verschiedenen Aktivitäten angepasst werden kann, sowie eine Terrasse mit Garten. Der Kindergarten und die Spielzimmer sind durch ein Atrium verbunden, das als Speisesaal dient und die Querlüftung im Innenraum fördert. Nach Süden und Norden ausgerichtete Glassteinwände erzeugen ein diffuses und homogenes Licht, das die Klassenzimmer und das Atrium taucht. Der Entwurf der Struktur mit multidirektionalen Portiken und Hohlkernplatten trägt dank ihrer Eigenschaften als Wärme- und Kältespeicher zum thermischen Komfort des Innenraums bei.

La conception de cette pépinière municipale accorde une importance particulière à la relation entre les espaces intérieurs et la cour extérieure verdoyante. C'est pourquoi la salle de jeux collective est située au rez-de-chaussée, dans le prolongement de cette cour. Le premier étage abrite les salles de classe du jardin d'enfants, dont la répartition peut être adaptée aux différentes activités grâce à la conception de son mobilier, et une terrasse avec un jardin. La crèche et les salles de jeux sont reliées par un atrium qui sert de salle à manger et favorise la ventilation transversale à l'intérieur. Les murs en briques de verre orientés au sud et au nord génèrent une lumière diffuse et homogène qui baigne les salles de classe et l'atrium. La conception de la structure avec des portiques multidirectionnels et des dalles creuses contribue au confort thermique de l'intérieur grâce à leurs propriétés d'accumulateurs de chaleur et de froid.

El diseño de esta guardería municipal otorga una especial importancia a la relación de los espacios interiores con el frondoso patio exterior. Por este motivo, la sala de juegos colectiva se sitúa en la planta baja como una continuación de este patio. El primer piso alberga las aulas de guardería, cuya distribución puede ajustarse a las diferentes actividades gracias al diseño de su mobiliario, y una terraza con un jardín. Las salas de guardería y de juegos se comunican a través de un atrio que sirve como comedor y que fomenta la ventilación cruzada en el interior. Unos paramentos de bloques de vidrio orientados a sur y a norte generan una luz difusa y homogénea que baña las aulas y el atrio. El diseño de la estructura con pórticos en varias direcciones y losas alveolares contribuye al confort térmico del interior gracias a sus propiedades como acumuladores de calor y frío.

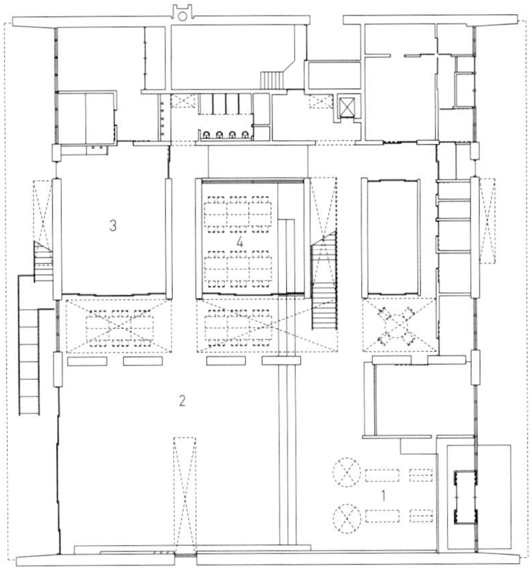

Ground floor plan

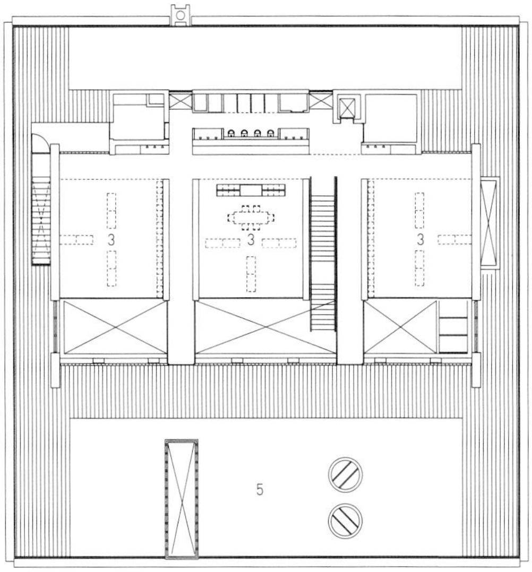

First floor plan

1. Entrance
2. Playroom
3. Childcare room
4. Aid-for-childcare room
5. Rooftop garden

ITOI ELEMENTARY SCHOOL

LOCATION: **SHIBETSU, HOKKAIDO, JAPAN**
PHOTOS: **© SHINKENCHIKU-SHA, KOJI SAKAI**

This small primary school located in a region of cold weather and frequent snowfalls aspires to become a symbol of the city for future generations. Its compact design allows most activities to take place inside and creates a family atmosphere among students and teachers. A mixed structure of concrete and steel and a continuous exposed ceiling of local laminated wood allows great freedom in the distribution of the floor and generates a continuous space where light and air flow without obstacles and where the circulation areas become part of the spaces dedicated to teaching. The project seeks the sustainability of the building by reducing the heating load, cross ventilation and the search for sunlight, which penetrates through the laminated wood openings creating different patterns of light and shade on the floor.

Cette petite école primaire située dans une région où il fait froid et où les chutes de neige sont fréquentes aspire à devenir un symbole de la ville pour les générations futures. Sa conception compacte permet à la plupart des activités de se dérouler à l'intérieur et crée une atmosphère familiale entre les élèves et les enseignants. Une structure mixte de béton et d'acier et un plafond apparent continu en bois lamellé local permettent une grande liberté dans la distribution du sol et génèrent un espace continu où la lumière et l'air circulent sans obstacle et où les zones de circulation font partie des espaces dédiés à l'enseignement. Le projet vise à assurer la durabilité du bâtiment en réduisant la charge de chauffage, la ventilation transversale et la recherche de la lumière du soleil, qui pénètre par les ouvertures en bois lamellé et crée différents motifs de lumière et d'ombre sur le sol.

Diese kleine Grundschule, die in einer Region mit kaltem Wetter und häufigen Schneefällen liegt, strebt danach, für künftige Generationen zu einem Symbol der Stadt zu werden. Sein kompaktes Design ermöglicht die meisten Aktivitäten im Inneren und schafft eine familiäre Atmosphäre zwischen Schülern und Lehrern. Eine gemischte Struktur aus Beton und Stahl und eine durchgehende Sichtdecke aus lokalem Brettschichtholz erlaubt eine große Freiheit bei der Verteilung des Bodens und erzeugt einen durchgehenden Raum, in dem Licht und Luft ohne Hindernisse strömen und in dem die Verkehrsflächen Teil der dem Unterricht gewidmeten Räume werden. Das Projekt bemüht sich um die Nachhaltigkeit des Gebäudes durch Reduzierung der Heizlast, Querlüftung und die Suche nach Sonnenlicht, das durch die Schichtholz-Öffnungen eindringt und unterschiedliche Licht- und Schattenmuster auf dem Boden erzeugt.

Esta pequeña escuela primaria ubicada en una región de clima frío y frecuentes nevadas aspira a convertirse en un símbolo de la ciudad para las generaciones futuras. Su diseño compacto permite desarrollar la mayoría de actividades en su interior y crea un ambiente familiar entre alumnos y maestros. Una estructura mixta de hormigón y acero y un techo continuo visto de madera laminada local permiten una gran libertad en la distribución de la planta y generan un espacio continuo donde luz y aire fluyen sin obstáculos y en el que las zonas de circulación se convierten en parte de los espacios dedicado a la enseñanza. El proyecto busca la sostenibilidad del edificio mediante la reducción de la carga de calefacción, la ventilación cruzada y la búsqueda de la luz solar, que penetra a través de las aberturas de madera laminada creando diferentes patrones de luz y sombra en el suelo.

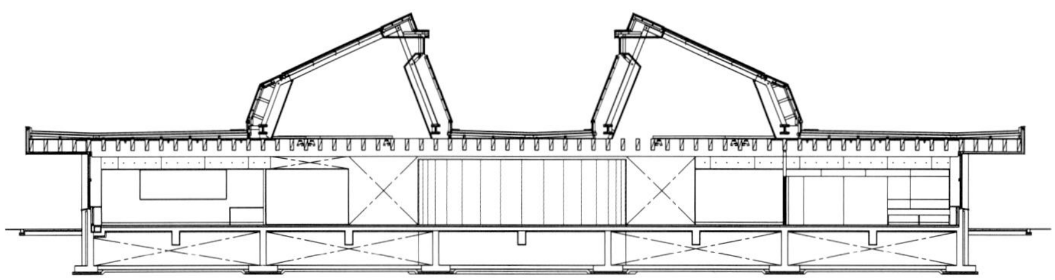

Classroom area section

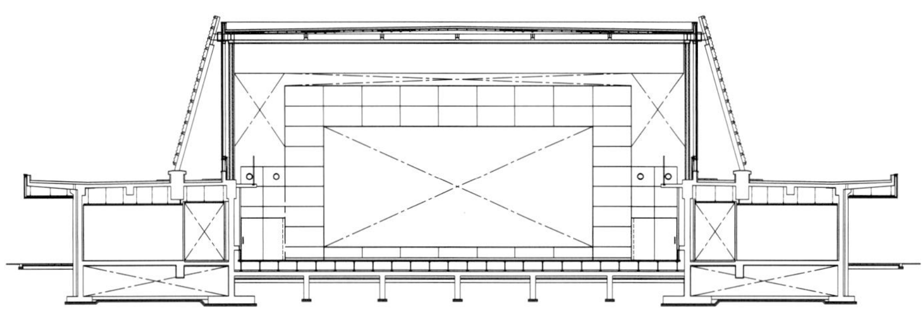

Gymnasium area section

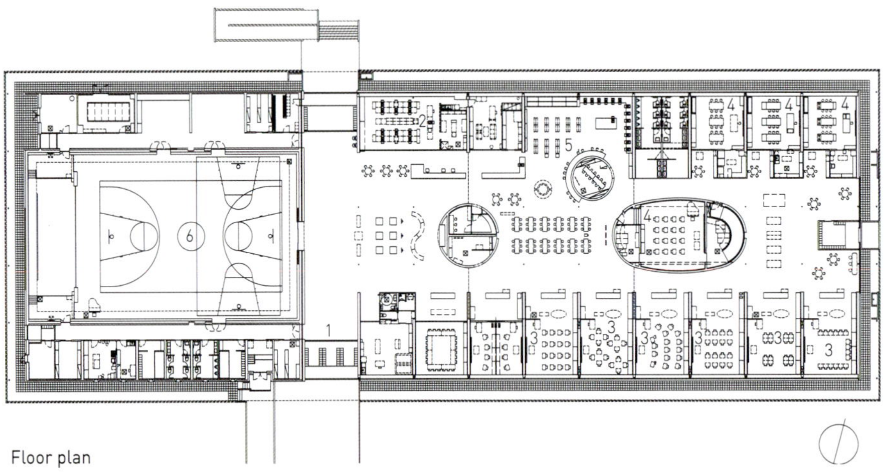

1. Entrance
2. Teacher room
3. Classroom
4. Special room
5. Media corner
6. Gymnasium

Floor plan

5

NUMATA ELEMENTARY SCHOOL

LOCATION: **NUMATA, HOKKAIDO, JAPAN**
PHOTOS: © **FUMIAKI SATO, KOJI SAKAI**

The location of this small school in a region of heavy snowfall generated a compact, rectangular-shaped design that houses a wide range of indoor activities for the children. Most of the building is on one level, except for a second floor classroom area that faces south. Its spaces are organized in a linear fashion in a north-south direction to create a deep and consecutive configuration, but the height and shape of the ceiling above these spaces vary to give the building a distinctive character. The core of the school is the "Field of Light", a double height atrium with a north-facing skylight in which the soft natural light is guided inwards to create a peaceful and serene space for the children. Inside, a wide staircase becomes a meeting place.

Die Lage dieser kleinen Schule in einer Region mit starkem Schneefall führte zu einem kompakten, rechteckigen Design, das eine Vielzahl von Aktivitäten für die Kinder in Innenräumen beherbergt. Der größte Teil des Gebäudes befindet sich auf einer Ebene, mit Ausnahme eines nach Süden ausgerichteten Klassenzimmerbereichs im zweiten Stock. Seine Räume sind in Nord-Süd-Richtung linear organisiert, um eine tiefe und aufeinander folgende Konfiguration zu schaffen, aber die Höhe und Form der Decke über diesen Räumen variieren, um dem Gebäude einen unverwechselbaren Charakter zu verleihen. Das Herzstück der Schule ist das „Feld des Lichts", ein Atrium von doppelter Höhe mit einem nach Norden gerichteten Oberlicht, in dem das weiche natürliche Licht nach innen gelenkt wird, um einen friedlichen und ruhigen Raum für die Kinder zu schaffen. Im Inneren wird eine breite Treppe zum Treffpunkt.

L'emplacement de cette petite école dans une région où les chutes de neige sont abondantes a donné naissance à une conception compacte de forme rectangulaire qui abrite un large éventail d'activités intérieures pour les enfants. La plus grande partie du bâtiment est de plain-pied, à l'exception d'une salle de classe au deuxième étage qui est orientée au sud. Ses espaces sont organisés de manière linéaire dans une direction nord-sud pour créer une configuration profonde et consécutive, mais la hauteur et la forme du plafond au-dessus de ces espaces varient pour donner au bâtiment un caractère distinctif. Le cœur de l'école est le « Champ de lumière », un atrium à double hauteur avec une lucarne orientée vers le nord dans laquelle la douce lumière naturelle est guidée vers l'intérieur pour créer un espace de paix et de sérénité pour les enfants. A l'intérieur, un large escalier devient un lieu de rencontre.

La ubicación de esta pequeña escuela en una región de fuertes nevadas generó un diseño compacto de planta rectangular que alberga una gran diversidad de actividades de interior para los niños. La mayor parte del edificio se desarrolla en un solo nivel, a excepción de una zona de aulas situada en un segundo piso y orientada a sur. Sus espacios se organizan de forma lineal en dirección norte-sur para crear una configuración profunda y consecutiva, pero la altura y la forma del techo sobre estos espacios varían para dar al edificio un carácter distintivo. El núcleo de la escuela lo constituye el «Campo de Luz», un atrio a doble altura con una claraboya orientada a norte en el que la suave luz natural es guiada hacia el interior para crear un espacio apacible y sereno para los niños. En su interior, una amplia escalinata se convierte en lugar de encuentro y reunión.

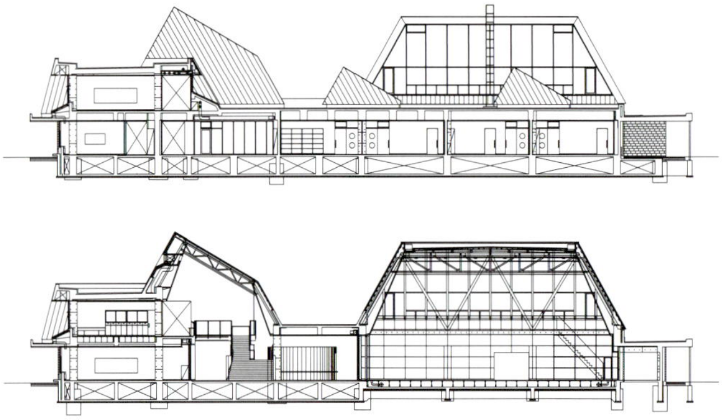

Sections

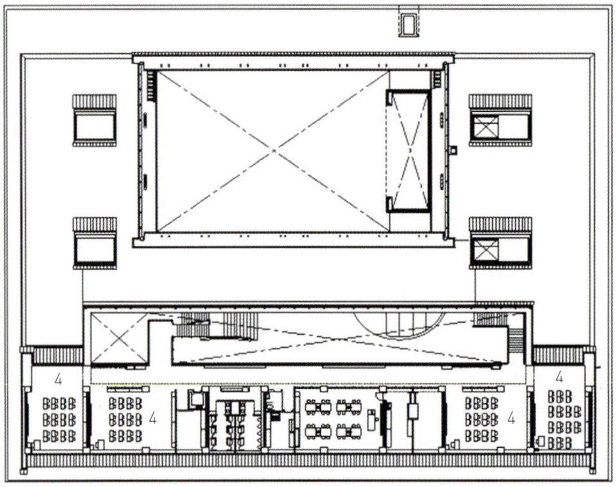

Second floor plan

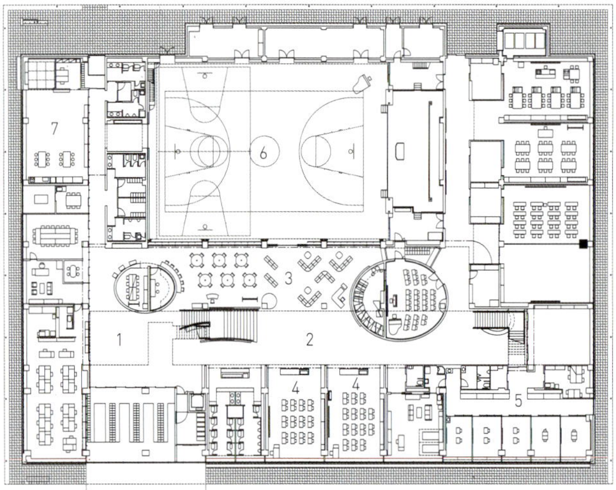

Ground floor plan

1. Entrance hall
2. Field of light
3. Library, computer corner
4. Classroom
5. Support classroom
6. Gymnasium
7. After school hours room

なかよく

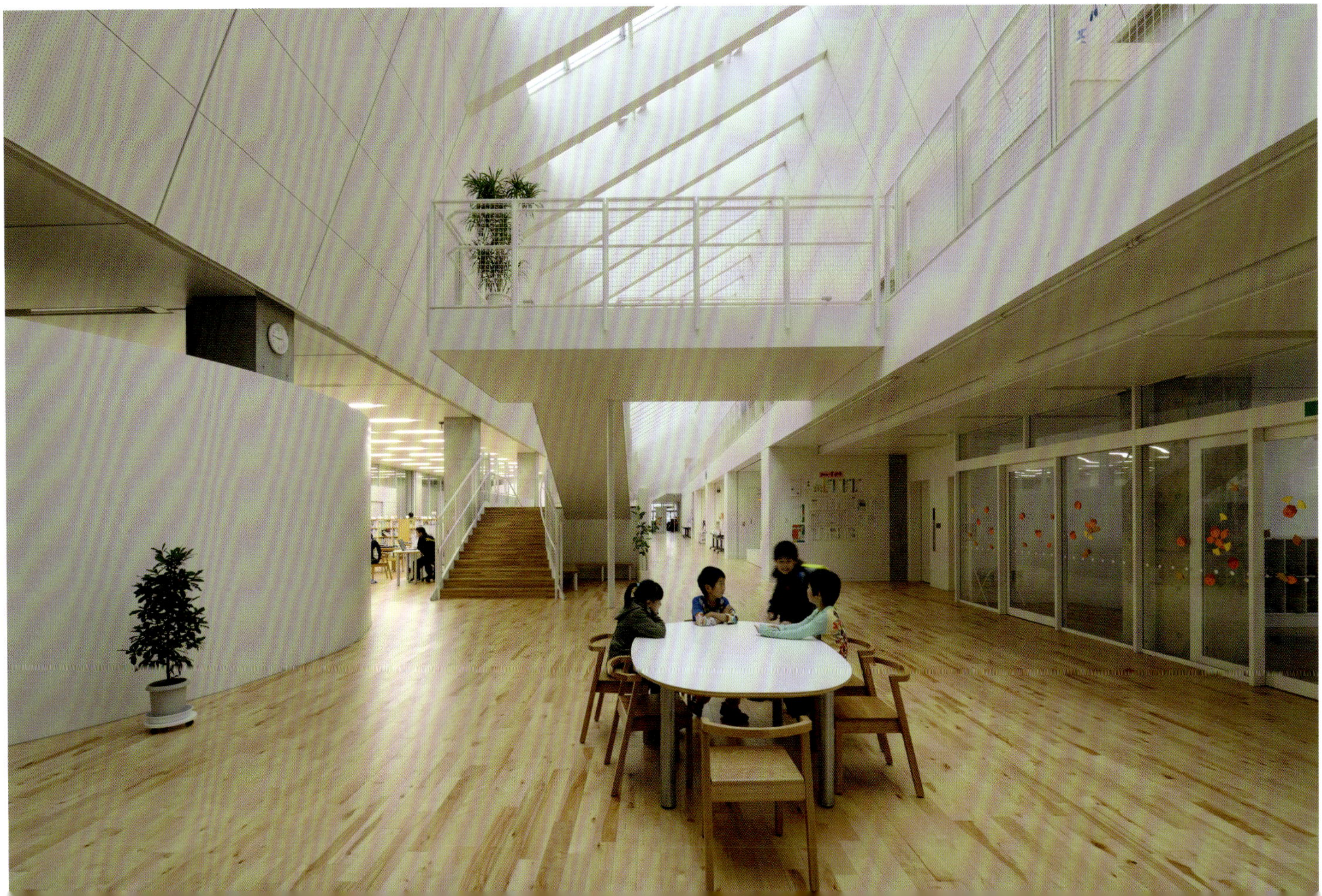

Barker Associates Architecture Office and 4|Mativ Design Studio

// PROJECTS //

1. MAPLE STREET SCHOOL
2. MI CASITA PRESCHOOL AND CULTURAL CENTER

www.baaostudio.com
www.4mativ.com

Barker Associates Architecture Office and 4|Mativ Design Studio

1.

2.

Barker Associates Architecture Office is an award-winning New York-based practice founded in 2006 by Alexandra Barker, AIA, LEED AP with a focus on exploring spatial and material approaches that adapt to the evolving contemporary relationships between inhabitants and the built environment. BAAO has worked on a range of projects that include townhouses, residential developments, ground-up private residences, interiors, and educational and retail projects in the New York area, regionally, and internationally.
4|MATIV is a woman-owned global design and architecture studio based in Brooklyn, New York and Nairobi, Kenya. It was founded in 2011 by Architect Priya Patel and Interior and Industrial Designer, Esther Beke. 4|MATIV specializes in a diverse range of projects from educational, multi residential, workplace, retail to commercial. Their design philosophy includes concepts of timelessness, functionality, innovation, simplicity and where appropriate playfulness.

Barker Associates Architecture Office est un cabinet primé basé à New York et fondé en 2006 par Alexandra Barker, AIA, LEED AP. Il se concentre sur l'exploration des approches spatiales et matérielles qui s'adaptent à l'évolution des relations contemporaines entre les habitants et l'environnement bâti. BAAO a travaillé sur une série de projets comprenant des maisons en rangée, des développements résidentiels, des résidences privées au sol, des intérieurs et des projets éducatifs et commerciaux dans la région de New York, au niveau régional et international.
4|MATIV est un studio de design et d'architecture global appartenant à des femmes, basé à Brooklyn, New York et Nairobi, Kenya. Il a été fondé en 2011 par l'architecte Priya Patel et la designer industrielle et d'intérieur Esther Beke. 4|MATIV se spécialise dans une gamme variée de projets, allant de l'éducation, du multi-residentiel, du lieu de travail, de la vente au détail et du commerce. Leur philosophie de conception inclut les concepts d'intemporalité, de fonctionnalité, d'innovation, de simplicité et, le cas échéant, de caractère ludique.

Barker Associates Architecture Office ist ein preisgekröntes New Yorker Büro, das 2006 von Alexandra Barker, AIA, LEED AP, gegründet wurde und sich auf die Erforschung räumlicher und materieller Ansätze konzentriert, die sich an die sich entwickelnden zeitgenössischen Beziehungen zwischen Bewohnern und gebauter Umwelt anpassen. BAAO hat an einer Reihe von Projekten gearbeitet, die Stadthäuser, Wohnsiedlungen, bebaute Privatwohnungen, Innenräume sowie Bildungs- und Einzelhandelsprojekte im Raum New York, regional und international umfassen.
4|MATIV ist ein von Frauen geführtes globales Design- und Architekturstudio mit Sitz in Brooklyn, New York, und Nairobi, Kenia. Es wurde 2011 von der Architektin Priya Patel und der Innen- und Industriedesignerin Esther Beke gegründet. 4|MATIV hat sich auf eine breite Palette von Projekten spezialisiert, die von Bildungs-, Multi-Wohn-, Arbeitsplatz-, Einzelhandels- bis hin zu kommerziellen Projekten reichen. Ihre Designphilosophie umfasst Konzepte der Zeitlosigkeit, Funktionalität, Innovation, Einfachheit und, wo angebracht, Verspieltheit.

La Barker Associates Architecture Office es un galardonado estudio con sede en Nueva York, fundado en 2006 por Alexandra Barker, AIA, LEED AP, que se centra en la exploración de enfoques espaciales y materiales que se adaptan a la evolución de las relaciones contemporáneas entre los habitantes y el entorno construido. La BAAO ha trabajado en una serie de proyectos que incluyen casas adosadas, urbanizaciones residenciales, residencias privadas subterráneas, interiores y proyectos educativos en la zona de Nueva York, pero también a nivel regional e internacional.
4|MATIV es un estudio femenino de diseño y arquitectura global con sede en Brooklyn, Nueva York y Nairobi, Kenia. Fue fundado en 2011 por la arquitecta Priya Patel y la diseñadora de interiores e industrial, Esther Beke. 4|MATIV se especializa en una diversa gama de proyectos, desde educativos, multiresidenciales, de oficinas, y comerciales. Su filosofía de diseño incluye conceptos de intemporalidad, funcionalidad, innovación, simplicidad y, en su caso, diversión.

MAPLE STREET SCHOOL

LOCATION: **BROOKLYN, NEW YORK, USA**
PHOTOS: **© LESLEY UNRUH**

Located on the second floor of a mixed-use building, this kindergarten's program includes three classrooms that open into a shared multipurpose space, and a playground located on the roof. The custom of scheduling daily group meetings at snack time led to the multipurpose space being organized around a kitchen that, like a food truck, displays windows and counters when in use. The classrooms are connected to each other by wide, high doors that open to create space for larger events. The bathrooms are conceived as focal points inserted inside the classrooms, designed to facilitate visibility for the teachers. The palette of materials is simple and the maple wood floors, doors and furniture give unity to the space, bring warmth to the interior and represent a wink to the name of the school.

Das Programm dieses Kindergartens befindet sich im zweiten Stock eines gemischt genutzten Gebäudes und umfasst drei Klassenzimmer, die sich zu einem gemeinsamen Mehrzweckraum öffnen, sowie einen Spielplatz auf dem Dach. Die Gewohnheit, tägliche Gruppentreffen zur Imbisszeit anzusetzen, führte dazu, dass der Mehrzweckbereich um eine Küche herum organisiert wurde, die wie ein Speisewagen Fenster und Theken zeigt, wenn sie benutzt wird. Die Klassenräume sind durch breite, hohe Türen miteinander verbunden, die sich öffnen, um Platz für größere Veranstaltungen zu schaffen. Die Toiletten sind als Brennpunkte konzipiert, die in die Klassenzimmer eingefügt wurden, um die Sichtbarkeit für die Lehrer zu erleichtern. Die Palette der Materialien ist schlicht und die Ahornholzböden, Türen und Möbel verleihen dem Raum Einheit, bringen Wärme in den Innenraum und stellen ein Augenzwinkern zum Namen der Schule dar.

Situé au deuxième étage d'un bâtiment à usage mixte, le programme de cette école maternelle comprend trois salles de classe qui s'ouvrent sur un espace polyvalent commun, et une aire de jeux située sur le toit. L'habitude de programmer les réunions de groupe quotidiennes à l'heure du goûter a conduit à organiser l'espace polyvalent autour d'une cuisine qui, comme un camion de nourriture, affiche des vitrines et des comptoirs lorsqu'elle est utilisée. Les salles de classe sont reliées entre elles par de larges et hautes portes qui s'ouvrent pour créer l'espace nécessaire à des événements plus importants. Les salles de bain sont conçues comme des points de convergence insérés à l'intérieur des salles de classe, conçus pour faciliter la visibilité des enseignants. La palette des matériaux est simple et les parquets, portes et meubles en érable donnent une unité à l'espace, apportent de la chaleur à l'intérieur et représentent un clin d'œil au nom de l'école.

Situada en el segundo piso de un edificio de uso mixto, el programa de este jardín de infancia incluye tres aulas que se abren hacia un espacio multiusos compartido, y un patio de juegos ubicado en la cubierta. La costumbre de programar las reuniones de grupo diarias a la hora de la merienda motivó que el espacio de usos múltiples se organizase alrededor de una cocina que, a modo de *food truck*, despliega ventanas y mostradores al estar en uso. Las aulas están conectadas entre sí por amplias puertas altas que al abrirse crean espacios para eventos más grandes. Los baños se conciben como puntos focales insertados dentro de las aulas, diseñados para facilitar la visibilidad a los maestros. La paleta de materiales es simple y los suelos, puertas y mobiliario de madera de arce dan unidad al espacio, aportan calidez al interior y representan un guiño al nombre de la escuela.

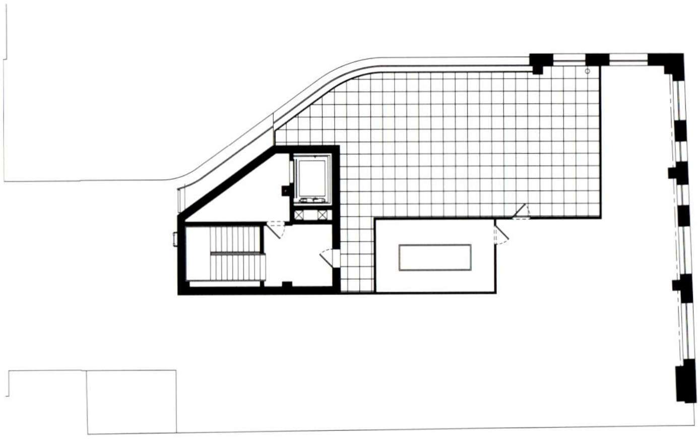

Rooftop floor plan

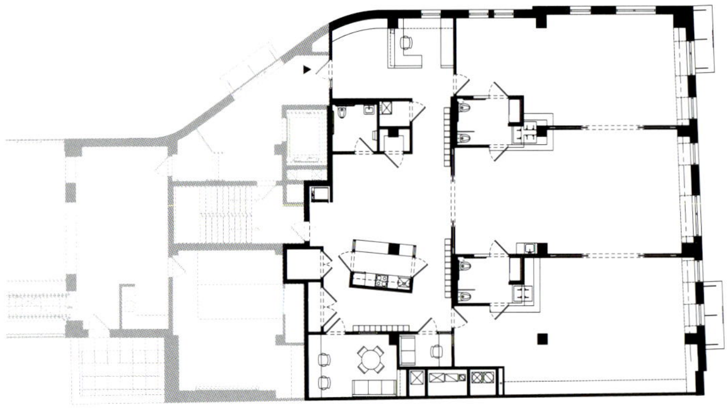

Classroom floor plan

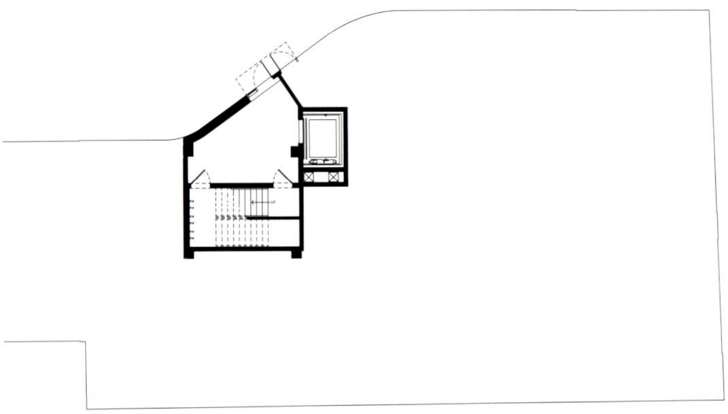

Entrance floor plan

MI CASITA PRESCHOOL AND CULTURAL CENTER

LOCATION: **BROOKLYN, NEW YORK, USA**
PHOTOS: © **LESLEY UNRUH**

This kindergarten and cultural centre is located on a ground floor with high ceilings. The program is organized around an L-shaped sink that becomes a meeting point. The separation between rooms by means of the design of the furniture provides flexibility when it comes to transforming the space for special events. The school's goal to be a "home away from home" and to learn from the different cultures that coexist in Brooklyn motivated the incorporation of graphic elements related to the home and the city in the interior design. Colours are also used to create suggestive effects: the turquoise of the ceiling and some light balloons give the impression of being under a bright sky, orange emphasises the cut-outs in the walls and orange-lined stairs lead to a lower level for support spaces.

Dieser Kindergarten und das Kulturzentrum befinden sich in einem Erdgeschoss mit hohen Decken. Das Programm ist um ein L-förmiges Waschbecken herum organisiert, das zu einem Treffpunkt wird. Die Trennung zwischen den Räumen durch die Gestaltung des Mobiliars bietet Flexibilität, wenn es darum geht, den Raum für besondere Veranstaltungen umzugestalten. Das Ziel der Schule, ein "Zuhause weit weg von zu Hause" zu sein und von den verschiedenen Kulturen zu lernen, die in Brooklyn nebeneinander existieren, motivierte die Schule dazu, grafische Elemente mit Bezug zum Zuhause und zur Stadt in die Innenarchitektur zu integrieren. Auch Farben werden eingesetzt, um suggestive Effekte zu erzeugen: Das Türkis der Decke und einige helle Luftballons erwecken den Eindruck, sich unter einem hellen Himmel zu befinden, Orange betont die Ausschnitte in den Wänden und orange gestrichene Treppen führen zu einer niedrigeren Ebene für Stützräume.

Ce jardin d'enfants et centre culturel est situé au rez-de-chaussée avec de hauts plafonds. Le programme est organisé autour d'un évier en forme de L qui devient un point de rencontre. La séparation entre les salles grâce à la conception du mobilier offre une certaine souplesse lorsqu'il s'agit de transformer l'espace pour des événements spéciaux. L'objectif de l'école d'être un « chez soi loin de chez soi » et d'apprendre des différentes cultures qui coexistent à Brooklyn a motivé l'incorporation d'éléments graphiques liés à la maison et à la ville dans la décoration intérieure. Les couleurs sont également utilisées pour créer des effets suggestifs : le turquoise du plafond et certains ballons lumineux donnent l'impression d'être sous un ciel lumineux, l'orange souligne les découpes dans les murs et les escaliers bordés d'orange mènent à un niveau inférieur pour les espaces de soutien.

Este jardín de infancia y centro cultural se desarrolla en una planta baja de techos altos. El programa se organiza alrededor de un lavamanos en forma de L que se convierte en punto de encuentro. La separación entre estancias mediante el diseño del mobiliario aporta flexibilidad a la hora de transformar el espacio para eventos especiales. El objetivo de la escuela de ser un «hogar lejos del hogar» y de aprender de las diferentes culturas que coexisten en Brooklyn motivó la incorporación de elementos gráficos relacionados con el hogar y la ciudad en el diseño interior. Así mismo, los colores son utilizados para crear efectos sugerentes: el turquesa del techo y unos globos de luz dan la impresión de estar bajo un cielo brillante, el naranja enfatiza los recortes en las paredes y unas escaleras revestidas de naranja conducen a un nivel inferior destinado a espacios de apoyo.

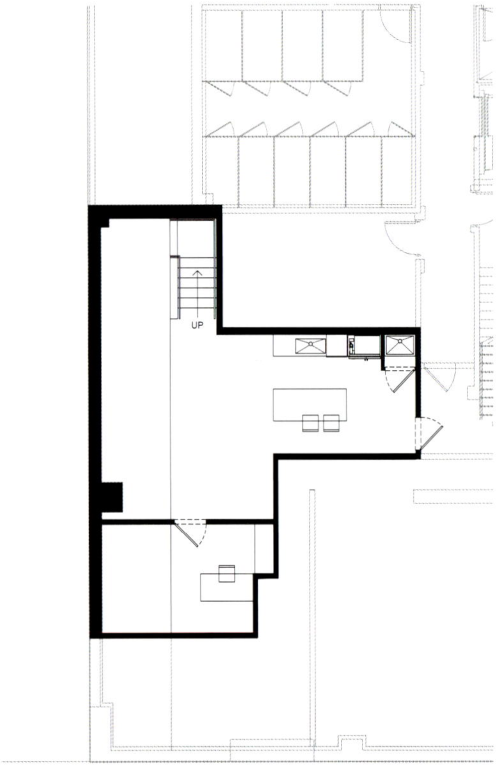

Basement floor plan

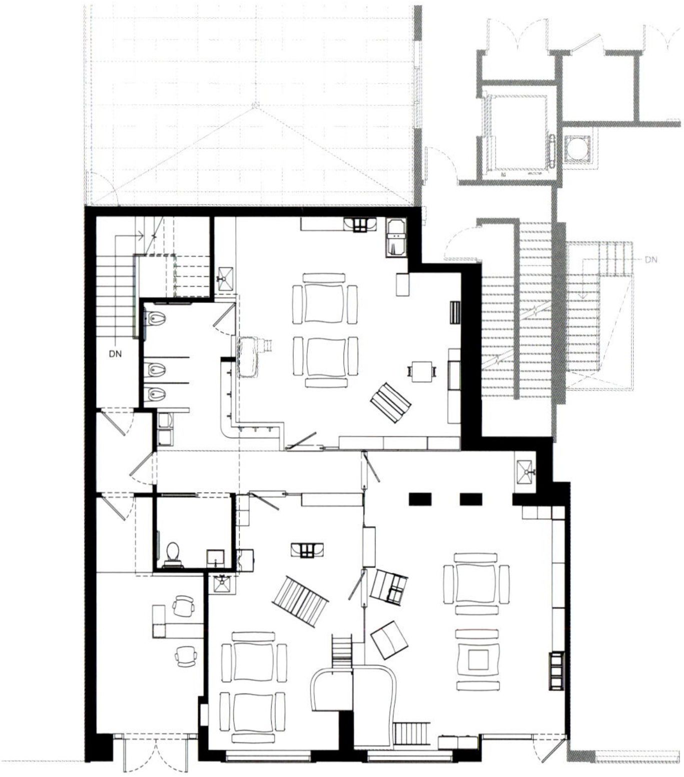

Ground floor plan

Challenge Design
Jie Lee

// PROJECTS //

1. TON WEN KINDERGARTEN
2. PARK LEGEND KINDERGARTEN

http://www.challenge-design.com

Challenge Design
Jie Lee

1.

2.

Graduated from School of Civil Engineering & Architecture of Nanchang University in 1995, Jie Lee was granted such national and vocational certifications as National Class 1 Registered Architects, National Certified Planner, International Certified Senior Green Engineer and, WACA Senior fellow. In April 2013, he founded "Challenge Design", and acted as the chief architect of Challenge Design Pte Ltd. (Class A architectural design office).
The aim of the company has been to provide "refined design and professional service" since its foundation. Challenge Design has been working to find a way for realization of harmonious co-existence between architecture, human being and the nature, hoping to find a possible way for bring renewed sense experience and creating new thoughts & spatial forms through creative thinking. The company has won many international awards, including 12th International Design Awards "Architect Design of the Year" and the "New Commercial Building Gold Award."

Diplômée de l'école de génie civil et d'architecture de l'université de Nanchang en 1995, Jie Lee a obtenu des certifications nationales et professionnelles telles que celle d'architecte national de classe 1, de planificateur national certifié, d'ingénieur écologique senior international certifié et de chercheur principal de la WACA. En avril 2013, il a fondé « Challenge Design », et a été l'architecte en chef de Challenge Design Pte Ltd. (bureau de conception architecturale de classe A).
L'objectif de l'entreprise est de fournir « un design raffiné et un service professionnel » depuis sa création. Challenge Design s'est efforcé de trouver un moyen de réaliser une coexistence harmonieuse entre l'architecture, l'être humain et la nature, en espérant trouver une manière possible d'apporter une expérience sensorielle renouvelée et de créer de nouvelles pensées et formes spatiales par la pensée créative. L'entreprise a remporté de nombreux prix internationaux, dont le 12e prix international de design « Architect Design of the Year » et le « New Commercial Building Gold Award ».

Jie Lee schloss 1995 die School of Civil Engineering & Architecture der Universität Nanchang ab und erhielt nationale und berufliche Zertifizierungen wie National Class 1 Registered Architects, National Certified Planner, International Certified Senior Green Engineer und WACA Senior Fellow. Im April 2013 gründete er „Challenge Design" und fungierte als Chefarchitekt von Challenge Design Pte Ltd. (Architekturbüro der Klasse A).
Das Ziel des Unternehmens ist es seit seiner Gründung, „verfeinertes Design und professionellen Service" zu bieten. Challenge Design hat daran gearbeitet, einen Weg zur Verwirklichung einer harmonischen Koexistenz zwischen Architektur, Mensch und Natur zu finden, in der Hoffnung, einen möglichen Weg zu finden, um durch kreatives Denken neue Sinneserfahrungen zu bringen und neue Gedanken & Raumformen zu schaffen. Das Unternehmen hat viele internationale Preise gewonnen, darunter den 12. Internationalen Designpreis „Architect Design of the Year" und den „New Commercial Building Gold Award".

Graduado de la Escuela de Ingeniería Civil y Arquitectura de la Universidad de Nanchang en 1995, a Jie Lee se le concedieron certificaciones nacionales y vocacionales tales como la National Class 1 Registered Architects, la National Certified Planner, el International Certified Senior Green Engineer y el WACA Senior fellow. En abril de 2013, fundó Challenge Design, y actuó como arquitecto jefe de Challenge Design Pte Ltd. (oficina de diseño arquitectónico de clase A).
El objetivo de la compañía ha sido proporcionar «diseño refinado y servicio profesional» desde su fundación. Challenge Design ha estado trabajando para encontrar una manera de realizar la coexistencia armoniosa entre la arquitectura, el ser humano y la naturaleza, con la esperanza de encontrar una posible manera de crear nuevos pensamientos y formas espaciales a través del pensamiento creativo. La empresa ha ganado muchos premios internacionales, entre ellos el 12º Premio Internacional de Diseño «Diseño de Arquitecto del Año» y el New Commercial Building Gold Award.

TON WEN KINDERGARTEN

LOCATION: **QUANZHOU CITY, FUJIAN PROVINCE, CHINA**
PHOTOS: © **WEIMIN YU**

The project is located on an irregular plot flanked to the north and west by high rise residential buildings. To soften the conflictive relationship with these, the kindergarten is developed around a central courtyard that provides a safe play area and a meeting place for daily activities. Wide open corridors connect all the spaces on each level and also act as a play area. Three types of windows open, producing different light and shade effects and enriching the indoor and outdoor visual experience. Skylights on the roofs of the third floor project a rainbow onto the white walls of each classroom every morning. The combinations of the building's sloping roofs create a visual game that generates a "fifth facade" for the residents of the neighboring buildings.

Das Projekt befindet sich auf einem unregelmäßigen Grundstück, das im Norden und Westen von hoch aufragenden Wohngebäuden flankiert wird. Um die konfliktreiche Beziehung zu diesen zu mildern, wird der Kindergarten um einen zentralen Hof herum entwickelt, der einen sicheren Spielbereich und einen Treffpunkt für die täglichen Aktivitäten bietet. Weite offene Korridore verbinden alle Räume auf jeder Ebene und dienen auch als Spielbereich. Drei Arten von Fenstern öffnen sich, erzeugen unterschiedliche Licht- und Schatteneffekte und bereichern das visuelle Erlebnis im Innen- und Außenbereich. Oberlichter auf den Dächern des dritten Stocks projizieren jeden Morgen einen Regenbogen auf die weißen Wände jedes Klassenzimmers. Die Kombinationen der Schrägdächer des Gebäudes erzeugen ein visuelles Spiel, das eine "fünfte Fassade" für die Bewohner der benachbarten Gebäude erzeugt.

Le projet est situé sur une parcelle irrégulière flanquée au nord et à l'ouest d'immeubles résidentiels de grande hauteur. Afin d'adoucir la relation conflictuelle avec ces derniers, le jardin d'enfants est développé autour d'une cour centrale qui offre une aire de jeu sûre et un lieu de rencontre pour les activités quotidiennes. De larges couloirs ouverts relient tous les espaces de chaque niveau et font également office d'aire de jeu. Trois types de fenêtres s'ouvrent, produisant des effets d'ombre et de lumière différents et enrichissant l'expérience visuelle à l'intérieur et à l'extérieur. Les lucarnes des toits du troisième étage projettent chaque matin un arc-en-ciel sur les murs blancs de chaque salle de classe. Les combinaisons des toits inclinés des bâtiments créent un jeu visuel qui génère une « cinquième façade » pour les résidents des bâtiments voisins.

El proyecto se ubica en una parcela irregular flanqueada al norte y al oeste por edificios residenciales de gran altura. Para suavizar la relación conflictiva con estos, el jardín de infancia se desarrolla en torno a un patio central que proporciona un área de juegos segura y un lugar de encuentro para las actividades diarias. Unos amplios corredores abiertos conectan todos los espacios de cada nivel y actúan también como zona de juegos. En ellos se abren tres tipos de ventanas, que producen diferentes efectos de luz y sombra y enriquecen la experiencia visual interior y exterior. Unos lucernarios dispuestos en las cubiertas del tercer piso proyectan cada mañana un arco iris sobre las paredes blancas de cada aula. Las combinaciones de las cubiertas inclinadas del edificio crean un juego visual que genera una «quinta fachada» para los residentes de las edificaciones vecinas.

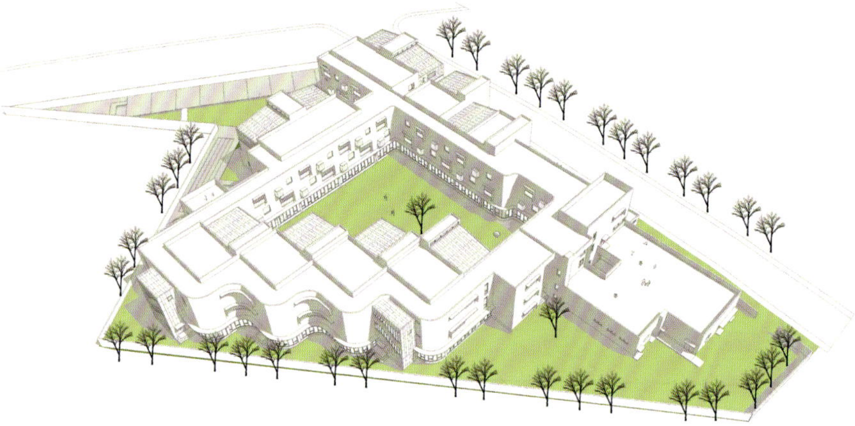

West-north Aerial View

Open corridor

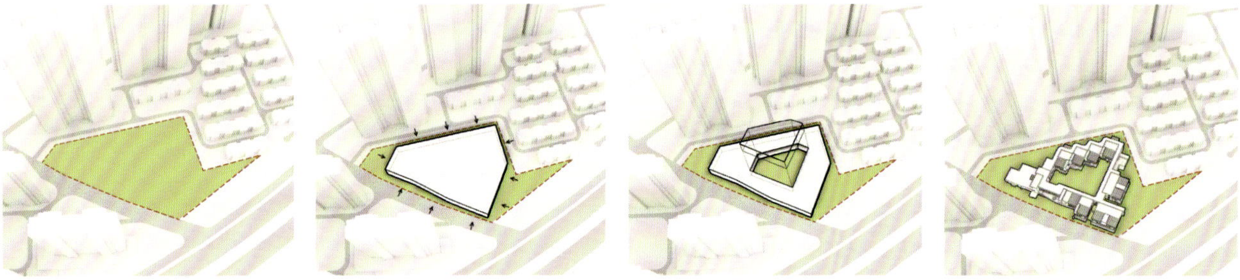

Concept diagrams

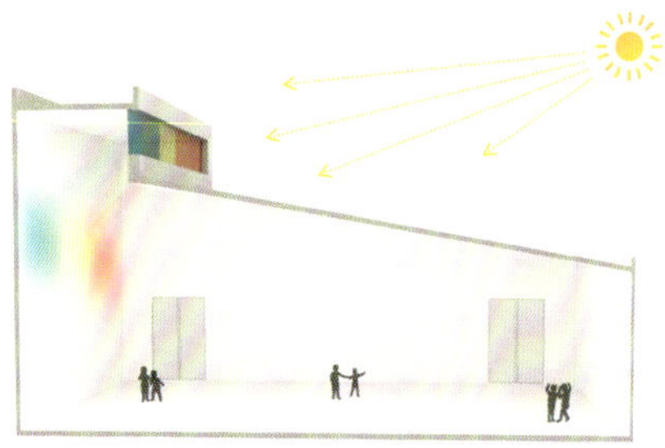

Skylight diagram

Floor plan

1. Activity room
2. Comunication room
3. Teacher's office
4. Kitchen
5. Function room
6. Reception room
7. Fire control room
8. Piano room

TAXI

PARK LEGEND KINDERGARTEN

LOCATION: **TIANFU NEW AREA, CHENGDU, CHINA**
PHOTOS: **© PRISM IMAGES/LUJING/XIONGHUAN**

The design of this kindergarten breaks with existing conventions and presents a pure and simple building that, following the dictates of Gestalt psychology, children perceive in all its complexity. The project creates a harmonious combination of nature and modernity, linking different buildings along a circular non-enclosed guideline, whose shape imitates the profiles of the surrounding mountains. The interior spaces are designed to break down the constraints of physical partitions and generate multifunctional areas for learning and children interaction. The predominant white colour gives prominence to the shapes of the whole and serves as a canvas for the surrounding nature, demonstrating that kindergartens do not necessarily need a colourful design to express life and beauty and to allow children to explore and learn.

Der Entwurf dieses Kindergartens bricht mit bestehenden Konventionen und präsentiert ein schlichtes und einfaches Gebäude, das die Kinder nach dem Diktat der Gestaltpsychologie in seiner ganzen Komplexität wahrnehmen. Das Projekt schafft eine harmonische Verbindung von Natur und Modernität, indem es verschiedene Gebäude entlang einer kreisförmigen, nicht umschlossenen Leitlinie verbindet, deren Form die Profile der umliegenden Berge imitiert. Die Innenräume sind so gestaltet, dass sie die Zwänge physischer Trennwände aufbrechen und multifunktionale Bereiche für das Lernen und die Interaktion zwischen den Kindern schaffen. Die vorherrschende weiße Farbe hebt die Formen des Ganzen hervor und dient als Leinwand für die umgebende Natur, was zeigt, dass Kindergärten nicht unbedingt ein farbenfrohes Design benötigen, um Leben und Schönheit auszudrücken und den Kindern zu ermöglichen, zu erforschen und zu lernen.

La conception de ce jardin d'enfants rompt avec les conventions existantes et présente un bâtiment pur et simple que, suivant les diktats de la psychologie de la Gestalt, les enfants perçoivent dans toute sa complexité. Le projet crée une combinaison harmonieuse de nature et de modernité, en reliant différents bâtiments le long d'une ligne directrice circulaire non fermée, dont la forme imite les profils des montagnes environnantes. Les espaces intérieurs sont conçus pour briser les contraintes des cloisons physiques et générer des zones multifonctionnelles pour l'apprentissage et l'interaction entre les enfants. La couleur blanche prédominante met en évidence les formes de l'ensemble et sert de toile pour la nature environnante, ce qui démontre que les jardins d'enfants n'ont pas nécessairement besoin d'un design coloré pour exprimer la vie et la beauté et pour permettre aux enfants d'explorer et d'apprendre.

El diseño de este jardín de infancia rompe con las convenciones existentes y presenta un edificio puro y simple que, siguiendo los dictados de la psicología de la Gestalt, los niños perciben en toda su complejidad. El proyecto crea una armoniosa combinación de naturaleza y modernidad, enlazando diferentes edificios a lo largo de una directriz circular no cerrada, cuya forma imita los perfiles de las montañas circundantes. Los espacios interiores se conciben para romper las restricciones de las particiones físicas y generar áreas multifuncionales de aprendizaje y de interacción entre los niños. El color blanco predominante da protagonismo a las formas del conjunto y sirve de lienzo para la naturaleza que lo rodea, demostrando que los jardines de infancia no necesitan por fuerza un diseño colorido para expresar vida y belleza y para permitir a los niños explorar y aprender.

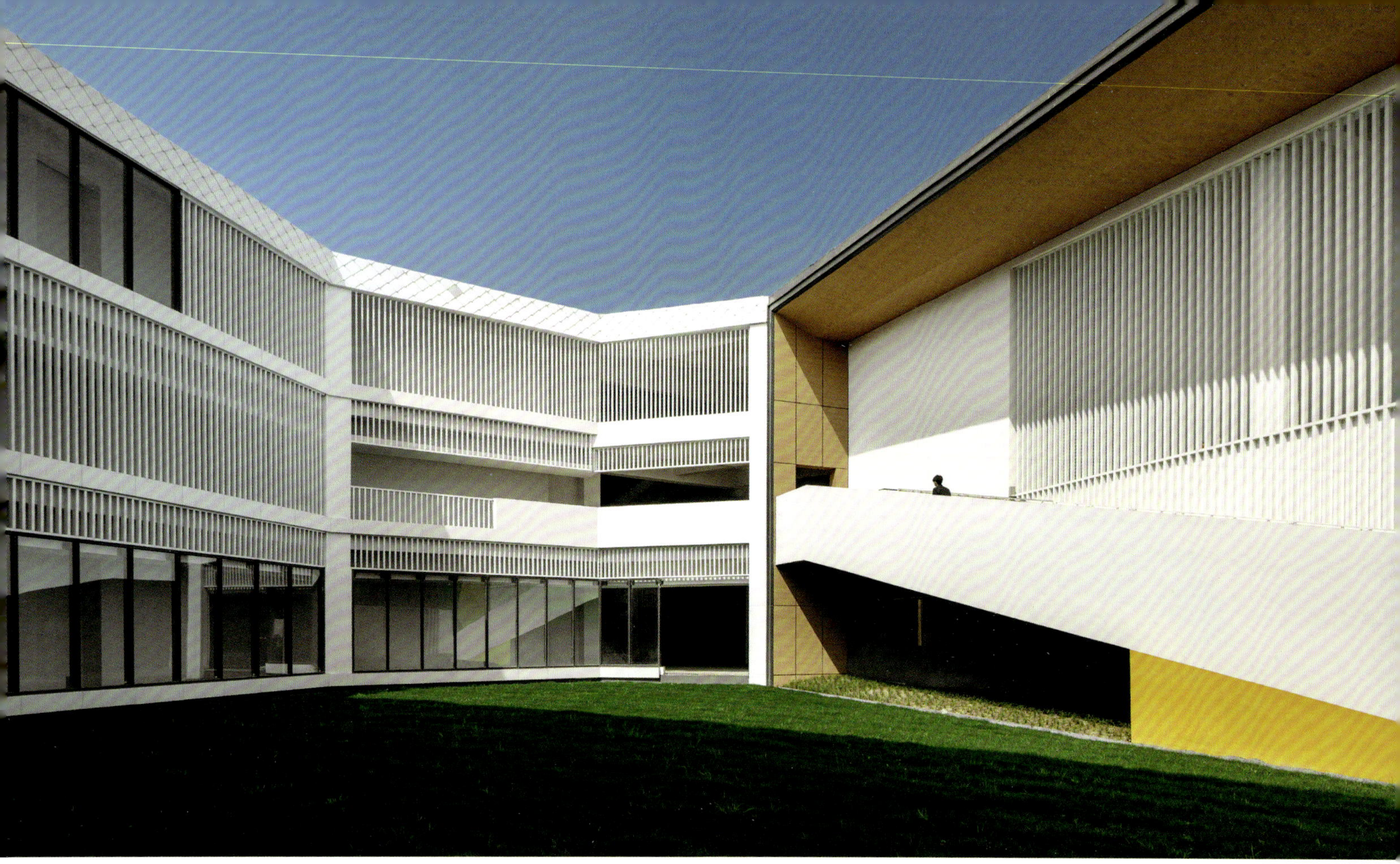

Master plan

1. City green belt
2. Residential area
3. Main entrance
4. Backdoor entrance
5. Open activity space
6. Playground
7. Second floor
8. Third floor

Floor plan

East elevation

South elevation

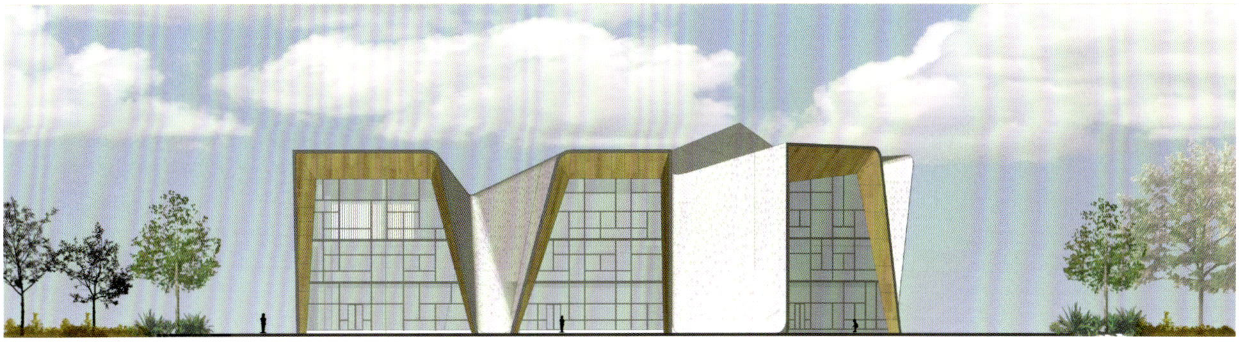

West elevation

North elevation

Cobe

// PROJECTS //

1. FORFATTERHUSET KINDERGARTEN
2. FREDERIKSVEJ KINDERGARTEN

www.cobe.dk

Cobe

1.

2.

Cobe was founded in 2006 by the architect Dan Stubbergaard. Based in Copenhagen, we have played a major role in the transformation of the Danish capital. Today, the company is a bustling international environment of more than 150 dedicated professionals devoted to creating extraordinary cities, buildings and landscapes that make a difference in everyday life.
We offer services within urban planning, architecture, landscape architecture and interior design. Every day we strive for extraordinary, long-lasting quality in the cities, buildings and landscapes we shape. Today, the building and construction sector account for 40% of the world's CO_2 emissions. We know that any newly built neighborhood, house or urban space requires a certain amount of our planet's resources, and we have a profound responsibility to exchange these into resilient, long-term solutions —cities, buildings and landscapes that are made to outlast our generation.

Cobe wurde 2006 vom Architekten Dan Stubbergaard gegründet. Mit Sitz in Kopenhagen haben wir eine wichtige Rolle bei der Umgestaltung der dänischen Hauptstadt gespielt. Heute ist das Unternehmen ein lebendiges internationales Umfeld mit mehr als 150 Fachleuten, die sich der Schaffung außergewöhnlicher Städte, Gebäude und Landschaften widmen, die im Alltag einen Unterschied machen.
Wir bieten Dienstleistungen in den Bereichen Stadtplanung, Architektur, Landschaftsarchitektur und Innenarchitektur an. Jeden Tag bemühen wir uns um außergewöhnliche und dauerhafte Qualität in den Städten, Gebäuden und Landschaften, die wir modellieren. Der Gebäudesektor ist heute für 40% der weltweiten CO_2-Emissionen verantwortlich. Wir wissen, dass jede neue Nachbarschaft, jedes neue Haus oder jeder neue städtische Raum einen bestimmten Anteil der Ressourcen unseres Planeten benötigt, und wir tragen eine große Verantwortung dafür, sie für langfristige, belastbare Lösungen zu verändern - Städte, Gebäude und Landschaften, die für eine längere Lebensdauer als unsere eigene Generation gemacht sind.

Cobe a été fondée en 2006 par l'architecte Dan Stubbergaard. Basés à Copenhague, nous avons joué un rôle majeur dans la transformation de la capitale danoise. Aujourd'hui, la société est un environnement international animé de plus de 150 professionnels dévoués qui se consacrent à la création de villes, de bâtiments et de paysages extraordinaires qui font une différence dans la vie quotidienne.
Nous offrons des services dans les domaines de l'urbanisme, de l'architecture, de l'architecture paysagère et de la décoration intérieure. Chaque jour, nous nous efforçons d'obtenir une qualité extraordinaire et durable dans les villes, les bâtiments et les paysages que nous façonnons. Aujourd'hui, le secteur du bâtiment et de la construction représente 40 % des émissions mondiales de CO_2. Nous savons que tout quartier, maison ou espace urbain nouvellement construit nécessite une certaine quantité de ressources de notre planète, et nous avons la profonde responsabilité de les échanger en solutions résilientes et à long terme - des villes, des bâtiments et des paysages qui sont faits pour durer plus longtemps que notre génération.

Cobe fue fundada en 2006 por el arquitecto Dan Stubbergaard. Con sede en Copenhague, hemos jugado un papel importante en la transformación de la capital danesa. Hoy en día, la empresa es un animado entorno internacional de más de ciento cincuenta profesionales dedicados a crear ciudades, edificios y paisajes extraordinarios que marcan la diferencia en la vida cotidiana.
Ofrecemos servicios dentro de la planificación urbana, la arquitectura, la arquitectura paisajística y el diseño de interiores. Cada día nos esforzamos por lograr una calidad extraordinaria y duradera en las ciudades, edificios y paisajes que modelamos. Hoy en día, el sector de la construcción representa el 40% de las emisiones de CO_2 en el mundo. Sabemos que cualquier vecindario, casa o espacio urbano de nueva construcción requiere una cierta cantidad de los recursos de nuestro planeta, y tenemos la profunda responsabilidad de cambiarlos por soluciones resistentes y a largo plazo: ciudades, edificios y paisajes hechos para durar más tiempo que nuestra propia generación.

FORFATTERHUSET KINDERGARTEN

LOCATION: **COPENHAGEN, DENMARK**
PHOTOS: © **ADAM MØRK AND RASMUS HJORTSHØJ**

Located in a historic neighborhood mainly populated by residences for the elderly, the establishment of this nursery represents a contrast in the vital dynamics of the area. The building consists of five small volumes with curved corners from one to three floors high, equipped with terraces and green areas on their roofs. Its facade features a cladding of thin ceramic pieces placed vertically that evokes the red brick facades of the area. This cladding surrounds all the volumes and extends to the roofs, the gardens and the playground, forming elements of protection and separation and giving the complex a uniform image. The interior space, dominated by a white colour that contrasts with the oxidised tone of the exterior, is organised around an atrium at a triple height delimited by a metallic mesh in whose interior a staircase rises.

Située dans un quartier historique principalement peuplé de résidences pour personnes âgées, l'implantation de cette crèche représente un contraste dans la dynamique vitale du quartier. Le bâtiment se compose de cinq petits volumes aux angles arrondis d'un à trois étages de hauteur, équipés de terrasses et d'espaces verts sur leurs toits. Sa façade présente un revêtement de fines pièces de céramique placées verticalement qui évoque les façades en briques rouges de la région. Ce revêtement entoure tous les volumes et s'étend aux toits, aux jardins et à l'aire de jeux, formant des éléments de protection et de séparation et donnant au complexe une image uniforme. L'espace intérieur, dominé par une couleur blanche qui contraste avec le ton oxydé de l'extérieur, s'organise autour d'un atrium à triple hauteur délimité par une grille métallique à l'intérieur de laquelle s'élève un escalier.

Die Einrichtung dieser Kinderkrippe in einem historischen Viertel, in dem hauptsächlich Seniorenresidenzen angesiedelt sind, stellt einen Kontrast in der vitalen Dynamik des Viertels dar. Das Gebäude besteht aus fünf kleinen Volumina mit geschwungenen Ecken von ein bis drei Stockwerken Höhe, die auf ihren Dächern mit Terrassen und Grünflächen ausgestattet sind. Seine Fassade weist eine Verkleidung aus dünnen, vertikal angeordneten Keramikstücken auf, die an die roten Backsteinfassaden der Gegend erinnert. Diese Verkleidung umschließt alle Volumen und erstreckt sich bis zu den Dächern, den Gärten und dem Spielplatz, bildet Schutz- und Trennelemente und verleiht der Anlage ein einheitliches Bild. Der Innenraum, der von einer weißen Farbe dominiert wird, die mit dem oxidierten Ton des Äußeren kontrastiert, ist um ein Atrium in dreifacher Höhe organisiert, das durch ein Metallgewebe begrenzt wird, in dessen Innern eine Treppe aufsteigt.

Situada en un barrio histórico poblado principalmente de residencias para mayores, la implantación de esta guardería supone un contraste en la dinámica vital de la zona. El edificio consta de cinco pequeños volúmenes de esquinas curvas de uno a tres pisos de altura, dotados de terrazas y zonas verdes en sus cubiertas. Su fachada presenta un revestimiento de delgadas piezas cerámicas colocadas en vertical que evoca las fachadas de ladrillo rojo de la zona. Este revestimiento rodea todos los volúmenes y se extiende hacia las cubiertas, los jardines y el patio de recreo, formando elementos de protección y separación y dotando al conjunto de una imagen uniforme. El espacio interior, dominado por un color blanco que contrasta con el tono oxidado del exterior, se organiza alrededor de un atrio a triple altura delmitado por una malla metálica en cuyo interior se eleva una escalera.

Front elevation

Section

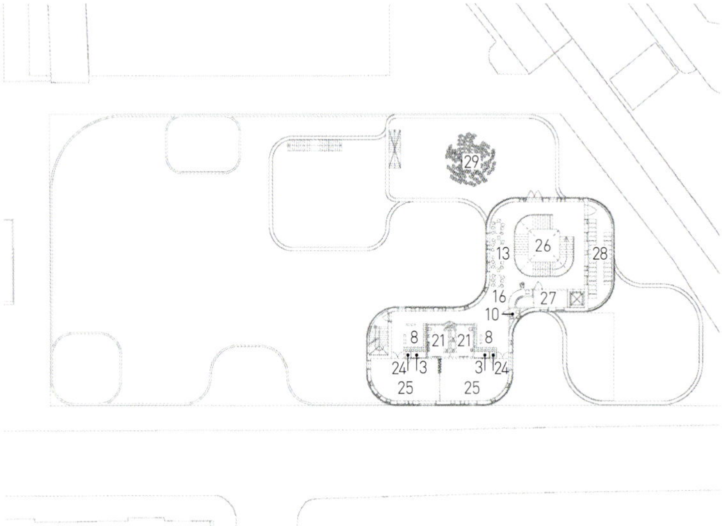

Second floor plan

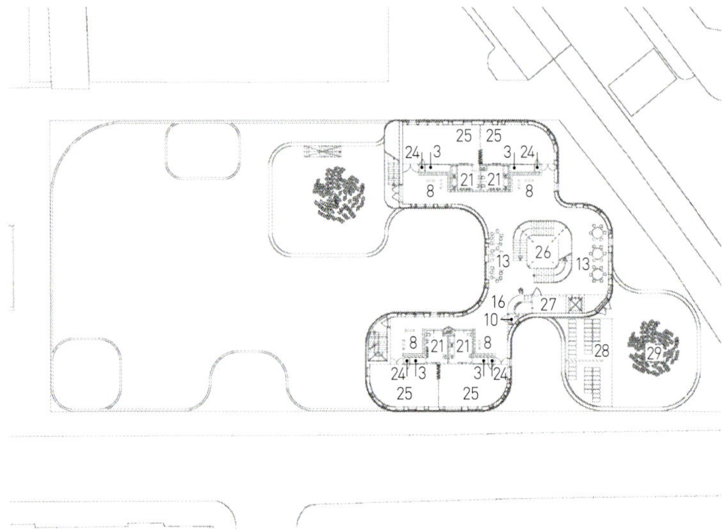

First floor plan

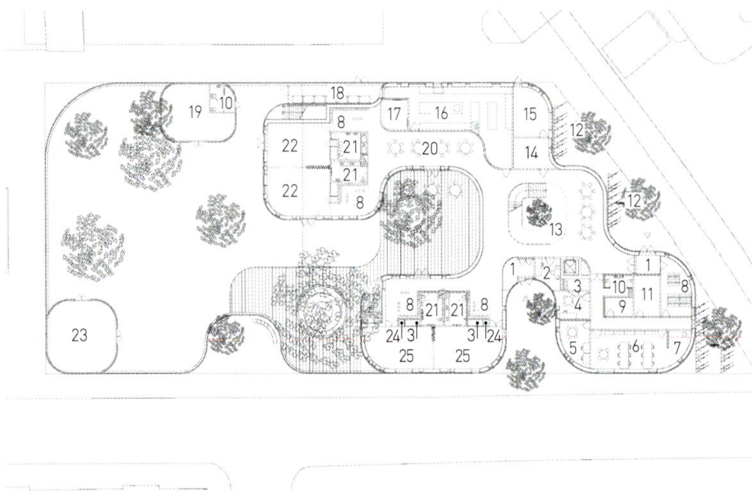

Ground floor plan

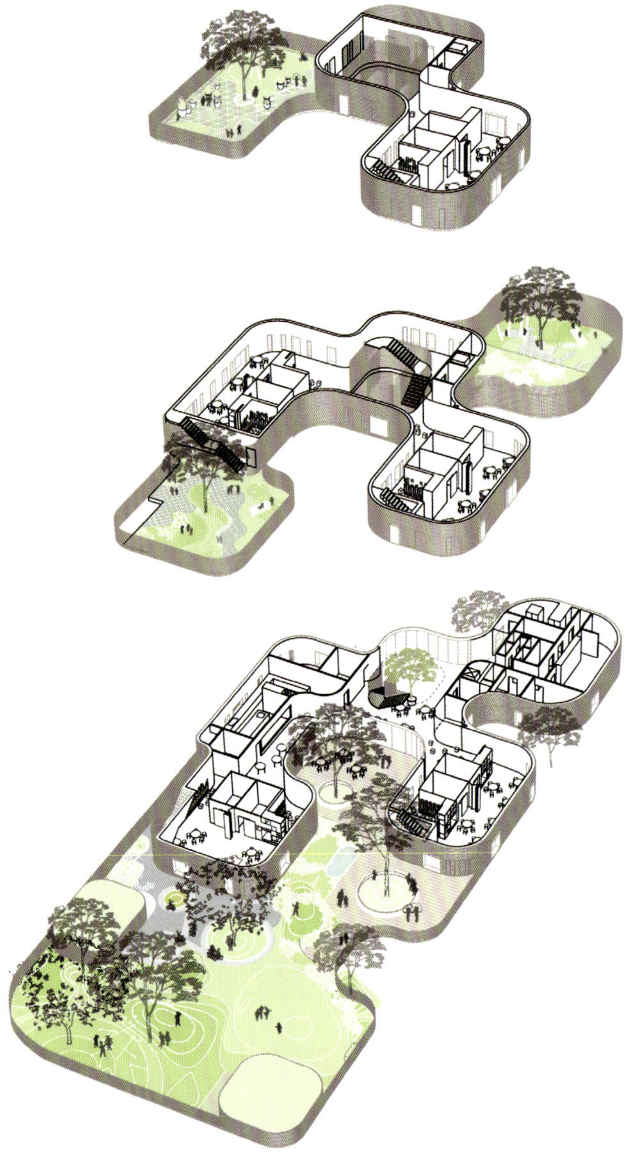

Axonometry

1. Porch
2. Administration
3. Depot
4. Meeting room
5. Management office
6. Staff room
7. Kitchenette
8. Wardrobe
9. Utility
10. Toilet
11. Cleaning rooms
12. Bicycle parking
13. Common rooms / workshops
14. Common storage
15. Technical room
16. Kitchen
17. Pantry
18. Renovation area
19. Utility room / shed
20. Educational project kitchen
21. Children's toilet
22. Kindergarten group room
23. Pram
24. Drying cabinet
25. Nursery group room
26. Atrium
27. Common depot
28. Bunk beds / cribs
29. Terrace

FREDERIKSVEJ KINDERGARTEN

LOCATION: **FREDERIKSBERG, DENMARK**
PHOTOS: **© ADAM MØRK AND RASMUS HJORTSHØJ**

The starting point of the project was to create a building from a child's point of view, for which the design was based on the concept of the traditional playhouse. The building is composed of eleven volumes that house various smaller houses with different sizes and functions, creating an architecture that is as comprehensible, simple and pure as a child's drawing, and whose size is progressively reduced to a playhouse. From small intimate play areas to larger rooms for common use, the diversity of spaces helps to create interesting and stimulating environments for all children despite their different personalities, preferences and needs. At the same time, the analogy of the sloping roofs of the different houses helps to unite the whole and creates a familiar and recognizable context for the children.

Le point de départ du projet était de créer un bâtiment du point de vue d'un enfant, dont la conception était basée sur le concept de la maison de jeux traditionnelle. Le bâtiment est composé de onze volumes principaux qui abritent plusieurs petites maisons de tailles et de fonctions différentes, créant une architecture aussi compréhensible, simple et pure qu'un dessin d'enfant, et dont la taille est progressivement réduite à une maison de jeux. Des petites aires de jeu intimes aux grandes pièces à usage commun, la diversité des espaces contribue à créer des environnements intéressants et stimulants pour tous les enfants, malgré leurs différentes personnalités, préférences et besoins. En même temps, l'homogénéité des toits en pente des différentes maisons contribue à unifier l'ensemble et crée un contexte familier et reconnaissable pour les enfants.

Ausgangspunkt des Projekts war die Schaffung eines Gebäudes aus der Sicht eines Kindes, wobei der Entwurf auf dem Konzept des traditionellen Spielhauses basierte. Das Gebäude besteht aus elf Hauptbaukörpern, die verschiedene kleinere Häuser mit unterschiedlichen Größen und Funktionen beherbergen. So entsteht eine Architektur, die so verständlich, einfach und rein wie eine Kinderzeichnung ist und deren Größe nach und nach zu einem Spielhaus reduziert wird. Von kleinen intimen Spielbereichen bis hin zu größeren Räumen zur gemeinsamen Nutzung hilft die Vielfalt der Räume dabei, interessante und anregende Umgebungen für alle Kinder zu schaffen, trotz ihrer unterschiedlichen Persönlichkeiten, Vorlieben und Bedürfnisse. Gleichzeitig trägt die Homogenität der Schrägdächer der verschiedenen Häuser zur Einheit des Ganzen bei und schafft einen vertrauten und erkennbaren Kontext für die Kinder.

El punto de partida del proyecto fue crear un edificio desde el punto de vista de un niño, para lo cual su diseño se basó en el concepto de la tradicional casita de juegos. El edificio se compone de once volúmenes principales que alojan diversas casas más pequeñas con diferentes tamaños y funciones, que crean una arquitectura comprensible, simple y pura como el dibujo de un niño y cuyo tamaño disminuye progresivamente hasta reducir el edificio a una casita de juegos. Desde pequeños ámbitos de juego íntimos hasta salas más grandes de uso común, la diversidad de espacios ayuda a crear ambientes interesantes y estimulantes para todos los niños a pesar de sus diferentes personalidades, preferencias y necesidades. A su vez, la homogeneidad en las cubiertas inclinadas de las diferentes casas ayuda a cohesionar el conjunto y crea un contexto familiar y reconocible para los niños.

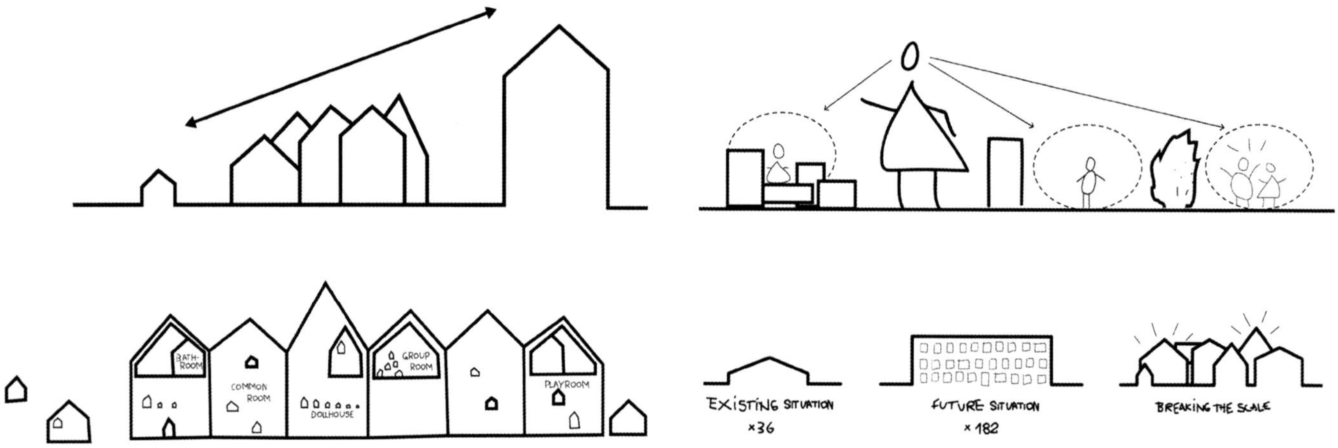

Concept diagrams

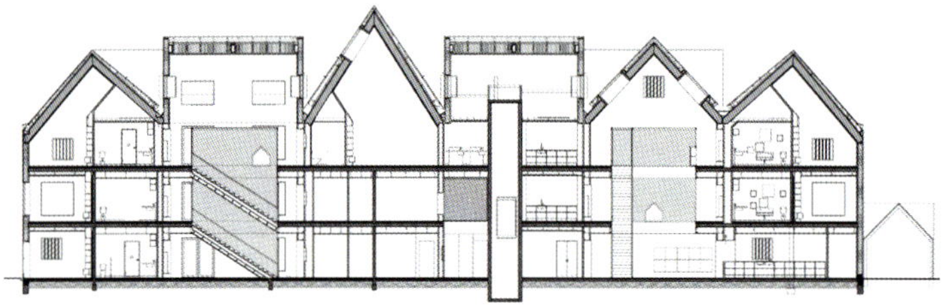

Section

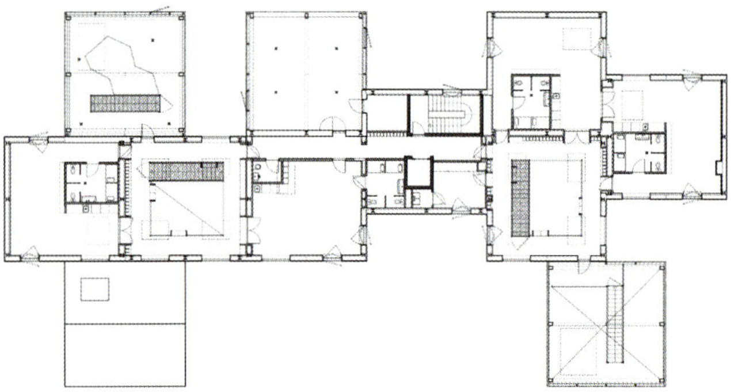

Second floor plan

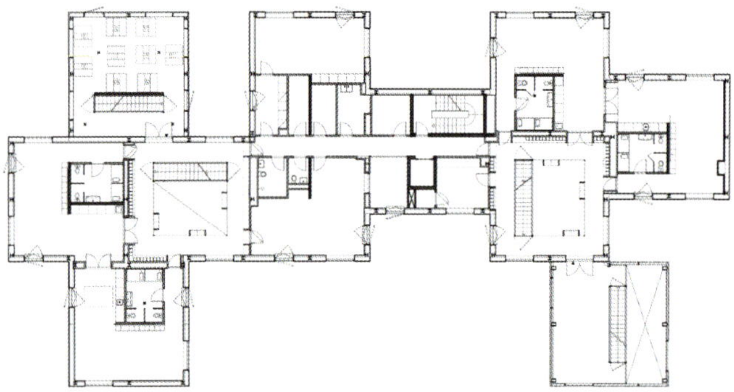

First floor plan

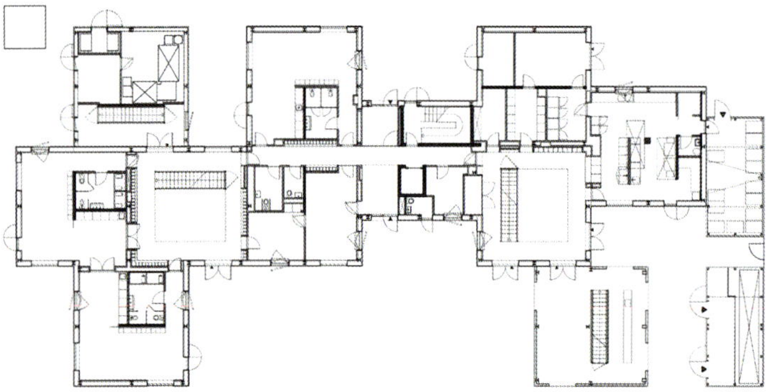

Ground floor plan

continiarchitettura
Marco Contini & Sara Chiari

// PROJECTS //

1. PRIMARY SCHOOL IN LOIANO
2. SCHOOL COMPLEX IN FELINO

www.continiarchitettura.net

continiarchitettura
Marco Contini & Sara Chiari

1.

2.

studio_ continiarchitettura, formed by the association of architects Marco Contini and Sara Chiari, is located in the village of Torrechiara, near the Parma Apennines in Italy. Most of its works are located in this unique area.
Marco Contini graduated in 1986 from the Istituto Universitario di Architettura in Venice, under the tutelage of Vittorio Gregotti. Sara Chiari graduated in 1995 from the Florence School of Architecture, and in 2010 she started her collaboration with studio_contini.
Her method of approaching projects is related to the interpretation of the historical and geographical context, and to the use of traditional materials and techniques combined with the application of innovative technologies. This method considers the constant presence of architects during the different phases of construction to be essential.

studio_ continiarchitettura, das von der Vereinigung der Architekten Marco Contini und Sara Chiari gegründet wurde, befindet sich im Dorf Torrechiara, in der Nähe des Parma-Apennins in Italien. Die meisten seiner Werke befinden sich in diesem charakteristischen Gebiet.
Marco Contini schloss 1986 sein Studium am Istituto Universitario di Architettura in Venedig unter der Leitung von Vittorio Gregotti ab. Sara Chiari schloss 1995 ihr Studium an der Architekturschule in Florenz ab und begann 2010 ihre Zusammenarbeit mit studio_contini.
Ihre Methode, an Projekte heranzugehen, bezieht sich auf die Interpretation des historischen und geographischen Kontextes sowie auf die Verwendung traditioneller Materialien und Techniken in Verbindung mit der Anwendung innovativer Technologien. Diese Methode erachtet die ständige Anwesenheit von Architekten während der verschiedenen Bauphasen als unerlässlich.

studio_ continiarchitettura, formé par l'association des architectes Marco Contini et Sara Chiari, est situé dans le village de Torrechiara, près des Apennins de Parme en Italie. La plupart de ses œuvres sont situées dans cette zone caractéristique.
Marco Contini est diplômé en 1986 de l'Istituto Universitario di Architettura de Venise, sous la direction de Vittorio Gregotti. Sara Chiari a obtenu son diplôme en 1995 à l'école d'architecture de Florence, et en 2010 elle a commencé sa collaboration avec studio_contini.
Sa méthode d'approche des projets est liée à l'interprétation du contexte historique et géographique, et à l'utilisation de matériaux et de techniques traditionnels combinée à l'application de technologies innovantes. Cette méthode considère comme essentielle la présence constante des architectes pendant les différentes phases de la construction.

studio_ continiarchitettura, formada por la asociación de los arquitectos Marco Contini y Sara Chiari, se ubica en el pueblo de Torrechiara, cerca de los Apeninos de Parma, en Italia. La mayor parte de sus obras se emplaza en este área característica.
Marco Contini se graduó en 1986 en el Istituto Universitario di Architettura de Venecia, siendo su tutor Vittorio Gregotti. Sara Chiari se graduó en 1995 en la facultad de Arquitectura de Florencia, y en 2010 comenzó su colaboración con studio_contini.
Su método de aproximación a los proyectos está relacionada con la interpretación del contexto histórico y geográfico, y con el uso de materiales y técnicas tradicionales combinados con la aplicación de tecnologías innovadoras. Este método considera esencial la constante presencia de los arquitectos durante las distintas fases de la construcción.

PRIMARY SCHOOL IN LOIANO

LOCATION: **LOIANO, BOLOGNA, ITALY**
PHOTOS: © **DAVIDE GALLI (HTTP://DAVIDEGALLIATELIER.COM/)**

In the design and implementation of this school, the architects sought the well-being of future users and a harmonious relationship with the geographical context. The building is partially buried in the ground to minimize its visual impact and to generate two levels with direct access to extensive green areas. Its programme proposes an adaptability of interior spaces that makes it possible to use it as a civic centre for the local community. The building meets NZB standards (zero emission energy consumption buildings) thanks to the high performance of its envelope and the use of photovoltaic energy. The façades are clad in stone at the base and coloured plaster at the top, differentiating the two levels and integrating the building into the environment. The wood of the interior coverings creates a calm perception and welcoming learning environments.

Bei der Planung und Umsetzung dieser Schule strebten die Architekten das Wohlbefinden der künftigen Nutzer und eine harmonische Beziehung zum geografischen Kontext an. Das Gebäude ist teilweise in den Boden eingegraben, um seine optische Wirkung zu minimieren und zwei Ebenen mit direktem Zugang zu ausgedehnten Grünflächen zu schaffen. Ihr Programm schlägt eine Anpassungsfähigkeit der Innenräume vor, die es ermöglicht, sie als bürgerliches Zentrum für die lokale Gemeinschaft zu nutzen. Das Gebäude erfüllt die NZB-Standards (Null-Emissions-Energieverbrauchs-Gebäude) dank der hohen Leistung seiner Hülle und der Nutzung von photovoltaischer Energie. Die Fassaden sind an der Basis mit Stein und an der Oberseite mit farbigem Putz verkleidet, wodurch die beiden Ebenen differenziert und das Gebäude in die Umgebung integriert wird. Das Holz der Innenverkleidungen schafft eine häusliche Wahrnehmung und einladende Lernumgebungen.

Dans la conception et la réalisation de cette école, les architectes ont recherché le bien-être des futurs utilisateurs et une relation harmonieuse avec le contexte géographique. Le bâtiment est partiellement enterré dans le sol afin de minimiser son impact visuel et de générer deux niveaux avec un accès direct à de vastes espaces verts. Son programme propose une adaptabilité des espaces intérieurs qui permet de l'utiliser comme un centre civique pour la communauté locale. Le bâtiment répond aux normes NZB (bâtiments à consommation d'énergie zéro émission) grâce à la haute performance de son enveloppe et à l'utilisation de l'énergie photovoltaïque. Les façades sont revêtues de pierre à la base et de plâtre coloré au sommet, ce qui permet de différencier les deux niveaux et d'intégrer le bâtiment dans l'environnement. Le bois des revêtements intérieurs crée une perception domestique et des environnements d'apprentissage accueillants.

En el diseño y la implementación de esta escuela, los arquitectos buscaron el bienestar de los futuros usuarios y una relación armoniosa con el contexto geográfico. El edificio se entierra parcialmente en el terreno para minimizar su impacto visual y generar dos niveles con acceso directo a extensas zonas verdes. Su programa plantea una adaptabilidad de espacios interiores que hace posible su uso como centro cívico de la comunidad local. El edificio cumple los estándares NZB (edificios de consumo energético con cero emisiones) gracias al alto rendimiento de su envolvente y al uso de energía fotovoltaica. Las fachadas se revisten de piedra en la base y de yeso coloreado en la parte superior, diferenciando los dos niveles e integrando el edificio en el entorno. La madera de los revestimientos interiores crea una percepción doméstica y unos ámbitos de aprendizaje acogedores.

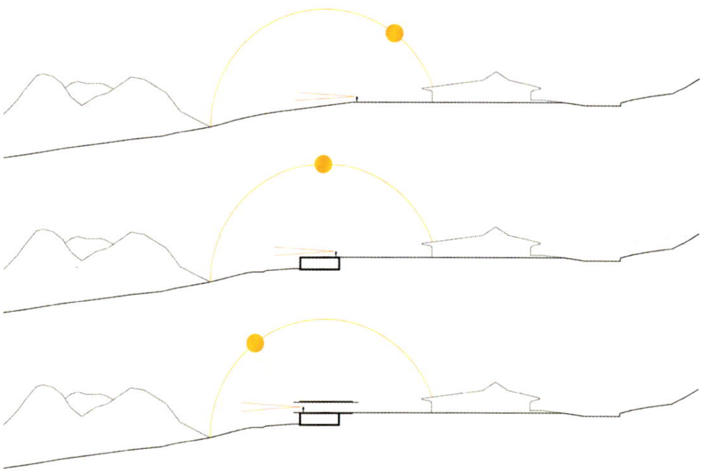

Concept diagram

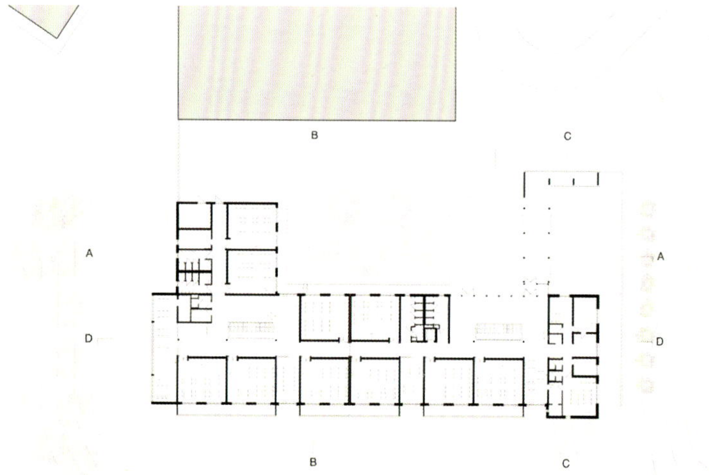

First floor plan

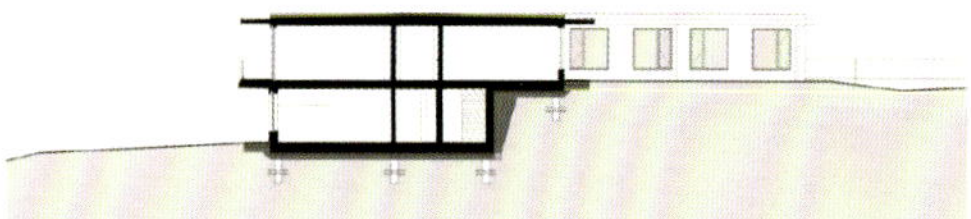

B-B section

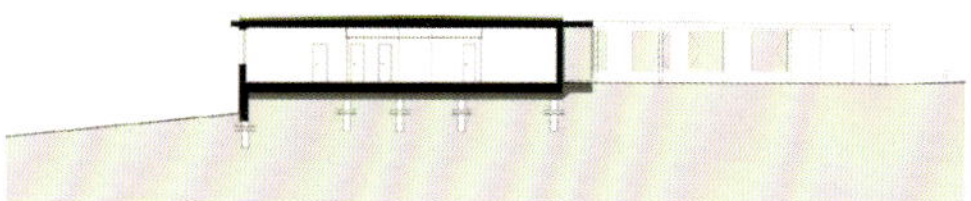

C-C section

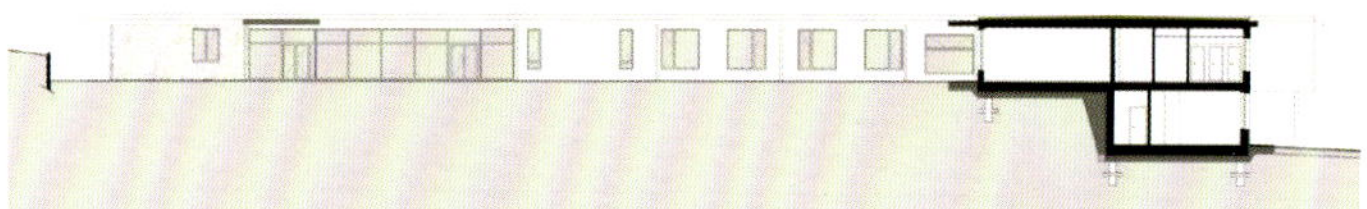

A-A section

D-D section

Ground floor plan

SCUOLA
PRIMARIA

3B

arte

SCHOOL COMPLEX IN FELINO

LOCATION: **FELINO, PARMA, ITALY**
PHOTOS: **© P.D.P., STEFANO VAIA**

This primary school constitutes the first phase of an educational center that will be characterized by its strong relationship with the future green areas foreseen in the urban planning. Its various buildings will be organized along a pedestrian and bicycle axis, which will connect them to the city centre and to sports facilities. Its interior is characterized by a double space visually and spatially connected to the exterior areas, which acts as an internal courtyard where students, teachers and parents interact. Used mainly for daily recreation, this space can also accommodate various educational activities and group meetings. The classrooms, special activity spaces and laboratories have large windows facing the surrounding green areas and their design evokes a sense of familiarity.

Diese Grundschule stellt die erste Phase eines Bildungszentrums dar, das sich durch seine starke Beziehung zu den künftigen, in der Stadtplanung vorgesehenen Grünflächen auszeichnen wird. Seine verschiedenen Gebäude werden entlang einer Fußgänger- und Fahrradachse organisiert, die sie mit dem Stadtzentrum und den Sportanlagen verbindet. Sein Inneres ist durch einen doppelten Raum gekennzeichnet, der visuell und räumlich mit den Außenbereichen verbunden ist und als Innenhof dient, in dem Schüler, Lehrer und Eltern interagieren. Dieser Raum, der hauptsächlich zur täglichen Erholung genutzt wird, kann auch für verschiedene Bildungsaktivitäten und Gruppentreffen genutzt werden. Die Klassenzimmer, speziellen Aktivitätsräume und Laboratorien haben große Fenster zu den umliegenden Grünflächen, und ihre Gestaltung ruft ein Gefühl der häuslichen Vertrautheit hervor.

Cette école primaire constitue la première phase d'un centre éducatif qui sera caractérisé par sa forte relation avec les futurs espaces verts prévus dans la planification urbaine. Ses différents bâtiments seront organisés le long d'un axe piétonnier et cyclable, qui les reliera au centre ville et aux installations sportives. Son intérieur est caractérisé par un double espace visuellement et spatialement relié aux zones extérieures, qui agit comme une cour intérieure où les étudiants, les enseignants et les parents interagissent. Utilisé principalement pour les loisirs quotidiens, cet espace peut également accueillir diverses activités éducatives et des réunions de groupe. Les salles de classe, les espaces d'activités spéciales et les laboratoires sont dotés de grandes fenêtres donnant sur les espaces verts environnants et leur conception évoque un sentiment de familiarité domestique.

Esta escuela primaria constituye la primera fase de un centro educativo que se caracterizará por su fuerte relación con las futuras áreas verdes previstas en el planeamiento urbano. Sus diversos edificios se organizarán a lo largo de un eje destinado a peatones y ciclistas, que los conectará con el centro de la ciudad y con equipamientos deportivos. Su interior se caracteriza por un doble espacio conectado visual y espacialmente con las áreas exteriores, que actúa como un patio interno donde se relacionan estudiantes, profesores y padres. Utilizado principalmente para el recreo diario, este espacio también puede albergar diversas actividades educativas y reuniones de grupo. Las aulas, los espacios para actividades especiales y los laboratorios tienen grandes ventanales orientados hacia las áreas verdes circundantes y su diseño evoca una sensación de familiaridad doméstica.

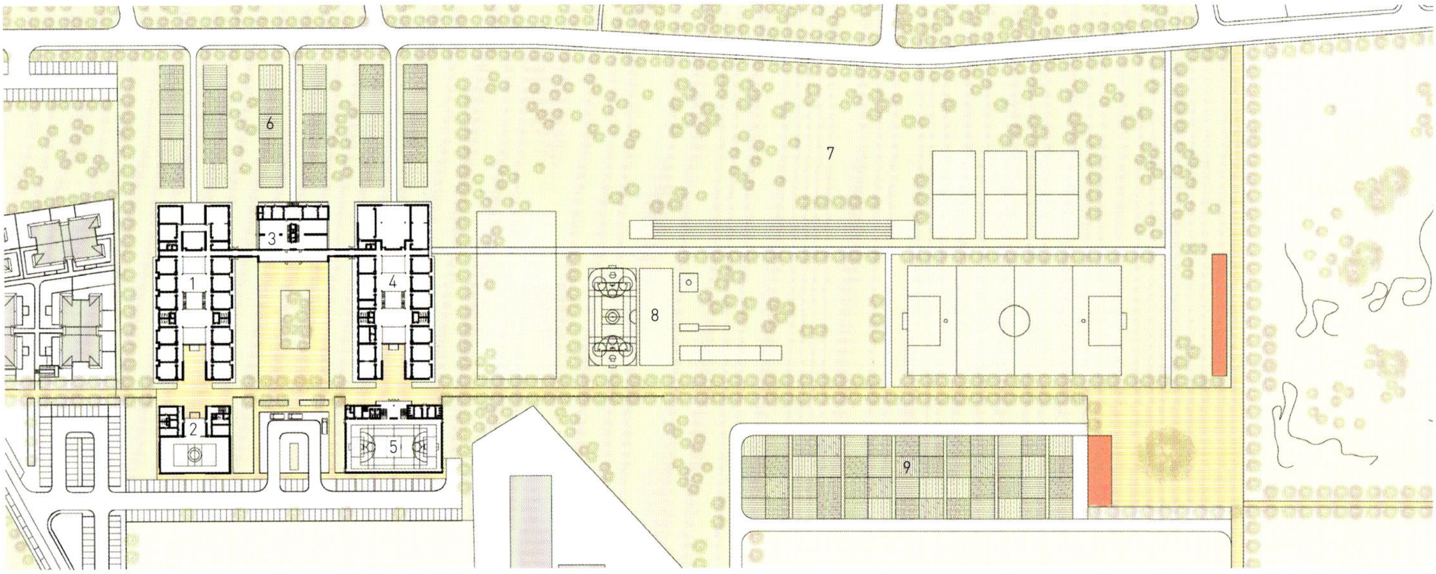

Complex plan

1. Primary school
2. Gymnasium
3. School canteen
4. Secondary school
5. Sports hall
6. Educational garden
7. Public park
8. Sports fields
9. urban gardens

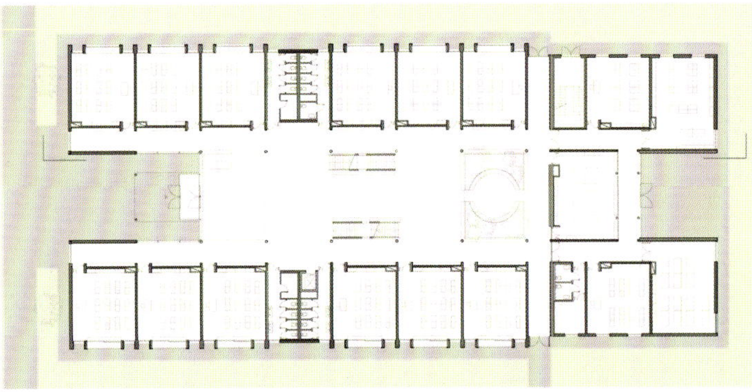

Ground floor plan

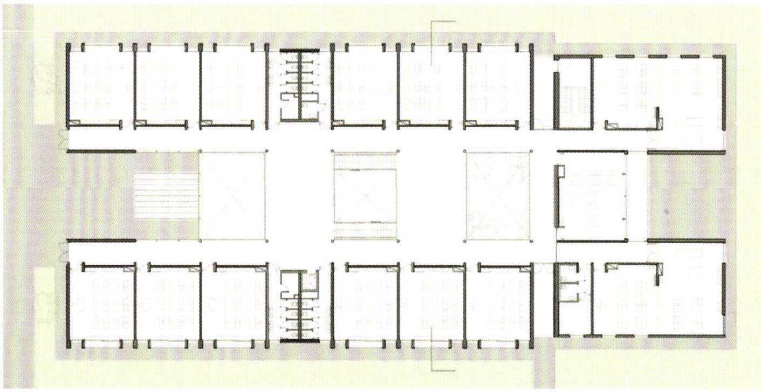

First floor plan

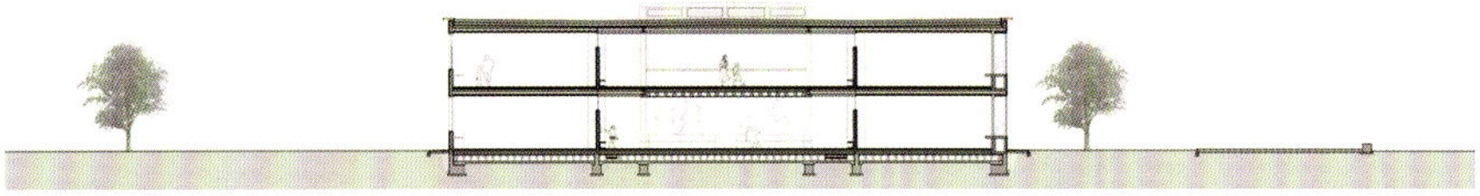

Cross section

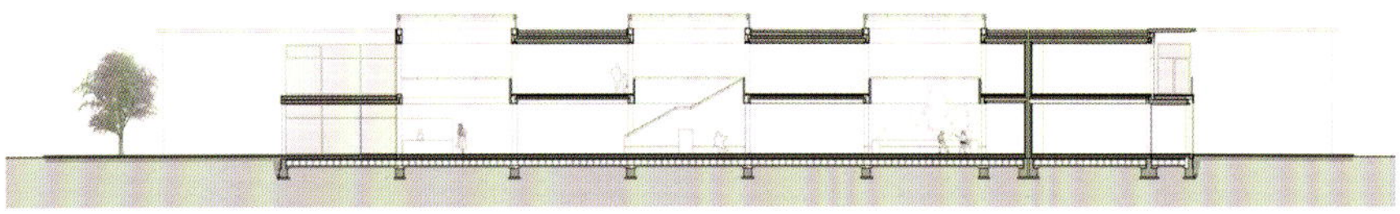

Longitudinal section

Daniel Valle Architects

// PROJECTS //

1. CLASSROOM RENOVATION AT THE GERMAN FOREIGN SCHOOL IN SEOUL
2. MAEBONG DAYCARE CENTER

www.danielvalle.com

Daniel Valle Architects

1.

2.

Daniel Valle Architects (DVA) was founded in Madrid in 2008 by Daniel Valle and ever since it has grown into an organization of international architects operating in the fields of interior, architecture and urban design. In the years previous to the establishment of the office, Daniel studied and worked in a number of countries between Asia and Europe weaving a large network of collaborators, partners and friends. The character of the office is a reflection of those experiences and connections done in the early years of Daniel's carrier. Our compromise to Architecture is not only to the discipline itself but rather to the world and society that is shaped by it. Architecture is our means to contribute to the design of a healthier, more optimistic and free environment.
Daniel Valle Architects operates between Madrid and Seoul. Europe became the early "playground" for DVA in the late 2000s. Later the work shifted to Asia with the branch office of Seoul acting as the magnet of our latest work.

Daniel Valle Arquitectos (DVA) a été fondé à Madrid en 2008 par Daniel Valle et est devenu depuis une organisation d'architectes internationaux opérant dans les domaines de l'intérieur, de l'architecture et de l'urbanisme. Dans les années précédant la création du bureau, Daniel a étudié et travaillé dans un certain nombre de pays entre l'Asie et l'Europe, tissant un vaste réseau de collaborateurs, de partenaires et d'amis. Le caractère du bureau est le reflet des expériences et des liens tissés au cours des premières années de la carrière de Daniel. Notre compromis avec l'architecture ne concerne pas seulement la discipline elle-même, mais plutôt le monde et la société qui sont façonnés par elle. L'architecture est notre moyen de contribuer à la conception d'un environnement plus sain, plus optimiste et plus libre.
Daniel Valle Arquitectos opère entre Madrid et Séoul. L'Europe est devenue le premier « terrain de jeu » de la DVA à la fin des années 2000. Plus tard, le travail s'est déplacé vers l'Asie, la succursale de Séoul étant l'aimant de notre dernier travail.

Daniel Valle Arquitectos (DVA) wurde 2008 von Daniel Valle in Madrid gegründet und hat sich seither zu einer Organisation internationaler Architekten entwickelt, die in den Bereichen Innenarchitektur, Architektur und Städtebau tätig sind. In den Jahren vor der Gründung des Büros hat Daniel in einer Reihe von Ländern zwischen Asien und Europa studiert und gearbeitet und dabei ein großes Netzwerk von Mitarbeitern, Partnern und Freunden geknüpft. Der Charakter des Büros spiegelt jene Erfahrungen und Verbindungen wider, die in den frühen Jahren von Daniels Karriere gemacht wurden. Unser Kompromiss gegenüber der Architektur ist nicht nur gegenüber der Disziplin selbst, sondern auch gegenüber der Welt und der Gesellschaft, die von ihr geprägt wird. Architektur ist unser Mittel, um zur Gestaltung einer gesünderen, optimistischeren und freieren Umwelt beizutragen.
Daniel Valle Arquitectos arbeitet zwischen Madrid und Seoul. Europa wurde in den späten 2000er Jahren zum frühen „Spielplatz" der DVA. Später verlagerte sich die Arbeit nach Asien, wobei das Zweigbüro in Seoul als Magnet unserer jüngsten Arbeit fungierte.

Daniel Valle Arquitectos (DVA) fue fundada en Madrid en 2008 por Daniel Valle y desde entonces ha crecido hasta convertirse en una organización de arquitectos internacionales que operan en los campos del interiorismo, la arquitectura y el diseño urbano. En los años anteriores a la creación del estudio, Daniel estudió y trabajó en varios países entre Asia y Europa tejiendo una gran red de colaboradores, socios y amigos. El carácter de la oficina es un reflejo de esas experiencias y conexiones hechas en los primeros años de su carrera. Nuestro compromiso con la Arquitectura no es solo con la disciplina en sí, sino con el mundo y la sociedad que está conformada por ella. La Arquitectura es nuestro medio para contribuir al diseño de un entorno más sano, optimista y libre.
Daniel Valle Arquitectos opera entre Madrid y Seúl. Europa se convirtió en el primer «patio de recreo» de DVA a finales de la década de 2000. Más tarde el trabajo se trasladó a Asia con la sucursal de Seúl actuando como imán de nuestro trabajo más reciente.

CLASSROOM RENOVATION AT THE GERMAN FOREIGN SCHOOL IN SEOUL

LOCATION: **YONGSAN-GU, SEOUL, SOUTH COREA**
PHOTOS: © **NAMSUN LEE**

The proposal for the renovation of two kindergarten classrooms tries to avoid programmatic duplicities. Many activities are taking place in each classroom simultaneously when those activities could be shared in a common space. Accordingly, the design proposes to reduce each of the two classrooms to the minimum size possible and create an in-between space that can be used by those common activities. This new space is understood as an extension of the classroom used by teachers and students at any given time.
The boundary between the classroom and the shared space is movable with a system of rotational walls that allow the interior space of the classroom expand towards the outside. These walls are glassed above 1,7 m extending the visuals from the interior of the classroom towards outside and allowing more natural light to penetrate inside the classroom.

Der Vorschlag zur Renovierung von zwei Kindergartenklassenräumen versucht, programmatische Doppelspurigkeiten zu vermeiden. Viele Aktivitäten finden in jedem Klassenzimmer gleichzeitig statt, wenn diese Aktivitäten in einem gemeinsamen Raum geteilt werden könnten. Dementsprechend schlägt der Entwurf vor, jedes der beiden Klassenzimmer auf die kleinstmögliche Größe zu reduzieren und einen Zwischenraum zu schaffen, der von diesen gemeinsamen Aktivitäten genutzt werden kann. Dieser neue Raum wird als eine Erweiterung des Klassenzimmers verstanden, das von Lehrern und Schülern zu einem bestimmten Zeitpunkt genutzt wird. Die Grenze zwischen dem Klassenzimmer und dem gemeinsamen Raum ist durch ein System von Drehwänden beweglich, die es ermöglichen, den Innenraum des Klassenzimmers nach außen zu erweitern. Diese Wände sind oberhalb von 1,7 m verglast, wodurch die Sicht vom Inneren des Klassenzimmers nach außen erweitert wird und mehr natürliches Licht in das Innere des Klassenzimmers eindringen kann.

La proposition de rénovation de deux salles de classe de maternelle tente d'éviter les doublons programmatiques. De nombreuses activités se déroulent simultanément dans chaque classe alors qu'elles pourraient être partagées dans un espace commun. En conséquence, la conception propose de réduire chacune des deux salles de classe à la taille minimale possible et de créer un espace intermédiaire qui peut être utilisé par ces activités communes. Ce nouvel espace est compris comme une extension de la salle de classe utilisée par les enseignants et les élèves à un moment donné. La limite entre la salle de classe et l'espace partagé est mobile grâce à un système de parois rotatives qui permettent à l'espace intérieur de la salle de classe de s'étendre vers l'extérieur. Ces murs sont vitrés au-dessus de 1,7 m, ce qui permet d'étendre les visuels de l'intérieur de la salle de classe vers l'extérieur et de faire pénétrer davantage de lumière naturelle à l'intérieur de la salle de classe.

La propuesta de renovación de dos aulas de jardín de infancia trata de evitar duplicidades programáticas. Muchas actividades se están llevando a cabo en cada aula de forma simultánea cuando esas actividades podrían ser compartidas en un espacio común. El diseño propone reducir cada una de las dos aulas al mínimo tamaño posible y crear un espacio intermedio que pueda ser utilizado por esas actividades comunes. Este nuevo espacio se entiende como una extensión del aula utilizada habitualmente por los profesores y los estudiantes. El límite entre el aula y el espacio compartido es desplazable con un sistema de paredes giratorias que permiten que el espacio interior del aula se expanda hacia el exterior. Estas paredes están acristaladas por encima de 1,7 m extendiendo las visuales desde el interior del aula hacia el exterior y permitiendo que penetre más luz natural en el interior del aula.

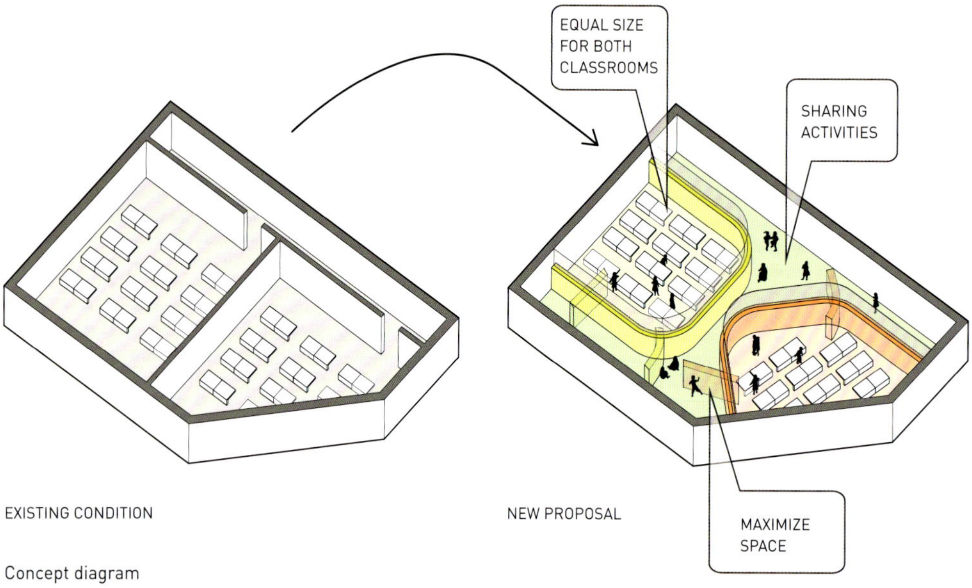

Concept diagram

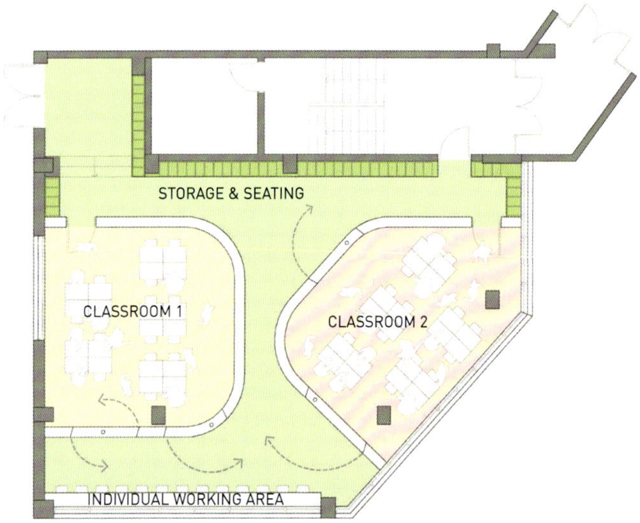

Floor plan. Closed classrooms

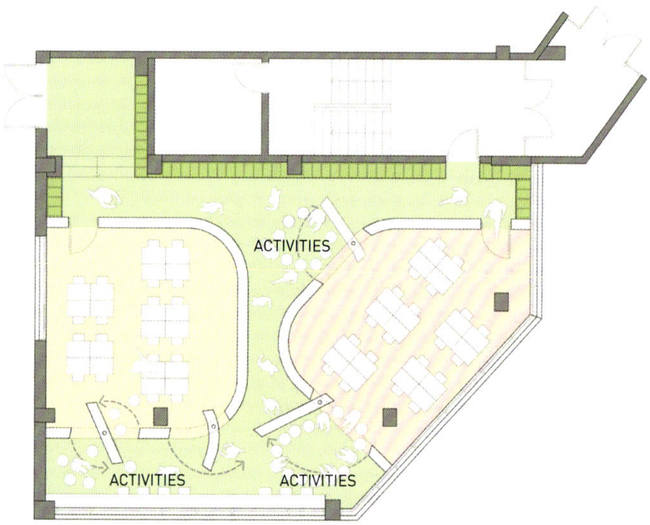

Floor plan. Common spaces

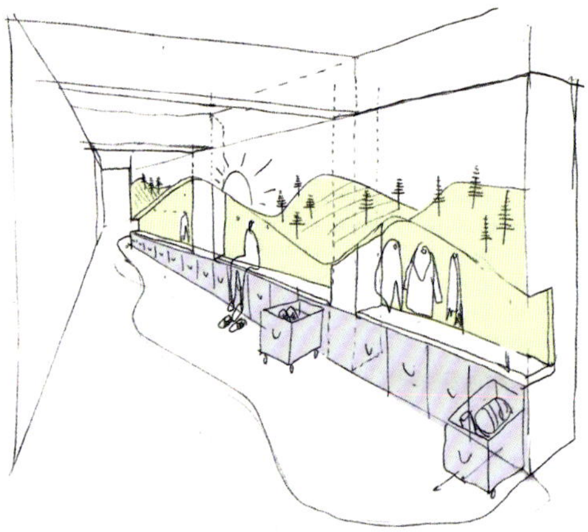

Sketches

6 5 4 3 2 1

MAEBONG DAYCARE CENTER

LOCATION: **SEONGDONG-GU, SEOUL, SOUTH COREA**
PHOTOS: **© NAMSUN LEE**

Children have a different scale perception than adults. At a young age, everything looks larger in size than when we see it as adults. The project focuses on the idea of scaling down the perception of the building so that children can relate more to it. In order to achieve this goal the massing of the building is divided into five smaller volumes. Each of them has a distinctive color, geometry and finishing material to emphasize the smaller volume among the overall mass of the building.
Subdividing the building in distinctive areas also allows students to establish a more intimate relationship with the environment they learn and play. Children need to find specific characteristics around them that can be identify as "theirs." Applying different colors to each of the classrooms' bathrooms will give a distinctive character to each room.

Kinder haben eine andere Skalenwahrnehmung als Erwachsene. In jungen Jahren sieht alles größer aus, als wenn wir es als Erwachsene sehen. Das Projekt konzentriert sich auf die Idee, die Wahrnehmung des Gebäudes zu verkleinern, damit Kinder sich mehr auf das Gebäude beziehen können. Um dieses Ziel zu erreichen, wird die Masse des Gebäudes in fünf kleinere Volumen unterteilt. Jedes von ihnen hat eine charakteristische Farbe, Geometrie und Ausbaumaterial, um das kleinere Volumen in der Gesamtmasse des Gebäudes hervorzuheben.
Die Unterteilung des Gebäudes in charakteristische Bereiche ermöglicht es den Schülern auch, eine intimere Beziehung zur Umgebung herzustellen, in der sie lernen und spielen. Die Kinder müssen spezifische Merkmale um sich herum finden, die als „ihre" identifiziert werden können. Die Verwendung unterschiedlicher Farben für die Badezimmer der Klassenzimmer verleiht jedem Raum einen eigenen Charakter.

Les enfants ont une perception de l'échelle différente de celle des adultes. À un jeune âge, tout semble plus grand que lorsque nous le voyons à l'âge adulte. Le projet se concentre sur l'idée de réduire la perception du bâtiment afin que les enfants puissent s'y identifier davantage. Afin d'atteindre cet objectif, la masse du bâtiment est divisée en cinq volumes plus petits. Chacun d'entre eux a une couleur, une géométrie et un matériau de finition distinctifs pour mettre en valeur le plus petit volume parmi la masse globale du bâtiment.

La subdivision du bâtiment en zones distinctes permet également aux étudiants d'établir une relation plus intime avec l'environnement dans lequel ils apprennent et jouent. Les enfants doivent trouver autour d'eux des caractéristiques spécifiques qui peuvent être identifiées comme « les leurs ». L'application de couleurs différentes dans les salles de bain de chacune des salles de classe donnera un caractère distinctif à chaque pièce.

Los niños tienen una percepción de escala diferente a la de los adultos. A una edad temprana, todo parece más grande en tamaño que cuando lo vemos como adultos. El proyecto se centra en la idea de reducir la percepción del edificio para que los niños puedan relacionarse más con él. Para lograr este objetivo, la masa del edificio se divide en cinco volúmenes más pequeños. Cada uno de ellos tiene un color, una geometría y un material de acabado distintivos para enfatizar el volumen más pequeño.

Esta subdivisión del edificio en áreas distintivas también permite a los estudiantes establecer una relación más íntima con el entorno en el que aprenden y juegan. Los niños necesitan encontrar características específicas a su alrededor que puedan ser identificadas como «suyas». Aplicar diferentes colores a cada uno de los baños de las aulas otorga un carácter distintivo a cada habitación.

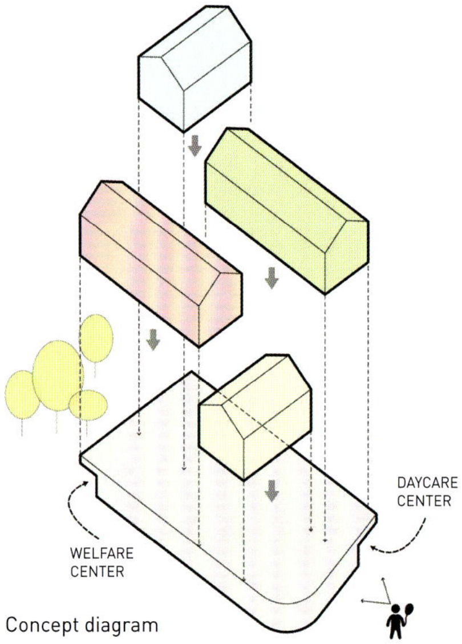

Concept diagram

Axonometry

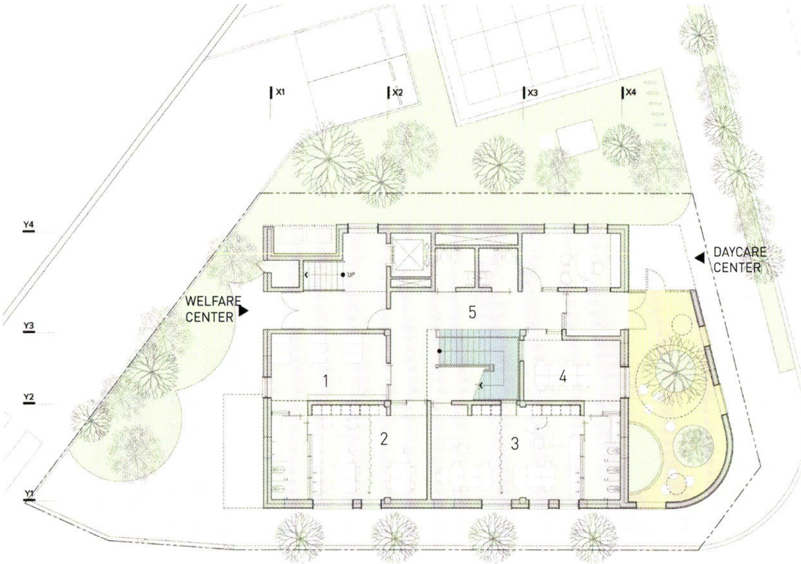

Entrance level plan

1. Daycare room (0-1 years)
2. Daycare room (1-2 years)
3. Daycare room (2-3 years)
4. Daycare room (temporary)
5. Playroom
6. Director room
7. Playground

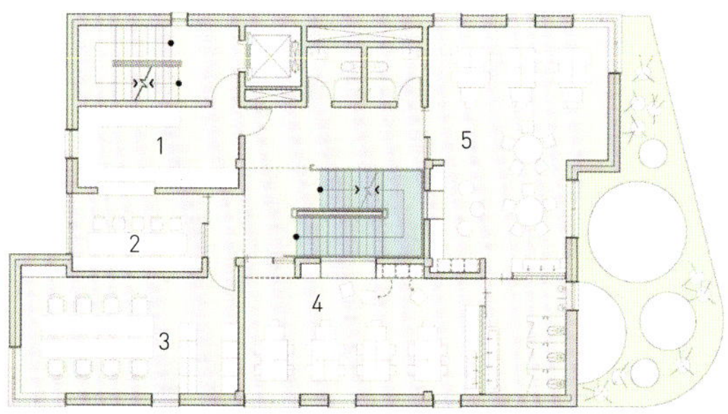

Second level plan

1. Kitchen
2. Cafeteria
3. Teachers room
4. Daycare room (4-5 years)
5. Daycare room (3-4 years)

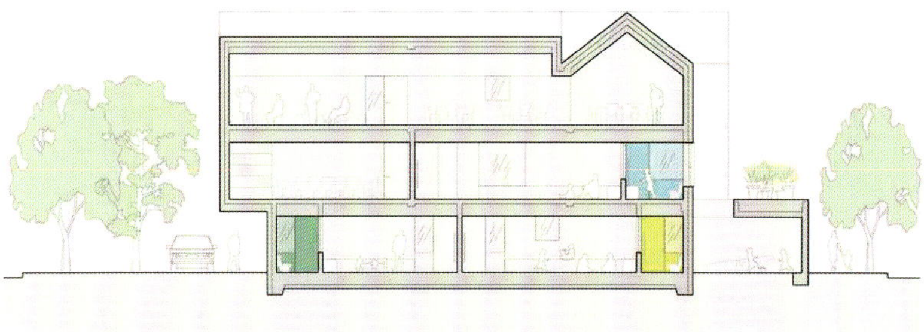

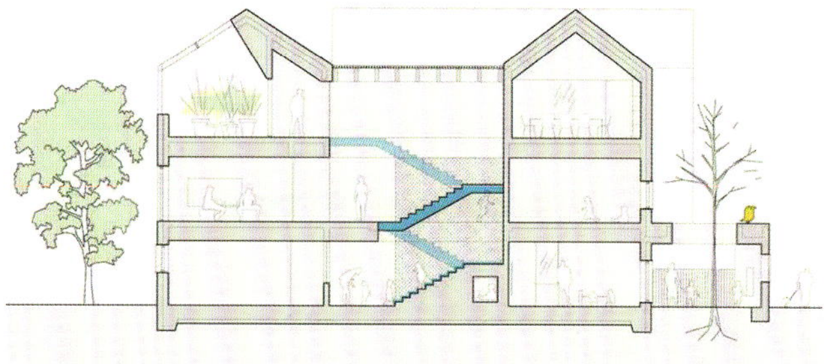

Sections

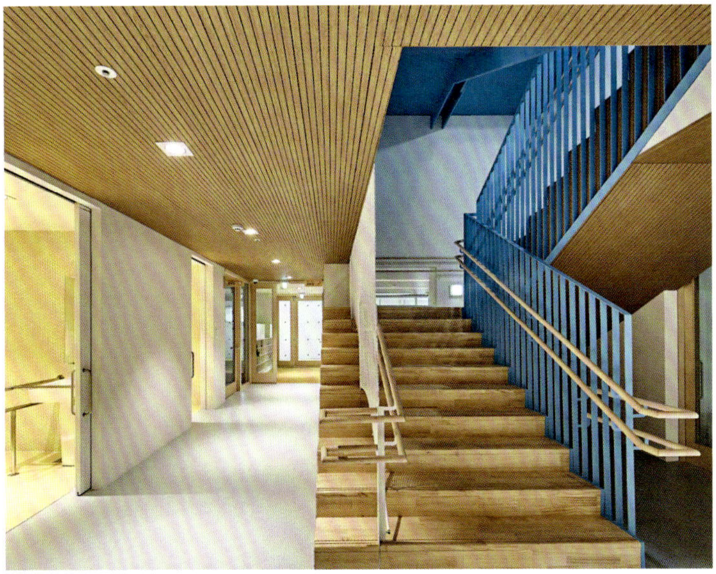

Dietrich | Untertrifaller Architekten

// PROJECTS //

1. MOBILE KINDERGARTEN INNSBRUCK
2. UNTERDORF ELEMENTARY SCHOOL HÖCHST
3. EDLACH ELEMENTARY SCHOOL DORNBIRN

www.dietrich.untertrifaller.com

1.

2.

3.

Our office, founded in 1994 by Helmut Dietrich and Much Untertrifaller, is one of the iconic agencies of the renowned School of Vorarlberg. It is led by Helmut Dietrich, Much Untertrifaller, Dominik Philipp and Patrick Stremler and employs an international team of 110 architects working in Austria, Switzerland, France and Germany. Our buildings are known for their humanistic approach, innovative and sustainable achievements, and their sympathetic relationship to urban context. We design with people in mind, and are motivated by creating landmarks that enhance their environments and serve their communities.
A decisive factor in all our work is the resource-saving and appropriate use of materials and structures, with a particular interest in and commitment to contemporary timber construction. We are well known for our expertise in timber design and construction and maintain this knowhow through relationships of dialogue and trust with clients, craftsmen and engineers.

Notre bureau, fondé en 1994 par Helmut Dietrich et Much Untertrifaller, est l'une des agences emblématiques de la célèbre école du Vorarlberg. Il est dirigé par Helmut Dietrich, Much Untertrifaller, Dominik Philipp et Patrick Stremler et emploie une équipe internationale de 110 architectes travaillant en Autriche, en Suisse, en France et en Allemagne. Nos bâtiments sont connus pour leur approche humaniste, leurs réalisations innovantes et durables, et leur relation sympathique avec le contexte urbain. Nous concevons en pensant aux gens et sommes motivés par la création de points de repère qui améliorent leur environnement et servent leurs communautés.
Un facteur décisif dans tout notre travail est l'économie des ressources et l'utilisation appropriée des matériaux et des structures, avec un intérêt et un engagement particuliers pour la construction contemporaine en bois. Nous sommes reconnus pour notre expertise en matière de conception et de construction en bois et nous entretenons ce savoir-faire grâce à des relations de dialogue et de confiance avec nos clients, artisans et ingénieurs.

Unser Büro, 1994 von Helmut Dietrich und Much Untertrifaller gegründet, ist eine der ikonischen Agenturen der renommierten Vorarlberger Schule. Es wird heute von Helmut Dietrich, Much Untertrifaller, Dominik Philipp und Patrick Stremler geleitet und beschäftigt ein internationales Team von 110 Architekten, die in Österreich, der Schweiz, Frankreich und Deutschland arbeiten. Unsere Gebäude sind bekannt für ihren humanistischen Ansatz, ihre innovativen und nachhaltigen Leistungen und ihre sympathische Beziehung zum städtischen Kontext. Wir entwerfen mit Blick auf den Menschen und sind motiviert, Wahrzeichen zu schaffen, die ihre Umgebung aufwerten und ihren Gemeinden dienen.
Ein entscheidender Faktor bei all unserer Arbeit ist der ressourcenschonende und angemessene Einsatz von Materialien und Konstruktionen, mit einem besonderen Interesse und Engagement für den zeitgenössischen Holzbau. Wir sind bekannt für unsere Fachkompetenz im Holzdesign und Holzbau und pflegen dieses Know-how im Dialog und in vertrauensvollen Beziehungen mit Bauherren, Handwerkern und Ingenieuren.

Nuestra oficina, fundada en 1994 por Helmut Dietrich y Much Untertrifaller, es una de las agencias icónicas de la renombrada Escuela de Vorarlberg. Está dirigida por Helmut Dietrich, Much Untertrifaller, Dominik Philipp y Patrick Stremler y emplea a un equipo internacional de 110 arquitectos que trabajan en Austria, Suiza, Francia y Alemania. Nuestros edificios son conocidos por su enfoque humanista, sus logros innovadores y sostenibles y su relación simpática con el contexto urbano. Diseñamos teniendo en cuenta a las personas, y nos motivamos creando puntos de referencia que mejoren sus entornos y sirvan a sus comunidades.
Un factor decisivo en todo nuestro trabajo es el ahorro de recursos y el uso apropiado de materiales y estructuras, con un interés y un compromiso particular en la construcción contemporánea en madera. Somos bien conocidos por nuestra experiencia en el diseño y la construcción en madera y mantenemos este conocimiento a través de relaciones de diálogo y confianza con clientes, artesanos e ingenieros.

MOBILE KINDERGARTEN INNSBRUCK

LOCATION: **INNSBRUCK, AUSTRIA**
PHOTOS: **© ANGELA LAMPRECHT, IKM/M. FREINHOFER**

The need to rapidly increase the number of kindergartens led the city of Innsbruck to promote the concept of a "mobile kindergarten". The building is temporarily located in the Olympic Village but can be relocated to another location, as the various prefabricated modules that make up the building can be easily assembled and dismantled. The kindergarten consists of three classrooms and several auxiliary spaces, whose arrangement along an axis allows playing with the modules to reduce or extend the building. The use of wood guarantees the recycling of its components, minimises the ecological footprint in the construction process and generates a warm and welcoming interior environment. On the outside, a façade of spruce slats extends over the entire building and links the individual modules to form a harmonious whole.

La nécessité d'augmenter rapidement le nombre de jardins d'enfants a conduit la ville d'Innsbruck à promouvoir le concept de « jardin d'enfants mobile ». Le bâtiment est temporairement situé dans le village olympique mais peut être déplacé vers un autre endroit, car les différents modules préfabriqués qui le composent peuvent être facilement assemblés et démontés. Le jardin d'enfants se compose de trois salles de classe et de plusieurs espaces auxiliaires, dont la disposition le long d'un axe permet de jouer avec les modules pour réduire ou agrandir le bâtiment. L'utilisation généralisée du bois garantit le recyclage de ses composants, minimise l'empreinte écologique dans le processus de construction et génère un environnement intérieur chaleureux et accueillant. À l'extérieur, une façade en lattes d'épicéa s'étend sur tout le bâtiment et relie les différents modules pour former un ensemble harmonieux.

Die Notwendigkeit, die Zahl der Kindergärten rasch zu erhöhen, veranlasste die Stadt Innsbruck, das Konzept eines „mobilen Kindergartens" zu fördern. Das Gebäude befindet sich derzeit im Olympischen Dorf, kann aber an einen anderen Standort verlegt werden, da die verschiedenen vorgefertigten Module, aus denen das Gebäude besteht, leicht auf- und abgebaut werden können. Der Kindergarten besteht aus drei Gruppenbereichen und mehreren Nebenräumen, deren Anordnung entlang einer Achse das Spiel mit den Modulen zur Verkleinerung oder Erweiterung des Gebäudes ermöglicht. Die allgemeine Verwendung von Holz garantiert das Recycling seiner Bestandteile, minimiert den ökologischen Fußabdruck im Bauprozess und erzeugt eine warme und einladende Innenumgebung. An der Außenseite erstreckt sich eine Fassade aus Fichtenlamellen über das gesamte Gebäude und verbindet die einzelnen Module zu einem harmonischen Ganzen.

La necesidad de incrementar rápidamente la dotación de jardines de infancia llevó a la ciudad de Innsbruck a promover el concepto de «guardería móvil». El edificio se sitúa temporalmente en la Villa Olímpica pero puede ser reubicado en otro emplazamiento, ya que los diferentes módulos prefabricados que lo componen pueden ensamblarse y desmantelarse fácilmente. El jardín de infancia consta de tres aulas y diversos espacios auxiliares, cuya disposición a lo largo de un eje permite jugar con los módulos para reducir o extender el edificio. El uso generalizado de la madera garantiza el reciclaje de sus componentes, minimiza la huella ecológica en el proceso constructivo y genera un ambiente interior cálido y acogedor. En el exterior, una fachada de lamas de madera de abeto se extiende sobre todo el edificio y enlaza los módulos individuales para formar un conjunto armonioso.

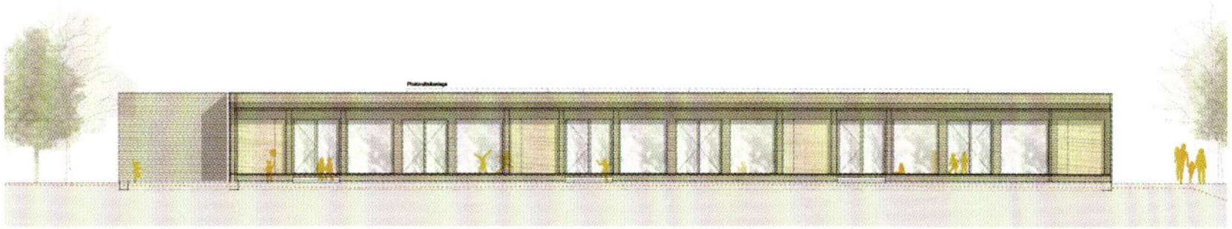

Southwest elevation

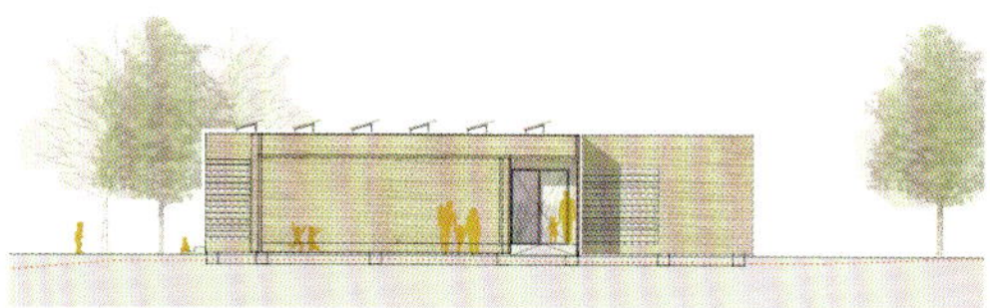

Southeast elevation

Northeast elevation

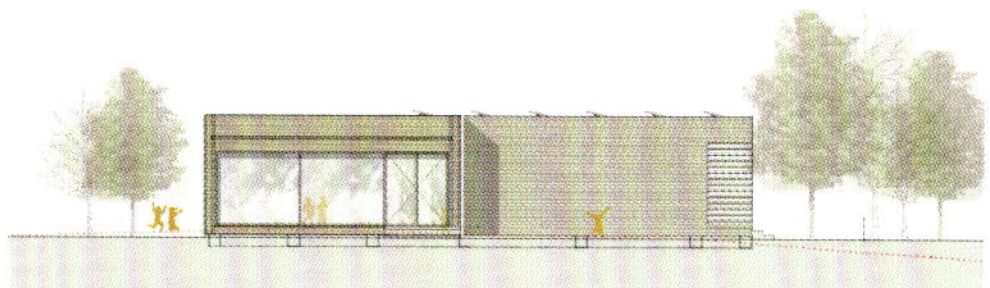

Northwest elevation

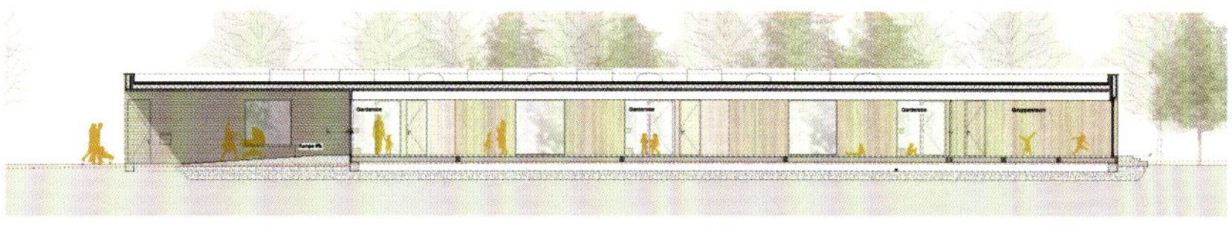

Longitudinal section

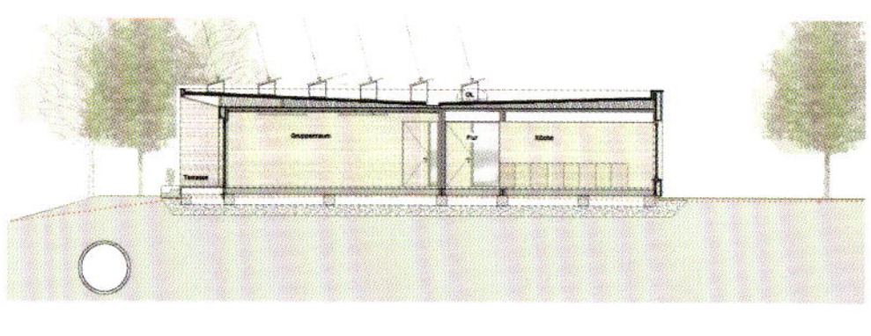

Longitudinal section

UNTERDORF ELEMENTARY SCHOOL HÖCHST

LOCATION: **HÖCHST, AUSTRIA**
PHOTOS: © **BRUNO KLOMFAR**

This primary school is a radical example of a modern and inclusive school, organized in clusters according to a model that promotes small group teaching, flexible use spaces and diversified open areas. Within a flat, elongated wooden building, four identical clusters are located along the east façade. The different areas of each one of them are organised around a common room with a high ceiling, illuminated from above and equipped with a direct exit to a private outdoor terrace. The large interior glass partitions provide transparency within each group and create visual axes that encourage the use of the central common space. The school is built entirely of uncoated wood, a renewable material that reduces the "grey" energy factor and creates a pleasant and warm atmosphere for the students.

Diese Grundschule ist ein radikales Beispiel für eine moderne und integrative Schule, die in Clustern nach einem Modell organisiert ist, das den Unterricht in kleinen Gruppen, flexibel nutzbare Räume und diversifizierte offene Bereiche fördert. Innerhalb eines flachen, langgestreckten Holzgebäudes befinden sich entlang der Ostfassade vier identische Cluster. Die verschiedenen Bereiche sind jeweils um einen Gemeinschaftsraum mit hoher Decke organisiert, der von oben beleuchtet und mit einem direkten Ausgang zu einer privaten Außenterrasse ausgestattet ist. Die großen Glastrennwände im Inneren sorgen für Transparenz innerhalb jeder Gruppe und schaffen Sichtachsen, die die Nutzung des zentralen Gemeinschaftsraums fördern. Die Schule ist vollständig aus unbeschichtetem Holz gebaut, einem erneuerbaren Material, das den „grauen" Energiefaktor reduziert und eine angenehme und warme Atmosphäre für die Schüler schafft.

Cette école primaire est un exemple radical d'école moderne et inclusive, organisée en grappes selon un modèle qui favorise l'enseignement en petits groupes, des espaces à usage flexible et des espaces ouverts diversifiés. À l'intérieur d'un bâtiment en bois plat et allongé, quatre grappes identiques sont situées le long de la façade est. Les différents espaces de chacun d'entre eux s'organisent autour d'une salle commune à haut plafond, éclairée par le haut et dotée d'une sortie directe vers une terrasse extérieure privée. Les grandes cloisons vitrées intérieures assurent la transparence au sein de chaque groupe et créent des axes visuels qui favorisent l'utilisation de l'espace commun central. L'école est entièrement construite en bois non revêtu, un matériau renouvelable qui réduit le facteur énergétique « gris » et crée une atmosphère agréable et chaleureuse pour les élèves.

Esta escuela primaria constituye un ejemplo radical de escuela moderna e inclusiva, organizada en *clusters* según un modelo que promueve una enseñanza en grupos pequeños, espacios de uso flexible y áreas abiertas diversificadas. Dentro de un edificio de madera plano y alargado, cuatro *clusters* idénticos se sitúan a lo largo de la fachada este. Los diferentes ámbitos de cada uno de ellos se organizan alrededor de una sala común de techo alto, iluminada cenitalmente y dotada de una salida directa hacia una terraza exterior privada. Las grandes particiones acristaladas interiores aportan transparencia dentro de cada grupo y crean ejes visuales que fomentan el uso del espacio central común. La escuela está enteramente construida en madera sin revestir, material renovable que reduce el factor de energía «gris» y que genera un ambiente agradable y cálido para los estudiantes.

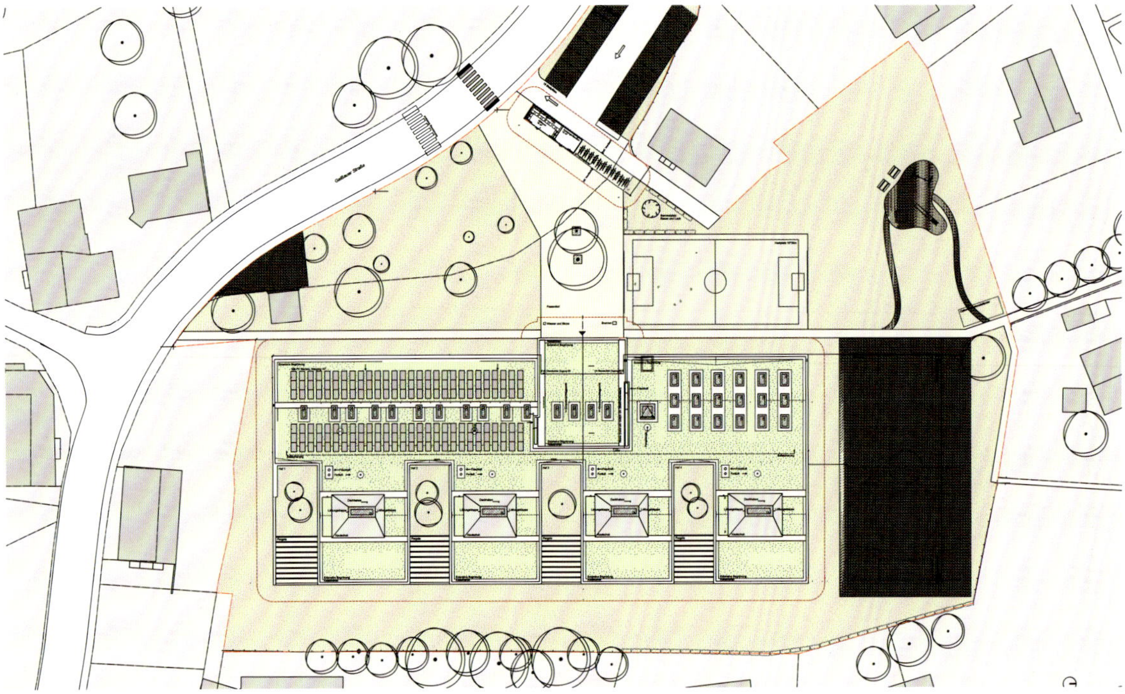

Site plan

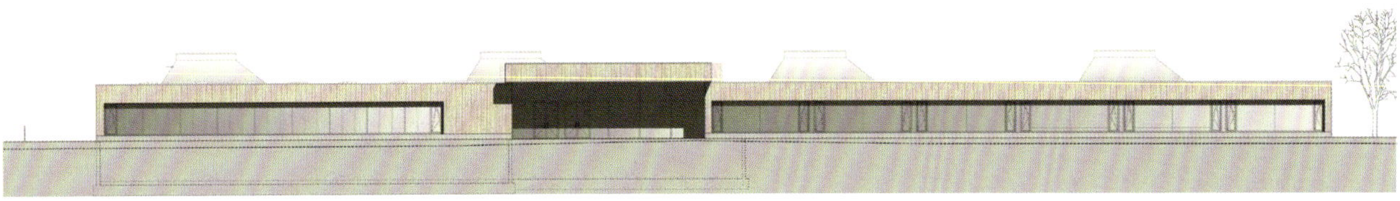

West elevation

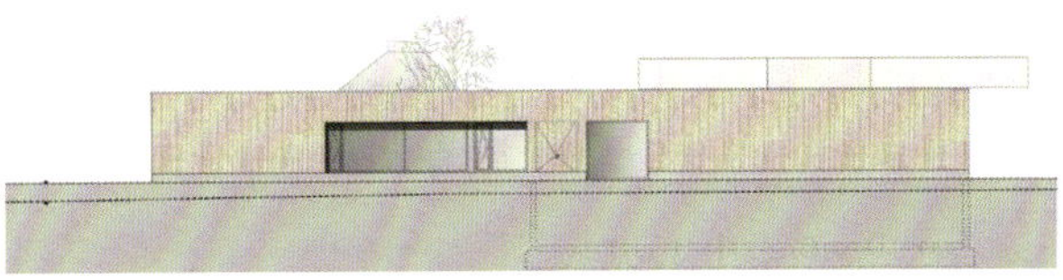

North elevation

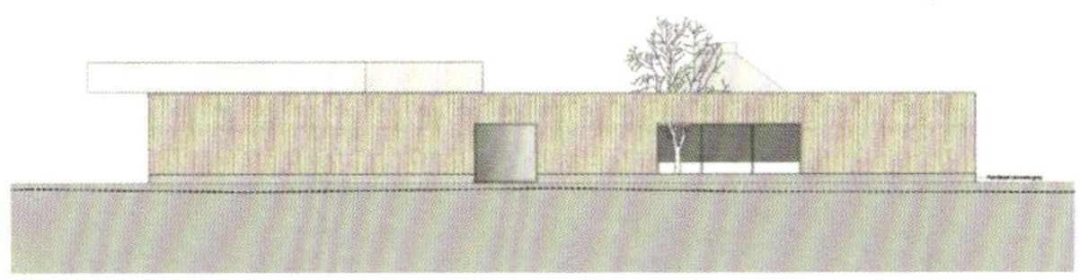

South elevation

East elevation

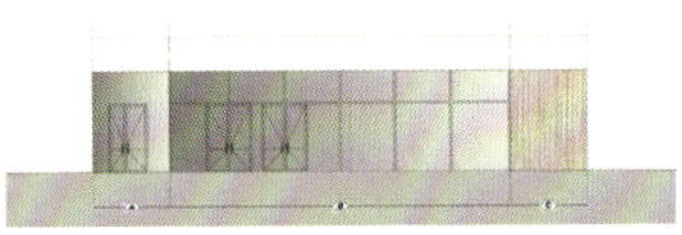

Main entrance elevation

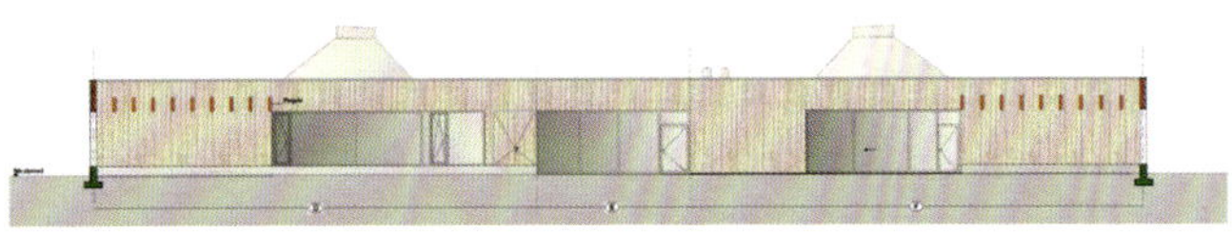

Inner court elevation

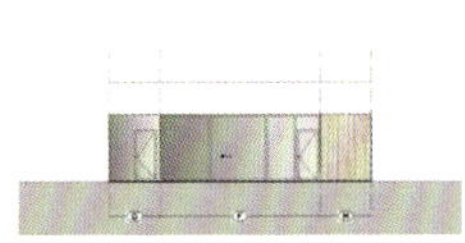

Terrace elevation

EDLACH ELEMENTARY SCHOOL DORNBIRN

LOCATION: **DORNBIRN, AUSTRIA**
PHOTOS: **© KURT HÖRBST, BRUNO KLOMFAR**

This new school has a linear configuration that distributes the classrooms on two levels and is connected to an existing gymnasium through a lower volume, which contains the main entrance and a glazed multifunctional room. The project implements the concept of an inclusive school by organizing it into four clusters and the possibility of creating different spatial design configurations. Each cluster consists of three classes, two group rooms and a central room. The use of wood is omnipresent in the construction and in the design of the façades, as well as in the interior finishes, which create a homely atmosphere. The project incorporates different measures aimed at sustainability, such as the use of ecological materials in construction, the use of photovoltaic energy or the minimisation of energy demand for heating.

Dieses neue Schulgebäude hat eine lineare Konfiguration, die die Klassenräume auf zwei Ebenen verteilt und durch ein niedrigeres Volumen mit einer bestehenden Turnhalle verbunden ist, die den Haupteingang und einen verglasten multifunktionalen Raum enthält. Das Projekt setzt das Konzept einer inklusiven Schule um, indem es sie in vier Cluster gliedert und die Möglichkeit bietet, verschiedene räumliche Gestaltungskonfigurationen zu schaffen. Jeder Cluster besteht aus drei Klassen, zwei Gruppenräumen und einem zentralen Raum. Die Verwendung von Holz ist in der Konstruktion und bei der Gestaltung der Fassaden sowie bei den Innenausbauten, die eine wohnliche Atmosphäre schaffen, allgegenwärtig. Das Projekt umfasst verschiedene Maßnahmen, die auf Nachhaltigkeit abzielen, wie z.B. die Verwendung ökologischer Materialien beim Bau, die Nutzung photovoltaischer Energie oder die Minimierung des Energiebedarfs für die Heizung.

Ce nouveau bâtiment scolaire a une configuration linéaire qui distribue les salles de classe sur deux niveaux et est relié à un gymnase existant par un volume plus bas, qui contient l'entrée principale et une salle multifonctionnelle vitrée. Le projet met en œuvre le concept d'école inclusive en l'organisant en quatre groupes et en offrant la possibilité de créer différentes configurations de conception spatiale. Chaque groupe se compose de trois classes, de deux salles de groupe et d'une salle centrale. L'utilisation du bois est omniprésente dans la construction et dans la conception des façades, ainsi que dans les finitions intérieures, qui créent une atmosphère chaleureuse. Le projet intègre différentes mesures visant à la durabilité, telles que l'utilisation de matériaux écologiques dans la construction, l'utilisation de l'énergie photovoltaïque ou la minimisation de la demande énergétique pour le chauffage.

Este nuevo edificio escolar presenta una configuración linear que distribuye las aulas en dos niveles y se une a un gimnasio existente a través de un volumen de menor altura, que contiene la entrada principal y una sala multifuncional acristalada. El proyecto implementa el concepto de escuela inclusiva mediante la organización en cuatro *clusters* y la posibilidad de crear diferentes configuraciones de diseño espacial. Cada *cluster* se compone de tres clases, dos salas de grupo y una sala central. El uso de la madera es omnipresente en la construcción y en el diseño de las fachadas, así como en los acabados interiores, que crean un ambiente hogareño. El proyecto incorpora diferentes medidas encaminadas a la sostenibilidad, como la utilización de materiales ecológicos en la construcción, el uso de energía fotovoltaica o la minimización de la demanda energética de calefacción.

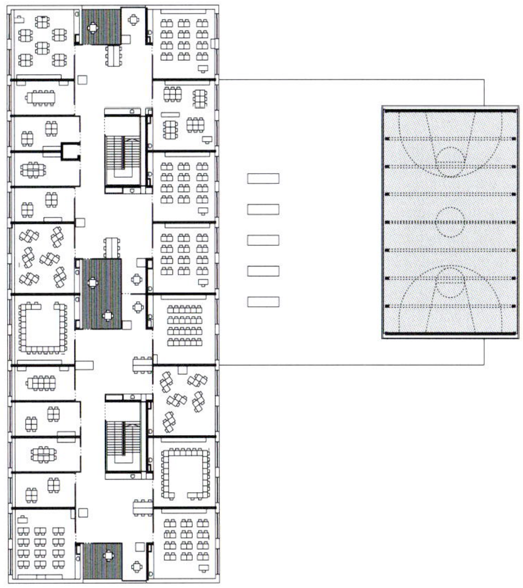

First floor plan

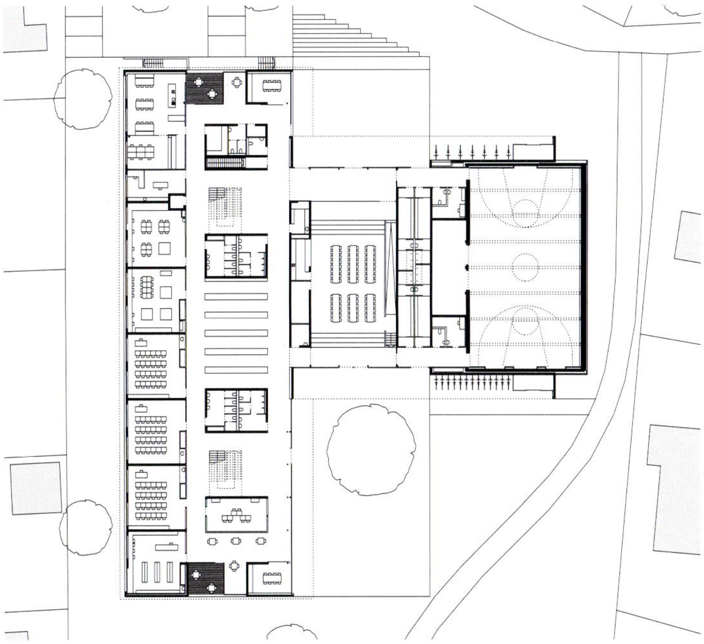

Ground floor plan

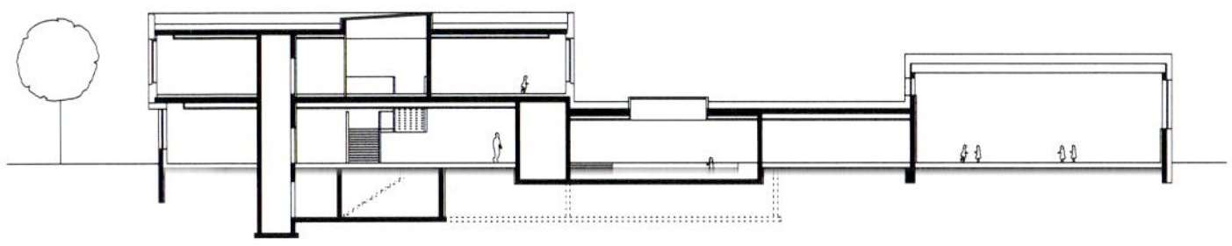

Section

Eduard Balcells Architecture+Urbanism +Landscape, Ignasi Rius, Daniel Tigges

// PROJECTS //

1. EL TIL·LER SCHOOL

www.behance.net/Eduard_Balcells
www.tiggesarchitekt.ch

Eduard Balcells Architecture+Urbanism+Landscape, Ignasi Rius, Daniel Tigges

1.

Eduard Balcells Architecture+Urbanism+Landscape is a practice based in Barcelona which provides research-based, cross-disciplinary and specifically tailored strategies and projects at all scales; from interiors to buildings, landscapes, public spaces and urban design projects. Its work has been extensively awarded, published and exhibited.
Ignasi Rius is a Barcelona-based architect, author of numerous public buildings, such as the Waldorf school El Til·ler, the high school in Cornudella de Montsant, the schools Can Roca and Torre Barona in Castelldefels, the Hospital Sagrat Cor in Barcelona, a CAP in Cerdanyola, a civic centre in Blanes, or eighty-one homes in Barberà el Vallès.
The office of Tigges Architekt, led by Barcelona-based Swiss Daniel Tigges, is characterized by the fusion of contemporary design with sustainable construction. His work has been awarded, published and certified, among others with the standards for low-energy houses Minergie and Passive House.

Eduard Balcells Architecture+Urbanism+Landscape ist ein in Barcelona ansässiges Büro, das interdisziplinäre, forschungsbasierte Strategien und Projekte entwirft, die für jeden Kunden und in allen Maßstäben spezifisch sind; von Innenräumen bis hin zu Gebäuden, Landschaften, öffentlichen Räumen und Stadtplanungsprojekten. Seine Arbeiten wurden vielfach ausgezeichnet, veröffentlicht und ausgestellt.
Ignasi Rius, Architekt aus Barcelona, ist Autor vieler öffentlicher Gebäude, wie die Waldorfschule El Til·ler, das Gymnasium in Cornudella de Montsant, die Schulen Can Roca und Torre Barona in Castelldefels, das Krankenhaus Sagrat Cor in Barcelona, ein CAP in Cerdanyola, ein Bürgerzentrum in Blanes oder einundachtzig Wohnungen in Barberà el Vallès.
Das Büro Tigges Architekt unter der Leitung des Schweizers Daniel Tigges hat seinen Sitz in Barcelona und zeichnet sich durch die Fusion von zeitgenössischem Design mit nachhaltigem Bauen aus. Sein Werk wurde ausgezeichnet, veröffentlicht und zertifiziert, u. a. mit den Niedrigenergiestandards Minergie und Passivhaus.

Eduard Balcells Architecture+Urbanism+Landscape est une agence avec siège à Barcelone, qui conçoit stratégies et projets interdisciplinaires fondés sur la recherche, spécifiquement adaptés aux différents clients et à toutes les échelles; intérieurs, bâtiments, paysages, espaces publics et aménagement urbain. Son travail a été largement exposé, lauréat et publié.
Ignasi Rius, architecte à Barcelone, est auteur de nombreux bâtiments publics, comme l'école Waldorf El Til·ler, le lycée de Cornudella de Montsant, les écoles Can Roca et Torre Barona à Castelldefels, l'hôpital Sagrat Cor à Barcelone, un CAP à Cerdanyola, un centre civique à Blanes, ou quatre-vingt-un logements à Barberà el Vallès.
Le bureau Tigges Architekt, dirigé par le Suisse Daniel Tigges, est basé à Barcelone et se caractérise par la fusion du design contemporain et de la construction durable. Son oeuvre a été lauréate, publiée et certifiée, entre autres avec les standards de maison à basse consommation d'énergie Minergie et Passivhaus.

Eduard Balcells Architecture+Urbanism+Landscape es un despacho con sede en Barcelona que diseña estrategias y proyectos interdisciplinarios, basados en la investigación, específicos para cada cliente y a todas las escalas; desde interiores hasta edificios, paisajes, espacios públicos y proyectos de urbanismo. Su trabajo ha sido ampliamente premiado, publicado y expuesto.
Ignasi Rius, arquitecto de Barcelona, es autor de numerosos edificios públicos, como la escuela Waldorf El Til·ler, el instituto de Cornudella de Montsant, las escuelas Can Roca y Torre Barona de Castelldefels, el Hospital Sagrat Cor de Barcelona, un CAP en Cerdanyola, un centro cívico en Blanes, u ochenta y una viviendas en Barberá el Vallés.
El despacho Tigges Architekt, dirigido por el suizo Daniel Tigges, tiene su sede en Barcelona y se caracteriza por la fusión del diseño contemporáneo con la construcción sostenible. Su obra ha sido premiada, publicada y certificada, entre otros con los estándares de bajo consumo energético Minergie y Passivhaus.

EL TIL·LER SCHOOL

LOCATION: **BELLATERRA, CERDANYOLA DEL VALLÈS, BARCELONA, SPAIN**
PHOTOS: **© ADRIÀ GOULA**

The El Til·ler School is carefully inserted in an old garden and organized along its main path. Five buildings are recycled, and the sixth building —which is presented here— houses the kindergarten and the common spaces.
The school embodies a contemporary expression of the Waldorf pedagogy adapted to the Mediterranean. Thus, life in the garden is maximized and there are no interior corridors. The views and natural light of each classroom vary, accompanying the experience of growth and learning.
Inside, alcoves at the scale of children adapt to the pedagogical needs of each space. Outside, these alcoves are contained within frames, visually reducing the scale of the building and bringing it closer to that of small children.
The facade evolves from a flat surface into an inhabited space, the classroom turns into a house and the school becomes a small village along a "rambla" —or Mediterranean high street.

Die Schule El Til·ler ist sorgfältig in einen alten Garten eingefügt und entlang seines Hauptweges organisiert. Fünf seiner Gebäude werden recycelt, und das sechste - auf diesen Seiten vorgestellt - beherbergt den Kindergarten und die Gemeinschaftsräume.
Die Schule verkörpert einen zeitgenössischen, dem Mittelmeerraum angepassten Ausdruck der Waldorfpädagogik. Auf diese Weise wird das Leben unter freiem Himmel maximiert und es gibt keine inneren Korridore. Die Aussichten und das natürliche Licht jedes Klassenzimmers variieren und begleiten das Wachstum und die Lernerfahrung.
Im Inneren sind die kindergerechten Öffnungen an die pädagogischen Bedürfnisse der einzelnen Räume angepasst. Im Außenbereich sind diese Räume in Rahmen eingefasst, wodurch das Gebäude optisch verkleinert und näher an den Maßstab von Kleinkindern herangeführt wird.
Die Fassade verwandelt sich von einer ebenen Fläche in einen bewohnten Raum, das Klassenzimmer wird zu einem Haus und die Schule zu einem kleinen Dorf entlang einer Promenade.

L'École El Til·ler est soigneusement insérée dans un ancien jardin et organisée le long de son chemin principal. Cinq bâtiments sont recyclés et le sixième bâtiment, présenté ici, abrite le jardin d'enfants et les espaces communs.
L'école incarne une expression contemporaine de la pédagogie Waldorf adaptée à la Méditerranée. Ainsi, la vie dans le jardin est maximisée et il n'y a pas de couloirs intérieurs. Les vues et la lumière naturelle de chaque classe changent, accompagnant l'expérience de la croissance et de l'apprentissage.
A l'intérieur, des alcôves à l'échelle des enfants s'adaptent aux besoins pédagogiques de chaque espace. À l'extérieur, ces alcôves sont contenues dans des cadres, réduisant visuellement l'échelle du bâtiment et la rapprochant à celle des petits enfants.
La façade évolue d'une surface plane en un espace habité, la salle de classe se transforme en une maison et l'école devient un petit village le long d'une « rambla » —ou promenade méditerranéenne.

La Escuela El Til·ler se inserta cuidadosamente en un antiguo jardín y se organiza a lo largo de su camino principal. Se reciclan cinco edificios, y el sexto -que se presenta aquí- alberga el jardín de infancia y los espacios comunes.
La escuela conforma una expresión contemporánea de la pedagogía Waldorf adaptada al Mediterráneo. Por lo tanto, la vida en el jardín se maximiza y no hay pasillos interiores. Las vistas y la luz natural de cada aula varían, acompañando la experiencia de crecimiento y aprendizaje.
En el interior, las alcobas a escala infantil se adaptan a las necesidades pedagógicas de cada espacio. En el exterior, estas alcobas están contenidos dentro de marcos, reduciendo visualmente la escala del edificio y acercándola a la de los niños pequeños.
La fachada deja de ser un plano para transformarse en un espacio habitado, el aula se convierte en una casa y la escuela en un pequeño pueblo a lo largo de una rambla.

1. New kindergarten and common spaces building
2. Kindergarten playground
3. Secondary school (recycled building)
4. Secondary school playground
5. Primary school (recycled buildings)
6. Primary school playground
7. Cantine and storage (recycled building)
8. Rambla (Mediterranean high street)
9. Square
10. Sports playground
11. Amphitheater
12. Vegetable garden
13. Reed ponds for on site waste water treatment

Overall plan

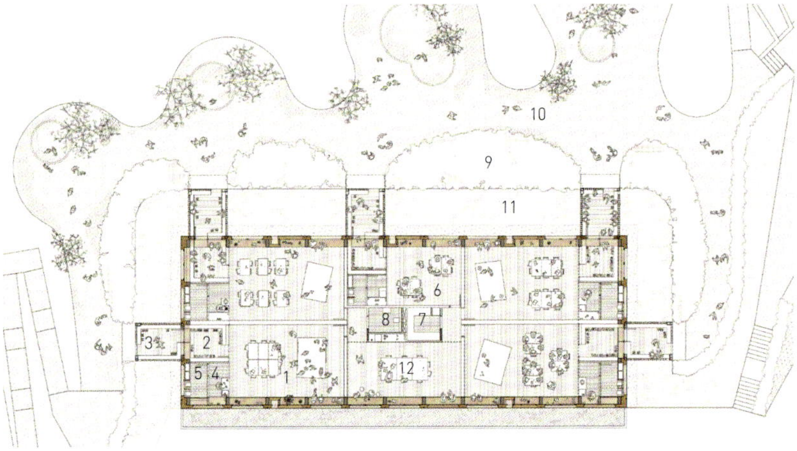

1. Kindergarten classroom
2. Vestibule
3. Access bridge / porch
4. Office
5. Classroom bathroom
6. Classroom 2-3 years old
7. Storage
8. Bathroom
9. Hedge (green railing)
10. Kindergarten playground
11. Green slope
12. Teacher's room

Common spaces & kindergarten building. First floor plan / upper level

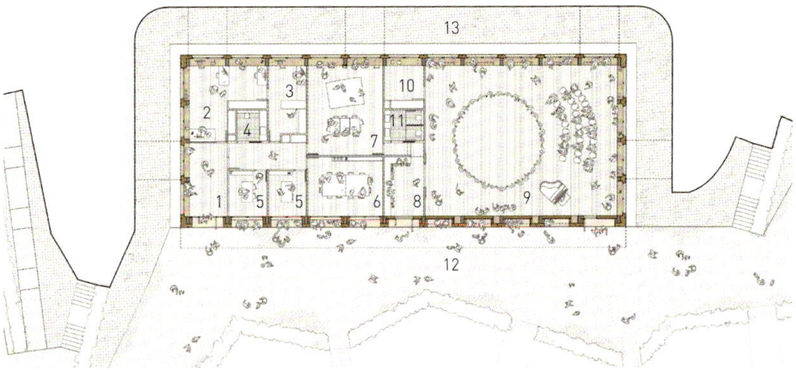

1. Reception
2. Administration
3. Management
4. Bathroom
5. Offices
6. Teacher's room
7. Support classroom
8. Eurythmics hall vestibule
9. Eurythmics hall
10. Storage
11. Bathroom
12. Rambla
13. Green slope

Common spaces & kindergarten building. Ground floor plan

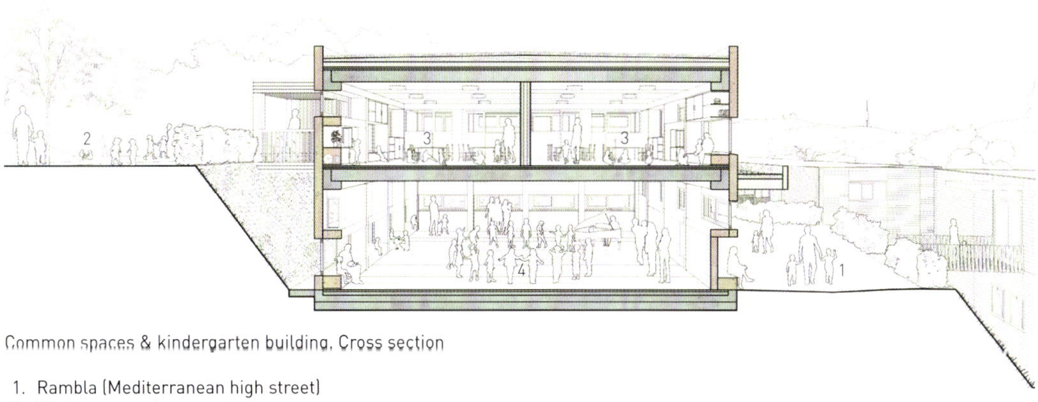

Common spaces & kindergarten building. Cross section

1. Rambla (Mediterranean high street)
2. Kindergarten playground
3. Kindergarten classrooms
4. Multipurpose / Eurythmics hall

Alcove & Frames, the facade as space.
Architecture as an expression of pedagogy

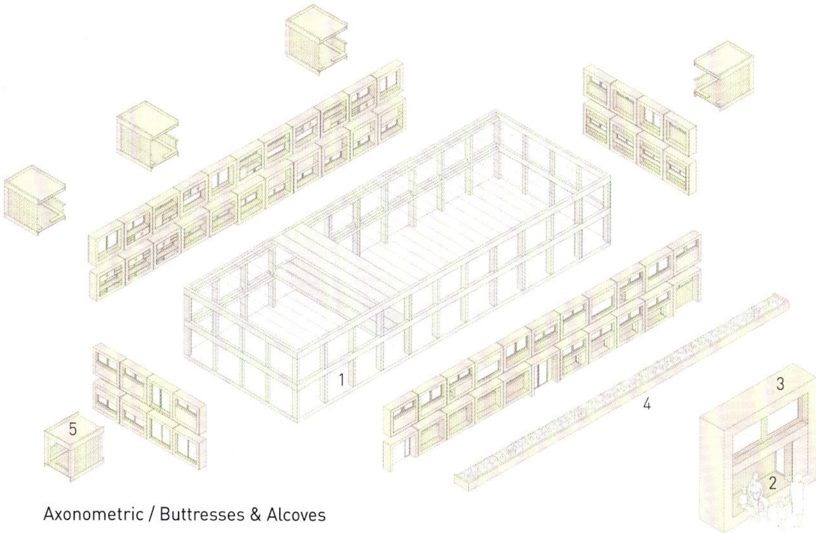

Axonometric / Buttresses & Alcoves

1. Structural buttress
2. Alcove
3. Frame
4. Porch (to be built at a later phase)
5. Access bridge & porch (to be built at a later phase)

Földes Architects

// PROJECTS //

1. NURSERY IN NAGYKOVÁCSI

www.foldesarchitects.hu

1.

Laszlo Földes founded Földes Architects in 1994 where he shares the work with 14 young architects. Projects of Földes Architects are both residential and public buildings. Their projects' identification lays in the use of natural and local materials (stone, brick, wood) and the belief in architectural continuity, however they are opened to new ideas. First time in history they built in "LiTraCon" (light transmitting concrete), Áron Losonczi's invention which received several awards. The office gained international recognition for the Kemenes Volcanopark Visitor Centre.
Laszlo Földes sees design commissions as answers addressing questions. His aim is to focus sharply on the substantial characteristics of the assignment. The better his comprehension, the more powerful the result is. Concentration offers him the possibility of an abstract, elementary solution. Apart from the expressional simplification the realized building should have a layer reflecting on and grow out of its cultural context.

Laszlo Földes gründete 1994 Földes Architects, wo er die Arbeit mit 14 jungen Architekten teilt. Projekte von Földes Architects sind sowohl Wohn- als auch öffentliche Gebäude. Ihre Projekte zeichnen sich durch die Verwendung von natürlichen und lokalen Materialien (Stein, Ziegel, Holz) und den Glauben an architektonische Kontinuität aus, sind jedoch offen für neue Ideen. Zum ersten Mal in der Geschichte bauten sie in „LiTraCon" (lichtdurchlässiger Beton), einer Erfindung von Áron Losonczi, die mehrfach ausgezeichnet wurde. Internationale Anerkennung erhielt das Büro für das Besucherzentrum des Kemenes Volcanopark.
Laszlo Földes sieht Designkommissionen als Antworten auf Fragen. Sein Ziel ist es, sich auf die wesentlichen Merkmale des Auftrags zu konzentrieren. Je besser sein Verständnis, desto aussagekräftiger ist das Ergebnis. Die Konzentration bietet ihm die Möglichkeit einer abstrakten, elementaren Lösung. Das realisierte Bauwerk soll neben der expressiven Vereinfachung eine Schicht haben, die seinen kulturellen Kontext reflektiert und aus ihm herauswächst.

Laszlo Földes a fondé Földes Architects en 1994 où il partage le travail avec 14 jeunes architectes. Les projets de Földes Architects sont à la fois des bâtiments résidentiels et publics. L'identification de leurs projets repose sur l'utilisation de matériaux naturels et locaux (pierre, brique, bois) et sur la croyance en la continuité architecturale, mais ils sont ouverts aux idées nouvelles. Pour la première fois dans l'histoire, ils ont construit en « LiTraCon » (béton transmettant la lumière), l'invention d'Áron Losonczi qui a reçu plusieurs prix. Le bureau a obtenu une reconnaissance internationale pour le Centre des visiteurs du volcan de Kemenes.
Laszlo Földes considère les commissions de conception comme des réponses à des questions. Son objectif est de se concentrer sur les caractéristiques essentielles de la mission. Plus sa compréhension est bonne, plus le résultat est puissant. La concentration lui offre la possibilité d'une solution abstraite et élémentaire. Outre la simplification de l'expression, le bâtiment réalisé doit avoir une couche de réflexion et sortir de son contexte culturel.

Laszlo Földes fundó Földes Architects en 1994 donde comparte el trabajo con catorce jóvenes arquitectos. Los proyectos de Földes Architects son tanto residenciales como edificios públicos. La identificación de sus proyectos se basa en el uso de materiales naturales y locales (piedra, ladrillo, madera) y la creencia en la continuidad arquitectónica; están sin embargo, abiertos a nuevas ideas. Por primera vez en la historia construyeron en «LiTraCon» (hormigón de transmisión de luz), el invento de Áron Losonczi que recibió varios premios. La oficina obtuvo reconocimiento internacional por el Centro de Visitantes del Parque Volcánico de Kemenes.
Laszlo Földes considera que los encargos de diseño son respuestas a las preguntas que tienen como objetivo el centrarse claramente en las características sustanciales del encargo. Cuanto mejor sea su comprensión, más poderoso será el resultado. La concentración le ofrece la posibilidad de una solución abstracta y elemental. Aparte de la simplificación expresiva, el edificio realizado debe tener una capa que refleje y crezca fuera de su contexto cultural.

NURSERY IN NAGYKOVÁCSI

LOCATION: **NAGYKOVÁCSI, HUNGARY**
PHOTOS: © **LEVENTE SIROKAI**

This three-building complex houses a day-care center, an obstetrics center and a dental office, and will be expanded with two additional wards to complete the complex. Its contemporary design is integrated into the rural environment where it is located, evoking the image of the traditional farms of the area. Although the height and volume of each of the buildings is different, the homogeneity of their exterior finishes gives the complex agility, freshness and playfulness, as well as an easily recognisable image as a public building. The proportions of the volumes transmit a sense of well-being reinforced by the sober brick cladding and the simple shapes of the windows. The porch that forms the main façade of the nursery is a clear reference to the oldest buildings in the village and invites conversation and the fostering of social relations.

Dieser dreigeteilte Gebäudekomplex beherbergt eine Kindertagesstätte, ein Geburtshilfezentrum und eine Zahnarztpraxis und wird um zwei zusätzliche Stationen erweitert, um den Komplex zu vervollständigen. Sein zeitgenössisches Design ist in die ländliche Umgebung, in der es sich befindet, integriert und erinnert an das Bild der traditionellen Bauernhöfe der Gegend. Obwohl die Höhe und das Volumen der einzelnen Gebäude unterschiedlich sind, verleiht die Homogenität ihrer äußeren Oberflächen der komplexen Anlage Agilität, Frische und Verspieltheit sowie ein leicht erkennbares Bild als öffentliches Gebäude. Die Proportionen der Gebäude vermitteln ein Gefühl des Wohlbefindens, das durch die nüchterne Ziegelverkleidung und die einfachen Formen der Fenster verstärkt wird. Der Vorbau, der die Hauptfassade des Kindergartens bildet, ist ein klarer Bezug zu den ältesten Gebäuden des Dorfes und lädt zum Gespräch und zur Pflege sozialer Beziehungen ein.

Ce complexe de trois bâtiments abrite une crèche, un centre d'obstétrique et un cabinet dentaire, et sera agrandi de deux salles supplémentaires pour compléter le complexe. Son design contemporain est intégré dans l'environnement rural où il est situé, évoquant l'image des fermes traditionnelles de la région. Bien que la hauteur et le volume de chacun des bâtiments soient différents, l'homogénéité de leurs finitions extérieures leur confère une agilité, une fraîcheur et un caractère ludique complexes, ainsi qu'une image facilement reconnaissable en tant que bâtiment public. Les proportions des bâtiments transmettent un sentiment de bien-être renforcé par le revêtement sobre en briques et les formes simples des fenêtres. Le porche qui forme la façade principale de la crèche fait clairement référence aux plus anciens bâtiments du village et invite à la conversation et au développement de relations sociales.

Este complejo de tres edificios alberga una guardería, un centro de obstetricia y un consultorio dental, y se ampliará con dos pabellones más que completarán el conjunto. Su diseño contemporáneo se integra en el entorno rural donde se ubica evocando la imagen de las granjas tradicionales de la zona. Si bien la altura y el volumen de cada uno de los edificios es diferente, la homogeneidad de sus acabados exteriores otorga al conjunto agilidad, frescura y ligereza lúdicas, así como una imagen fácilmente reconocible como edificio público. Las proporciones de los edificios transmiten un bienestar reforzado por el sobrio revestimiento de ladrillo y las formas sencillas de las ventanas. El porche que conforma la fachada principal de la guardería constituye una clara referencia a los edificios más antiguos del pueblo e invita a la conversación y a fomentar las relaciones sociales.

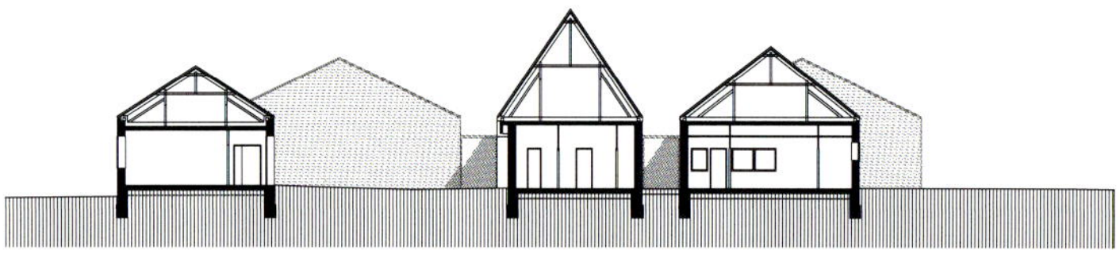

Cross section

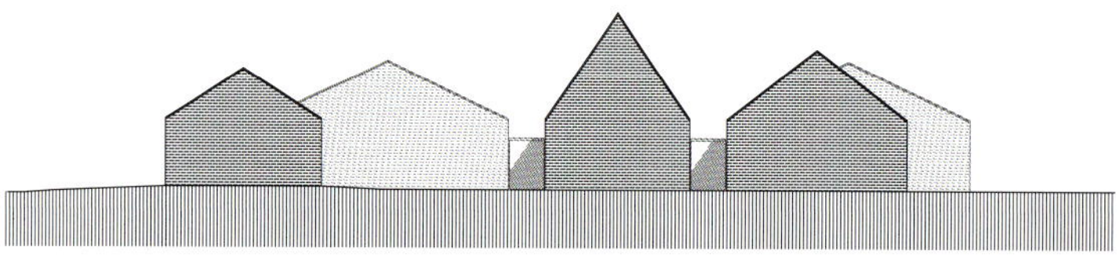

North facade

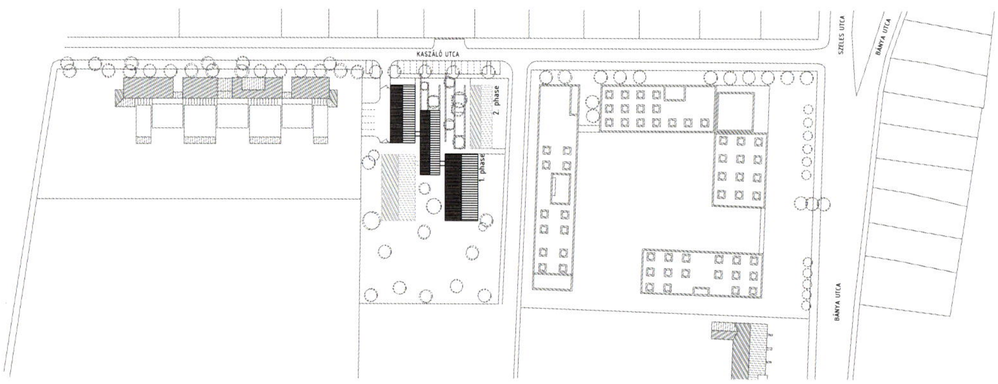

Site plan

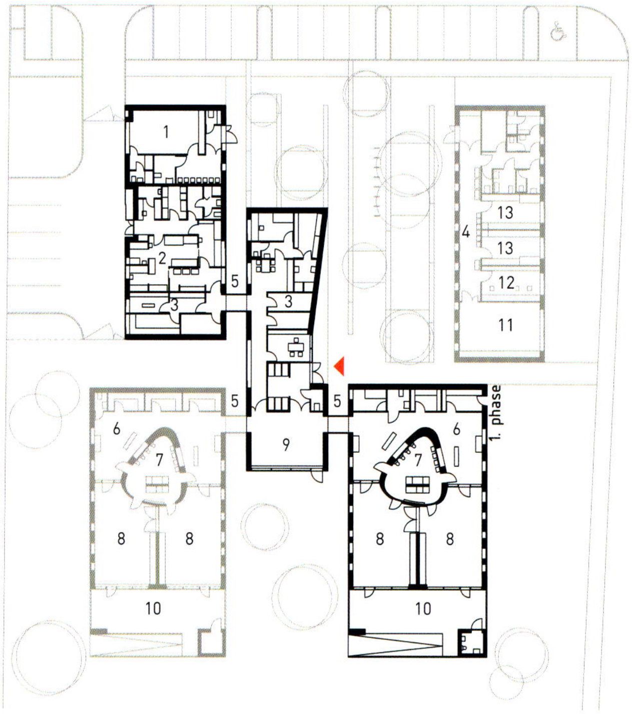

Floor plan

1. Dentist's office
2. Kitchen
3. Office block
4. Traffic
5. Bridge
6. Clothing
7. Washbasin
8. Group room
9. Development room
10. Exterior covered layer
11. Community park
12. Workshop
13. Consultation room

HIBINOSEKKEI + Youji no Shiro + KIDS DESIGN LABO

// PROJECTS //

1. YM NURSERY
2. HN NURSERY
3. KM KINDERGARTEN AND NURSERY

https://hibinosekkei.com
https://e-ensha.com
https://kidsdesignlabo.com

1.

2.

3.

Founded in 1972, HIBINO SEKKEI has designed and supervised the construction sites of various types of architecture. After a considerable amount of experiences, in 2001, the company became an architectural designing office that specializes in two building categories: welfare facilities and children's facilities.
As of today, the company have designed more than five hundred children's facilities. "Youji no Shiro", the children's facilities designing section of the company, now receives inquiries from all around the world. Also, in 2016, the company formed a separate company called KIDS DESIGN LABO, which designs 'everything other than architecture' about children's facilities such as furniture, uniform, CI and so on.
Through the operation of both Youji no Shiro and KIDS DESIGN LABO, we are trying to make contributions to the society. Together with more and more clients who we can share the thoughts for the children, we are moving forward in generating a better environment for children.

HIBINO SEKKEI wurde 1972 gegründet und hat architektonische Arbeiten verschiedener Art entworfen und betreut. Nach einer beträchtlichen Menge an Erfahrung wurde das Unternehmen 2001 zu einem Architekturbüro, das sich auf zwei Gebäudekategorien spezialisiert hat: Sozialeinrichtungen und Kindergebäude.
Bis heute hat das Unternehmen über fünfhundert Kindereinrichtungen entworfen. „Youji no Shiro", die Abteilung für die Gestaltung von Kindereinrichtungen des Unternehmens, erhält nun Anfragen aus der ganzen Welt. Im Jahr 2016 gründete das Unternehmen ein separates Unternehmen mit dem Namen KIDS DESIGN LABO, das „alles andere als Architektur" für Kindereinrichtungen, wie Möbel und Uniformen, entwirft.
Sowohl durch Youji no Shiro als auch durch das KIDS DESIGN LABO „versuchen wir, einen Beitrag zur Gesellschaft zu leisten. Gemeinsam mit immer mehr Kunden können wir Ideen für Gebäude für Kinder austauschen und so Fortschritte bei der Schaffung einer besseren Umwelt für sie erzielen."

Fondée en 1972, HIBINO SEKKEI a conçu et supervisé des chantiers de construction de différents types d'architecture. Après de nombreuses expériences, la société est devenue en 2001 un bureau d'études architecturales spécialisé dans deux catégories de bâtiments : les équipements sociaux et les équipements pour enfants.
À ce jour, la société a conçu plus de cinq cents installations pour enfants. «Youji no Shiro», la section de conception d'installations pour enfants de la société, reçoit désormais des demandes de renseignements du monde entier. En 2016, la société a également créé une société distincte appelée KIDS DESIGN LABO, qui conçoit «tout sauf l'architecture» pour les installations pour enfants, comme le mobilier, les uniformes, les infrastructures essentielles, etc.
Par le biais de Youji no Shiro et de KIDS DESIGN LABO, nous essayons d'apporter notre contribution à la société. En collaboration avec de plus en plus de clients qui nous permettent de partager nos pensées pour les enfants, nous progressons dans la création d'un meilleur environnement pour les enfants.

Fundada en 1972, HIBINO SEKKEI ha diseñado y supervisado obras de arquitectura de diversa tipología. Después de una considerable cantidad de experiencias, en 2001, la compañía se convirtió en una oficina de diseño arquitectónico que se especializa en dos categorías de edificios: instalaciones de bienestar e edificios para niños.
Hasta hoy, la compañía ha diseñado más de quinientas instalaciones para niños. Youji no Shiro, la sección de diseño de instalaciones infantiles de la empresa, ahora recibe consultas de todo el mundo. En 2016, la compañía formó una empresa separada llamada KIDS DESIGN LABO, que diseña «todo lo que no sea arquitectura» sobre instalaciones infantiles, como muebles y uniformes.
A través de ambas empresas, Youji no Shiro y KIDS DESIGN LABO, «estamos tratando de hacer contribuciones a la sociedad. Junto con más y más clientes podemos compartir ideas para edificios destinados a los niños, avanzando en la consecución de un mejor ambiente para ellos».

YM NURSERY

LOCATION: **YONAGO, TOTTORI, JAPAN**
PHOTOS: © **STUDIO BAUHAUS**

"Feel the nature, develop the sensitivity." Despite being located in an area surrounded by sea and mountains, the location of this new nursery did not allow the perception of the natural environment. To solve this, the design of the building promotes the meaningful use of materials through three different approaches. The use of natural materials that stimulate the senses and encourage children's sensitivity, imagination and development; the use of local materials that integrate children into their immediate environment, such as Chizu Cedar wood for the handrails or traditional Yumihama Gasuri cloth for the classroom signs, and the re used materials from the old kindergarten buildings, which bring warmth, evoke the ancient landscape and make the children aware of how to care for things.

„Fühle die Natur, entwickle die Sensibilität". Obwohl diese neue Kinderkrippe in einem Gebiet liegt, das von Meer und Bergen umgeben ist, erlaubte der Standort dieser neuen Kinderkrippe nicht die Wahrnehmung dieser natürlichen Umgebung. Um dieser Tatsache abzuhelfen, fördert die Gestaltung des Gebäudes den sinnvollen Einsatz von Materialien durch drei verschiedene Ansätze. Der erste Ansatz konzentriert sich auf die Verwendung von natürlichen Materialien, die die Sinne anregen und die Sensibilität, Phantasie und Entwicklung der Kinder fördern. Zum anderen sollen lokale Materialien verwendet werden, die die Kinder in ihre unmittelbare Umgebung integrieren, wie z.B. Chizu-Zedernholz für die Handläufe oder traditionelles Yumihama-Gasuri-Tuch für die Schilder im Klassenzimmer. Die dritte ist die Wiederverwendung von Materialien aus den alten Kindergartengebäuden, die Wärme bringen, an die alte Landschaft erinnern und den Kindern bewusst machen, wie man sich um die Dinge kümmert.

« Sentir la nature, développer la sensibilité ». Bien que située dans une zone entourée de mer et de montagnes, l'emplacement de cette nouvelle pépinière ne permettait pas la perception de cet environnement naturel. Pour remédier à ce fait, la conception du bâtiment favorise l'utilisation judicieuse des matériaux par le biais de trois approches différentes. La première approche se concentre sur l'utilisation de matériaux naturels qui stimulent les sens et encouragent la sensibilité, l'imagination et le développement des enfants. La seconde consiste à utiliser des matériaux locaux qui intègrent les enfants dans leur environnement immédiat, comme le bois de cèdre Chizu pour les rampes ou le tissu traditionnel Yumihama Gasuri pour les panneaux de classe. La troisième consiste à réutiliser les matériaux des anciens bâtiments du jardin d'enfants, qui apportent de la chaleur, évoquent le paysage ancien et sensibilisent les enfants à la manière de prendre soin des choses.

«Sentir la naturaleza, desarrollar la sensibilidad». A pesar de estar situada en una zona rodeada de mar y de montañas, el emplazamiento de esta nueva guardería no permitía percibir este entorno natural. Para subsanar este hecho, el diseño del edificio promueve el empleo significativo de los materiales mediante tres enfoques diferentes. El primero se centra en el uso de materiales naturales que estimulen los sentidos y fomenten la sensibilidad, la imaginación y el desarrollo de los niños. El segundo utiliza materiales locales que integran a los niños en su entorno más inmediato, como la madera de Cedro de Chizu de los pasamanos o la tela tradicional Yumihama Gasuri de los letreros de las clases. El tercero reutiliza materiales de los antiguos edificios de la guardería, que aportan calidez, evocan el antiguo paisaje y sensibilizan a los niños hacia el cuidado de las cosas.

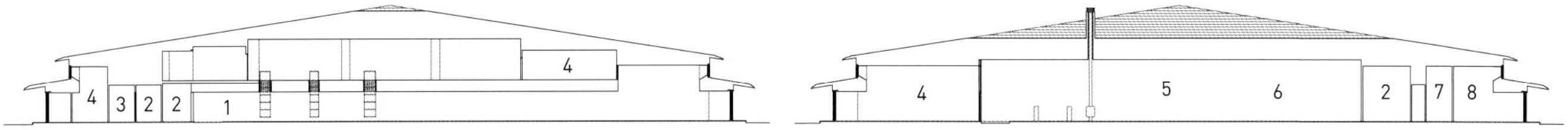

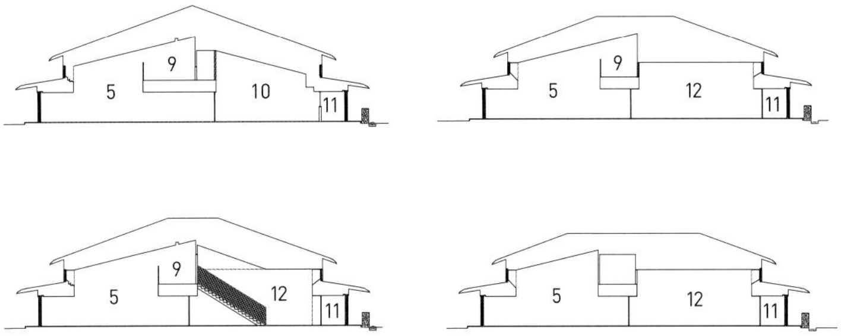

1. Entrance
2. Edge side corridor
3. Locker room
4. 0-2 years old childcare room
5. Dining room
6. Play room
7. Charging room
8. Children's toilet
9. Corridor
10. Kitchen
11. Edge side corridor
12. Nursery room

Sections

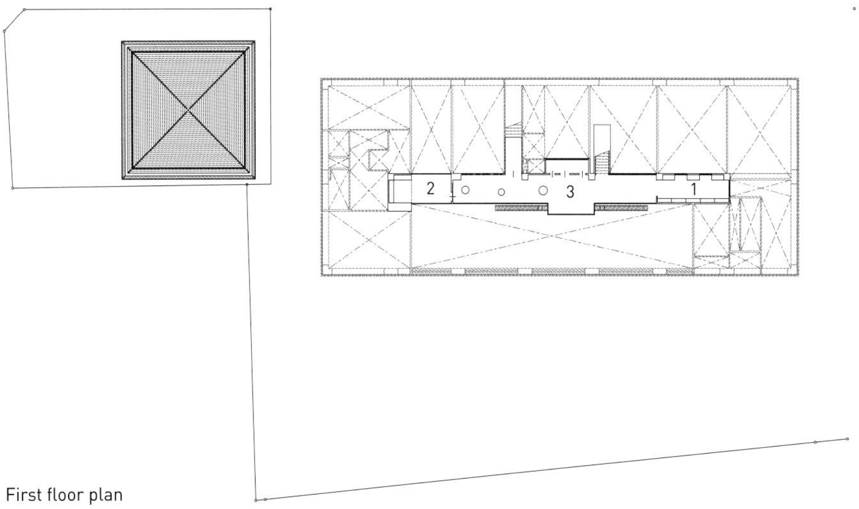

1. Picture book / library
2. Changing room
3. Corridor

First floor plan

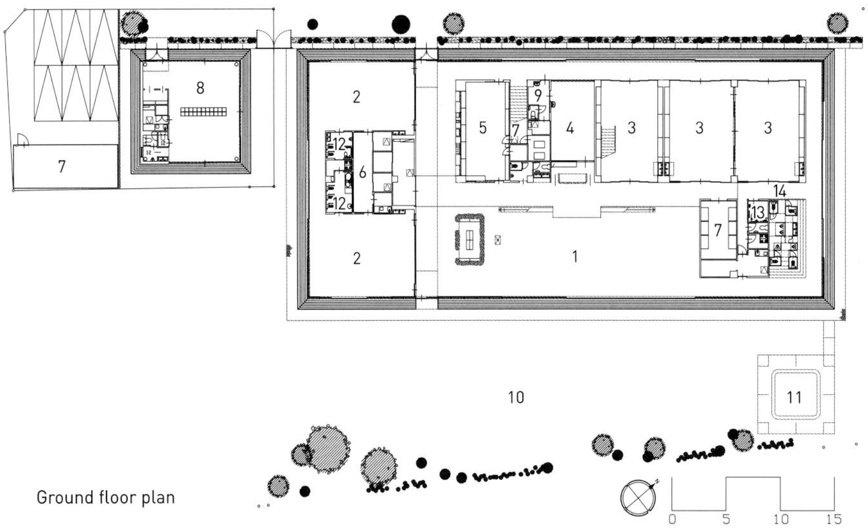

1. Dining room
2. 0-2 years old childcare room
3. Nursery room
4. Kitchen
5. Staff room
6. Locker room
7. Storage
8. After school children's club
9. Inspection room
10. Playground
11. Pool
12. Children's toilet
13. Toilet
14. Corridor

Ground floor plan

HN NURSERY

LOCATION: **KANAGAWA, JAPAN**
PHOTOS: © **TOSHINARI SOGA (STUDIO BAUHAUS)**

The design of this nursery focuses on creating a place where children can perceive nature from any point and throughout the day, and play in an environment full of motivation that develop their sensitivity and creativity. In contrast to the usual programmed and less flexible activities of indoor spaces, the outdoor activities allow children to become aware of the multiple incentives from the outside that encourage the desire to discover and think for themselves, such as the changes in seasons and climate, the touch of the ground and even the smell of flowers. Elements such as the tree planted inside one of the rooms, the glass roof that provides natural light and allows children to see the sky, or the five-metre high hill in the outdoor playground provide children with a rich natural setting in which to develop their own stories.

La conception de cette crèche est axée sur la création d'un lieu où les enfants peuvent percevoir la nature à tout moment et tout au long de la journée, et jouer dans un environnement plein de stimuli qui développent leur sensibilité et leur créativité. Contrairement aux activités habituellement programmées et moins flexibles des espaces intérieurs, les activités de plein air permettent aux enfants de prendre conscience des multiples stimuli de l'extérieur qui favorisent l'envie de découvrir et de penser par eux-mêmes, comme les changements de saisons et de climat, le toucher du sol et même l'odeur des fleurs. Des éléments tels que l'arbre planté dans l'une des pièces, le toit en verre qui fournit de la lumière naturelle et permet aux enfants de voir le ciel, ou la colline de cinq mètres de haut dans la cour de récréation extérieure offrent aux enfants un cadre naturel riche dans lequel ils peuvent développer leurs propres histoires.

Die Gestaltung dieser Kinderkrippe konzentriert sich darauf, einen Ort zu schaffen, an dem die Kinder die Natur von jedem Punkt aus und den ganzen Tag über wahrnehmen und in einer Umgebung voller Anreize spielen können, die ihre Sensibilität und Kreativität entwickelt. Im Gegensatz zu den üblichen programmierten und weniger flexiblen Aktivitäten in Innenräumen ermöglichen die Aktivitäten im Freien den Kindern, sich der vielfältigen Reize von außen bewusst zu werden, die den Wunsch zum Entdecken und selbstständigen Denken fördern, wie z.B. die Veränderungen der Jahreszeiten und des Klimas, die Berührung des Bodens und sogar der Blumenduft. Elemente wie der in einem der Räume gepflanzte Baum, das Glasdach, das natürliches Licht spendet und den Kindern den Blick in den Himmel ermöglicht, oder der fünf Meter hohe Hügel im Außenbereich des Spielplatzes bieten den Kindern eine reiche natürliche Umgebung, in der sie ihre eigenen Geschichten entwickeln können.

El diseño de esta guardería se centra en crear un lugar donde los niños perciban la naturaleza desde cualquier punto y durante todo el día y jueguen en un entorno lleno de estímulos que desarrollen su sensibilidad y creatividad. En contraste con las habituales actividades programadas y menos flexibles de los espacios interiores, las actividades al aire libre permiten que los niños se sensibilicen frente a los múltiples estímulos del exterior que fomentan las ganas de descubrir y pensar por ellos mismos, como los cambios de estaciones y de clima, el tacto del terreno e incluso el olor de las flores. Elementos como el árbol plantado en el interior de unas de las salas, el techo acristalado que aporta luz natural y permite ver el cielo, o la colina de cinco metros de altura del patio exterior brindan a los niños un rico escenario natural donde desarrollar sus propias historias.

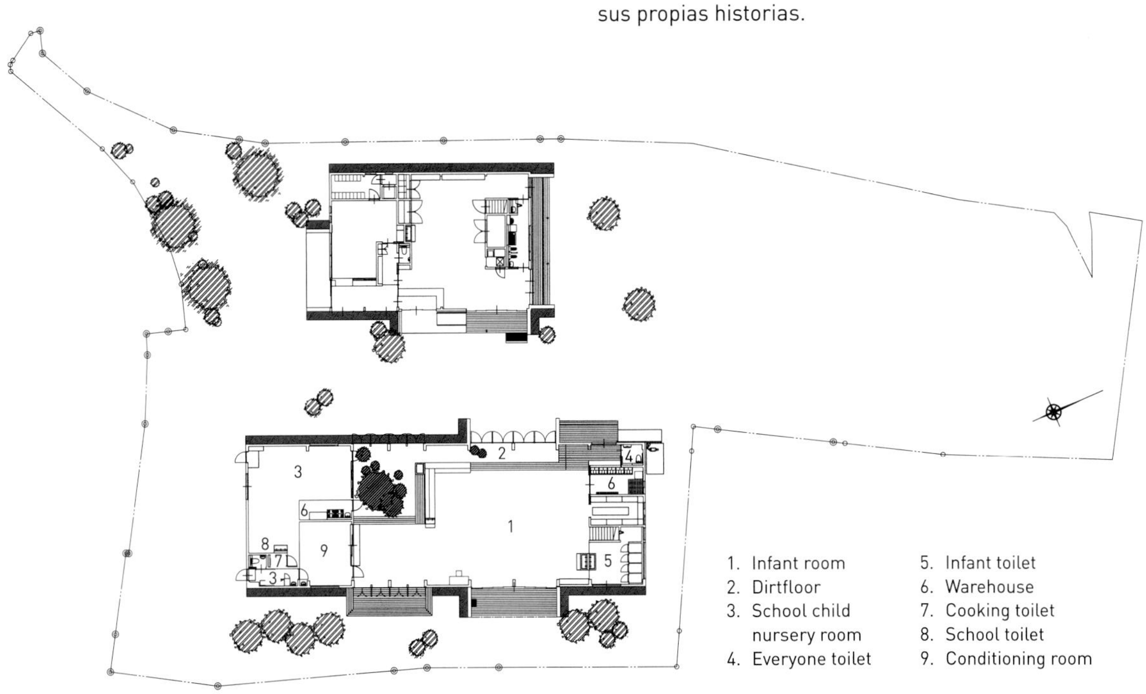

1. Infant room
2. Dirtfloor
3. School child nursery room
4. Everyone toilet
5. Infant toilet
6. Warehouse
7. Cooking toilet
8. School toilet
9. Conditioning room

Floor plan

KM KINDERGARTEN AND NURSERY

LOCATION: **OSAKA, JAPAN**
PHOTOS: **© STUDIO BAUHAUS, RYUJI INOUE**

The commission consisted of the complete renovation of a kindergarten located in an area with an important textile industrial past. The project focused on two objectives: to promote physical exercise in children despite the reduced space of the plot and to help them learn about their place of residence by introducing aspects of the region's textile past into the design of the building. To achieve the first goal, an undulating environment was created that promotes children's movement in a natural way and an ascending roof designed to become a playground that, by connecting with a staircase that returns to the lower level, becomes part of a chase and race circuit. To achieve the second objective, fabrics were used in small elements of the design and in coverings of some walls, and they were integrated in some games.

La commission a consisté en la rénovation complète d'un jardin d'enfants situé dans une zone au passé industriel textile important. Le projet s'est concentré sur deux objectifs : promouvoir l'exercice physique chez les enfants malgré l'espace réduit du terrain et les aider à connaître leur lieu de résidence en introduisant des aspects du passé textile de la région dans la conception du bâtiment. Pour atteindre le premier objectif, on a créé un environnement vallonné qui favorise le mouvement des enfants de manière naturelle et un toit ascendant conçu pour devenir un terrain de jeu qui, en se connectant avec un escalier qui revient au niveau inférieur, devient une partie d'un circuit de course et de poursuite. Pour atteindre le second objectif, des tissus ont été utilisés dans de petits éléments du dessin et dans les revêtements de certains murs, et ils ont été intégrés dans certains jeux.

Der Auftrag bestand in der vollständigen Renovierung eines Kindergartens in einem Gebiet mit einer bedeutenden textilindustriellen Vergangenheit. Das Projekt konzentrierte sich auf zwei Ziele: die Förderung der körperlichen Bewegung von Kindern trotz des reduzierten Platzes auf dem Grundstück und die Unterstützung beim Kennenlernen des Wohnortes durch die Einführung von Aspekten der textilen Vergangenheit der Region in die Gestaltung des Gebäudes. Um das erste Ziel zu erreichen, wurde eine wellenförmige Umgebung geschaffen, die die Bewegung der Kinder auf natürliche Weise fördert, sowie ein ansteigendes Dach, das zu einem Spielplatz wird, der durch eine Verbindung mit einer Treppe, die in die untere Ebene zurückführt, Teil einer Verfolgungs- und Rennstrecke wird. Um das zweite Ziel zu erreichen, wurden Stoffe in kleinen Elementen des Designs und in Verkleidungen einiger Wände verwendet und in einigen Spielen integriert.

El encargo consistió en la completa remodelación de un jardín de infancia situado en una zona con un importante pasado industrial textil. El proyecto se centró en dos objetivos: fomentar el ejercicio físico en los niños a pesar del reducido espacio de la parcela y ayudarles a aprender sobre su lugar de residencia introduciendo aspectos del pasado textil de la región en el diseño del edificio. Para lograr el primer objetivo se crearon un entorno ondulado que promueve el movimiento infantil de forma natural y una cubierta ascendente diseñada para convertirse en patio de juegos que, al conectar con una escalera que vuelve a comunicar con el nivel inferior, se convierte en parte de un circuito de persecución y carrera. Para lograr el segundo objetivo se utilizaron tejidos en pequeños elementos del diseño y en revestimientos de algunos muros, y se integraron en algunos juegos.

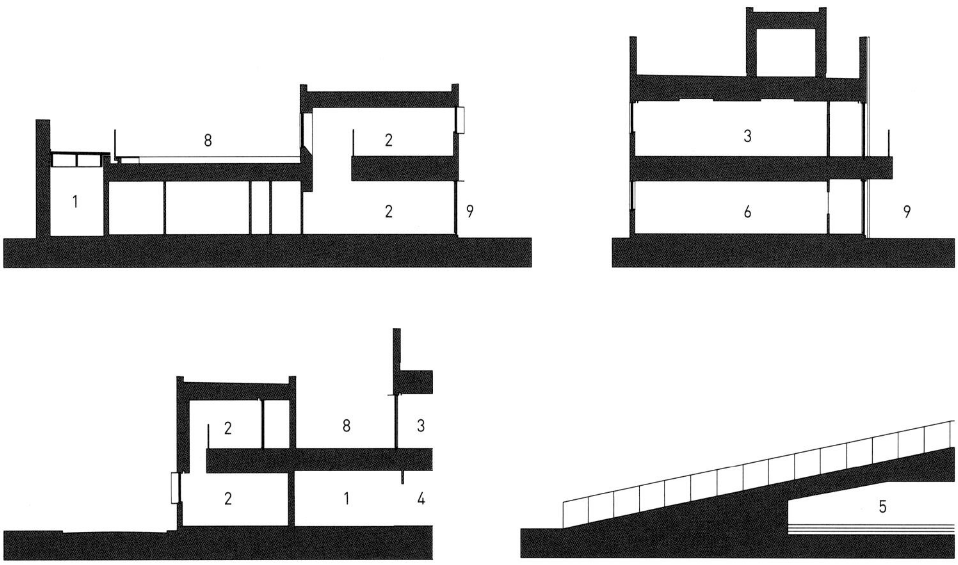

1. Entrance
2. Office
3. Childcare room
4. Gymnasium
5. Atelier
6. Kitchen
7. Slope
8. Play terrace
9. Courtyard

Sections

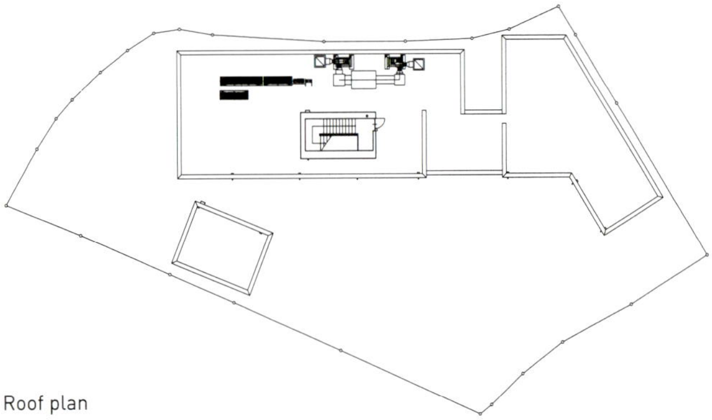

Roof plan

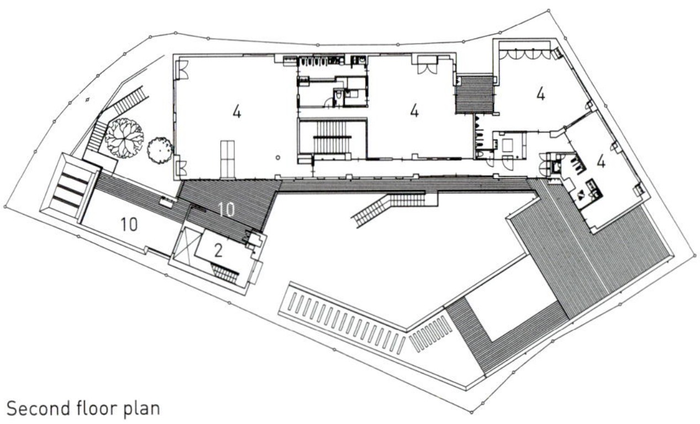

Second floor plan

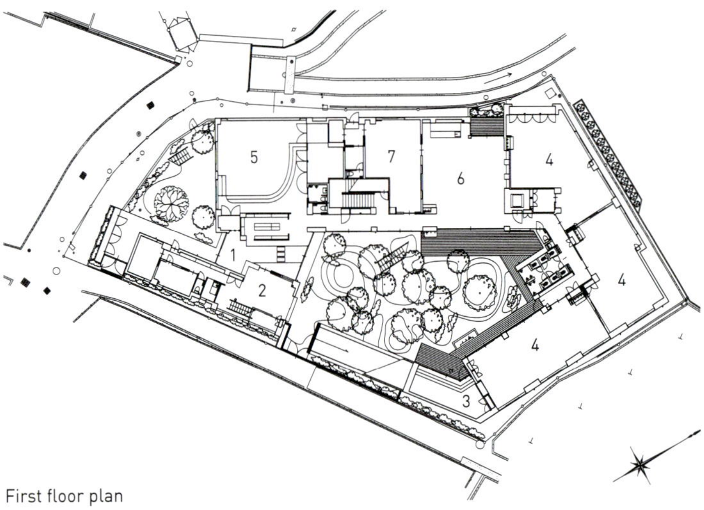

First floor plan

1. Entrance
2. Office
3. Restroom
4. Childcare room
5. Gymnasium
6. Dining room
7. Kitchen
8. Atelier
9. Play hole
10. Play terrace
11. Slope

ISON Architects
Jean Son

// PROJECTS //

1. IDDEUL KINDERGARTEN

www.isonarch.com

ISON Architects
Jean Son

1.

Jean Son is an architect who is working in South Korea. He graduated from Hongik University in Korea and moved to Italy in 1987 to study at Università Iuav di Venezia until 1992. Since 1993, he has gained three years of working experience at the Francesco Venetian office in Naples. After returning his home country, he established ISON architecture in 1997 with Min Lee, where he has worked on numerous projects in South Korea. He won the 2008 "Kim Soo-Geun Cultural Prize," 2004, 2008, 2015 "Architects Association Award," and 2015 "Seoul Metropolitan Government Architecture Award."

Jean Son ist ein in Südkorea tätiger Architekt. Er schloss sein Studium an der Hongik-Universität in Korea ab und zog 1987 nach Italien, um bis 1992 an der Università Iuav di Venezia zu studieren. Seit 1993 sammelte er drei Jahre Berufserfahrung im Büro von Francesco Venetian in Neapel. Nach der Rückkehr in sein Heimatland gründete er 1997 zusammen mit Min Lee ISON, wo er an zahlreichen Projekten in Südkorea mitgearbeitet hat. Er gewann den „Kim Soo-Geun-Kulturpreis 2008", den „Architectural Association Award 2004, 2008, 2015" und den „Seoul Metropolitan Government Architecture Award 2015".

Jean Son est un architecte qui travaille en Corée du Sud. Il est diplômé de l'université Hongik en Corée et s'est installé en Italie en 1987 pour étudier à l'université Iuav di Venezia jusqu'en 1992. Depuis 1993, il a acquis une expérience professionnelle de trois ans au sein du bureau Francesco Venetian à Naples. De retour dans son pays, il a créé ISON architecture en 1997 avec Min Lee, où il a travaillé sur de nombreux projets en Corée du Sud. Il a remporté le prix culturel Kim Soo-Geun en 2008, le prix de l'association des architectes en 2004, 2008 et 2015 et le prix d'architecture du gouvernement métropolitain de Séoul en 2015.

Jean Son es un arquitecto que trabaja en Corea del Sur. Se graduó en la Universidad de Hongik en Corea y se trasladó a Italia en 1987 para estudiar en la Università Iuav de Venecia hasta 1992. Desde 1993, obtuvo tres años de experiencia laboral en la oficina de Francesco Venetian en Nápoles. Después de regresar a su país de origen, estableció ISON en 1997 con Min Lee, donde ha trabajado en numerosos proyectos en Corea del Sur. Ganó el Premio Cultural Kim Soo-Geun 2008, el Premio de la Asociación de Arquitectos 2004, 2008, 2015 y el Premio de Arquitectura del Gobierno Metropolitano de Seúl 2015.

IDDEUL KINDERGARTEN

LOCATION: **SUJI-GU, YONGIN-SI, GYEONGGI-DO, SOUTH KOREA**
PHOTOS: © **JONGOH KIM**

Designed to accommodate nearly four hundred children, this kindergarten organizes its extensive program taking advantage of the characteristics of the site. To this end it places the auxiliary spaces in the underground and distributes the classrooms into four articulated "boxes" arranged on a rectangular platform that adapts to the topography and that becomes a meeting point between the exterior and interior spaces. A fifth black metal box is inserted at the base of the building and contains the main entrance. The different positions of the boxes on the platform give them a unique spatial identity and create a variety of outdoor environments. Inside, the bright colours of the floors are inspired by specific concepts that are adapted to the characteristics of each plant and express the unique vibrant and childlike gesture of the kindergarten.

Dieser Kindergarten, der für fast vierhundert Kinder ausgelegt ist, organisiert sein umfangreiches Programm unter Ausnutzung der Besonderheiten des Ortes. Zu diesem Zweck platziert sie die Nebenräume im Untergrund und verteilt die Klassenräume in vier gegliederte „Boxen", die auf einer rechteckigen Plattform angeordnet sind, die sich der Topographie anpasst und zu einem Treffpunkt zwischen Außen- und Innenraum wird. Ein fünfter schwarzer Metallkasten ist an der Basis des Gebäudes eingefügt und enthält den Haupteingang. Die verschiedenen Positionen der Boxen auf der Plattform verleihen ihnen eine einzigartige räumliche Identität und schaffen eine Vielzahl von Außenumgebungen. Im Inneren sind die hellen Farben der Böden von spezifischen Konzepten inspiriert, die an die Eigenschaften der einzelnen Pflanzen angepasst sind und die einzigartige, lebendige und kindliche Geste des Kindergartens zum Ausdruck bringen.

Conçu pour accueillir près de quatre cents enfants, ce jardin d'enfants organise son vaste programme en profitant des caractéristiques du site. À cette fin, il place les espaces auxiliaires dans le sous-sol et distribue les salles de classe en quatre « boîtes » articulées disposées sur une plate-forme rectangulaire qui s'adapte à la topographie et qui devient un point de rencontre entre les espaces extérieurs et intérieurs. Une cinquième boîte métallique noire est insérée à la base du bâtiment et contient l'entrée principale. Les différentes positions des boîtes sur la plate-forme leur confèrent une identité spatiale unique et créent une variété d'environnements extérieurs. À l'intérieur, les couleurs vives des sols s'inspirent de concepts spécifiques adaptés aux caractéristiques de chaque plante et expriment le geste unique, vibrant et enfantin, du jardin d'enfants.

Diseñado para acomodar a cerca de cuatrocientos niños, este jardín de infancia organiza su extenso programa aprovechando las características del solar. Para ello, coloca los espacios auxiliares en el subsuelo y distribuye las aulas en cuatro «cajas» articuladas, dispuestas sobre una plataforma rectangular que se adapta a la topografía y que deviene un punto de encuentro entre los espacios exteriores y el interior. Una quinta caja de metal negro se inserta en la base del edificio y contiene la entrada principal. Las diferentes posiciones de las cajas sobre la plataforma otorgan a estas una identidad espacial única y crean gran variedad de ámbitos exteriores. En el interior, los colores vivos de los suelos se inspiran en conceptos específicos que se adaptan a las características de cada una de las plantas y expresan el gesto vibrante e infantil único del jardín de infancia.

Site plan

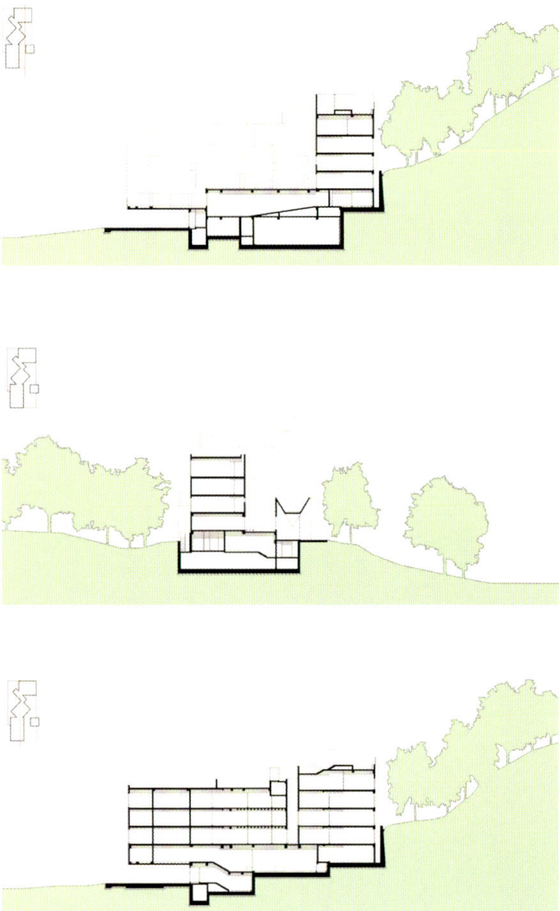

Sections

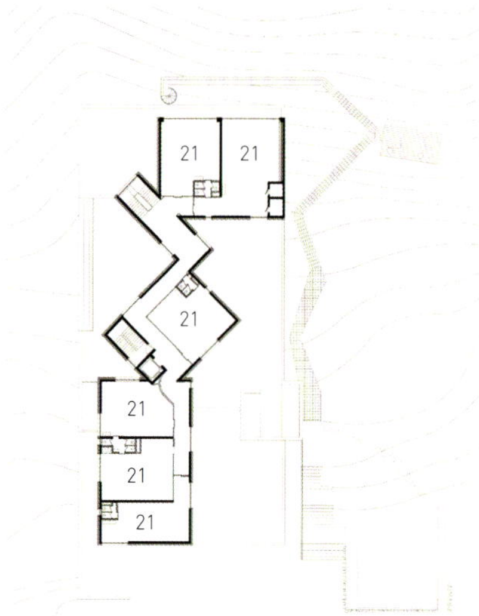

Second and third floor plan

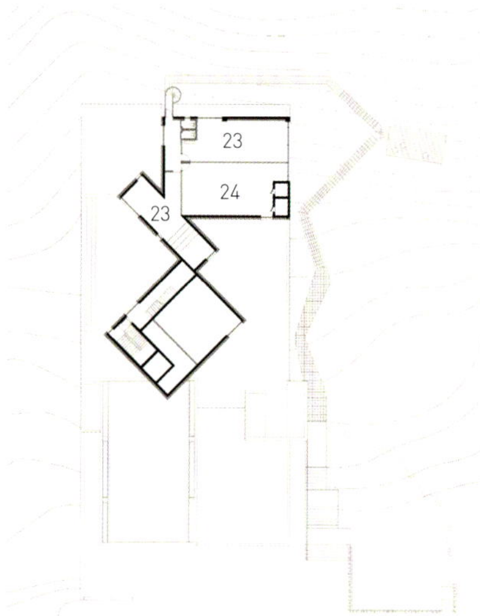

Fourth floor plan

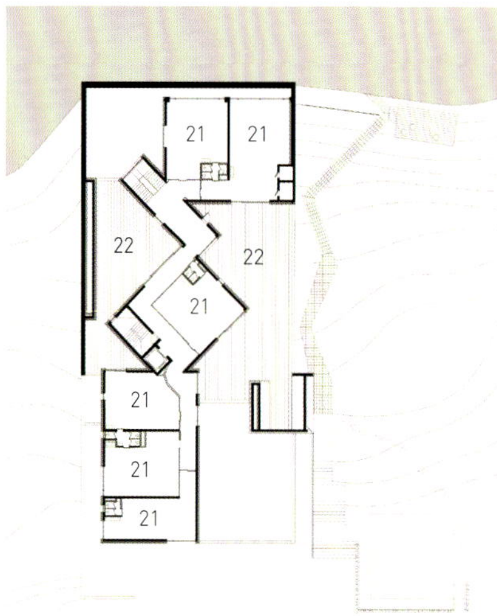

First floor plan

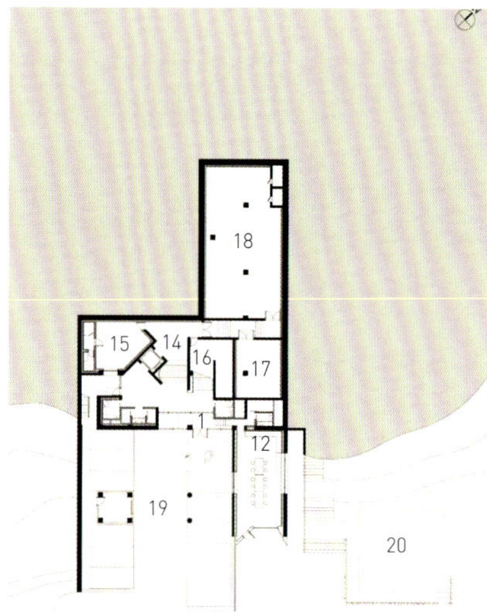

Basement 2

Basement 1

1. Entrance
2. Lobby
3. Auditorium
4. Teacher's room
5. Director room / health room
6. Article room
7. Reference room
8. Indoor playground
9. Kitchen
10. Outdoor playground
11. Sunken
12. Lounge-1(cafe)
13. Hall-1
14. Hall-2
15. Staff lounge
16. Storage-1
17. Electrical room
18. Mechanical room
19. Lounge-2
20. Garden
21. Classroom
22. Yard
23. Language lab
24. Art room-2

Klab architecture

// PROJECTS //

1. PUBLIC NURSERY IN GLYFADA, ATHENS

www.klab.gr

Klab architecture

1.

KLAB architecture (kinetic lab of architecture), was founded in 2001 by Konstantinos Labrinopoulos. It is a group of highly qualified and motivated architects who seek opportunities to create unique and intriguing urban events. KLAB architecture deals with a diverse field of projects, from large planning schemes to furniture design.
KLAB's work has been published widely in architectural magazines and books internationally. Notably, in 2008, KLAB architecture achieved international recognition when Wallpaper magazine included it among the fifty most upcoming architectural firms in the world. In 2010 KLAB works were included in the book STARCHITECTS by Collins design editions and in 2013 Placebo pharmacy was featured at Architecture Now! Vol 9 book by Taschen. Klab architecture has won among others, the X International Award by Domus Russia for Placebo Pharmacy and has been nominated twice for the MiesEU Award for Urban stripes in Koukaki in 2015 and for Public Nursery in Glyfada in 2019.

KLAB architecture (laboratoire cinétique d'architecture), a été fondé en 2001 par Konstantinos Labrinopoulos. Il s'agit d'un groupe d'architectes hautement qualifiés et motivés qui recherchent des opportunités de créer des événements urbains uniques et intrigants. KLAB architecture s'occupe d'un large éventail de projets, allant des grands projets d'urbanisme à la conception de mobilier.
Les travaux de KLAB ont été largement publiés dans des magazines et des livres d'architecture au niveau international. En 2008, l'architecture de KLAB a notamment été reconnue internationalement lorsque le magazine Wallpaper l'a incluse parmi les cinquante cabinets d'architecture les plus prometteurs du monde. En 2010, les travaux de KLAB ont été inclus dans le livre STARCHITECTS by Collins Design et en 2013, la pharmacie Placebo a été présentée à Architecture Now ! Vol 9 de Taschen. Klab architecture a remporté, entre autres, le Xe prix international de Domus Russie pour la pharmacie Placebo et a été nominé deux fois pour le prix MiesEU pour les bandes urbaines à Koukaki en 2015 et pour la pépinière publique à Glyfada en 2019.

KLAB architecture (kinetisches Labor der Architektur), wurde 2001 von Konstantinos Labrinopoulos gegründet. Es handelt sich um eine Gruppe hochqualifizierter und motivierter Architekten, die nach Möglichkeiten suchen, einzigartige und faszinierende städtische Ereignisse zu schaffen. KLAB architecture beschäftigt sich mit einem vielfältigen Bereich von Projekten, von großen Planungen bis hin zum Möbeldesign.
Die Arbeit von KLAB wurde international in Architekturmagazinen und Büchern veröffentlicht. Bemerkenswert ist, dass KLAB architecture im Jahr 2008 internationale Anerkennung erlangte, als die Zeitschrift Wallpaper sie unter die fünfzig aufstrebenden Architekturbüros der Welt aufnahm. Im Jahr 2010 wurden KLAB-Werke in das Buch STARCHITECTS by Collins Design aufgenommen und 2013 wurde Placebo Pharmacy bei Architecture Now! Band 9 von Taschen vorgestellt. Klab architecture hat unter anderem den X International Award von Domus Russia für Placebo Pharmacy gewonnen und wurde zweimal für den MiesEU Award for Urban Stripes in Koukaki im Jahr 2015 und für Public Nursery in Glyfada im Jahr 2019 nominiert.

KLAB architecture (laboratorio cinético de arquitectura), fue fundado en 2001 por Konstantinos Labrinopoulos. Es un grupo de arquitectos altamente cualificados y motivados que buscan oportunidades para crear eventos urbanos únicos e intrigantes. KLAB arquitectura se ocupa de un campo diverso de proyectos, desde grandes esquemas de planificación hasta diseño de mobiliario.
El trabajo de KLAB ha sido publicado ampliamente en revistas y libros de arquitectura a nivel internacional. Cabe destacar que en 2008, KLAB architecture obtuvo reconocimiento internacional cuando la revista Wallpaper la incluyó entre los cincuenta estudios de arquitectura más destacados del mundo. En 2010 los trabajos de KLAB fueron incluidos en el libro STARCHITECTS de Collins Design y en 2013 la farmacia Placebo fue presentada en Architecture Now! Vol. 9, libro de la editorial Taschen. Klab architecture ha ganado, entre otros, el X Premio Internacional de Domus Rusia para la Farmacia Placebo y ha sido nominado dos veces para el Premio EUmies de franjas urbanas en Koukaki en 2015 y para la Guardería Pública en Glyfada en 2019.

PUBLIC NURSERY IN GLYFADA, ATHENS

LOCATION: **GLYFADA, ATHENS, GREECE**
PHOTOS: © **MARIANA BISTI**

This nursery consists of different prefabricated modules, each built with a different roof, whose design is inspired by the archetypal drawing of a house as perceived by a child. The idea of the project was to create an urban village generated by the same materials and architectural principles where, on a child's scale, the classrooms represent the houses and the courtyard is the square. Thus, the program consists of four classrooms designed to have three open sides, which are organized around a central courtyard and have two or three balconies with wooden pergolas. Two of the classrooms can be joined together for special events, and smaller courtyards provide light and views of the common areas. The project tries to break with the concept of an overprotective environment, creating a place that encourages fun and play, mixed with a touch of adventure.

Diese Kinderkrippe besteht aus verschiedenen vorgefertigten Modulen, jedes mit einem anderen Dach gebaut, deren Design von der archetypischen Zeichnung eines Hauses inspiriert ist, wie es von einem Kind wahrgenommen wird. Die Idee des Projekts bestand darin, ein städtisches Dorf zu schaffen, das aus denselben Materialien und nach denselben architektonischen Prinzipien entstanden ist, in dem die Klassenzimmer im Maßstab eines Kindes die Häuser und der Hof den Platz darstellen. So besteht das Programm aus vier Klassenzimmern mit drei offenen Seiten, die um einen zentralen Innenhof herum angeordnet sind und zwei oder drei Balkone mit Holzpergolen haben. Zwei der Klassenzimmer können für besondere Anlässe miteinander verbunden werden, und kleinere Innenhöfe sorgen für Licht und Ausblicke auf die Gemeinschaftsräume. Das Projekt versucht, mit dem Konzept einer überfürsorglichen Umgebung zu brechen und einen Ort zu schaffen, der Spaß und Spiel fördert, gemischt mit einem Hauch von Abenteuer.

Cette crèche est composée de différents modules préfabriqués, chacun construit avec un toit différent, dont la conception s'inspire du dessin archétypal d'une maison telle qu'elle est perçue par un enfant. L'idée du projet était de créer un village urbain généré par les mêmes matériaux et principes architecturaux où, à l'échelle d'un enfant, les salles de classe représentent les maisons et la cour est la place. Ainsi, le programme se compose de quatre salles de classe conçues pour avoir trois côtés ouverts, qui s'organisent autour d'une cour centrale et possèdent deux ou trois balcons avec des pergolas en bois. Deux des salles de classe peuvent être réunies pour des événements spéciaux, et des cours plus petites offrent de la lumière et des vues sur les zones communes. Le projet tente de rompre avec le concept d'un environnement surprotecteur, en créant un lieu qui encourage le plaisir et le jeu, mélangé à une touche d'aventure.

Esta guardería se compone de diferentes módulos prefabricados, cada uno de ellos construido con una cubierta diferente, cuyo diseño se inspira en el dibujo arquetípico de una casa tal como la percibe un niño. La idea del proyecto fue crear un pueblo urbano generado por los mismos materiales y principios arquitectónicos donde, a escala infantil, las aulas representan las casas y el patio es la plaza. De este modo, el programa consta de cuatro aulas diseñadas para tener tres lados abiertos, que se organizan alrededor de un patio central y que disponen de dos o tres balcones con pérgolas de madera. Dos de las aulas pueden unirse para eventos especiales, y unos patios más pequeños aportan luz y vistas a las zonas comunes. El proyecto intenta romper con el concepto de entorno sobreprotector, creando un lugar que fomenta la diversión y el juego, mezclados con un toque de aventura.

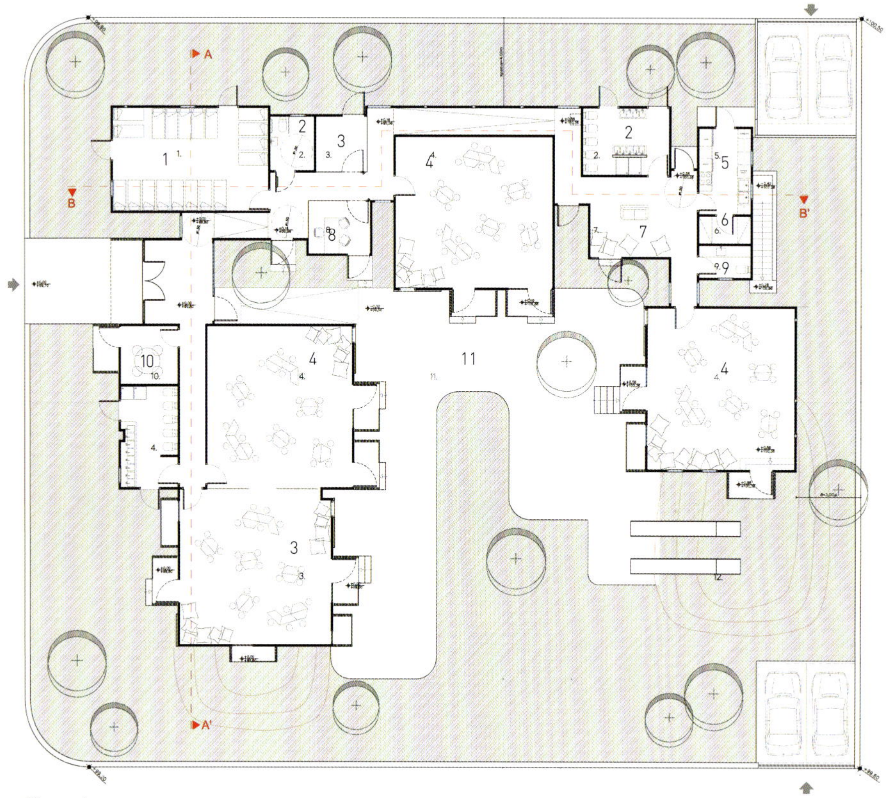

Floor plan

1. Sleeping room
2. Toilet room
3. Isolation room
4. Nursery room
5. Kitchen
6. Storage room
7. Multi-purpose room
8. Administration
9. Teachers' toilet room
10. Teachers' office
11. Playing field
12. Slopes

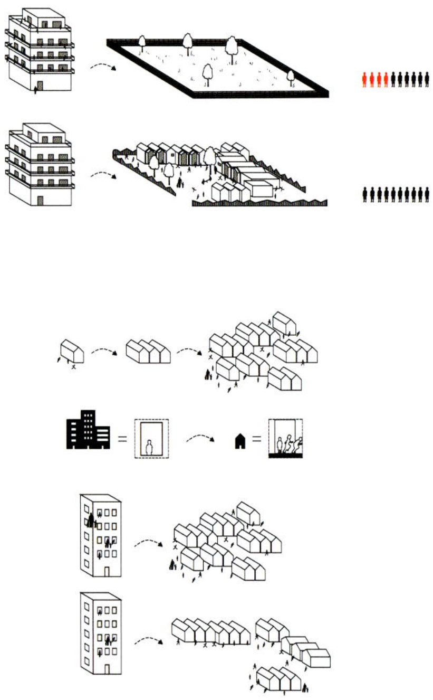

Concept diagram

Elevations

ΜΟΥΣΙΚΗ ΓΩΝΙΑ

Luca Peralta
PERALTA design & consulting

// PROJECTS //

1. KINDERGARDEN SCHOOL "SANDRO PERTINI"

www.lucaperalta.com

Luca Peralta
PERALTA design & consulting

1.

"PERALTA – design & consulting", is an award winning practice specialized in the design of public and private architecture, interior design, urban and landscape design with a specific interest in experimentation and application of environmentally sensitive technologies. The studio has an internal staff of architects and engineers and, along with a network of important consultants and collaborators in Italy and abroad, has successfully collaborated on many projects. Luca Peralta, the founder and the director, is a registered engineer and architect: member of the Italian Association of Building and Environmental Engineers and the Architects Registration Board of London, UK.

« PERALTA – design & consulting », est un cabinet primé, spécialisé dans la conception d'architecture publique et privée, de design d'intérieur, de design urbain et paysager, avec un intérêt particulier pour l'expérimentation et l'application de technologies sensibles à l'environnement. Le studio dispose d'une équipe interne d'architectes et d'ingénieurs et, avec un réseau d'importants consultants et collaborateurs en Italie et à l'étranger, a collaboré avec succès à de nombreux projets. Luca Peralta, le fondateur et le directeur, est un ingénieur et un architecte agréé : il est membre de l'Association italienne des ingénieurs du bâtiment et de l'environnement et du Conseil d'enregistrement des architectes de Londres, au Royaume-Uni.

„PERALTA – design & consulting", ist ein anerkanntes und ausgezeichnetes Unternehmen, das sich auf das Design von öffentlicher und privater Architektur, Innenarchitektur, Stadt- und Landschaftsgestaltung spezialisiert hat und ein besonderes Interesse an der Erprobung und Anwendung umweltsensibler Technologien hat. Das Studio verfügt über einen internen Stab von Architekten und Ingenieuren und hat zusammen mit einem Netzwerk von wichtigen Beratern und Mitarbeitern in Italien und im Ausland an vielen anderen Projekten erfolgreich mitgearbeitet. Luca Peralta, der Gründer und Direktor, ist Ingenieur und eingetragener Architekt: Mitglied des italienischen Verbands der Bau- und Umweltingenieure und des Architects' Register Council of London, Großbritannien.

PERALTA – design & consulting, es una reconocida y premiada empresa especializada en el diseño de arquitectura pública y privada, diseño de interiores, diseño urbano y paisajístico con un interés específico en la experimentación y aplicación de tecnologías sensibles al medio ambiente. El estudio cuenta con una plantilla interna de arquitectos e ingenieros y, junto con una red de importantes consultores y colaboradores en Italia y en el extranjero, ha colaborado con éxito en muchos otros proyectos. Luca Peralta, el fundador y director, es ingeniero y arquitecto colegiado: miembro de la Asociación Italiana de Ingenieros de Construcción y Medio Ambiente y del Consejo de Registro de Arquitectos de Londres, Reino Unido.

KINDERGARDEN SCHOOL SANDRO PERTINI

LOCATION: **BISCEGLIE (BT), ITALY**
PHOTOS: © **ALESSANDRO PERALTA, LUCA PERALTA, LUIGI FILETICI**

The project includes the construction of a nursery and a public square in a new residential area. The floor plan of the building is structured in a succession of parallel walls that define an alternation between public and service areas. This rigid scheme is mixed with a more fluid element, materialized in an exterior central courtyard around which a glassed-in circulation corridor connects the building's functional programs. The project evokes a link with Mother Nature through the ethereal features of the central courtyard and through the orchard and fruit tree gardens that incorporate environmental education into the academic environment. The use of sustainable materials and passive energy-saving systems or the production and consumption of renewable energy are factors that reflect the project's sensitivity to the environment.

Das Projekt umfasst den Bau eines Kindergartens und eines öffentlichen Platzes in einem neuen Wohngebiet. Der Grundriss des Gebäudes ist in eine Abfolge von parallelen Wänden gegliedert, die einen Wechsel zwischen öffentlichen und Servicebereichen definieren. Dieses starre Schema wird mit einem flüssigeren Element gemischt, das sich in einem zentralen Außenhof materialisiert, um den herum ein verglaster Zirkulationskorridor die Funktionsprogramme des Gebäudes verbindet. Das Projekt evoziert eine Verbindung mit Mutter Natur durch die ätherischen Merkmale des zentralen Hofes und durch den Obst- und Obstbaumgarten, die die Umwelterziehung in das akademische Umfeld integrieren. Die Verwendung nachhaltiger Materialien und passiver Energiesparsysteme oder die Produktion und der Verbrauch erneuerbarer Energien sind Faktoren, die die Sensibilität des Projekts gegenüber der Umwelt widerspiegeln.

Le projet comprend la construction d'une crèche et d'une place publique dans un nouveau quartier résidentiel. Le plan du bâtiment est structuré en une succession de murs parallèles qui définissent une alternance entre les espaces publics et les espaces de service. Ce schéma rigide est mélangé à un élément plus fluide, matérialisé par une cour centrale extérieure autour de laquelle un couloir de circulation vitré relie les programmes fonctionnels du bâtiment. Le projet évoque un lien avec Mère Nature à travers les caractéristiques éthérées de la cour centrale et à travers le verger et les jardins d'arbres fruitiers qui intègrent l'éducation à l'environnement dans le milieu universitaire. L'utilisation de matériaux durables et de systèmes passifs d'économie d'énergie ou la production et la consommation d'énergie renouvelable sont des facteurs qui reflètent la sensibilité du projet à l'environnement.

El proyecto integra la construcción de una guardería y una plaza pública en una nueva zona residencial. La planta del edificio se estructura en una sucesión de muros paralelos que define una alternancia entre zonas públicas y de servicio. Este rígido esquema intersecciona con un elemento más fluido, materializado en un patio central exterior alrededor del cual un corredor de circulación acristalado conecta los programas funcionales del edificio. El proyecto evoca un vínculo con la Madre Naturaleza a través de las características etéreas del patio central y a través de los jardines de huertos y árboles frutales que incorporan la educación medioambiental al ámbito académico. El uso de materiales sostenibles y de sistemas pasivos de ahorro de energía o la producción y consumo de energías renovables son factores que reflejan la sensibilidad del proyecto hacia el medio ambiente.

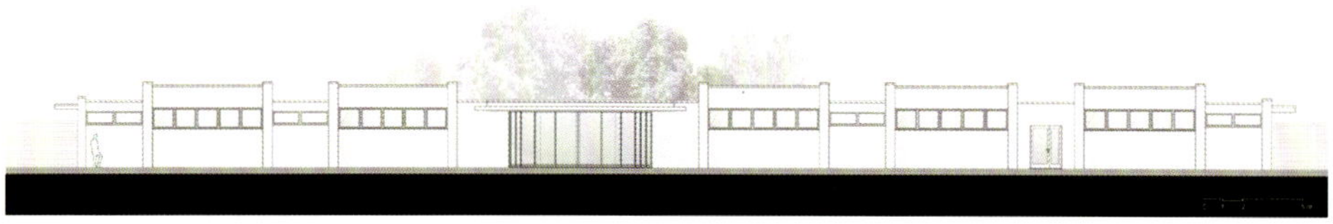

North elevation

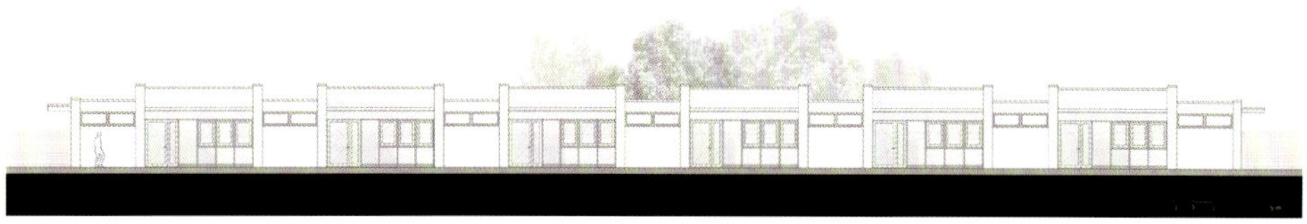

South elevation

Central courtyard section

Classrooms section

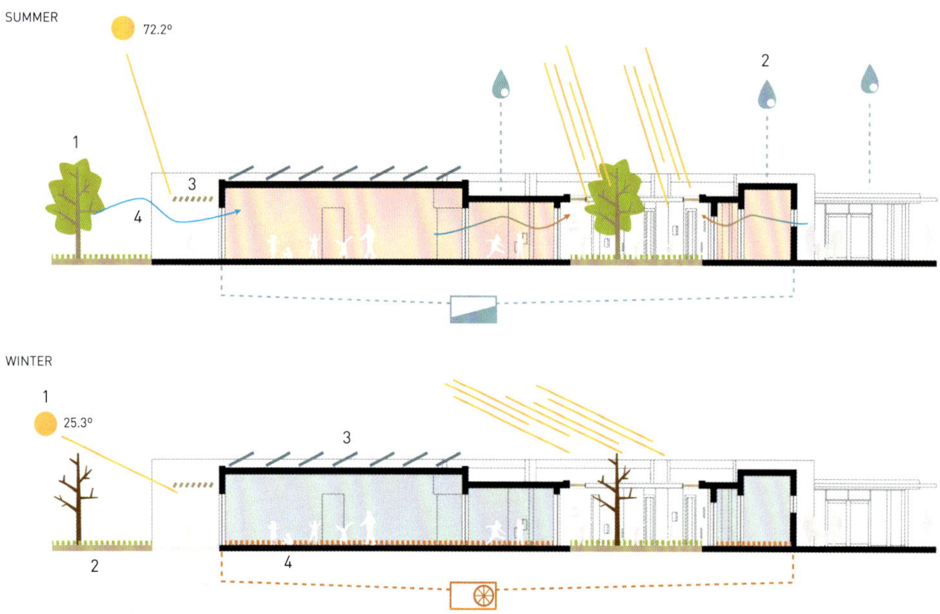

1. Trees of feeble leaves
2. Rainwater recovery
3. Sunscreen
4. Passive cooling

1. Free solar supplies
2. Draining surface
3. Photovoltaic panels
4. Radiant flooring

Bioclimatic sectional study

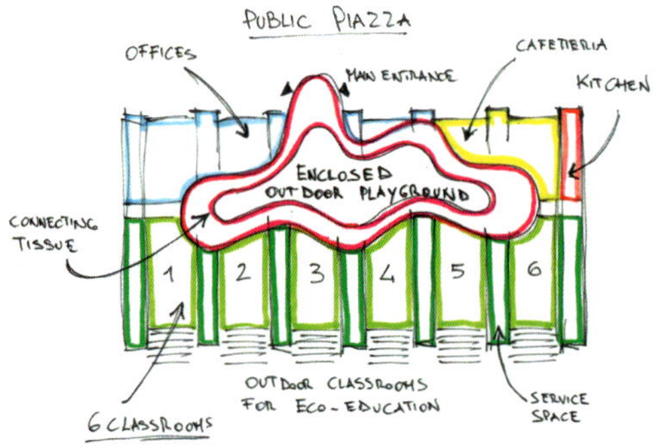

Initial concept sketch by Luca Peralta

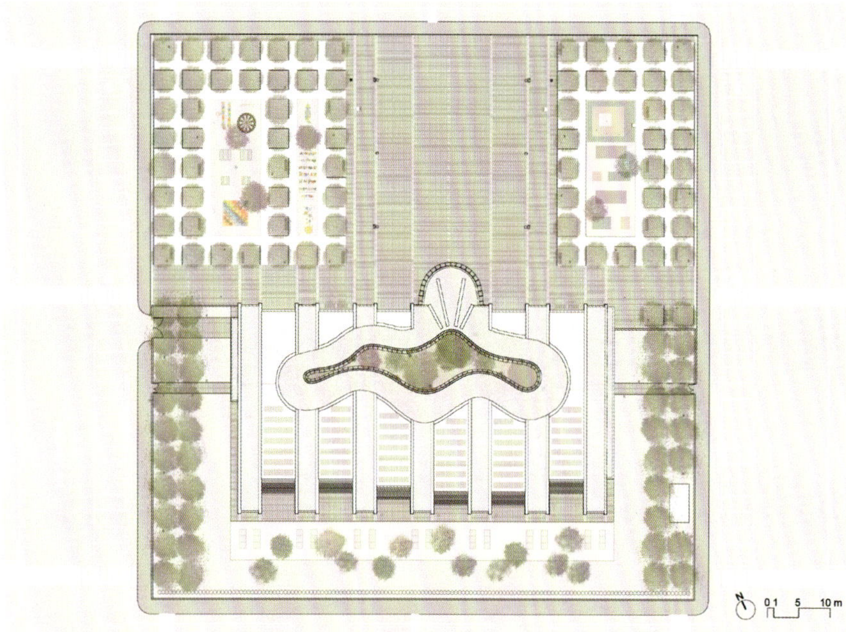

Plan of the kindergarten, of the school garden and of the public piazza

Interior design floor plan with furnitures layout

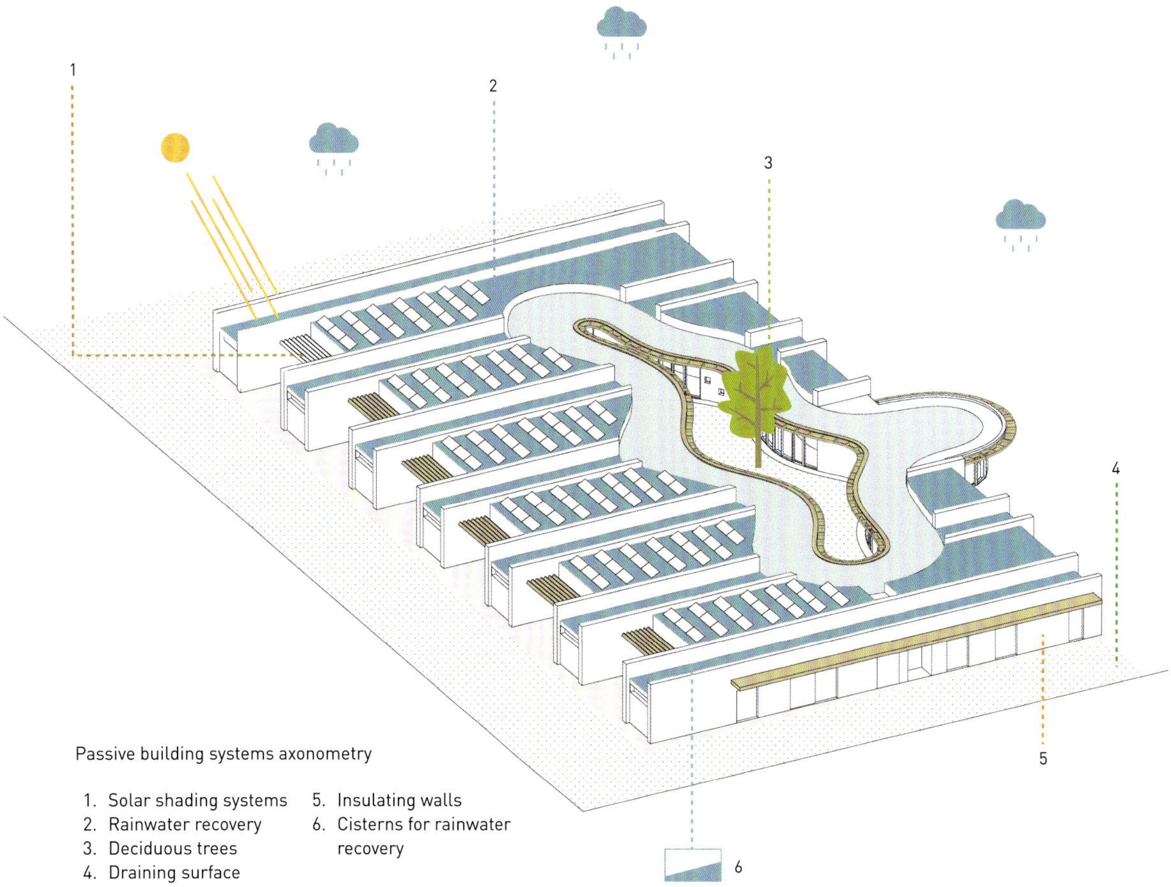

Passive building systems axonometry

1. Solar shading systems
2. Rainwater recovery
3. Deciduous trees
4. Draining surface
5. Insulating walls
6. Cisterns for rainwater recovery

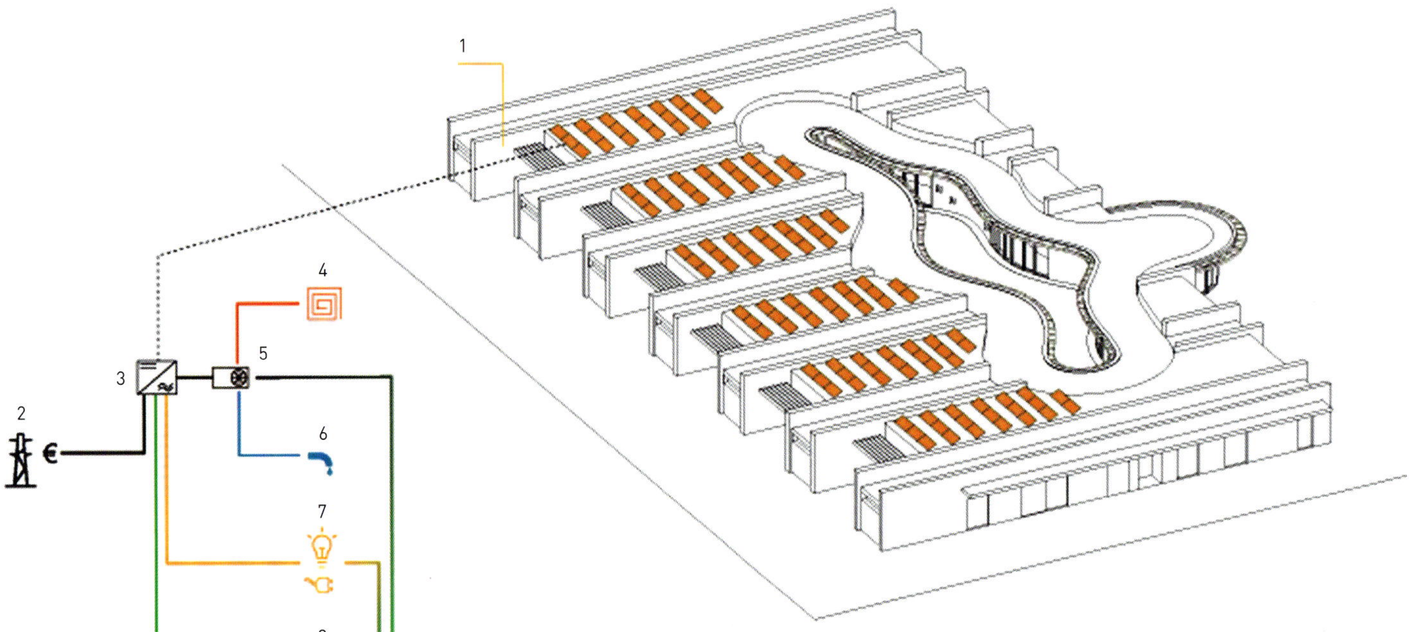

Active building systems axonometry

1. Photovoltaic panels 40 kWp
2. Red eléctrica
3. Inverter
4. Underfloor heating system
5. Heat pump
6. ACS
7. Electricity
8. Accumulator battery

Naf Architect & Design
Akio Nakasa

// PROJECTS //

1. SEIWA KINDERGARTEN
2. small pond

www.naf-aad.com

Naf Architect & Design
Akio Nakasa

1.

2.

naf architect & design was established in 2000 by Akio Nakasa and Tetsuya Nakazono, who both studied architecture at Hiroshima University. Prior to its establishment, Nakasa earned his master's degree at Waseda University in Tokyo and worked at Riken Yamamoto. Since 2001, Nakasa has been Tokyo Office representative mainly working with clients in eastern Japan, while Nakazono continued in Hiroshima to work on projects in western Japan.
They have designed a wide range of projects from private home, clinics, nursery schools and apartment buildings, all of which are concept oriented reflecting the philosophy of the clients. Their goal in design is how best architectural expression and solution are materialized in the project.
Among many awards received, "small village" nursery school received GOOD DESIGN, JIA award, Kids Design and exhibited during Milano triennale, and "A House Made of Two", private home, and "Machida Shizen Kindergarten" received JIA award.

naf architect & design wurde im Jahr 2000 von Akio Nakasa und Tetsuya Nakazono, der an der Universität Hiroshima Architektur studierte, gegründet. Vor seiner Gründung erwarb Nakasa seinen Master-Abschluss an der Waseda-Universität in Tokio und arbeitete bei Riken Yamamoto. Seit 2001 ist Nakasa ein Vertreter des Büros in Tokio und arbeitet vor allem mit Kunden im Osten Japans, während Nakazono in Hiroshima blieb und an Projekten im Westen Japans arbeitete.
Sie haben eine breite Palette von Projekten entworfen, von Privathäusern, Kliniken, Kindertagesstätten und Mehrfamilienhäusern, die alle auf Konzepte ausgerichtet sind, die die Philosophie der Auftraggeber widerspiegeln. Ihr Ziel beim Entwurf ist es, sicherzustellen, dass der beste architektonische Ausdruck und die beste Lösung im Projekt realisiert werden.
Unter den vielen erhaltenen Auszeichnungen erhielt die „Kleinstadtgärtnerei" die Auszeichnung „GOOD DESIGN" von JIA, die während der Triennale von Mailand ausgestellt wurde. Auch „Ein Haus aus zweien", ein Privathaus, und die „Machida Shizen Nursery" erhielten die JIA-Auszeichnung.

naf architect & design a été créé en 2000 par Akio Nakasa et Tetsuya Nakazono, qui ont tous deux étudié l'architecture à l'université d'Hiroshima. Avant sa création, Nakasa a obtenu sa maîtrise à l'université Waseda de Tokyo et a travaillé chez Riken Yamamoto. Depuis 2001, Nakasa est le représentant du bureau de Tokyo et travaille principalement avec des clients dans l'est du Japon, tandis que Nakazono a continué à Hiroshima pour travailler sur des projets dans l'ouest du Japon.
Ils ont conçu un large éventail de projets allant de la maison privée aux cliniques, en passant par les écoles maternelles et les immeubles d'habitation, tous orientés vers des concepts reflétant la philosophie des clients. Leur objectif en matière de conception est de trouver la meilleure expression et la meilleure solution architecturale pour le projet.
Parmi les nombreux prix reçus, l'école maternelle du « petit village » a reçu le prix GOOD DESIGN, le prix JIA, Kids Design et a été exposée pendant la triennale de Milan, et « A House Made of Two », maison privée, et « Machida Shizen Kindergarten » ont reçu le prix JIA.

naf architect & design fue establecido en 2000 por Akio Nakasa y Tetsuya Nakazono, quienes estudiaron arquitectura en la Universidad de Hiroshima. Antes de su establecimiento, Nakasa obtuvo su máster en la Universidad de Waseda en Tokio y trabajó en Riken Yamamoto. Desde 2001, Nakasa ha sido representante de la Oficina de Tokio, trabajando principalmente con clientes en el Japón oriental, mientras que Nakazono siguió en Hiroshima trabajando en proyectos en el Japón occidental.
Han diseñado una amplia gama de proyectos, desde casas particulares, clínicas, guarderías y edificios de apartamentos, todos ellos orientados a conceptos que reflejan la filosofía de los clientes. Su objetivo en el diseño es conseguir que la mejor expresión y solución arquitectónica se materializan en el proyecto.
Entre los muchos premios recibidos, la «Guardería de un Pequeño Pueblo» recibió el premio Good Design de JIA, siendo exhibida durante la trienal de Milán. «A House Made of Two», casa privada, y la «Guardería Machida Shizen» recibieron asimismo el premio JIA.

SEIWA KINDERGARTEN

LOCATION: **MACHIDA-CITY, TOKYO, JAPAN**
PHOTOS: **© TOSHIYUKI YANO**

This is a project to rebuild a day care center located at the end of a residential complex from the late 1960s, which seeks to extend its relationship to neighboring communities. The complex consists of two gently curved buildings between which is a terrace covered by a membrane roof, used as part of the cafeteria, transit area, classroom and entrance hall. Building A is the longest and contains the classrooms, all of which have direct access to the garden resulting from the demolition of the old building. Building B faces the main street and houses the multipurpose room and kitchen. The new garden was planned maintaining as much as possible the existing trees, planting 350 new ones and creating small hills and a well, and aims to achieve the complicity of the children in the care of the natural environment.

Il s'agit d'un projet de reconstruction d'une garderie située à l'extrémité d'un complexe résidentiel de la fin des années 1960, qui cherche à étendre ses relations avec les communautés voisines. Le complexe se compose de deux bâtiments légèrement courbés entre lesquels se trouve une terrasse couverte d'un toit en membrane, utilisée comme partie de la cafétéria, de la zone de transit, de la salle de classe et du hall d'entrée. Le bâtiment A est le plus long et contient les salles de classe, qui ont toutes un accès direct au jardin résultant de la démolition de l'ancien bâtiment. Le bâtiment B fait face à la rue principale et abrite la salle polyvalente et la cuisine. Le nouveau jardin a été planifié en maintenant autant que possible les arbres existants, en plantant 350 nouveaux arbres et en créant des petites collines et un puits, et vise à obtenir la complicité des enfants dans le soin de l'environnement naturel.

Dabei handelt es sich um ein Projekt zum Wiederaufbau einer Kindertagesstätte am Ende eines Wohnkomplexes aus den späten 1960er Jahren, das seine Beziehungen zu den Nachbargemeinden ausweiten will. Der Komplex besteht aus zwei sanft geschwungenen Gebäuden, zwischen denen sich eine mit einem Membrandach überdachte Terrasse befindet, die als Teil der Cafeteria, des Transitbereichs, des Klassenzimmers und der Eingangshalle genutzt wird. Gebäude A ist das längste und enthält die Klassenzimmer, die alle einen direkten Zugang zum Garten haben, der durch den Abriss des alten Gebäudes entstanden ist. Gebäude B liegt zur Hauptstraße und beherbergt den Mehrzweckraum und die Küche. Der neue Garten wurde so geplant, dass die vorhandenen Bäume so weit wie möglich erhalten bleiben, 350 neue Bäume gepflanzt und kleine Hügel und ein Brunnen angelegt werden.

Este es un proyecto de reconstrucción de una guardería ubicada en el extremo de un complejo residencial de finales de la década de 1960, que busca extender su relación hacia las comunidades vecinas. El conjunto se compone de dos edificios suavemente curvados entre los que se sitúa una terraza cubierta por un techo de tela de membrana, utilizada como parte de la cafetería, zona de paso, aula y hall de entrada. El edificio A es el más largo y contiene las aulas, todas ellas con acceso directo al jardín resultante de la demolición del antiguo edificio. El edificio B se orienta a la calle principal y alberga la sala de usos múltiples y la cocina. El nuevo jardín se planificó manteniendo en la medida de lo posible los árboles existentes, plantando 350 nuevos y creando pequeñas colinas y un pozo, y aspira a lograr la complicidad de los niños en el cuidado del entorno natural.

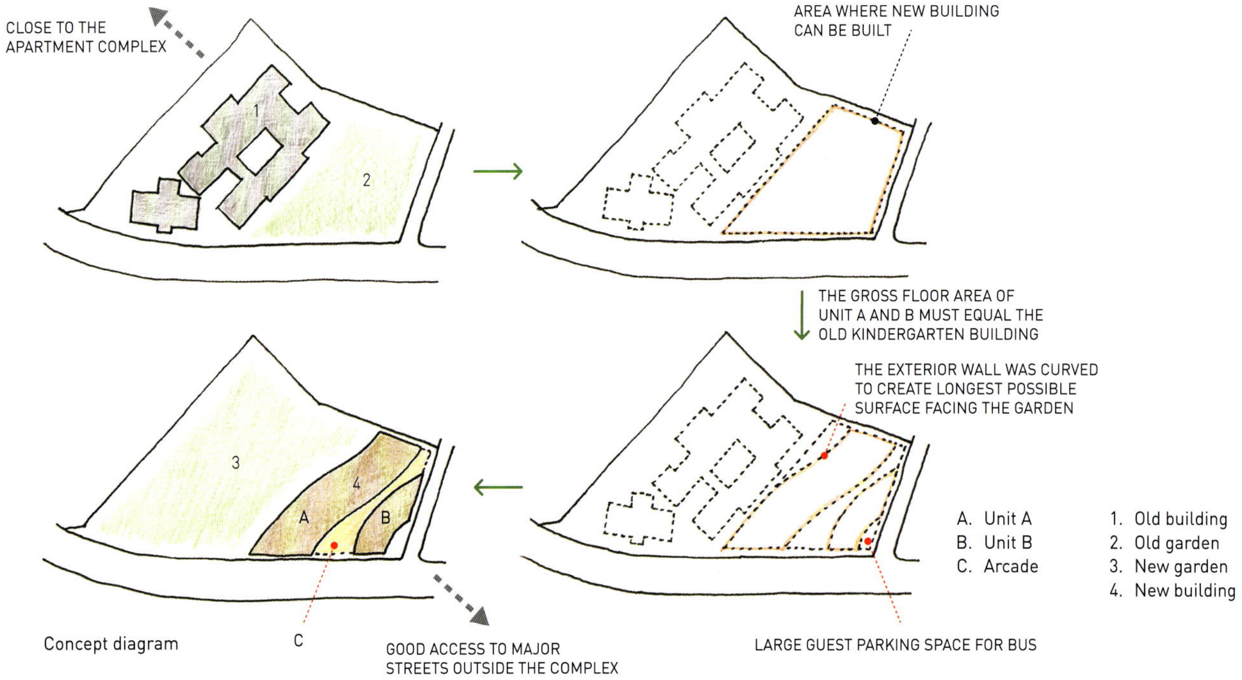

Concept diagram

せいわようちえん

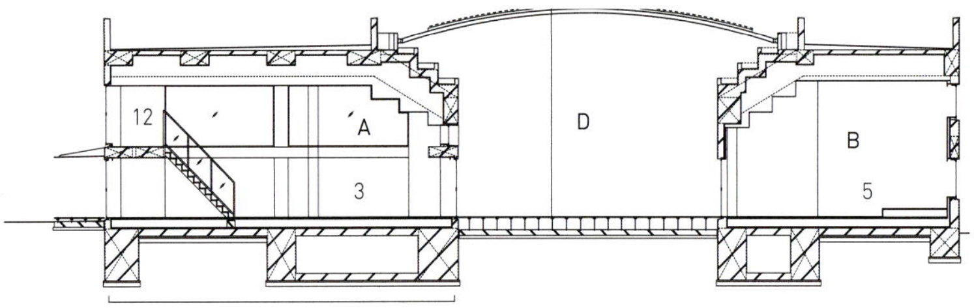

Section

Floor plan

A. Unit A
B. Unit B
C. Garden
D. Arcade
E. Parking lot for housing complex
F. Meeting place for housing complex

1. Main entrance
2. Entrance for parents
3. Nursery room 1
4. Nursery room 2-7
5. Playroom
6. Kitchen
7. Staff room
8. Parking
9. Demolished building location
10. Retaining wall
11. Large guest parking space for bus
12. Teaching material preparation room

small pond

LOCATION: **SETAGAYA WARD, TOKYO, JAPAN**
PHOTOS: © **TOSHIYUKI YANO**

Based on a methodology that defends the potential of children to learn by themselves, the project seeks to create a place where they can meet, within a safe environment and where they feel the nature. The name of the nursery (small pond) reflects the hope that the children will be as spontaneous as the water flowing from the pond. Its design is sensitive to the surrounding environment by arranging, as a buffer zone, buildings of different heights in the areas around the perimeter of the plot adjacent to the neighbouring buildings. This frees up a central space destined for a garden that preserves the contemplation of the sky. Inside, each classroom has a unique spatial composition that creates different entrances for wind and light. The flexible zoning of the floors allows for a total connection between the interior and exterior.

Basierend auf einer Methodik, die das Potenzial der Kinder, selbstständig zu lernen, verteidigt, versucht das Projekt, einen Ort zu schaffen, an dem sie sich in einer sicheren Umgebung treffen können und wo sie die Natur spüren. Der Name des Kindergartens (kleiner Teich) spiegelt die Hoffnung wider, dass die Kinder so spontan sind wie das Wasser, das aus dem Teich fließt. Seine Gestaltung reagiert sensibel auf die Umgebung, indem es als Pufferzone unterschiedlich hohe Gebäude in den Bereichen um den Grundstücksrand herum, die an die Nachbargebäude angrenzen, anordnet. Dadurch wird ein zentraler Raum frei, der für einen Garten bestimmt ist, der die Kontemplation des Himmels bewahrt. Im Inneren hat jedes Klassenzimmer eine einzigartige räumliche Komposition, die verschiedene Eingänge für Wind und Licht schafft. Die flexible Zonierung der Stockwerke ermöglicht eine totale Verbindung zwischen innen und außen.

Basé sur une méthodologie qui défend le potentiel des enfants à apprendre par eux-mêmes, le projet cherche à créer un lieu où ils peuvent se rencontrer, dans un environnement sûr et où ils ressentent la nature. Le nom de la crèche (petit étang) reflète l'espoir que les enfants seront aussi spontanés que l'eau qui coule de l'étang. Sa conception est sensible à l'environnement environnant en disposant, comme zone tampon, des bâtiments de différentes hauteurs dans les zones du périmètre de la parcelle adjacentes aux bâtiments voisins. Cela libère un espace central destiné à un jardin qui préserve la contemplation du ciel. À l'intérieur, chaque classe a une composition spatiale unique qui crée des entrées différentes pour le vent et la lumière. Le zonage flexible des étages permet une connexion totale entre l'intérieur et l'extérieur.

Basándose en una metodología que defiende el potencial de los niños para aprender por sí mismos, el proyecto busca crear un lugar donde éstos puedan reunirse, dentro de un ambiente seguro y en el que sientan la naturaleza. El nombre de la guardería (pequeño estanque) refleja la esperanza de que los niños sean espontáneos como el agua que brota del estanque. Su diseño es sensible al entorno que la rodea mediante la disposición, a modo de zona de amortiguación, de edificios de diferentes alturas en las zonas del perímetro de la parcela colindantes con las edificaciones vecinas. Este hecho libera un espacio central destinado a jardín que preserva la contemplación del cielo. En el interior, cada aula presenta una composición espacial única que crea diferentes entradas de viento y luz. La zonificación flexible de las plantas permite la total conexión entre interior y exterior.

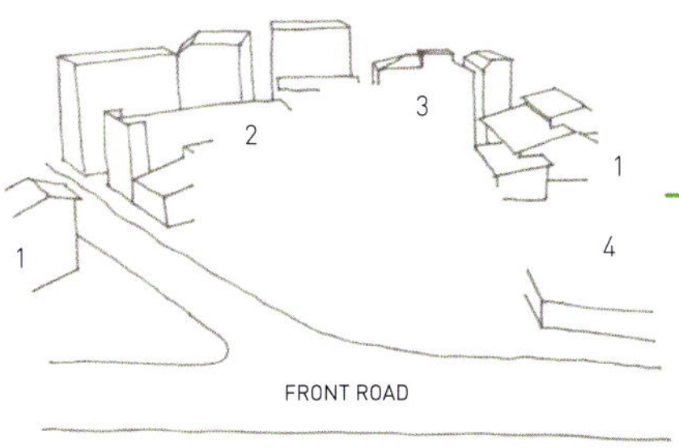

Surrounding environment

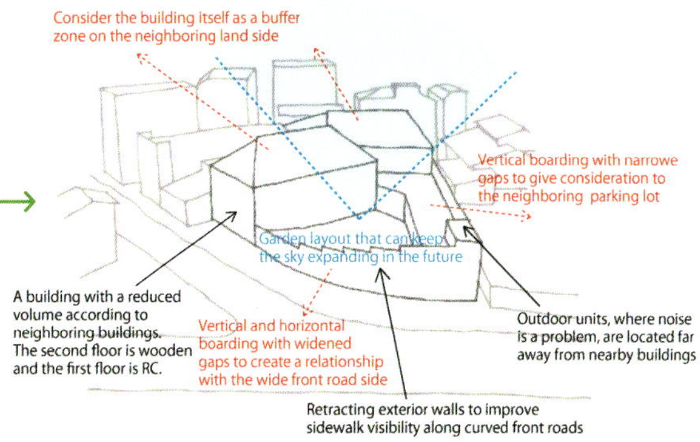

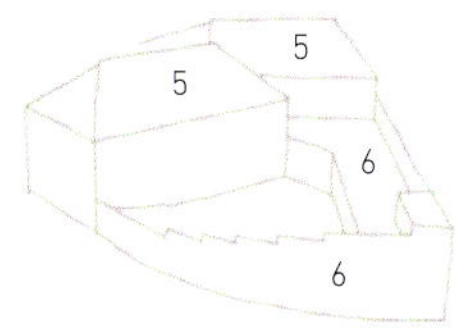

Building layout in consideration of surrounding environment

Concept diagram

1. Neighboring house
2. Neighboring store
3. Neighboring apartment
4. Neighboring parking
5. Colonial-style roof
6. Vertical board fence
7. Horizontal board fence

Elevations

Sections

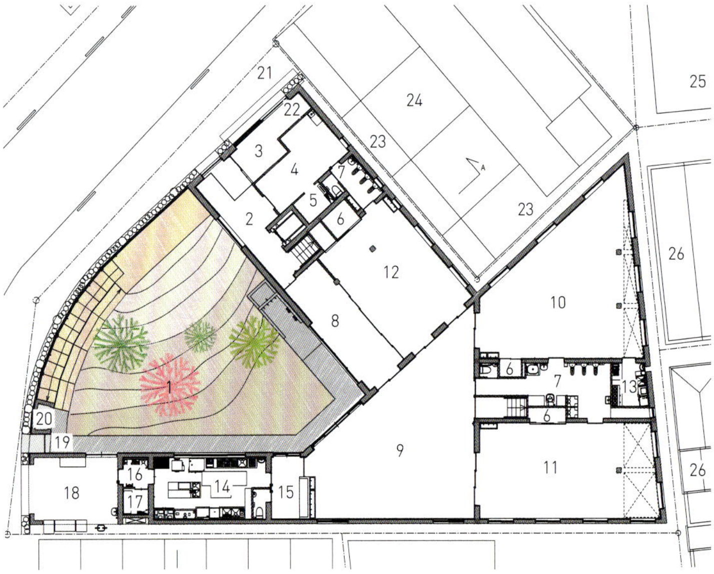

Ground floor plan

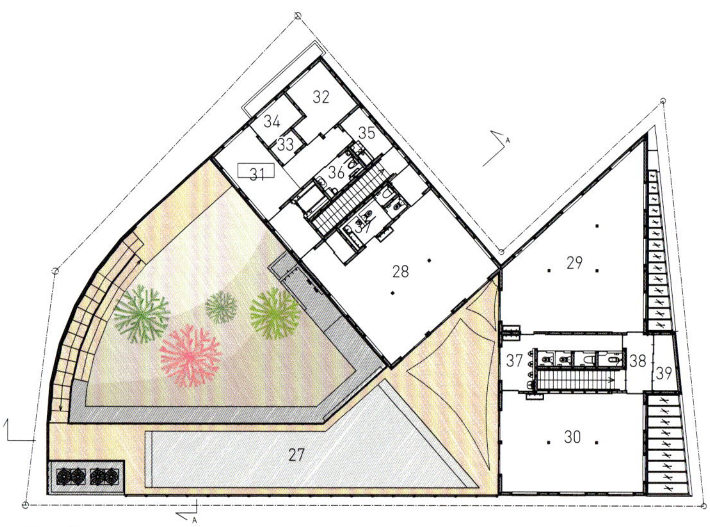

First floor plan

1. Courtyard
2. Entrance
3. Porch
4. Office
5. Medical office
6. Storage
7. Restroom
8. Corridor
9. Hall
10. Nursery room A
11. Nursery room B
12. Nursery room C
13. Milk preparation room
14. Kitchen room
15. Serving corner
16. Inspection room
17. Food storage
18. Parking
19. Sub entrance
20. Buggy storage
21. Stroller storage area
22. Bicycle parking
23. Neighborhood border
24. Neighborhood store (Motorcycle shop)
25. Neighborhood apartment
26. Neighboring house
27. Roof balcony
28. Nursery room D
29. Nursery room E
30. Nursery room F
31. Staff room
32. Changing room (women)
33. Changing room (men)
34. Wardhouse
35. Utility room
36. Accessible restroom
37. Restroom
38. Corridor
39. Storage

NAYA ARCHITECTS
Manabu Naya, Arata Naya

// PROJECTS //

1. SHOWA EARLY CHILDHOOD EDUCATION AND CARE CENTER, SHOWA WOMAN'S UNIVERSITY

www.naya1993.com

NAYA ARCHITECTS
Manabu Naya, Arata Naya

1.

NAYA architects is the award winning architecture and design firm of two brothers, Arata and Manabu Naya, based in Kanagawa Japan. They approach architecture through a simple and modern lens, focusing on existing site conditions and human centered design. Since forming in 1993, NAYA architects has designed on many scales from residential housing to interstate rest areas while also being exhibited, reviewed and published widely.
Recently, Naya architects engaged in a large scale exhibition highlighting their work from the past 26 years, playfully titled "We Know it's Sudden! But We Will be Moving to Tokyo for Two Weeks" which gained large critical acclaim as a living exhibition in which the process of creating architecture was exhibited alongside the work.

NAYA architects est le cabinet d'architecture et de design primé de deux frères, Arata et Manabu Naya, basé à Kanagawa au Japon. Ils abordent l'architecture à travers une lentille simple et moderne, en se concentrant sur les conditions existantes du site et sur un design centré sur l'homme. Depuis sa création en 1993, NAYA architects a conçu des projets à de nombreuses échelles, allant des logements résidentiels aux aires de repos interétatiques, tout en étant largement exposés, examinés et publiés.
Récemment, les architectes de Naya ont participé à une exposition à grande échelle mettant en valeur leurs travaux des 26 dernières années, intitulée de manière ludique « We Know it's Sudden ! Mais nous allons déménager à Tokyo pendant deux semaines », qui a été largement saluée par la critique en tant qu'exposition vivante dans laquelle le processus de création de l'architecture était exposé en même temps que l'œuvre.

NAYA Architects ist das preisgekrönte Architektur- und Designbüro zweier Brüder, Arata und Manabu Naya, mit Sitz in Kanagawa Japan. Sie nähern sich der Architektur durch eine einfache, moderne Linse und konzentrieren sich dabei auf die vorhandenen Bodenverhältnisse und eine auf den Menschen ausgerichtete Gestaltung. Seit ihrer Gründung im Jahr 1993 haben NAYA-Architekten in vielen Maßstäben entworfen, von Wohnhäusern bis hin zu zwischenstaatlichen Ruhezonen, und wurden vielfach veröffentlicht.
Kürzlich nahmen die Architekten von Naya an einer großen Ausstellung teil, die ihre Arbeit der letzten 26 Jahre unter dem spielerischen Titel „We Know It's Sudden! Aber wir ziehen für zwei Wochen nach Tokio", die von der Kritik als eine lebende Ausstellung gefeiert wurde, in der der Entstehungsprozess von Architektur neben ihrem Werk gezeigt wurde.

NAYA Architects es la galardonada firma de arquitectura y diseño de dos hermanos, Arata y Manabu Naya, con sede en Kanagawa Japón. Se acercan a la arquitectura a través de una lente simple y moderna, centrándose en las condiciones del terreno existente y el diseño centrado en el ser humano. Desde su formación en 1993, los arquitectos de NAYA han diseñado a muchas escalas, desde viviendas residenciales hasta áreas de descanso interestatales, siendo ampliamente publicados.
Recientemente, los arquitectos de Naya participaron en una exposición a gran escala que destacaba su trabajo de los últimos veintiséis años, titulada de forma divertida «¡Sabemos que es repentino! Pero nos mudaremos a Tokio durante dos semanas», que obtuvo una gran aclamación de la crítica como una exposición viva en la que el proceso de creación de la arquitectura se exhibió junto con su obra.

SHOWA EARLY CHILDHOOD EDUCATION AND CARE CENTER

LOCATION: **SETAGAYA-KU, TOKYO, JAPAN**
PHOTOS: © **SHINICHI OSAWA**

This early childhood education facility is located on the campus of Showa Women's University. It accommodates 12 classes, 223 children, ranging in age from 0 to 5 years old. The plans include raising the school yard to the 2nd floor level to capture more light and create a sense of openness and not to give a strong impact on the surroundings and the townscape as well. The gently sloping yard on the west by the road is great for running around. There is a bright enclosed courtyard, rooms arranged for a smooth flow between activities, and a large staircase which has become a landmark within the campus. We hope this facility will tie cherished memories of the previous building to a new, beloved representative of the campus and the community.

Dieses Kinderbildungszentrum befindet sich auf dem Campus der Showa Women's University. Es bietet Platz für 12 Klassen mit 223 Kindern im Alter von 0-5 Jahren. Es ist geplant, den Schulhof auf das Niveau des zweiten Stocks anzuheben, um mehr Licht einzufangen und ein Gefühl der Offenheit zu schaffen und nicht auch die dörfliche Umgebung und Landschaft stark zu beeinträchtigen. Der sanft abfallende Spielplatz im Westen, neben der Straße, ist ideal zum Laufen. Es gibt einen hellen, geschlossenen Innenhof, Räume, die für einen reibungslosen Ablauf zwischen den Aktivitäten angeordnet sind, und eine große Treppe, die zu einem Wahrzeichen des Campus geworden ist. Wir hoffen, dass diese Einrichtungen geschätzte Erinnerungen an das alte Gebäude mit einem neuen und geliebten Vertreter des Campus und der Gemeinschaft zusammenbringen werden.

Ce centre d'éducation de la petite enfance est situé sur le campus de l'université féminine de Showa. Il accueille 12 classes, 223 enfants, dont l'âge varie de 0 à 5 ans. Il est prévu de surélever la cour de l'école au niveau du deuxième étage afin de capter plus de lumière et de créer un sentiment d'ouverture et de ne pas avoir un impact trop fort sur l'environnement et le paysage urbain. La cour en pente douce à l'ouest, près de la route, est idéale pour courir. On y trouve une cour fermée et lumineuse, des pièces disposées de manière à faciliter la circulation entre les activités, et un grand escalier qui est devenu un point de repère au sein du campus. Nous espérons que cette installation permettra de lier les souvenirs chers du bâtiment précédent à un nouveau représentant bien-aimé du campus et de la communauté.

Este centro de educación infantil está situado en el campus de la Universidad de Mujeres Showa. Tiene capacidad para doce clases, 223 niños, de edades comprendidas entre 0 y 5 años. Los planes incluyen elevar el patio de la escuela al nivel del segundo piso para captar más luz y crear una sensación de apertura y no dar un fuerte impacto en el entorno y el paisaje del pueblo también. El patio con una suave pendiente al oeste, junto a la carretera, es ideal para correr. Hay un luminoso patio cerrado, habitaciones dispuestas para un flujo suave entre las actividades y una gran escalera que se ha convertido en un punto de referencia dentro del campus. Esperamos que estas instalaciones unan los recuerdos queridos del edificio anterior con un nuevo y querido representante del campus y de la comunidad.

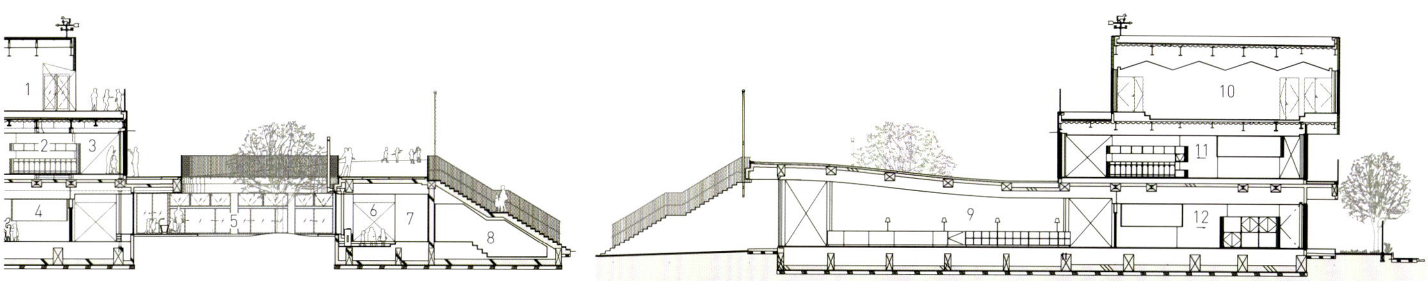

Cross sections

1. Terrace
2. 4 year old nursery room
3. Open space
4. 3 year old nursery room
5. Inner court
6. Stove corner
7. Picture book corner
8. Storage
9. Teachers' room
10. Playroom
11. 5 year old nursery room
12. 0 year old nursery room

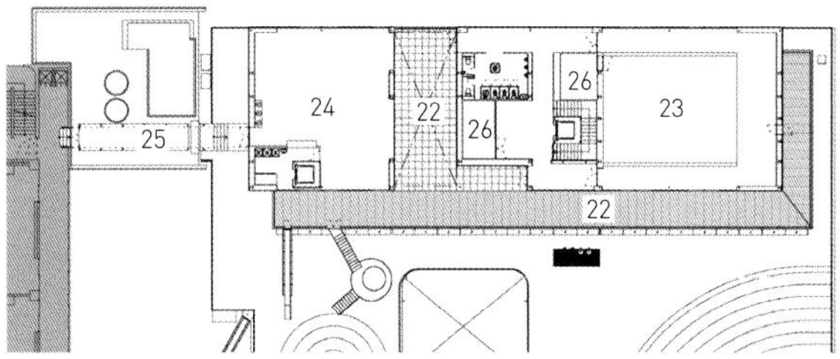

Third floor plan

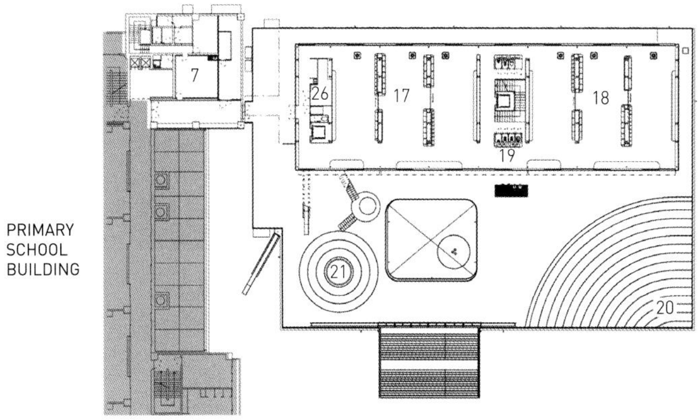

Second floor plan

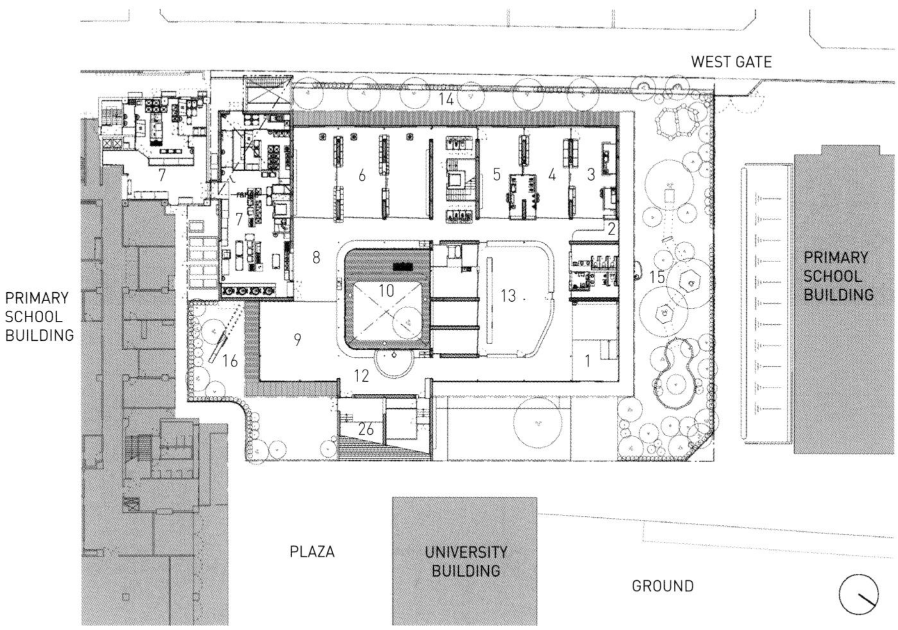

First floor plan

1. Entrance
2. Sub entrance
3. 0 year old nursery room
4. 1 year old nursery room
5. 2 year old nursery room
6. 3 year old nursery room
7. Kitchen
8. Dining room
9. Play room
10. Inner court
11. Stove corner
12. Picture book corner
13. Teachers' room
14. Garden+Farm
15. Forest garden
16. Edible garden
17. 4 year old nursery room
18. 5 year old nursery room
19. Open space
20. Hill
21. Mountain
22. Terrace
23. Play room
24. Primary school dining room
25. Passage
26. Storage

opus Architekten BDA / Prof. Anke Mensing, Andreas Sedler

// PROJECTS //

1. NEW BUILDING +E KITA (PLUS-ENERGY- /SOLAR-BUILDING) MARBURG

www.opus-architekten.de

opus Architekten BDA /
Prof. Anke Mensing, Andreas Sedler

1.

The office opus Architekten BDA was founded in 1989 by Prof. Anke Mensing and Dipl.-Ing. Andreas Sedler. City, architecture, design, art —meaning designed environment is everywhere. You cannot avoid it. It is largely responsible for the function and quality of our society and for our well-being. The designed environment is our field of activity. We are aware of our responsibility and consider it a challenge. Opus works on urban planning, architectural and interior design projects. Our main focus thereby is on educational facilities for children. From time to time, the artistic engagement with the environment sharpens our view of things. The assignment structure is accordingly diverse. It ranges from development planning to buildings for industry, administration, culture and housing to refurbishments and conversions. Opus works closely with various other disciplines and engineers to achieve optimal results for our clients and to give independent, sometimes unexpected solutions a chance.

Le bureau Opus Architekten BDA a été fondé en 1989 par le professeur Anke Mensing et l'ingénieur diplômé Andreas Sedler. La ville, l'architecture, le design, l'art - c'est-à-dire que l'environnement conçu est partout. Vous ne pouvez pas l'éviter. Il est largement responsable de la fonction et de la qualité de notre société et de notre bien-être. L'environnement conçu est notre domaine d'activité. Nous sommes conscients de notre responsabilité et considérons qu'il s'agit d'un défi. Opus travaille sur des projets d'urbanisme, d'architecture et de design d'intérieur. Nous nous concentrons donc principalement sur les installations éducatives pour les enfants. De temps en temps, l'engagement artistique avec l'environnement aiguise notre vision des choses. La structure des missions est donc diversifiée. Elle va de la planification du développement à la construction de bâtiments pour l'industrie, l'administration, la culture et le logement, en passant par les rénovations et les transformations. Opus travaille en etroite collaboration avec diverses autres disciplines et ingenieurs afin d'obtenir des résultats optimaux pour nos clients et de donner une chance à des solutions indépendantes, parfois inattendues.

Das büro Opus Architekten BDA wurde 1989 von Prof. Anke Mensing und Dipl.-Ing. Andreas Sedler gegründet. Stadt, Architektur, Design, Kunst - das heißt gestaltete Umwelt ist überall. Man kann sich ihr nicht entziehen. Sie ist weitgehend verantwortlich für die Funktion und Qualität unserer Gesellschaft und für unser Wohlergehen. Die gestaltete Umwelt ist unser Betätigungsfeld. Wir sind uns unserer Verantwortung bewusst und sehen sie als Herausforderung. Opus arbeitet an städtebaulichen, architektonischen und innenarchitektonischen Projekten. Unser Hauptaugenmerk liegt dabei auf Bildungseinrichtungen für Kinder. Die künstlerische Auseinandersetzung mit der Umwelt schärft von Zeit zu Zeit unseren Blick für die Dinge. Entsprechend vielfältig ist die Auftragsstruktur. Sie reicht von der Bebauungsplanung über Bauten für Industrie, Verwaltung, Kultur und Wohnen bis hin zu Sanierungen und Umbauten. Opus arbeitet eng mit verschiedenen anderen Disziplinen und Ingenieuren zusammen, um optimale Ergebnisse für unsere Kunden zu erzielen und unabhängigen, manchmal unerwarteten Lösungen eine Chance zu geben.

La oficina Opus Architekten BDA fue fundada en 1989 por el Prof. Anke Mensing y el Dipl.-Ing. Andreas Sedler. En la ciudad, en la arquitectura, en el diseño, en el arte... el diseño está en todas partes, no se puede evitar. Es en gran parte responsable de la función y la calidad de nuestra sociedad y de nuestro bienestar. El entorno diseñado es nuestro campo de actividad. Somos conscientes de nuestra responsabilidad y lo consideramos un desafío. Opus trabaja en proyectos de urbanismo, arquitectura y diseño interior, centrándonos principalmente en instalaciones educativas para niños. De vez en cuando, el compromiso artístico con el medio ambiente agudiza nuestra visión de las cosas. La estructura de la asignación es, por consiguiente, diversa. Va desde la planificación del desarrollo a edificios para la industria, la administración, la cultura y la vivienda hasta las reformas y rehabilitaciones. Opus trabaja estrechamente con otras disciplinas e ingenieros para lograr resultados óptimos para nuestros clientes y para dar una oportunidad a soluciones independientes, a veces inesperadas.

NEW BUILDING +E KITA (PLUS-ENERGY- /SOLAR-BUILDING) MARBURG

LOCATION: **MARBURG, GERMANY**
PHOTOS: **© EIBE SÖNNECKEN**

The kindergarten is located within the former premises of the Vitos Klinik, a 19th century psychiatric institution structured in several pavilions distributed within a garden. Its position, in a sloping meadow, generates a semi-buried and compact two-storey building that stands out for its striking folded glass façade that reflects the green of the park and for a roof that is also folded and favours the installation of photovoltaic panels. The school's programme includes five classrooms, a multifunctional room and auxiliary spaces located at the back of the ground floor. The adjacent historical chapel is used as a multifunctional room. The careful design of the different interior spaces makes the children feel good about identifying with their respective environments and, at the same time, develops their interest in architecture.

Der Kindergarten befindet sich auf dem ehemaligen Gelände der Vitos-Klinik, einer psychiatrischen Einrichtung aus dem 19. Jahrhundert, die in mehrere, in einem Garten verteilte Pavillons gegliedert ist. Durch seine Lage in einer geneigten Wiese entsteht ein halbverdecktes und kompaktes zweigeschossiges Gebäude, das sich durch seine markante gefaltete Glasfassade, die das Grün des Parks widerspiegelt, und durch ein ebenfalls gefaltetes Dach, das die Installation von Photovoltaikmodulen begünstigt, auszeichnet. Das Programm der Schule umfasst fünf Klassenzimmer, einen Multifunktionsraum und Nebenräume, die sich im hinteren Teil des Erdgeschosses befinden, und nutzt auch die angrenzende historische Kapelle als Multifunktionsraum. Die sorgfältige Gestaltung der verschiedenen Innenräume gibt den Kindern ein gutes Gefühl der Identifikation mit ihrer jeweiligen Umgebung und fördert gleichzeitig ihr Interesse an der Architektur.

Le jardin d'enfants est situé dans les anciens locaux de la Vitos Klinik, une institution psychiatrique du XIXe siècle structurée en plusieurs pavillons répartis dans un jardin. Sa position, dans une prairie en pente, génère un bâtiment de deux étages semi enterré et compact qui se distingue par sa façade en verre plié frappante qui reflète le vert du parc et par un toit également plié qui favorise l'installation de panneaux photovoltaïques. Le programme de l'école comprend cinq salles de classe, une salle multifonctionnelle et des espaces auxiliaires situés à l'arrière du rez-de-chaussée, et utilise également la chapelle historique adjacente comme salle multifonctionnelle. La conception soignée des différents espaces intérieurs permet aux enfants de s'identifier à leur environnement respectif et, en même temps, de développer leur intérêt pour l'architecture.

El jardín de infancia se ubica dentro del antiguo recinto de la Vitos Klinik, una institución psiquiátrica del siglo XIX estructurada en varios pabellones distribuidos dentro de un jardín. Su posición, en un prado inclinado, genera un edificio semienterrado y compacto de dos plantas, que destaca por una llamativa fachada plegada de vidrio que refleja el verde del parque y por una cubierta también plegada que favorece la implantación de paneles fotovoltaicos. El programa de la escuela incluye cinco aulas, una sala multifuncional y espacios auxiliares situados en la parte posterior de la planta baja, y utiliza también la capilla histórica contigua como sala multifuncional. El cuidado diseño de los diferentes espacios interiores hace que los niños se sientan bien al identificarse con sus ámbitos respectivos y, al mismo tiempo, desarrolla su interés por la arquitectura.

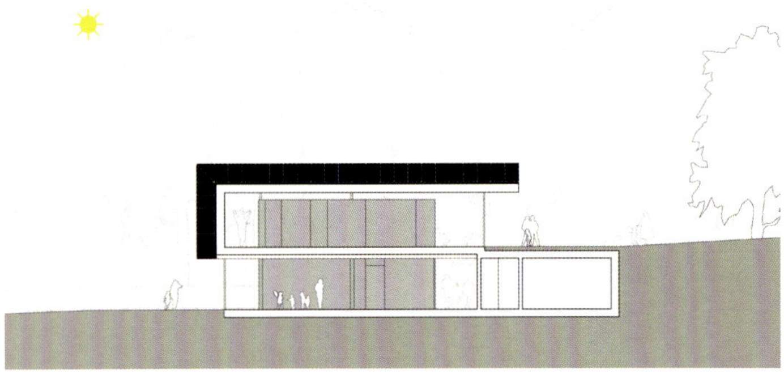

Cross section

Longitudinal section

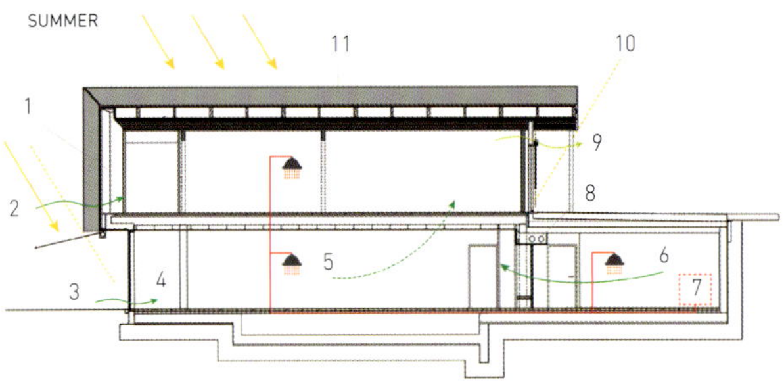

Schematic section with energetic effects in summer

1. Reinforced north orientation of the west facade to protect against overheating
2. Natural shading by cantilever
3. Sun protection
4. Facade ventilation
5. Airflow over the stairwell
6. Air supply through the courtyard
7. Water heater
8. Regulated kitchen exhaust air
9. Exhaust flap
10. Natural shading by cantilever
11. PV area

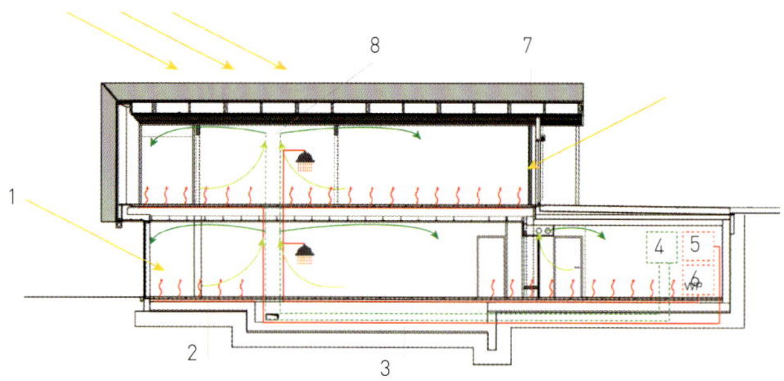

Schematic section with energetic effects in winter

1. Solar use for passive heat
2. Radiant heating system
3. Central distribution shaft
4. Heat recovery ventilation
5. Heating WP
6. Water heater
7. PV area
8. Central ventilation with heat recovery
9. Exhaust flap
10. Natural shading by cantilever
11. PV area

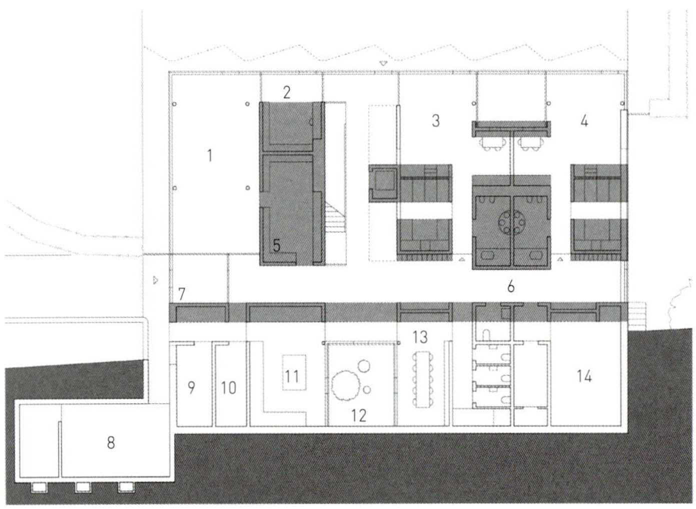

Ground floor plan

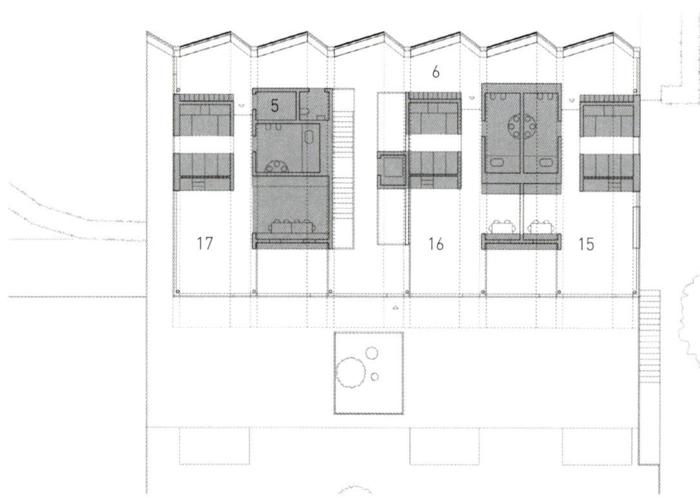

First floor plan

1. Multipurpose room
2. Office
3. Group 1
4. Group 2
5. Storage
6. Play hall
7. Entrance
8. Baby carts
9. Utility room
10. Pantry
11. Kitchen
12. Courtyard
13. Staff room
14. Technical room
15. Group 3
16. Group 4
17. Group 5

Pierre-Alain Dupraz Architecte ETS FAS

// PROJECTS //

1. ÉCOLE ENFANTINE ET UAPE
2. CRÈCHE DE SAINT-JEAN

www.padupraz.ch

Pierre-Alain Dupraz Architecte
ETS FAS

1.

2.

Pierre-Alain Dupraz is an architect, member of the Federation of Swiss Architects (FAS). He has won numerous competitions for architecture, urban planning and engineering structures, including four major competitions in Geneva: the pedestrian and bicycle crossing of the harbour, the masterplan for the PAV Etoile, the development of the harbour, and the Cité de la Musique. He is regularly invited as a competition jury and expert at the universities of architecture and has taught at the HEIA in Fribourg. He has also been awarded several nominations and distinctions for the Prangins School (Die Besten 2015, Arc Award 2016 and Best architects 17), as well as the SIA Geneva 2016 distinction for the Peace Bridge.
His projects, of different sizes, have several aspects in common. Their design is as much a result of the context as of the construction methods. The topography in which they are built is inseparable from the project and often becomes its central theme.

Pierre-Alain Dupraz est un architecte, membre de la Fédération des Architectes Suisses (FAS). Il remporte de nombreux concours d'architecture, d'urbanisme, et d'ouvrages d'art et notamment quatre concours d'importance à Genève : la traversée piétonne et cycliste de la rade, le masterplan du PAV Etoile, l'aménagement de la rade, et la Cité de la Musique. Il est régulièrement invité en tant que jury de concours et expert dans les hautes écoles d'architecture et a enseigné à la HEIA de Fribourg. Il a également été récompensé par plusieurs nominations et distinctions pour l'école de Prangins (Die Besten 2015, Arc Award 2016 et Best architects 17), ainsi que la distinction SIA Genève 2016 pour la passerelle de la Paix.
Ses projets, de tailles différentes ont plusieurs aspects en commun. Leur conception est aussi bien issue du contexte que des méthodes de construction. La topographie dans laquelle s'inscrivent ses réalisations est indissociable du projet et en devient souvent le thème central.

Pierre-Alain Dupraz ist Architekt und Mitglied des Schweizerischen Architektenverbandes (FAS). Er hat zahlreiche Wettbewerbe in den Bereichen Architektur, Stadtplanung und Ingenieurbauwerke gewonnen, darunter vier große Wettbewerbe in Genf: den Fußgänger- und Fahrradübergang des Hafens, den Masterplan PAV Etoile, die Hafenentwicklung und die Cité de la Musique. Er wird regelmässig als Wettbewerbsrichter und Experte an Architekturhochschulen eingeladen und hat am HEIA in Fribourg gelehrt. Er hat auch mehrere Nominierungen und Auszeichnungen für die Prangins-Schule erhalten (Die Besten 2015, Arc Award 2016 und Beste Architekten 17) sowie die Auszeichnung des SIA Genf 2016 für die Friedensbrücke.
Ihre Projekte, die unterschiedlich groß sind, haben mehrere Aspekte gemeinsam. Ihre Gestaltung ergibt sich ebenso aus dem Kontext wie aus den Baumethoden. Die Topographie, in der sie gebaut werden, ist untrennbar mit dem Projekt verbunden und wird oft zu seinem zentralen Thema.

Pierre-Alain Dupraz es un arquitecto miembro de la Federación de Arquitectos Suizos (FAS). Ha ganado numerosos concursos de arquitectura, urbanismo y estructuras de ingeniería, incluidos cuatro importantes concursos en Ginebra: el cruce peatonal y de bicicletas del puerto, el plan maestro del PAV Etoile, el desarrollo del puerto y la Cité de la Musique. Es invitado regularmente como jurado de concursos y experto en las universidades de arquitectura y ha enseñado en la HEIA de Friburgo. También ha sido galardonado con varias nominaciones y distinciones para la Escuela Prangins (Die Besten 2015, Arc Award 2016 y Best architects 17), así como con la distinción SIA Ginebra 2016 por el Puente de la Paz.
Sus proyectos, de diferentes tamaños, tienen varios aspectos en común. Su diseño es tanto resultado del contexto como de los métodos de construcción. La topografía en la que se construyen es inseparable del proyecto y a menudo se convierte en su tema central.

ÉCOLE ENFANTINE ET UAPE

LOCATION: **PRANGINS, SWITZERLAND**
PHOTOS: © **THOMAS JANTSCHER, FERNANDO GUERRA**

Prangins' new nursery school has been designed to look like a large house perched on a sloping plot of land. The building's shape asserts its independence from the surrounding built environment.
It's a design that creates rooms with differing aspects, which are emphasised by generously sized windows. The four wings of the building, each offset by a third of a storey and interlocking with one another, reduce perceptions of the building's size. The central staircase, which features ramps, is a playful element and a key piece in the interior space. A separate entrance at the top of the plot helps ensure unfettered access to the childcare centre, while exposed concrete inside and out enables the building to blend into the topography.

Der neue Kindergarten von Prangins ist als großes Haus an einem Hanggrundstück konzipiert. Die Form des Gebäudes bekräftigt eine Unabhängigkeit vom gebauten Kontext.
Die Volumetrie begünstigt eine abwechslungsreiche Ausrichtung der Räume, die durch die großzügigen Fenster noch verstärkt wird. Die vier um ein Drittel einer Ebene versetzten und ineinander verschachtelten Volumen reduzieren die Wahrnehmung und den Maßstab des Gebäudes. Die zentrale Treppe, die mit den Handläufen verbunden ist, ist ein spielerisches und grundlegendes Element des Innenraumes. Ein unabhängiger Zugang von der Oberseite des Geländes gewährleistet den reibungslosen Ablauf der UAPE. Das Sichtbetonmaterial, das sowohl innen als auch außen zum Ausdruck kommt, verankert das Gebäude in seiner Topographie.

La nouvelle école enfantine de Prangins est conçue comme une grande maison posée sur un terrain en pente. La forme du bâtiment affirme une indépendance par rapport au contexte bâti.
La volumétrie favorise une orientation diversifiée des salles, mise en valeur par les généreuses baies vitrées. Les 4 volumes décalés d'un tiers de niveau et emboités les uns aux autres, diminuent la perception et l'échelle du bâtiment. L'escalier central, connecté aux rampes, est un élément ludique et fondamental de la spatialité intérieure. Un accès indépendant depuis le haut de la parcelle, assure le bon fonctionnement de l'UAPE. La matérialité en béton apparent, exprimé à l'intérieur et à l'extérieur, ancre le bâtiment dans sa topographie.

La nueva escuela infantil de Prangins está diseñada como una gran casa en un terreno inclinado. La forma del edificio afirma una independencia del contexto construido.
La volumetría favorece una orientación diversificada de las habitaciones, realzada por los generosos ventanales. Los cuatro volúmenes, compensados por un tercio de nivel y anidados entre sí, reducen la percepción y la escala del edificio. La escalera central, conectada a las barandillas, es un elemento lúdico y fundamental de la espacialidad interior. Un acceso independiente desde la parte superior del terreno asegura el buen funcionamiento de la UAPE. La materialidad de hormigón visto, expresada en el interior y en el exterior, ancla el edificio en su topografía.

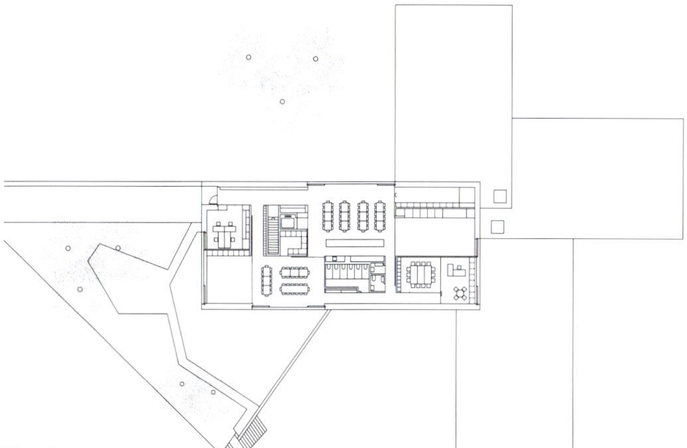

First floor plan

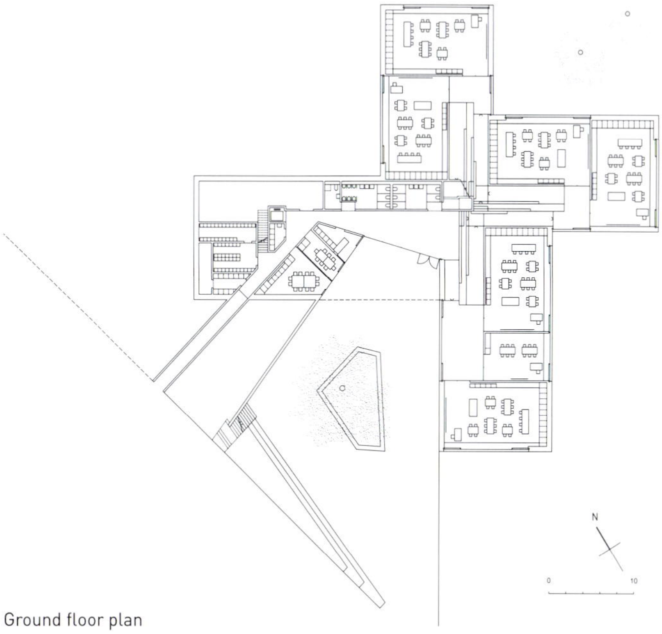

Ground floor plan

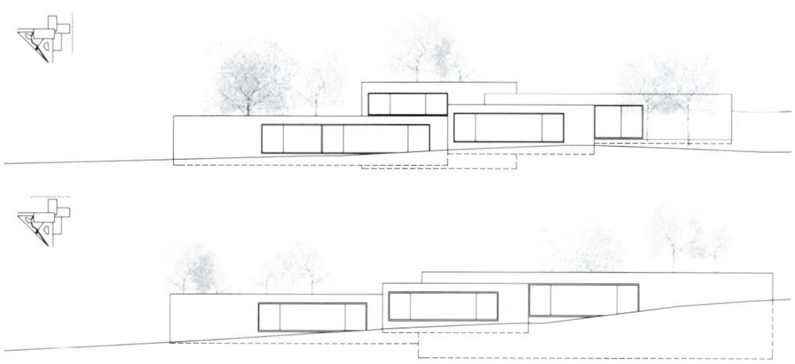

Elevations

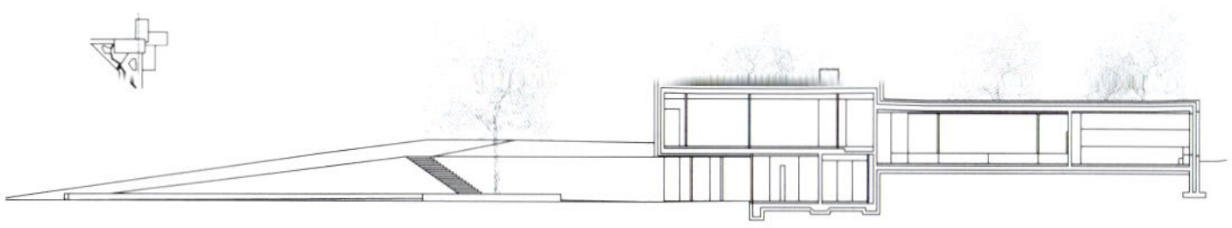

Section

CRÈCHE DE SAINT-JEAN

LOCATION: **GENEVA, SWITZERLAND**
PHOTOS: © **SERGES FRUEHAUF**

Built on a level below the public park, the new crèche building houses all of the activity rooms directly overlooking a secure private garden. The public park, where no new structures are to be built, is a place where locals can enjoy green surroundings.
The existing building contains the crèche's dining room and administrative facilities. The tunnel link between the two entities gives the building an independent touch, yet still enables the crèche to run smoothly. A ramp provides access to the new section. The various areas benefit from plenty of natural light, while visual contact is encouraged through an appropriate level of transparency. Sand-blasted reinforced concrete in dark grey adds the finishing touch to this new structure.

Das unter dem öffentlichen Park errichtete neue Kindergartengebäude enthält alle Aktivitätsräume in direkter Beziehung zum Garten. Der öffentliche Park, befreit von jeglichem auftauchenden Volumen, bietet den Bewohnern des Viertels eine Grünfläche.
Das bestehende Haus beherbergt den Speisesaal und das Verwaltungsbüro des Kindergartens. Die unterirdische Verbindung zwischen den beiden Entitäten stärkt die Unabhängigkeit des Hauses und ermöglicht ein optimales Funktionieren. Der Zugang zum neuen Teil erfolgt über eine Rampe. Die verschiedenen Sektoren profitieren vom großzügigen natürlichen Licht durch den Garten, das den Sichtkontakt begünstigt. Der dunkelgraue, sandgestrahlte Stahlbeton materialisiert diesen neuen Band.

Construit sous le parc public, le nouveau bâtiment de la crèche contient toutes les pièces d'activité en relation directe avec le jardin sécurisé. Le parc public, libéré de toute volumétrie émergente, offre un espace vert aux habitants du quartier.
La maison existante abrite la salle-à-manger et l'administration de la crèche. La liaison souterraine entre les deux entités renforce l'indépendance de la maison tout en permettant un fonctionnement optimal du programme. L'accès à la nouvelle partie est assuré par une rampe. Les différents secteurs bénéficient d'une lumière naturelle généreuse. La transparence voulue au travers du jardin incite les contacts visuels. Un béton armé gris foncé et sablé matérialise ce nouveau volume.

Construido bajo el parque público, el nuevo edificio de la guardería contiene todas las salas de actividades en relación directa con el jardín. El parque público, liberado de cualquier volumen emergente, ofrece un espacio verde a los habitantes del barrio.
La casa existente alberga el comedor y la oficina de administración de la guardería. El enlace subterráneo entre las dos entidades refuerza la independencia de la casa y permite un funcionamiento óptimo. El acceso a la nueva parte se realiza mediante una rampa. Los diversos sectores se benefician de una generosa luz natural a través del jardín que favorece el contacto visual. El hormigón armado gris oscuro y arenado materializa este nuevo volumen.

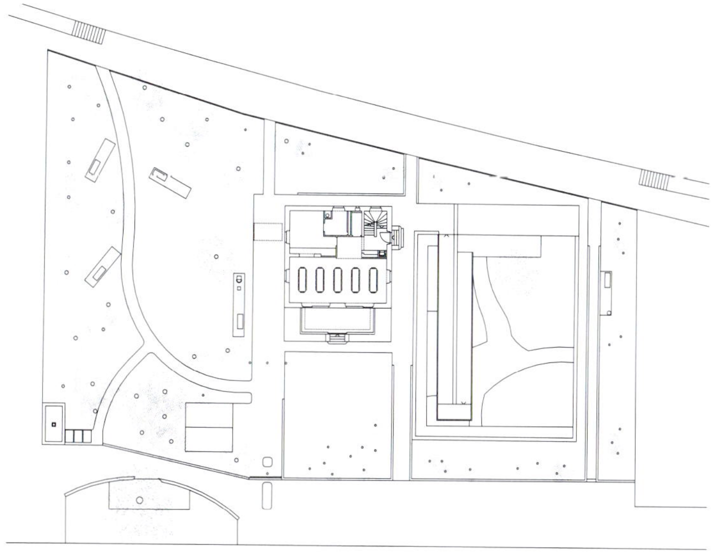

Upper floor plan

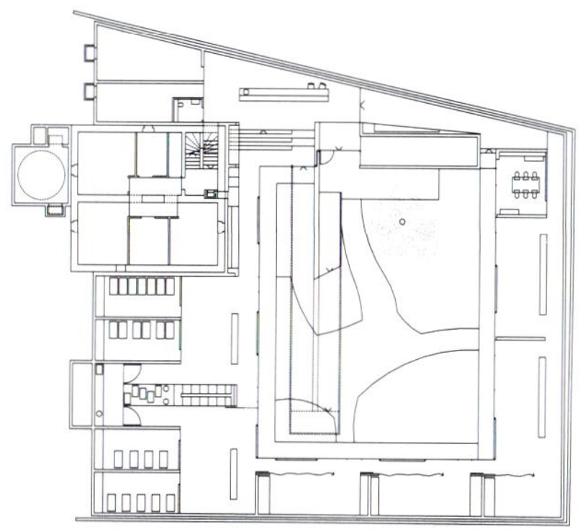

Lower floor plan

Sections

SOA architekti

// PROJECTS //

1. **ELEMENTARY SCHOOL AMOS FOR PSÁRY AND DOLNÍ JIRČANY**

www.s-o-a.cz

SOA architekti

1.

Working from Wenceslas Square at the heart of Prague's New Town, SOA architekti was established in 2015 by architects Ondrej Pihrt, Stefan Sulek and Ondrej Laciga.
Originally focused on interior design, hospitality and residential projects SOA have been developing a specialism in school and educational structures recently.
Their name, SOA, is an acronym standing for Sons of Architecture.

Vom Wenzelsplatz im Herzen der Prager Neustadt aus arbeitend, wurde SOA Architekti 2015 von den Architekten Ondrej Pihrt, Stefan Sulek und Ondrej Laciga gegründet.
Ursprünglich auf Innenarchitektur, Gastgewerbe und Wohnprojekte ausgerichtet, hat SOA in letzter Zeit eine Spezialisierung auf Schul- und Bildungsstrukturen entwickelt.
Ihr Name, SOA, ist ein Akronym, das für „Sons of Architecture" steht.

Installé sur la place Venceslas, au cœur de la Nouvelle Ville de Prague, SOA architekti a été créé en 2015 par les architectes Ondrej Pihrt, Stefan Sulek et Ondrej Laciga.
Initialement axée sur la décoration intérieure, l'hôtellerie et les projets résidentiels, SOA a récemment développé une spécialisation dans les structures scolaires et éducatives.
Leur nom, SOA, est un acronyme signifiant « Sons of Architecture » (fils de l'architecture).

Trabajando desde la Plaza Wenceslao en el corazón de la Ciudad Nueva de Praga, SOA architekti fue fundada en 2015 por los arquitectos Ondrej Pihrt, Stefan Sulek y Ondrej Laciga.
Originalmente enfocado en el diseño de interiores, hospitalidad y proyectos residenciales, SOA ha estado desarrollando su especialidad recientemente en el ámbito de las estructuras escolares y educativas.
Su nombre, SOA, es un acrónimo que significa «Sons of Architecture» (Hijos de la Arquitectura).

ELEMENTARY SCHOOL AMOS FOR PSÁRY AND DOLNÍ JIRČANY

LOCATION: **PSÁRY, CZECH REPUBLIC**
PHOTOS: © **BOYSPLAYNICE**

This primary school, designed as a passive house and which also functions as a community centre, is naturally integrated into its spatial and functional context. Located on a gentle slope, a multi-volume arrangement adapts it to the scale of its surroundings. Its appearance is determined by four white volumes that present a minimalist image inspired in rural typology and that house classrooms and administrative spaces. An intermediate volume, with a flat roof and clad in larch strips, links the four buildings and houses the entrance and the common areas. The interior is designed as a "learning landscape", a fluid space flooded with light that creates naturally defined zones, with different levels of privacy depending on the use of the space. The abundant use of wood in the interior gives a warm and homely feeling to the whole building.

Diese als Passivhaus konzipierte Grundschule, die auch als Gemeindezentrum fungiert, ist selbstverständlich in ihren räumlichen und funktionalen Kontext integriert. An einem sanften Hang gelegen, passt es sich durch eine mehrbändige Anordnung dem Maßstab seiner Umgebung an. Sein Erscheinungsbild wird von vier weißen Bänden bestimmt, die ein minimalistisches, von der ländlichen Typologie inspiriertes Bild präsentieren und Klassenzimmer und Verwaltungsräume beherbergen. Ein Zwischenvolumen mit einem Flachdach und mit Lärchenstäben verkleidet verbindet die vier Gebäude und beherbergt den Eingang und die Gemeinschaftsbereiche. Der Innenraum ist als „Lernlandschaft" konzipiert, ein flüssiger, lichtdurchfluteter Raum, der natürlich definierte Zonen schafft, die je nach Nutzung des Raumes unterschiedlich viel Privatsphäre bieten. Die reichliche Verwendung von Holz im Inneren verleiht dem gesamten Gebäude ein warmes und wohnliches Gefühl.

Cette école primaire, conçue comme une maison passive et qui fonctionne également comme un centre communautaire, est naturellement intégrée dans son contexte spatial et fonctionnel. Situé sur une pente douce, un aménagement en plusieurs volumes l'adapte à l'échelle de son environnement. Son apparence est déterminée par quatre volumes blancs qui présentent une image minimaliste inspirée de la typologie rurale et qui abritent des salles de classe et des espaces administratifs. Un volume intermédiaire, à toit plat et revêtu de lamelles de mélèze, relie les quatre bâtiments et abrite l'entrée et les parties communes. L'intérieur est conçu comme un « paysage d'apprentissage », un espace fluide inondé de lumière qui crée des zones naturellement définies, avec différents niveaux d'intimité selon l'utilisation de l'espace. L'utilisation abondante de bois à l'intérieur donne un sentiment de chaleur et d'intimité à l'ensemble du bâtiment.

Esta escuela primaria, diseñada como casa pasiva y que funciona también como centro comunitario, se integra con naturalidad en su contexto espacial y funcional. Situada en una pendiente suave, una disposición en varios volúmenes la adapta a la escala de su entorno. Su apariencia la determinan cuatro volúmenes de color blanco que presentan una imagen minimalista inspirada en la tipología rural y que alojan aulas y espacios administrativos. Un volumen intermedio, de cubierta plana y revestido con listones de alerce, enlaza los cuatro edificios y alberga la entrada y las áreas comunes. El interior está diseñado como «paisaje de aprendizaje», un espacio fluido inundado de luz que crea zonas definidas naturalmente, con diferentes niveles de privacidad según el uso del espacio. El uso abundante de la madera en el interior otorga una sensación cálida y hogareña a todo el edificio.

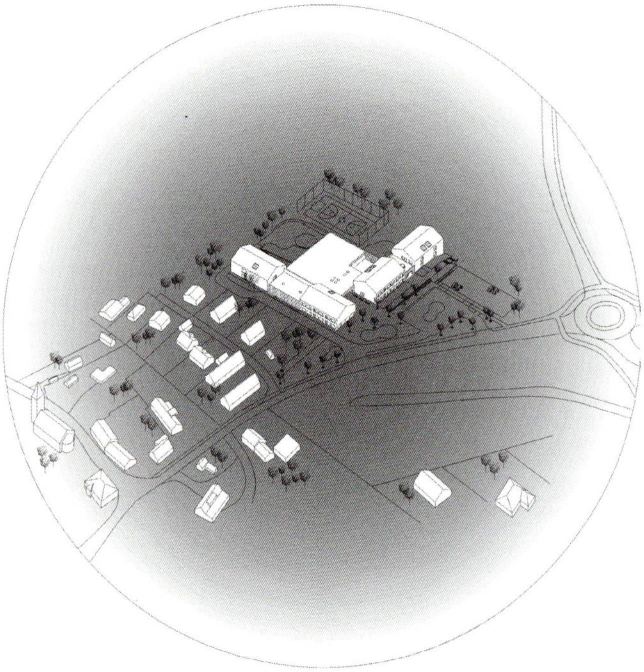

Site plan

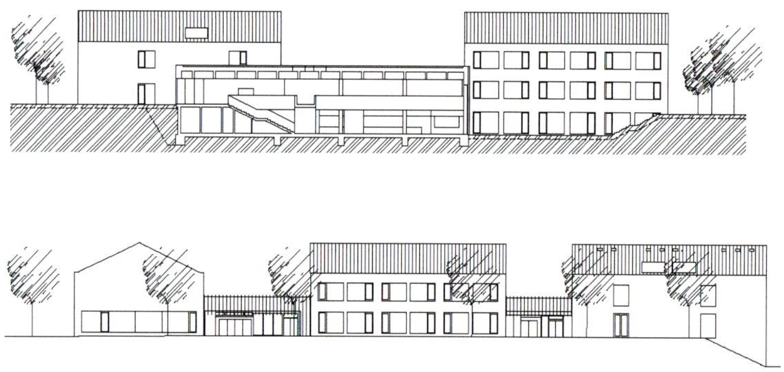

Elevations

ZŠ AMOS

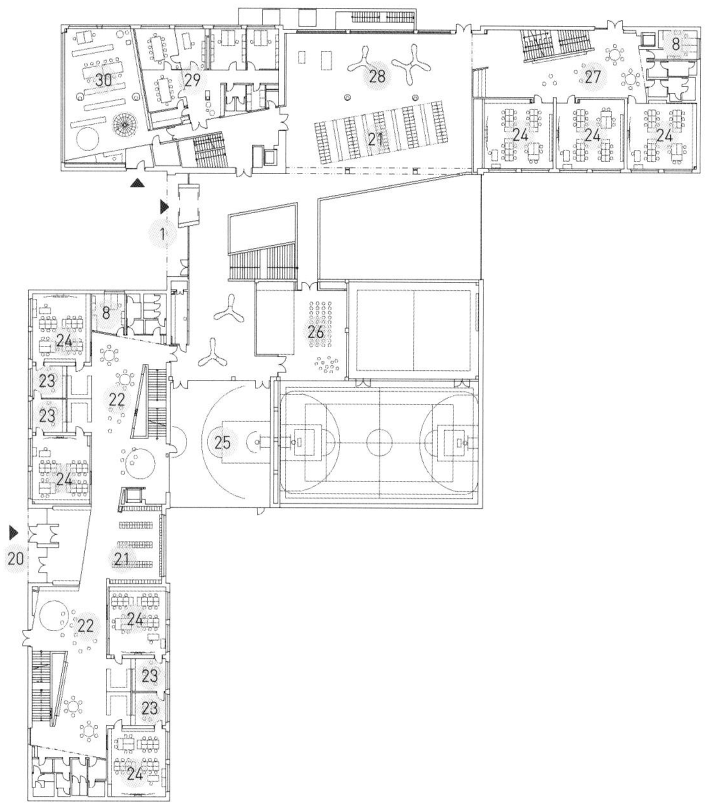

Ground floor plan

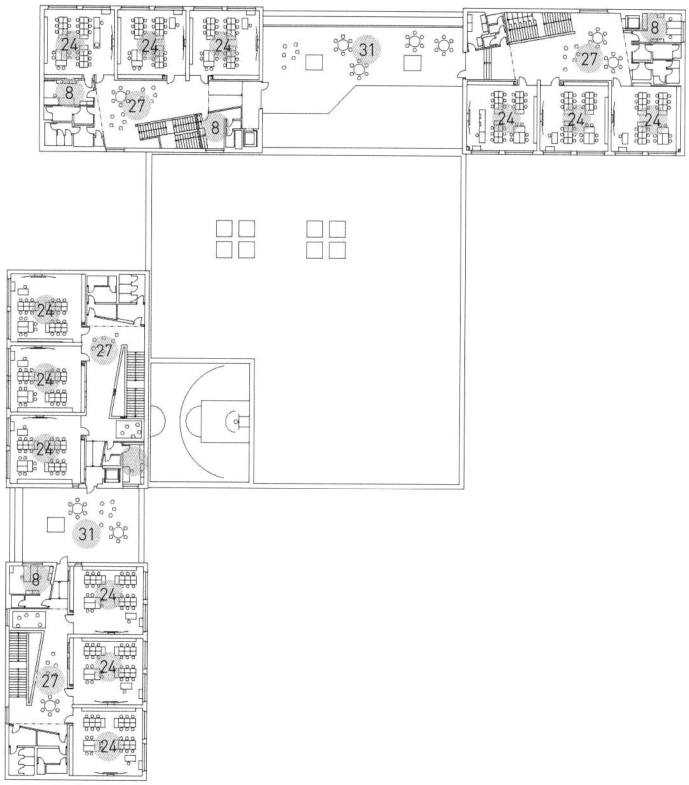

First floor plan

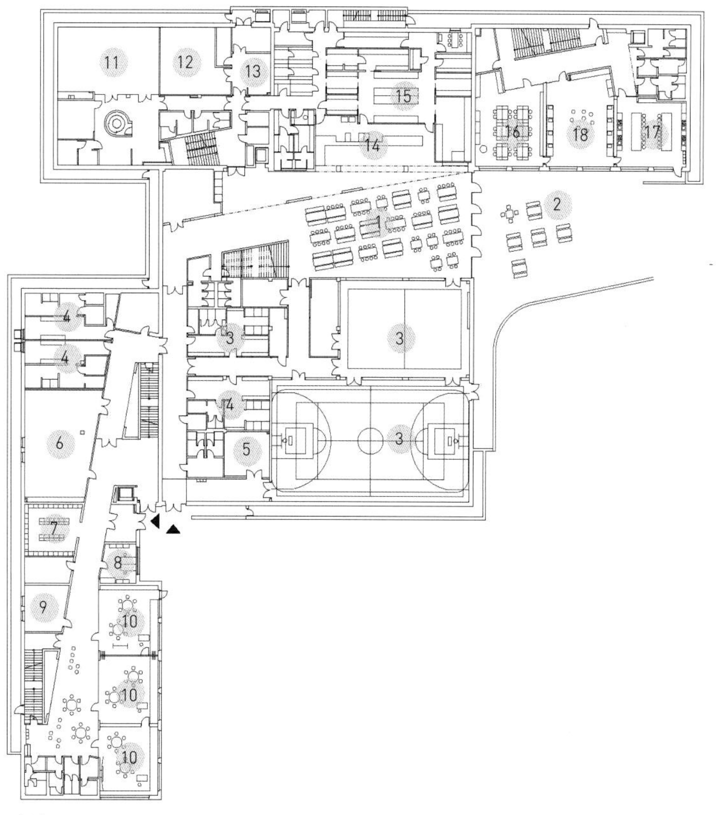

First basement plan

1. Canteen / auditorium
2. Outdoor terrace
3. Gymnasium
4. Cloakroom
5. Storage
6. Dance studio
7. Afterschool club cloakroom
8. Teacher's room
9. Reading room
10. Afterschool club
11. Multimedia lab
12. Mechanical room
13. Janitor's workshop
14. Dispensing counter
15. Kitchen
16. Art class
17. Training kitchen
18. Workshop
19. Main entrance
20. Entrance 1st grade
21. Cloakroom / locker room
22. Cluster 1st grade
23. Play area
24. Classroom
25. Atrium
26. School club / music room
27. Cluster 2nd grade
28. Break hall
29. School administration / principal
30. Library
31. Roof terrace

Sulkin Askenazi

// PROJECTS //

1. NIA SCHOOL BOSQUES
2. NIA SCHOOL PIRULES

sulkinaskenazi.com

Sulkin Askenazi

1.

2.

Sulkin Askenazi is an architecture and design studio based in Mexico City. Jack Sulkin and Gabriel Askenazi created the studio in 2016, forming a group of creative people who are passionate about architecture, becoming known for their fresh and timeless designs that transform the user's life.
The work methodology is based on the commitment to improve the environment, generating a sensory experience in the inhabitant.
Sulkin Askenazi is formed by a team of architects obsessed with design, spatial quality and economic commitment. The studio has commercial, residential, office and educational projects that are backed by architectural awards and recognition.

Sulkin Askenazi ist ein Architektur- und Designstudio mit Sitz in Mexiko-Stadt. Jack Sulkin und Gabriel Askenazi gründeten das Studio im Jahr 2016 und bildeten eine Gruppe kreativer Menschen, die sich für Architektur begeistern und für ihre frischen und zeitlosen Designs bekannt wurden, die das Leben des Benutzers verändern.
Die Arbeitsmethodik basiert auf der Verpflichtung, die Umwelt zu verbessern und beim Benutzer eine sensorische Erfahrung zu erzeugen.
Sulkin Askenazi wird von einem Team von Architekten gebildet, die von Design, räumlicher Qualität und wirtschaftlichem Engagement besessen sind. Das Studio hat Geschäfts-, Wohn-, Büro- und Bildungsprojekte, die durch Architekturpreise und Anerkennungen unterstützt werden.

Sulkin Askenazi est un studio d'architecture et de design basé à Mexico. Jack Sulkin et Gabriel Askenazi ont créé le studio en 2016, formant un groupe de créatifs passionnés d'architecture, qui se sont fait connaître par leurs designs frais et intemporels qui transforment la vie de l'utilisateur.
La méthodologie de travail est basée sur l'engagement à améliorer l'environnement, en générant une expérience sensorielle chez l'utilisateur.
Sulkin Askenazi est formé par une équipe d'architectes obsédés par le design, la qualité spatiale et l'engagement économique. Le studio a des projets commerciaux, résidentiels, de bureau et éducatifs qui sont soutenus par des prix et des reconnaissances architecturales.

Sulkin Askenazi es un estudio de arquitectura y diseño establecido en la Ciudad de México. Jack Sulkin y Gabriel Askenazi crean el estudio en el año 2016, formando un grupo de creativos apasionados por la arquitectura, dándose a conocer por sus diseños frescos y atemporales que transforman el vivir del usuario.
La metodología de trabajo se basa en el compromiso de mejorar el entorno, generando una experiencia sensorial en el usuario.
Sulkin Askenazi es formado por un equipo de arquitectos obsesionados con el diseño, la calidad espacial y el compromiso económico. El estudio cuenta con proyectos comerciales, habitacionales, de oficinas y educativos que son respaldados por reconocimientos y premios arquitectónicos.

NIA SCHOOL BOSQUES

LOCATION: **MEXICO CITY, MEXICO**
PHOTOS: © **ALDO C GRACIA**

This learning space seeks to release the creative potential of children between the ages of two and eight through design and to encourage interactive teaching through different environments that allow them to develop their skills. The layout allows the children to move freely and has areas of movement to exercise the body and mind, as well as two rooms that integrate nature into the interior. The design of the furniture and finishes creates a comfortable and natural environment for learning. The sensory room promotes a dynamic game that encourages learning through exploration, experimentation and discovery. Materials that are soft to the touch, such as cork and oak wood, form elements designed for children to climb, jump and assemble, developing different skills.

Cet espace d'apprentissage cherche à libérer le potentiel créatif des enfants de deux à huit ans par le biais de la conception et à encourager l'enseignement interactif par le biais de divers environnements qui leur permettent de développer leurs compétences. L'aménagement permet aux enfants de se déplacer librement entre les différents environnements et dispose de zones de mouvement pour exercer le corps et l'esprit, ainsi que de deux pièces qui intègrent la nature dans les espaces intérieurs. La conception du mobilier et des finitions crée un environnement confortable et naturel pour l'apprentissage. La salle sensorielle propose un jeu dynamique qui encourage l'apprentissage par l'exploration, l'expérimentation et la découverte. Des matériaux doux au toucher, tels que le liège et le bois de chêne, forment des éléments conçus pour que les enfants puissent grimper, sauter et s'assembler, développant ainsi différentes aptitudes.

Dieser Lernraum versucht, das kreative Potenzial von Kindern im Alter zwischen zwei und acht Jahren durch Gestaltung freizusetzen und den interaktiven Unterricht durch verschiedene Umgebungen zu fördern, die es ihnen ermöglichen, ihre Fähigkeiten zu entwickeln. Das Layout erlaubt es den Kindern, sich frei zwischen den verschiedenen Umgebungen zu bewegen, und verfügt über Bewegungsbereiche, um Körper und Geist zu trainieren, sowie über zwei Räume, die die Natur in die Innenräume integrieren. Das Design der Möbel und Oberflächen schafft eine komfortable und natürliche Lernumgebung. Der Sinnesraum fördert ein dynamisches Spiel, das zum Lernen durch Erkunden, Experimentieren und Entdecken anregt. Materialien, die sich weich anfühlen, wie z.B. Kork und Eichenholz, bilden Elemente, die für Kinder zum Klettern, Springen und Zusammenbauen gedacht sind und verschiedene Fähigkeiten entwickeln.

Este espacio de aprendizaje busca liberar el potencial creativo de niños de entre dos y ocho años mediante el diseño y fomentar una enseñanza interactiva a través de varios ambientes que les permitan desarrollar sus habilidades. La distribución permite a los niños desplazarse libremente entre los diferentes ambientes y cuenta con zonas de movimiento para ejercitar el cuerpo y la mente, así como dos salas que integran la naturaleza en los espacios interiores. El diseño del mobiliario y de los acabados genera un entorno cómodo y natural para el aprendizaje. El salón sensorial promueve un juego dinámico que fomenta el aprendizaje a través de la exploración, la experimentación y el descubrimiento. Materiales suaves al tacto como el corcho y la madera de encino conforman elementos concebidos para que los niños escalen, salten y armen, desarrollando diferentes habilidades.

Cross section

Longitudinal section

Second floor plan

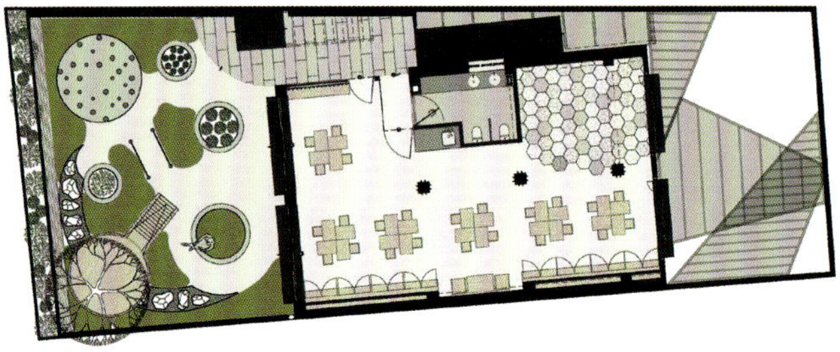

First floor plan

Ground floor plan

NIA SCHOOL PIRULES

LOCATION: **MEXICO CITY, MEXICO**

The project of this nursery is oriented towards a personalized education for children between two and eight years old. Its main objective is to create flexible spaces that allow free mobility focused on self-learning and encourage curiosity, creativity and collaboration. All the design elements seek to encourage the independence and self-discipline of the students and stimulate their sensory development. The movement room is a space for physical and mental development where children experience creativity and curiosity together, by overcoming the ponderable design exercises available. Nature is integrated into the project through the windows that open the main classroom to a terrace with trees and vegetable gardens where the children learn about caring for the environment and the surroundings.

Le projet de cette crèche est orienté vers une éducation personnalisée pour les enfants entre deux et huit ans. Son principal objectif est de créer des espaces flexibles qui permettent une libre mobilité axée sur l'auto-apprentissage et qui encouragent la curiosité, la créativité et la collaboration. Tous les éléments de conception visent à encourager l'indépendance et l'autodiscipline des élèves et à stimuler leur développement sensoriel. La salle de mouvement est un espace de développement physique et mental où les enfants font l'expérience, vivent ensemble et utilisent leur curiosité et leur créativité pour surmonter les défis et les exercices conçus. La nature est intégrée dans le projet par les fenêtres qui ouvrent la salle de classe principale sur une terrasse avec des arbres et des potagers où les enfants apprennent à prendre soin de l'environnement et des alentours.

Das Projekt dieser Kinderkrippe ist auf eine personalisierte Erziehung für Kinder zwischen zwei und acht Jahren ausgerichtet. Ihr Hauptziel ist es, flexible Räume zu schaffen, die eine freie, auf das Selbstlernen ausgerichtete Mobilität ermöglichen und Neugier, Kreativität und Zusammenarbeit fördern. Alle Gestaltungselemente sollen die Unabhängigkeit und Selbstdisziplin der Schülerinnen und Schüler fördern und ihre sensorische Entwicklung anregen. Der Bewegungsraum ist ein Raum für die körperliche und geistige Entwicklung, in dem die Kinder ihre Neugier und Kreativität erleben, zusammenleben und ihre Neugier und Kreativität nutzen, um die entworfenen Herausforderungen und Übungen zu bewältigen. Die Natur wird in das Projekt durch die Fenster integriert, die den Hauptklassenraum zu einer Terrasse mit Bäumen und Gemüsegärten öffnen, wo die Kinder lernen, sich um die Umwelt und die Umgebung zu kümmern.

El proyecto de esta guardería se orienta hacia una educación personalizada, dirigida a niños de entre dos y ocho años. Su principal objetivo es crear espacios flexibles que permitan una movilidad libre enfocada hacia el autoaprendizaje y fomenten la curiosidad, la creatividad y la colaboración. Todos los elementos del diseño buscan incentivar la independencia y la autodisciplina de los alumnos y estimular su desarrollo sensorial. El salón de movimiento constituye un espacio destinado al desarrollo físico y mental donde los niños experimentan, conviven y usan su curiosidad y creatividad para superar los retos y ejercicios diseñados. La naturaleza se integra en el proyecto a través de los ventanales que abren el salón de clases hacia una terraza dotada de árboles y huertos en la que los niños aprenden sobre el cuidado del medio ambiente y el entorno que los rodea.

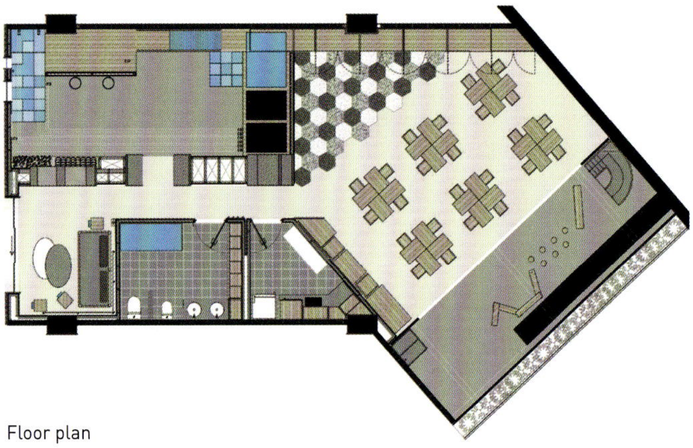

Floor plan

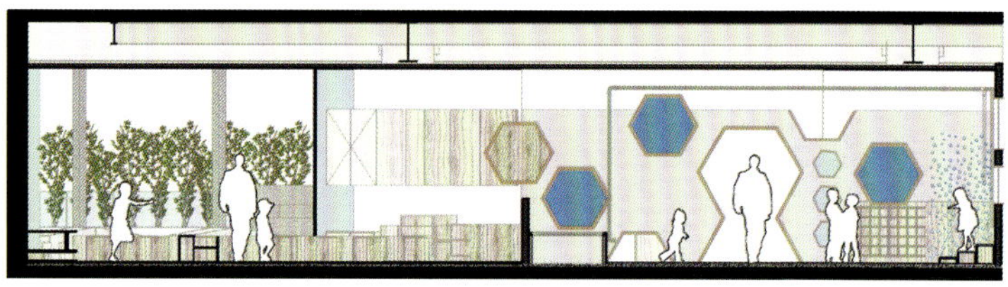

Section

NIA
Montessori

syntax architecture

// PROJECTS //

1. HUGGING THE GARDEN

www.syntax-architecture.com

syntax architecture

1.

Syntax architecture was founded in 2006 by Michael Barth, Martina Barth Sedelmayer and Alexander Spauwen.
"Syntax" in its original meaning stands for compilation and is the essence of the syntax architecture team.
The quality of work is not only finding a form, it's more the flexibility in functional and structural solutions. For a successful project it is also very important to find out about the needs of people and integrate them within the concept and design. All projects are deeply rooted in the local context and reinforce the genius loci.
Idea, form, structure, organisation and function are directly connected to each other. Therefore it's necessary to get the ideal balance between these factors —to find the "syntax" of the project.

SYNTAX Architecture a été fondée en 2006 par Michael Barth, Martina Barth Sedelmayer et Alexander Spauwen.
« Syntax » dans son sens original signifie compilation et constitue l'essence de l'équipe d'architecture syntaxique.
La qualité du travail n'est pas seulement de trouver une forme, c'est aussi la flexibilité des solutions fonctionnelles et structurelles. Pour la réussite d'un projet, il est également très important de connaître les besoins des gens et de les intégrer dans le concept et la conception. Tous les projets sont profondément ancrés dans le contexte local et renforcent le genius loci.
L'idée, la forme, la structure, l'organisation et la fonction sont directement liées les unes aux autres. Il est donc nécessaire d'obtenir l'équilibre idéal entre ces facteurs - pour trouver la « syntax » du projet.

Syntax architecture wurde 2006 von Michael Barth, Martina Barth Sedelmayer und Alexander Spauwen gegründet.
„Syntax" in seiner ursprünglichen Bedeutung steht für Kompilierung und ist die Essenz des Syntaxarchitektur-Teams.
Die Qualität der Arbeit liegt nicht nur in der Formfindung, sondern vielmehr in der Flexibilität in funktionalen und strukturellen Lösungen. Für ein erfolgreiches Projekt ist es auch sehr wichtig, die Bedürfnisse der Menschen herauszufinden und sie in das Konzept und den Entwurf zu integrieren. Alle Projekte sind tief im lokalen Kontext verwurzelt und stärken den genius loci.
Idee, Form, Struktur, Organisation und Funktion sind direkt miteinander verbunden. Deshalb ist es notwendig, die ideale Balance zwischen diesen Faktoren zu finden - die „Syntax" des Projekts zu finden.

SYNTAX Architecture fue fundada en 2006 por Michael Barth, Martina Barth Sedelmayer y Alexander Spauwen.
«Syntax» en su significado original significa compilación y es la esencia del equipo.
La calidad del trabajo no es solo encontrar una forma, sino más bien la flexibilidad en las soluciones funcionales y estructurales. Para que un proyecto tenga éxito es también muy importante conocer las necesidades de las personas e integrarlas en el concepto y el diseño. Todos los proyectos están profundamente arraigados en el contexto local y refuerzan el genio de los loci.
La idea, la forma, la estructura, la organización y la función están directamente conectadas entre sí. Por lo tanto, es necesario conseguir el equilibrio ideal entre estos factores para encontrar la «sintaxis» del proyecto.

HUGGING THE GARDEN

LOCATION: **KLOSTERNEUBURG, AUSTRIA**
PHOTOS: **© HERTA HURNAUS, ROMAN BÖNSCH**

To maximize the garden space and preserve an old beech tree, the concept of this project is based on pushing the new building of this primary school towards the northern edge of the plot and connecting it to an existing building next door. This scheme integrates the building into the slope of the plot and ensures generous natural lighting for all the group rooms, which are south-facing and arranged in a zigzag pattern. The idea of free forms of the classrooms encourages interaction between the students and the connection to the garden, which merges with the building through large windows. The design breaks the lines of the façades and roofs to generate a smaller volume that adapts to the scale of the surrounding single-family homes. According to the client, the project incorporated different measures to reduce the building's CO_2 footprint.

Um den Gartenraum zu maximieren und eine alte Buche zu erhalten, basiert das Konzept dieses Projekts darauf, das neue Gebäude dieser Grundschule an den nördlichen Rand des Grundstücks zu schieben und es mit einem bestehenden Gebäude nebenan zu verbinden. Dieses Schema integriert das Gebäude in den Hang des Grundstücks und sorgt für eine großzügige natürliche Belichtung aller Gruppenräume, die nach Süden ausgerichtet und im Zickzackmuster angeordnet sind. Die Idee der freien Formen der Klassenräume fördert die Interaktion zwischen den Schülern und die Verbindung zum Garten, der durch große Fenster mit dem Gebäude verschmilzt. Der Entwurf des Gebäudes durchbricht die Linien der Fassaden und Dächer, um ein kleineres Volumen zu erzeugen, das sich an den Maßstab der umliegenden Einfamilienhäuser anpasst. Nach Angaben des Bauherrn umfasste das Projekt verschiedene Maßnahmen zur Reduzierung des CO_2-Fußabdrucks des Gebäudes.

Pour maximiser l'espace du jardin et préserver un vieux hêtre, le concept de ce projet est basé sur le fait de pousser le nouveau bâtiment de cette école primaire vers la limite nord du terrain et de le relier à un bâtiment existant situé à côté. Ce projet intègre le bâtiment dans la pente du terrain et assure un éclairage naturel généreux pour toutes les salles de groupe, qui sont orientées au sud et disposées en zigzag. L'idée de formes libres des salles de classe encourage l'interaction entre les étudiants et le lien avec le jardin, qui se fond avec le bâtiment par de grandes fenêtres. La conception du bâtiment brise les lignes des façades et des toits pour générer un volume plus petit qui s'adapte à l'échelle des maisons unifamiliales environnantes. Selon le client, le projet comprenait différentes mesures visant à réduire l'empreinte de CO_2 du bâtiment.

Para maximizar el espacio del jardín y conservar una vieja haya, el concepto de este proyecto se basa en empujar el nuevo edificio de esta escuela primaria hacia el límite norte de la parcela y conectarlo a un edificio existente contiguo. Este esquema integra el edificio en la pendiente del solar y garantiza una generosa iluminación natural de todas las salas de grupo, orientadas al sur y dispuestas en forma de zigzag. La idea de formas libres de las aulas fomenta la interacción entre los alumnos y la conexión con el jardín, que se funde con el edificio a través de grandes ventanales. El diseño del edificio rompe las líneas de fachadas y cubiertas para generar un volumen más reducido que se adapte a la escala de las viviendas unifamiliares del entorno. De acuerdo con el cliente, el proyecto incorporó diferentes medidas para reducir la huella de CO_2 del edificio.

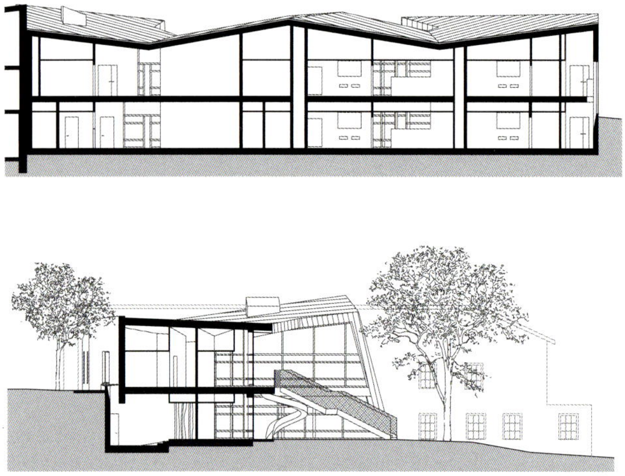

Sections

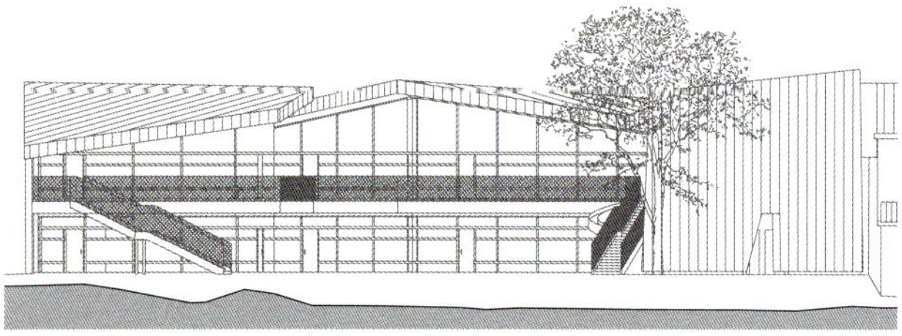

South elevation

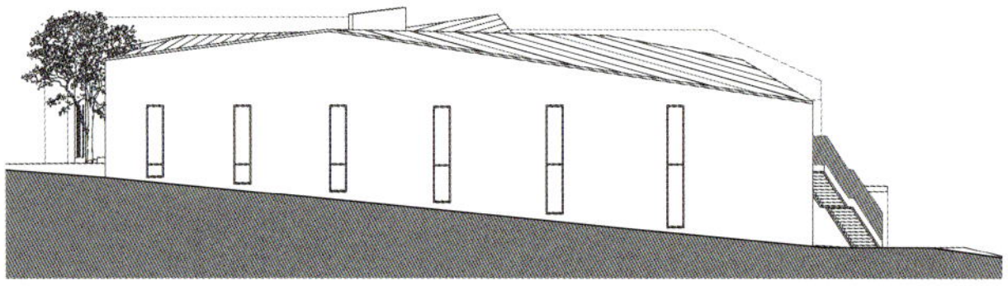

West elevation

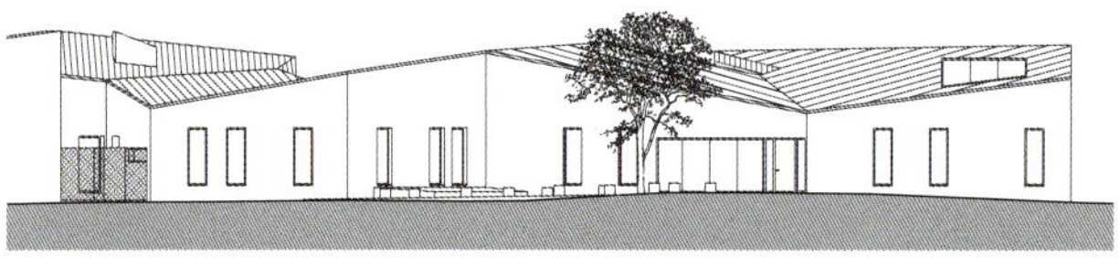

North elevation

Render

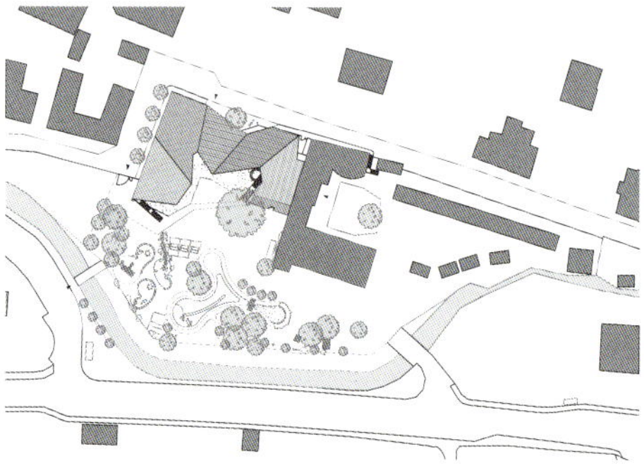

Site plan

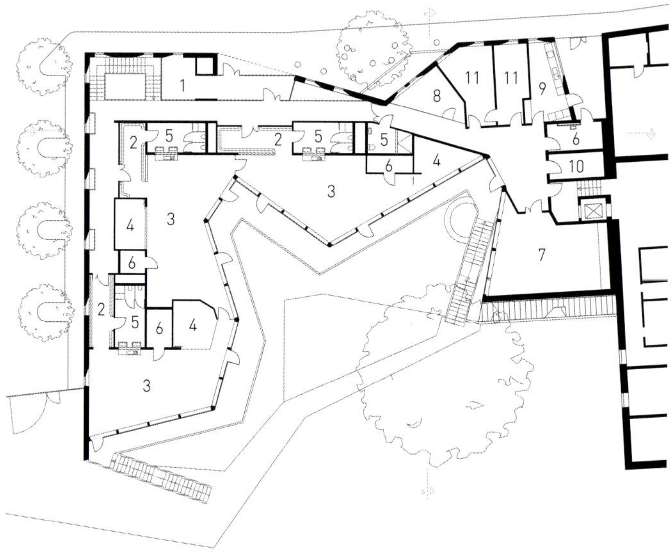

First floor plan / entrance level

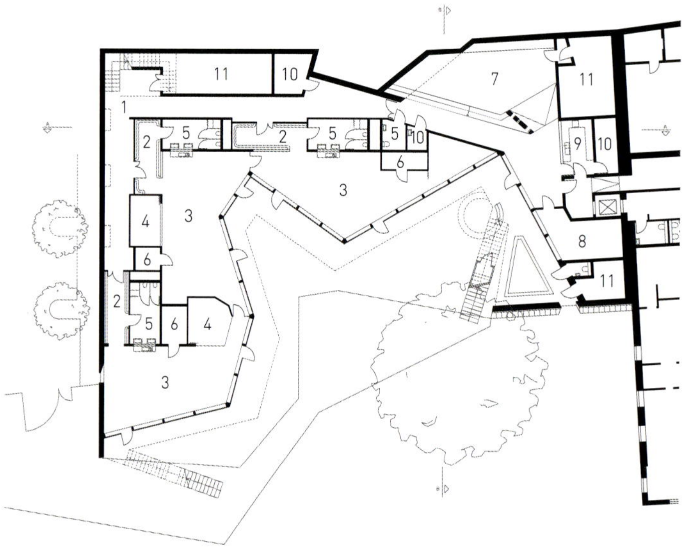

Ground floor plan

1. Porch
2. Cloakroom
3. Classroom
4. Rest area
5. Bathroom facilities
6. Storeroom
7. Fitness and movement room
8. Workshop
9. Kitchen
10. Storage
11. Plant room
12. Office
13. Staff

Taller Viga Maestra

// PROJECTS //

1. ESCUELA RURAL CANTINO
2. JARDIN INFANTIL LAS ABEJITAS

www.instagram.com/tallervigamaestra/

Taller Viga Maestra

1.

2.

Jaime Gatica Martínez has been an architect at the School of Architecture of the Universidad Autónoma de Chile since 2005 and obtained a Master's degree in Energy Efficiency and Sustainable Construction at the School of Architecture of the Universidad Mayor in 2010.
In the year 2016, he created El Taller Viga Maestra, developing the management and design of public and private projects focused on sustainability and urban design, highlighting the execution of buildings with a high standard in energy savings applied mainly to medium-scale public construction. The Viga Maestra Workshop is committed to a more handcrafted design process, generating personalized links with the communities where it operates, and has stood out for focusing its action on complex social contexts, its base of operations being the Araucanía Region located in the south of Chile, a region that has a high intercultural component and social vulnerability added to a unique and singular landscape.

Jaime Gatica Martínez est architecte à l'école d'architecture de l'Universidad Autónoma de Chile depuis 2005 et a obtenu un master en efficacité énergétique et construction durable à l'école d'architecture de l'Universidad Mayor en 2010.
En 2016, il crée El Taller Viga Maestra, qui développe la gestion et la conception de projets publics et privés axés sur la durabilité et la conception urbaine, en mettant l'accent sur l'exécution de bâtiments avec un niveau élevé d'économie d'énergie appliqué principalement aux constructions publiques de taille moyenne. L'atelier Viga Maestra s'est engagé dans un processus de conception plus artisanale, générant des liens personnalisés avec les communautés où il opère, et s'est distingué en concentrant son action sur des contextes sociaux complexes, sa base d'opération étant la région d'Araucanía située au sud du Chili, une région qui présente une forte composante interculturelle et une vulnérabilité sociale ajoutée à un paysage unique et singulier.

Jaime Gatica Martínez ist seit 2005 Architekt an der Fakultät für Architektur der Universidad Autónoma de Chile und erwarb 2010 einen Master-Abschluss in Energieeffizienz und nachhaltigem Bauen an der Fakultät für Architektur der Universidad Mayor.
Im Jahr 2016 gründet er El Taller Viga Maestra und entwickelt das Management und die Planung von öffentlichen und privaten Projekten, die sich auf Nachhaltigkeit und Stadtgestaltung konzentrieren, wobei er die Ausführung von Gebäuden mit einem hohen Standard an Energieeinsparungen hervorhebt, die hauptsächlich im öffentlichen Bauwesen mittlerer Größe Anwendung finden. Der Viga Maestra Workshop ist einem eher handwerklich geprägten Designprozess verpflichtet, der persönliche Verbindungen zu den Gemeinden, in denen er tätig ist, herstellt, und hat sich dadurch hervorgetan, dass er seine Aktionen auf komplexe soziale Kontexte konzentriert. Seine Operationsbasis ist die Region Araucanía im Süden Chiles, eine Region mit einer hohen interkulturellen Komponente und sozialer Verwundbarkeit, die zu einer einzigartigen und einzigartigen Landschaft beiträgt.

Jaime Gatica Martínez es arquitecto de la Escuela de Arquitectura de la Universidad Autónoma de Chile desde 2005 y obtiene el grado de Magíster en Eficiencia Energética y Construcción Sustentable en la Escuela de Arquitectura de la Universidad Mayor en el año 2010.
En el año 2016, crea El Taller Viga Maestra, desarrollando la gestión y diseño de proyectos públicos y privados enfocados a la sostenibilidad y el diseño urbano, destacando la ejecución de edificios con un alto estándar en ahorro energético aplicado principalmente a la edificación publica de mediana escala. El Taller Viga Maestra apuesta por una factura más artesanal en los procesos de diseño, generando vínculos personalizados con las comunidades donde opera, y se ha destacado por enfocar su acción en contextos sociales complejos, siendo su base de operaciones la Región de la Araucanía emplazada en el sur de Chile, región que tiene un alto componente intercultural y de vulnerabilidad social sumado a un paisaje singular y único.

ESCUELA RURAL CANTINO

LOCATION: **COMUNIDAD INDÍGENA JUAN TRAIPI, CODINHUE / HIJUELA 61, COMUNA DE VILCUN REGIÓN DE LA ARAUCANIA, CHILE**

PHOTOS: **© RODRIGO PASTOR PENSA**

Located in an domestic community, this school synthesizes different variables of the spatial organization of the Mapuche people, although its volumetry evokes a southern architecture of compact and simple volumes that act as references within the landscape. The predominant use of wood integrates the building in the place, condensing rurality and simplicity. The building is organised on the basis of a central space situated on a west-east axis, which establishes relations that range from the public to the private. Located on the north-south axis, the access opens up to the street enhancing its public role as an iconic point within the community. The building has high standards of passive design and energy efficiency, forced by a context of cold winters and hot summers, which generates a building with low energy demand and a high level of indoor environmental comfort.

In einer indigenen Gemeinschaft gelegen, synthetisiert diese Schule verschiedene Variablen der räumlichen Organisation des Mapuche-Volkes, obwohl ihre Volumetrie an eine südliche Architektur aus kompakten und einfachen Volumen erinnert, die als Referenzen innerhalb der Landschaft fungieren. Die vorherrschende Verwendung von Holz integriert das Gebäude in den Ort und verdichtet Ländlichkeit und Schlichtheit. Das Gebäude ist auf der Grundlage eines zentralen, auf einer West-Ost-Achse gelegenen Raumes organisiert, der Beziehungen herstellt, die von öffentlich bis privat reichen. Auf der Nord-Süd-Achse gelegen, öffnet sich der Zugang zur Straße, wodurch ihre öffentliche Rolle als ikonischer Punkt innerhalb der Gemeinde gestärkt wird. Das Gebäude weist hohe Standards in Bezug auf passives Design und Energieeffizienz auf, die durch einen Kontext kalter Winter und heißer Sommer erzwungen werden, wodurch ein Gebäude mit niedrigem Energiebedarf und einem hohen Maß an Innenumweltkomfort entsteht.

Située dans une communauté indigène, cette école synthétise différentes variables de l'organisation spatiale du peuple mapuche, bien que sa volumétrie évoque une architecture méridionale de volumes compacts et simples qui servent de références dans le paysage. L'utilisation prédominante du bois intègre le bâtiment dans le lieu, condensant la ruralité et la simplicité. Le bâtiment est organisé sur la base d'un espace central situé sur un axe ouest-est, qui établit des relations allant du public au privé. Situé sur l'axe nord-sud, l'accès s'ouvre sur la rue, renforçant ainsi son rôle public en tant que point emblématique de la communauté. Le bâtiment répond à des normes élevées de conception passive et d'efficacité énergétique, imposées par un contexte d'hivers froids et d'étés chauds, ce qui génère un bâtiment à faible demande énergétique et un niveau élevé de confort environnemental intérieur.

Situada en una comunidad indígena, esta escuela sintetiza diferentes variables de la organización espacial del pueblo Mapuche, si bien su volumetría evoca una arquitectura sureña, de volúmenes compactos y simples que actúan como referentes dentro del paisaje. El uso predominante de la madera integra al edificio en el lugar, condensando ruralidad y sencillez. El edificio se organiza a partir de un espacio central situado en un eje oeste-este, que establece relaciones que van desde lo público a lo privado. Situado en el eje norte-sur, el acceso se abre hacia la calle potenciando su rol público como punto icónico dentro de la comunidad. La obra cuenta con altos estándares de diseño pasivo y eficiencia energética obligados por un contexto de inviernos fríos y veranos calurosos, que generan un edificio de baja demanda energética y un alto nivel de confort ambiental interior.

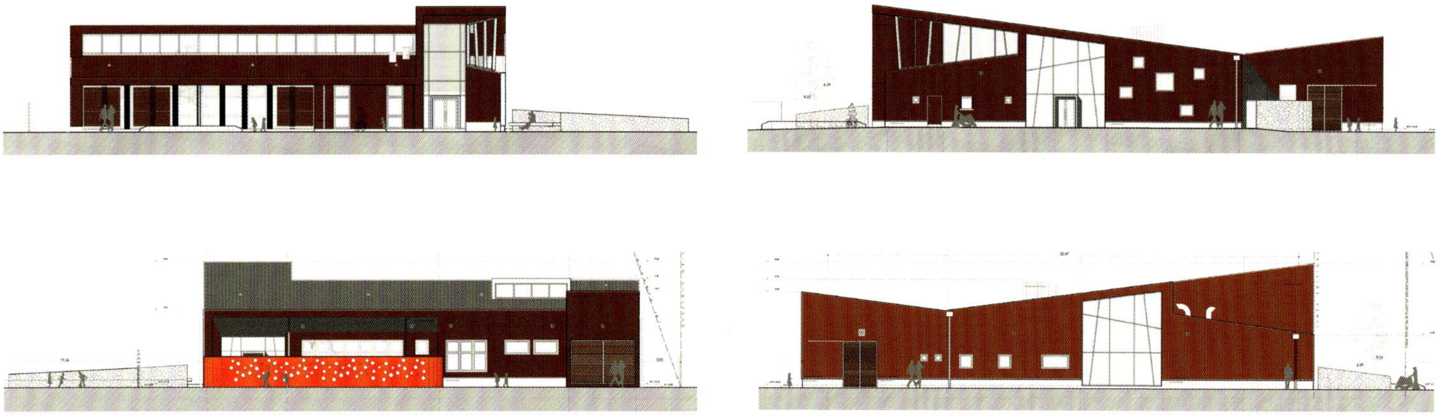

Elevations

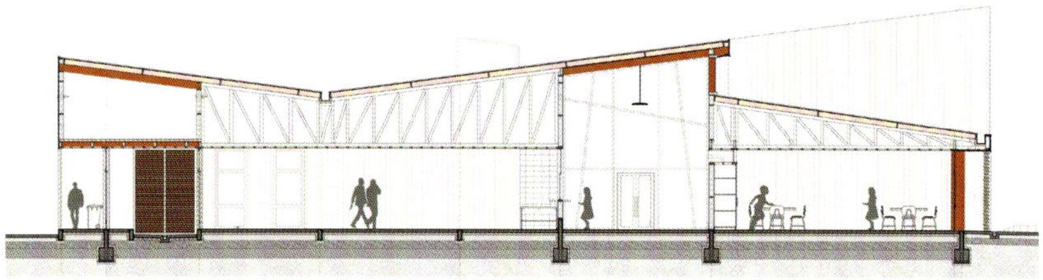

Section

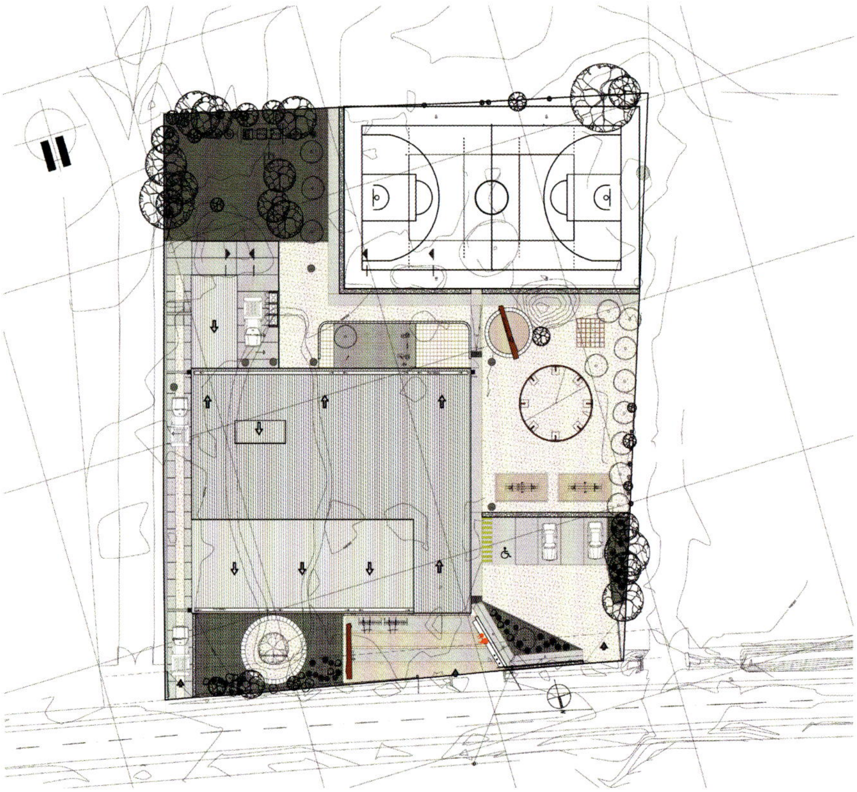

Roof plan

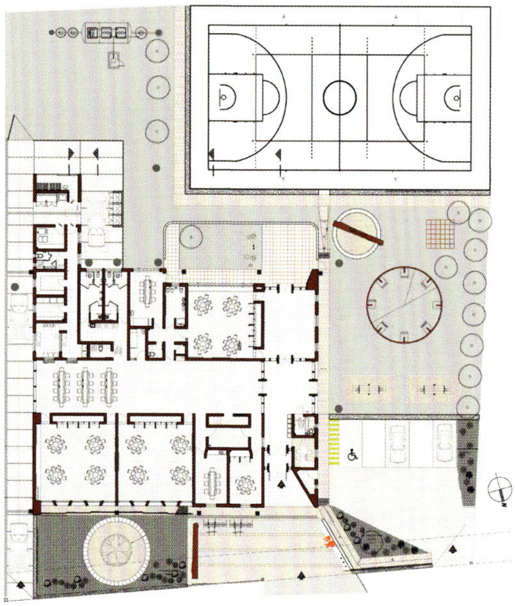

Floor plan

JARDIN INFANTIL LAS ABEJITAS

LOCATION: **TEMUCO / REGIÓN DE LA ARAUCANIA, CHILE**
PHOTOS: **© RODRIGO PASTOR PENSA**

The insertion of this kindergarten in a low-rise residential area transforms it into a reference point within an orphaned sector of public facilities, necessary to improve the quality of life of this dense sector called La Rivera. Its architectural image seeks to adapt to its main use, promoting the idea of wanting to be an entertaining, playful and didactic building for children's learning. On the other hand, it takes up again the idea of the gabled community image, reinterpreting it in a contemporary language within a context of simple houses, with sloping roofs and volumes that do not exceed two floors in height. The work is developed under criteria of high energy efficiency and incorporates active and passive elements that contribute to improving the environmental comfort of the building and the quality of life of the children and the neighborhood.

Die Einfügung dieses Kindergartens in ein niedriges Wohngebiet verwandelt ihn in einen Referenzpunkt innerhalb eines verwaisten Sektors öffentlicher Einrichtungen, der notwendig ist, um die Lebensqualität in diesem dichten Sektor namens La Rivera zu verbessern. Sein architektonisches Erscheinungsbild soll sich seiner Hauptnutzung anpassen und die Idee fördern, ein unterhaltsames, spielerisches und didaktisches Gebäude für das Lernen von Kindern sein zu wollen. Andererseits greift sie die Idee des giebelartigen Gemeinschaftsbildes wieder auf und interpretiert es in einer zeitgenössischen Sprache im Kontext einfacher Häuser mit schrägen Dächern und Volumina, die zwei Stockwerke in der Höhe nicht überschreiten, neu. Die Arbeit wird unter Kriterien hoher Energieeffizienz entwickelt und beinhaltet aktive und passive Elemente, die dazu beitragen, den Umweltkomfort des Gebäudes und die Lebensqualität der Kinder und der Nachbarschaft zu verbessern.

L'insertion de ce jardin d'enfants dans une zone résidentielle de faible hauteur le transforme en un point de référence au sein d'un secteur orphelin d'équipements publics, nécessaire pour améliorer la qualité de vie de ce secteur dense appelé La Rivera. Son image architecturale cherche à s'adapter à son utilisation principale, en promouvant l'idée de vouloir être un bâtiment divertissant, ludique et didactique pour l'apprentissage des enfants. D'autre part, il reprend l'idée de l'image de la communauté à pignon, et la réinterprète dans un langage contemporain dans un contexte de maisons simples, avec des toits en pente et des volumes qui ne dépassent pas deux étages de hauteur. Le travail est développé selon des critères de haute efficacité énergétique et intègre des éléments actifs et passifs qui contribuent à améliorer le confort environnemental du bâtiment et la qualité de vie des enfants et du quartier.

La inserción de este jardín infantil en un barrio de escala habitacional baja lo transforma en un referente dentro de un sector huérfano de equipamientos públicos, necesarios para mejorar la calidad de vida de este denso sector denominado La Rivera. Su imagen arquitectónica busca adecuarse a su uso principal, potenciando la idea de querer ser un edificio entretenido, lúdico y didáctico para el aprendizaje de los niños. Por otro lado, se retoma la idea de la imagen de barrio a dos aguas, y se reinterpreta en un lenguaje contemporáneo dentro de un contexto de casas simples, con cubiertas inclinadas y volúmenes que no sobrepasan los dos pisos de altura. La obra se desarrolla bajo criterios de alta eficiencia energética e incorpora elementos activos y pasivos que contribuyen a mejorar el confort ambiental del edificio y la calidad de vida de los niños y el barrio.

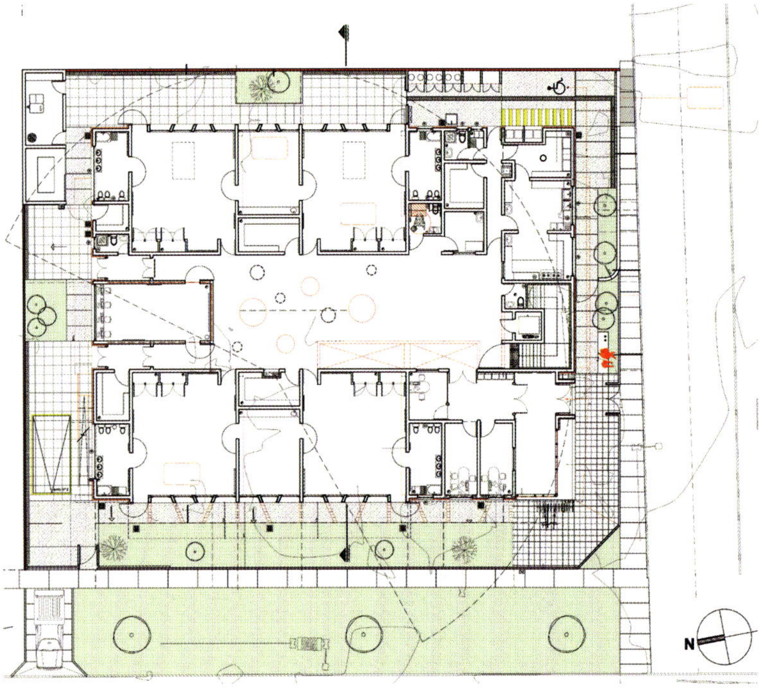

First level plan

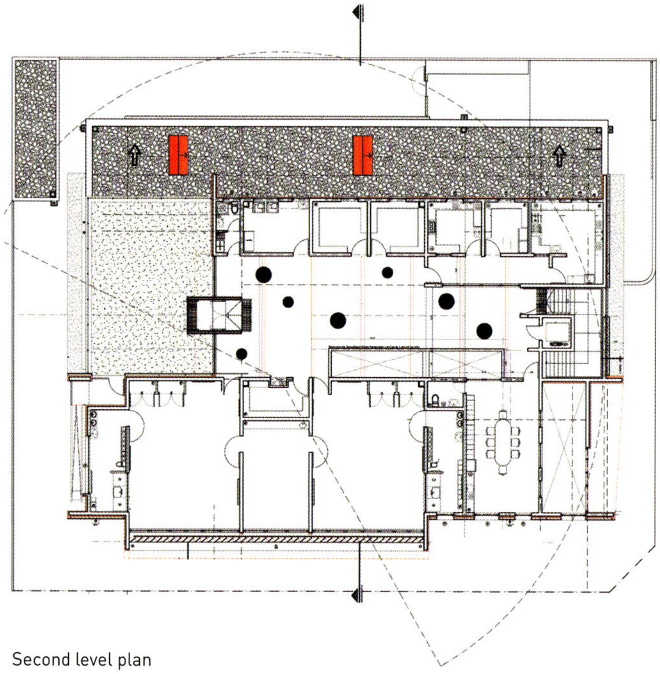

Second level plan

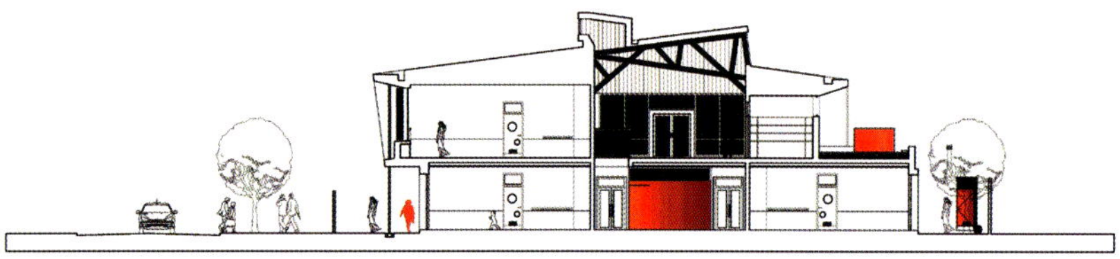

Section

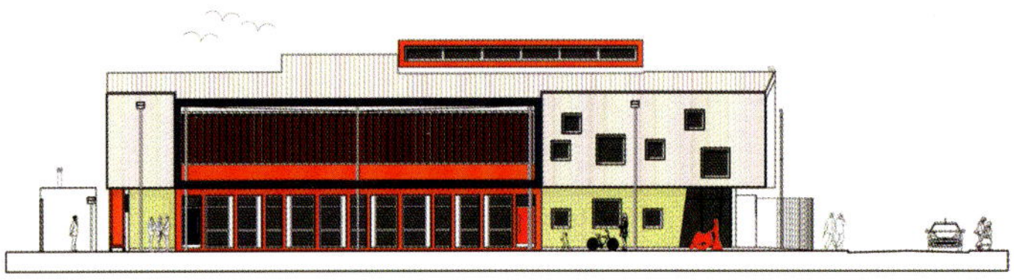

Street elevation

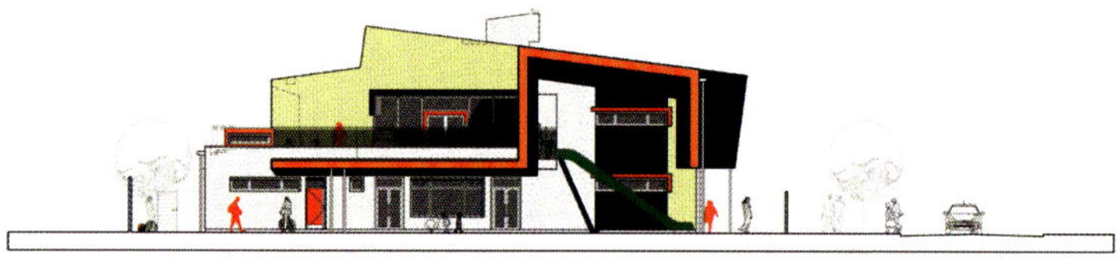

North elevation

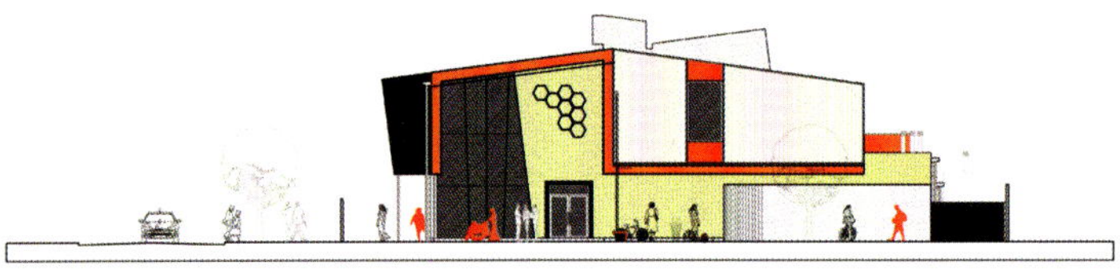

Street elevation

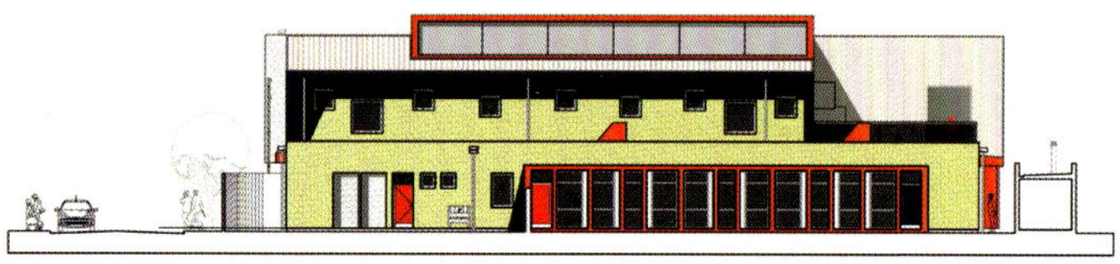

East elevation

SALIDA

Tekhnê Architectes et Urbanistes

// PROJECTS //

1. **REQUALIFICATION DU GROUPE SCOLAIRE MARCELLIN BERTHELOT**
2. **GROUPE SCOLAIRE MATERNELLE ET PRIMAIRE SIMONE VEIL**

http://www.tekhne-architectes.com

Tekhnê Architectes et Urbanistes

1.

2.

The studio, founded in 1990, brings together the multidisciplinary skills of some twenty employees, who, by exercising their collaborative intelligence, share the desire to experiment on a daily basis with architecture and urban planning that is at the service of people who respect the environment. The close dialogue established with our clients, combined with our environmental skills, has always led to the creation of rich and innovative projects that meet current and future challenges. This philosophy and practice are at the service of energy-saving projects (Positive Energy School Group, Passive Offices and Day Hospital...) but not only!
Global cost is our permanent research focus, encompassing project economics (investment, operation, maintenance), use value (comfort and simplicity of systems), materials (grey energy, health), well-being and enhancement (architectural aesthetics, landscape and bio-diversity, water management...).

L'agence fondée en 1990, réunit les compétences pluridisciplinaires d'une vingtaine de collaborateurs, qui partagent en exerçant leur intelligence collaborative, le désir d'expérimenter quotidiennement une architecture et un urbanisme au service des hommes respectueux de l'environnement. Le dialogue étroit instauré avec nos maîtres d'ouvrages allié à nos compétences environnementales, a toujours permis la naissance de projets riches et innovants, répondant aux enjeux actuels et à venir. Cette philosophie et cette pratique sont au service de projets économes en énergie (Groupe Scolaire à Energie Positive, Bureaux et Hôpital de Jour Passifs...) mais pas seulement !
Le coût global est notre axe permanent de recherche, englobant économie de projet (investissement, fonctionnement, maintenance), valeur d'usage (conforts et simplicité des systèmes), matériaux (énergie grise, santé), bien-être et valorisation (esthétique architecturale, paysage et bio-diversité, gestion de l'eau...)...

Die 1990 gegründete Agentur vereint die multidisziplinären Kompetenzen von etwa zwanzig Mitarbeitern, die durch die Ausübung ihrer kooperativen Intelligenz den Wunsch teilen, täglich mit Architektur und Stadtplanung zu experimentieren, die im Dienste von Menschen stehen, die die Umwelt respektieren. Der enge Dialog mit unseren Kunden, kombiniert mit unseren Fähigkeiten im Umweltbereich, hat stets zur Schaffung reichhaltiger und innovativer Projekte geführt, die den aktuellen und zukünftigen Herausforderungen gerecht werden. Diese Philosophie und Praxis stehen im Dienst von Energiesparprojekten (Schulgruppe Positive Energie, Passivbüros und Tagesklinik...), aber nicht nur!
Die globalen Kosten sind unser ständiger Forschungsschwerpunkt, der die Projektwirtschaft (Investition, Betrieb, Wartung), den Nutzwert (Komfort und Einfachheit der Systeme), die Materialien (graue Energie, Gesundheit), das Wohlbefinden und die Verbesserung (architektonische Ästhetik, Landschaft und biologische Vielfalt, Wassermanagement...) umfasst...

La compañía, fundada en 1990, reúne las competencias multidisciplinarias de una veintena de colaboradores que, ejerciendo su inteligencia de colaboración, comparten el deseo de experimentar diariamente con la arquitectura y el urbanismo al servicio de personas respetuosas del medio ambiente. El estrecho diálogo establecido con nuestros clientes, combinado con nuestras habilidades ambientales, nos lleva a la creación de proyectos ricos e innovadores que satisfacen los desafíos actuales y futuros. Esta filosofía y práctica están al servicio de proyectos de ahorro de energía (Grupo Escolar de Energía Positiva, Oficinas Pasivas y Hospital de Día...) ¡pero no solo eso !
El coste global es nuestro foco de investigación, abarcando la economía del proyecto (inversión, operación, mantenimiento), el valor del uso (confort y simplicidad de los sistemas), los materiales (energía gris, salud), el bienestar y la mejora (estética arquitectónica, paisaje y biodiversidad, gestión del agua...).

REQUALIFICATION DU GROUPE SCOLAIRE MARCELLIN BERTHELOT

LOCATION: **VILLEURBANNE, LYON, FRANCE**
PHOTOS: **© RENAUD ARAUD**

The intervention consists of the extension of an early 20th century school complex from 18 to 25 classrooms. To do this, the extension was designed as a bridge building, raising it off the ground to return it to the playground. The structure, built entirely of wood, connects the two existing schools, forms a courtyard and marks the entrance to the school complex. The street front of the building reflects the two great challenges of ultramodernity, the ecological and the digital. The façade of the second new building is made up of wood-clad pavilions, arranged in a discontinuous fashion to fit in with the continuity of the neighbourhood. The street façade of the bridge building, the focal point of the complex, abandons materials of biological origin to offer an image more in keeping with the digital culture characteristic of the 21st century.

Die Intervention besteht in der Erweiterung eines Schulkomplexes aus dem frühen 20. Jahrhundert von 18 auf 25 Klassenzimmer. Zu diesem Zweck wurde der Erweiterungsbau als Brückenbau konzipiert, indem er vom Boden abgehoben wurde, um ihn wieder auf den Spielplatz zu bringen. Der vollständig aus Holz errichtete Bau verbindet die beiden bestehenden Schulen, bildet einen Innenhof und markiert den Eingang zum Schulkomplex. Die Straßenfront des Gebäudes spiegelt die beiden großen Herausforderungen der Ultramodernität wider, die ökologische und die digitale. Die Fassade des zweiten neuen Gebäudes besteht aus holzverkleideten Pavillons, die diskontinuierlich angeordnet sind, um sich in die Kontinuität des Viertels einzufügen. Die Straßenfassade des Brückengebäudes, dem Mittelpunkt des Komplexes, verzichtet auf Materialien biologischen Ursprungs, um ein Bild zu bieten, das der für das 21. Jahrhundert charakteristischen digitalen Kultur besser entspricht.

L'intervention consiste en l'agrandissement d'un complexe scolaire du début du XXe siècle de 18 à 25 salles de classe. À cette fin, l'extension est conçue en bâtiment pont et libère le sol pour le restituer à la cour de récréation. L'ouvrage, construit entièrement en bois, relie les deux écoles existantes, forme un préau et marque l'entrée du groupe scolaire. La façade vers la rue du complexe reflète les deux grands défis de l'ultramodernité, l'écologique et le numérique. La façade du deuxième nouveau bâtiment est composée de pavillons revêtus de bois, disposés de manière discontinue pour s'inscire dans la continuité du voisinage. La façade sur rue du bâtiment pont, point de convergence des équipements, abandonne les matériaux biosourcés pour offrir une image plus conforme à la culture numérique caractéristique du XXIe siècle.

La intervención consiste en la ampliación de un complejo escolar de principios del siglo XX de 18 a 25 aulas. Para ello, la extensión se diseñó como un edificio puente, elevándolo del suelo para devolverlo al patio de recreo. La estructura, construida totalmente de madera, conecta las dos escuelas existentes, forma un patio y marca la entrada al complejo escolar. El frente de la calle del edificio refleja los dos grandes desafíos de la ultramodernidad, el ecológico y el digital. La fachada del segundo nuevo edificio se compone de pabellones revestidos de madera, dispuestos de forma discontinua para encajar en la continuidad del barrio. La fachada de la calle del edificio del puente, el punto focal del conjunto, abandona los materiales de origen biológico para ofrecer una imagen más acorde con la cultura digital característica del siglo XXI.

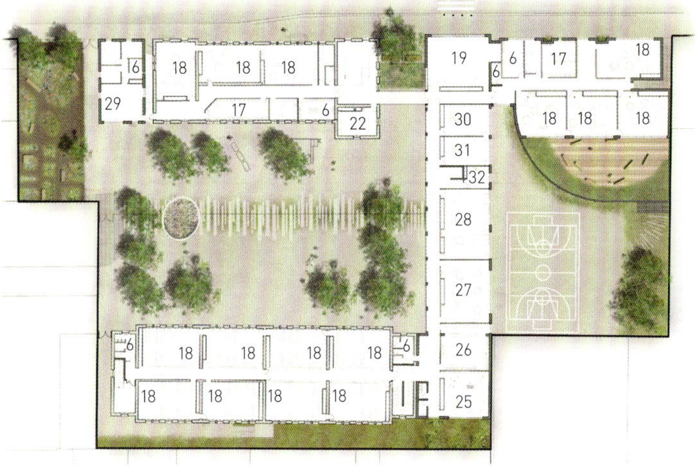

First floor plan

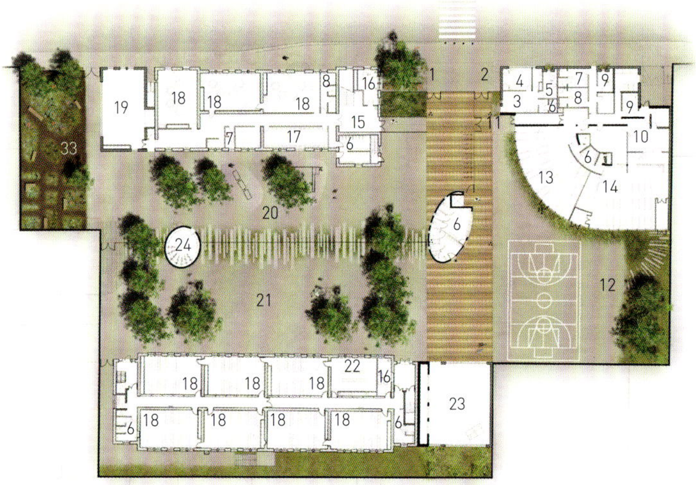

Ground floor plan

1. Preschool entry
2. Primary school entry
3. Hall
4. Nurse's office
5. First aid room
6. Toilet room
7. Boys' changing room
8. Girls' changing room
9. Box
10. Cold store
11. Covered entry to preschool dining hall
12. Entry to primary school dining hall
13. Preschool dining hall
14. Primary school dining hall
15. Hall
16. School principal's office
17. Resting room
18. Classroom
19. Motor-skills development room
20. Preschool playground
21. Primary school playground
22. Staff room
23. Gymnasium
24. Bikes and toys storage
25. Multipurpose room
26. Computer room
27. Visual arts
28. Library
29. Kitchen/living area
30. Reinforcement room
31. CLAD room
32. Psychologist's office
33. Vegetable garden

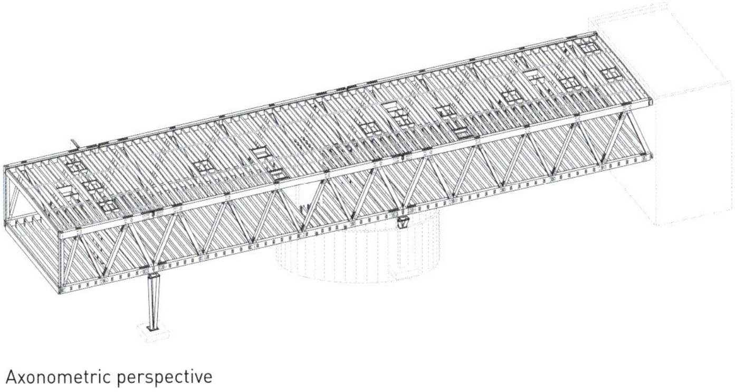

Axonometric perspective

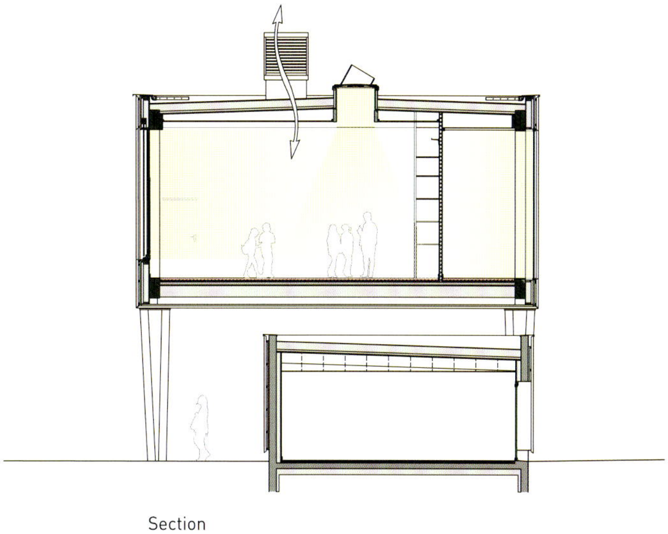

Section

GROUPE SCOLAIRE MATERNELLE ET PRIMAIRE SIMONE VEIL

LOCATION: **BOURGOIN JALLIEU, FRANCE**
PHOTOS: © **RENAUD ARAUD**

This school group is located next to an urban park, along a promenade that waters the conversion of an industrial area in the process of transformation. It is structured in two parallel blocks, corresponding to the nursery and primary school, connected by a bridge anchored to the land by means of an organic volume that houses the auxiliary spaces. This construction layout allows the view of the park to be maintained from the playgrounds and the two courtyards on the ground floor. The fixed wooden brise-soleil on the north and south façades creates a smooth transition to the west side, where the predominant wood establishes a polite relationship with the park. The project integrates different bioclimatic strategies for energy efficiency. Thanks to an insulated envolture, natural light is abundant in all rooms. Natural ventilation is achieved by means of a tower that causes passive cooling during the hours when there is no sunlight.

Diese Schulgruppe befindet sich neben einem städtischen Park, entlang einer Promenade, die die Umwandlung eines Industriegebiets im Transformationsprozess begleitet. Es ist in zwei parallele Blöcke gegliedert, die dem Kindergarten und der Grundschule entsprechen und durch eine Brücke verbunden sind, die durch ein organisches Volumen, das die Nebenräume beherbergt, im Gelände verankert ist. Diese Bauweise ermöglicht es, den Blick auf den Park von den Spielplätzen und den beiden Höfen im Erdgeschoss aus aufrecht zu erhalten. Der feste hölzerne Sonnenschirm an der Nord- und Südfassade schafft einen fließenden Übergang zur Westfassade, wo das vorherrschende Holz eine höfliche Beziehung zum Park herstellt. Das Projekt integriert verschiedene bioklimatische Strategien für Energieeffizienz. Dank einer isolierten Hülle ist natürliches Licht in allen Räumen reichlich vorhanden. Die natürliche Belüftung wird durch einen Turm erreicht, der in den sonnenlichtlosen Stunden eine passive Kühlung bewirkt.

Ce groupe scolaire est situé à côté d'un parc urbain, le long d'une promenade qui irrigue la reconversion d'une zone industrielle en transformation. Il est structuré en deux blocs parallèles, correspondant à la maternelle et à l'école primaire, reliés par un pont ancré au terrain au moyen d'un volume organique qui abrite les espaces auxiliaires. Cette disposition constructive permet de conserver la vue sur le parc depuis les aires de jeux et de créer deux préaux au rez-de-chaussée. Les brise-soleil en bois fixes des façades nord et sud créent une transition en douceur vers la façade ouest, où le bois prédominant établit une relation de courtoisie avec le parc. Le projet intègre différentes stratégies bioclimatiques pour l'efficacité energétique et le confort d'été. L'enveloppe est surisolée, la lumière naturelle est abondante dans tous les locaux et circulations, et la ventilation naturelle assistée par tourelles permet le rafraichissement passif nocturne.

Este grupo escolar está situado junto a un parque urbano, a lo largo de un paseo que riega la reconversión de una zona industrial en fase de transformación. Se estructura en dos bloques paralelos, correspondientes a la guardería y a la escuela primaria, conectados por un puente anclado al terreno mediante un volumen orgánico que alberga los espacios auxiliares. Esta disposición constructiva permite mantener la vista del parque desde los patios de recreo y los dos patios de la planta baja. El parasol de madera fijo en las fachadas norte y sur crea una transición suave a la fachada oeste, donde la madera predominante establece una relación cortés con el parque. El proyecto integra diferentes estrategias bioclimáticas para la eficiencia energética. Gracias a una envoltura aislada, la luz natural es abundante en todas las habitaciones. La ventilación natural se consigue por medio de una torreta que provoca un enfriamiento pasivo durante las horas sin luz solar.

Site plan

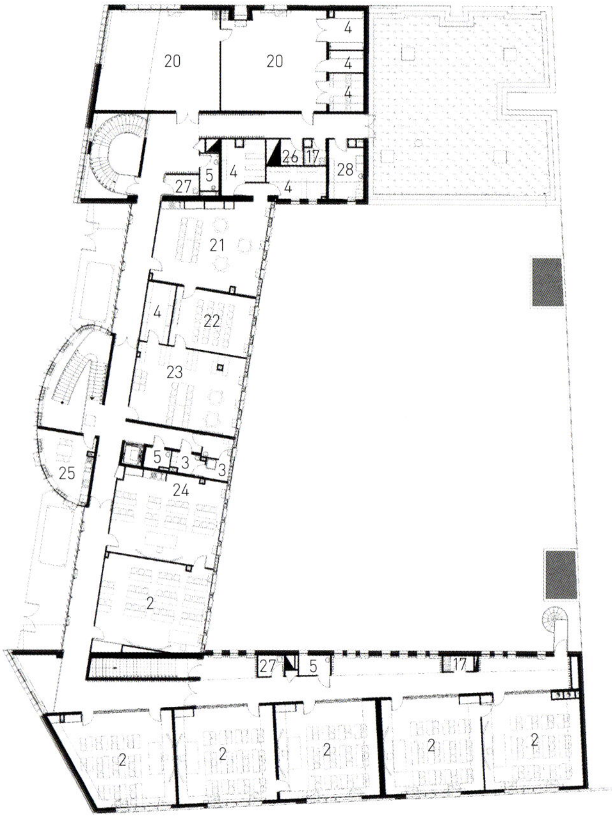

First floor plan

Sustainability diagram

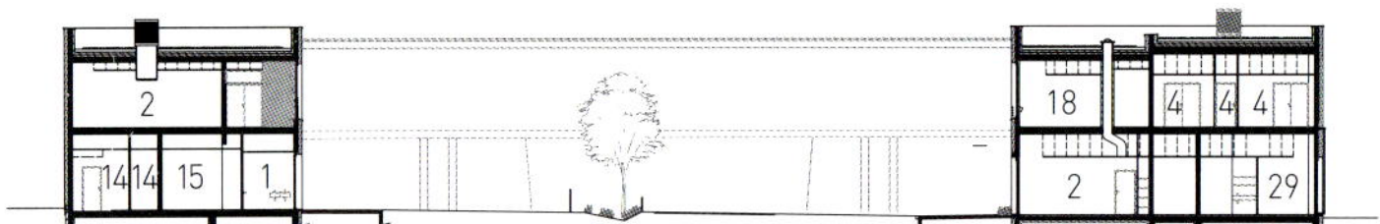

Cross section

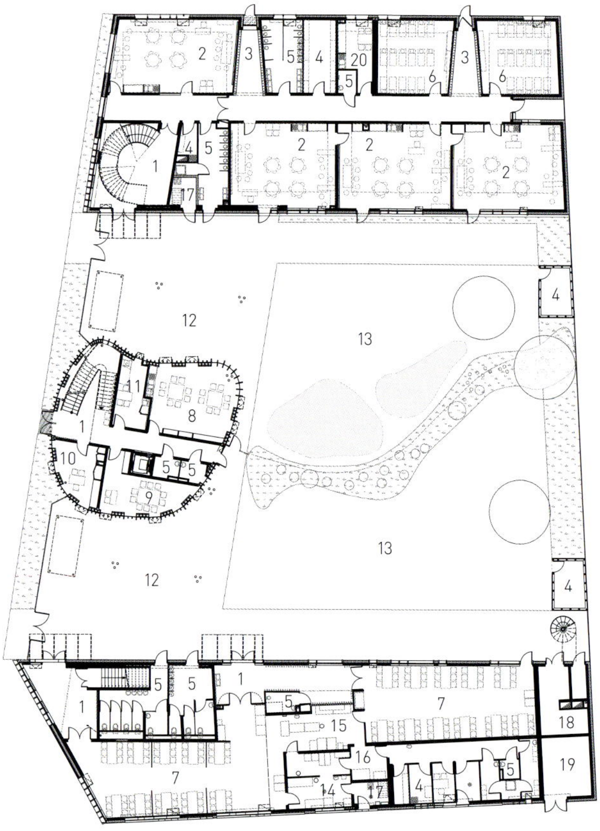

Ground floor plan

1. Entry
2. Classroom
3. Changing room
4. Storage
5. Toilet room
6. Break room
7. Dining hall
8. Educational team room
9. Specialized Support Network for Students with Difficulties
10. Principal's office
11. Nurse's office
12. Covered playground
13. Playgrounds
14. Launderette
15. Preparation / reheating
16. Cold room
17. Garbage
18. Ventilation
19. Boiler room
20. Motor-skills development room
21. Music and arts classroom
22. Audiovisual classroom
23. Library
24. Inclusive education classroom
25. Staff room
26. VDI room, (Voice, Data, Image)
27. Housekeeping room
28. Launderette
29. Specialized Territorial Agent for Nursery Schools

UArchitects
Misak Terzibasiyan

© MARIJKE KREKELS

// PROJECTS //

1. IKC DE GELUKSVOGEL
2. SCHOOL 'T HOFKE
3. SCHOOL DE BRUG

www.uarchitects.com

UArchitects
Misak Terzibasiyan

1.

2.

3.

UArchitects is fascinated by the interplay of levels of scale and imagination: the scale of the city and the scale of the individual; imagination in the abstract and imagination in concrete form. They do not look for the interconnection in just one relentless, dogmatic theme; they prefer to investigate it in a range of different concepts. Their design philosophy remains recognizable throughout: intuitive and reflective and always based on the fascination for people and places. It is not a typical critical regionalism, but a more sensitive open approach of the context.
The founder and owner of UArchitects, Misak Terzibasiyan, is personally and professionally focusing on an international context as well as on the influence of cultural themes. He is convinced that architecture is all about people and their cultural environment. Architecture of modesty and humanity are key words in his approach. This can only be achieved through permanent communication with users and clients in an open dialogue.

UArchitects est fasciné par l'interaction des niveaux d'échelle et de l'imagination : l'échelle de la ville et l'échelle de l'individu ; l'imagination dans l'abstrait et l'imagination dans le concret. Ils ne recherchent pas l'interconnexion dans un seul thème dogmatique et implacable ; ils préfèrent l'étudier dans une série de concepts différents. Leur philosophie de conception reste reconnaissable entre toutes : intuitive et réfléchie et toujours basée sur la fascination pour les gens et les lieux. Il ne s'agit pas d'un régionalisme critique typique, mais d'une approche plus sensible et ouverte du contexte.
Le fondateur et propriétaire d'UArchitects, Misak Terzibasiyan, se concentre personnellement et professionnellement sur un contexte international ainsi que sur l'influence des thèmes culturels. Il est convaincu que l'architecture est une affaire de personnes et de leur environnement culturel. Architecture de la modestie et de l'humanité sont les mots clés de sa démarche. Cela ne peut être réalisé que par une communication permanente avec les utilisateurs et les clients dans un dialogue ouvert.

UArchitects ist fasziniert von der Interaktion der Ebenen von Maßstab und Imagination: der Maßstab der Stadt und der Maßstab des Individuums; Imagination im Abstrakten und Imagination im Konkreten. Sie suchen nicht die Verbindung in einem einzigen schonungslosen dogmatischen Thema, sondern ziehen es vor, es in einer Reihe verschiedener Konzepte zu untersuchen. Seine Designphilosophie bleibt jederzeit erkennbar: intuitiv und durchdacht und immer von der Faszination für Menschen und Orte getragen. Es handelt sich nicht um einen typischen kritischen Regionalismus, sondern um einen offenen, kontextsensitiveren Ansatz.
Der Gründer und Eigentümer von UArchitects, Misak Terzibasiyan, konzentriert sich persönlich und beruflich auf einen internationalen Kontext sowie auf den Einfluss kultureller Fragen. Er ist überzeugt, dass es in der Architektur um den Menschen und sein kulturelles Umfeld geht. Die Architektur der Bescheidenheit und Menschlichkeit sind Schlüsselwörter in seinem Ansatz. Dies kann nur durch permanente Kommunikation mit Nutzern und Kunden in einem offenen Dialog erreicht werden.

UArchitects está fascinado por la interacción de los niveles de escala e imaginación: la escala de la ciudad y la escala del individuo; la imaginación en lo abstracto y la imaginación en lo concreto. No buscan la interconexión en un solo tema dogmático implacable, sino que prefieren investigarlo en una serie de conceptos diferentes. Su filosofía de diseño sigue siendo reconocible en todo momento: intuitiva y reflexiva y siempre basada en la fascinación por la gente y los lugares. No se trata de un típico regionalismo crítico, sino de un enfoque abierto más sensible del contexto.
El fundador y propietario de UArchitects, Misak Terzibasiyan, se centra personal y profesionalmente en un contexto internacional, así como en la influencia de los temas culturales. Está convencido de que la arquitectura es todo acerca de las personas y su entorno cultural. La arquitectura de la modestia y la humanidad son palabras clave en su enfoque. Esto solo puede lograrse mediante una comunicación permanente con los usuarios y clientes en un diálogo abierto.

IKC DE GELUKSVOGEL

LOCATION: **MAASTRICHT, THE NETHERLANDS**
PHOTOS: **© DAAN DIJKMEIJER**

This is a building that includes a kindergarten, primary school, gymnasium and library, the result of the merger of two nearby schools. The resulting modern school implements a new digital education system that promotes learning about the environment, nature and sustainability. This new way of teaching and the new virtual reality in which we live are reflected in the architecture of the building through the brick elements of the façades, which compose random messages in binary code. Both the design of the school and the building escape the classical educational systems and use a concept of free movement and free use of space based on the idea of the movement of a flock of birds. Educational spaces are not limited to classrooms and can be extended to other open spaces for different purposes.

Il s'agit d'un bâtiment qui comprend un jardin d'enfants, une école primaire, un gymnase et une bibliothèque, résultat de la fusion de deux écoles voisines. L'école moderne qui en résulte met en œuvre un nouveau système d'éducation numérique qui favorise l'apprentissage de l'environnement, de la nature et de la durabilité. Cette nouvelle façon d'enseigner et la nouvelle réalité virtuelle dans laquelle nous vivons se reflètent dans l'architecture du bâtiment à travers les éléments de brique des façades, qui composent des messages aléatoires en code binaire. La conception de l'école et du bâtiment échappe aux systèmes éducatifs classiques et utilise un concept de libre circulation et de libre utilisation de l'espace basé sur l'idée du mouvement d'une volée d'oiseaux. Les espaces éducatifs ne sont pas limités aux salles de classe et peuvent être étendus à d'autres espaces ouverts à des fins différentes.

Es handelt sich um ein Gebäude, das einen Kindergarten, eine Grundschule, eine Turnhalle und eine Bibliothek umfasst, die aus der Zusammenlegung von zwei nahe gelegenen Schulen hervorgegangen ist. Die daraus entstandene moderne Schule implementiert ein neues digitales Bildungssystem, das das Lernen über Umwelt, Natur und Nachhaltigkeit fördert. Diese neue Art des Unterrichts und die neue virtuelle Realität, in der wir leben, spiegeln sich in der Architektur des Gebäudes durch die Ziegelsteinelemente der Fassaden wider, die zufällige Nachrichten im Binärcode zusammensetzen. Sowohl die Gestaltung der Schule als auch des Gebäudes entziehen sich den klassischen Bildungssystemen und verwenden ein Konzept der freien Bewegung und der freien Raumnutzung, das auf der Idee der Bewegung eines Vogelschwarms basiert. Bildungsräume sind nicht auf Klassenzimmer beschränkt und können für verschiedene Zwecke auf andere offene Räume ausgedehnt werden.

Este es un edificio que engloba jardín de infancia, escuela primaria, gimnasio y biblioteca, fruto de la fusión de dos escuelas próximas. La moderna escuela resultante implanta un nuevo sistema de educación digital que fomenta el aprendizaje sobre el medio ambiente, la naturaleza y la sostenibilidad. Esta nueva forma de enseñanza y la nueva realidad virtual en la que vivimos se reflejan en la arquitectura del edificio a través los elementos de ladrillo de las fachadas, que componen mensajes aleatorios en código binario. Tanto el diseño de la escuela como el del edificio huyen de los sistemas educativos clásicos y utilizan un concepto de libre circulación y uso libre de espacios basado en la idea del movimiento de una bandada de pájaros. Los espacios educativos no están limitados a las aulas y pueden prolongarse hacia otros espacios abiertos con fines diferentes.

Ground floor plan

1. Entrance
2. Multifunctional room
3. Day care
4. Reception / library
5. Meeting room
6. Playroom
7. Mutlifunctional room
8. Classroom
9. Dressing room
10. Gym

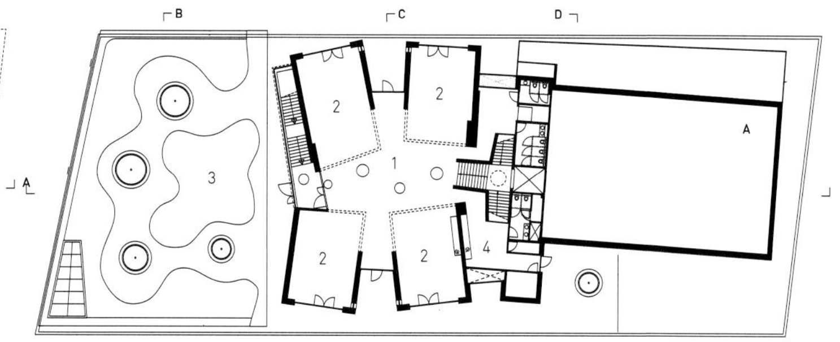

First floor plan

SCHOOL 'T HOFKE

LOCATION: EINDHOVEN, THE NETHERLANDS
PHOTOS: © DAAN DIJKMEIJER

This primary school houses facilities dedicated to teaching, childcare, sports and neighbourhood activities, and replaces a highly regarded school in the neighbourhood. The project evokes the old school through the design of a central open space that distributes the users and which is manifested in the façade, and through the exterior brick cladding, which evokes the white colour of the old school and whose texture imitates the barks of the monumental trees in the surroundings. The white spaces alternate with areas clad in wood, which show a texture based on the rhythm of the trees and on the cane mats that protect them. A process of seeking links with the context, reflected in the interior and exterior design, generates an image of the building that inspires confidence and makes the children feel at home.

Diese Grundschule beherbergt Einrichtungen für Unterricht, Kinderbetreuung, Sport und Nachbarschaftsaktivitäten und ersetzt eine hoch angesehene Schule in der Nachbarschaft. Das Projekt erinnert an die alte Schule durch die Gestaltung eines zentralen offenen Raumes, der die Nutzer verteilt und sich in der Fassade manifestiert, und durch die äußere Verkleidung aus Ziegelsteinen, die an die weiße Farbe der alten Schule erinnert und deren Textur die Rinden der monumentalen Bäume in der Umgebung imitiert. Die weißen Flächen wechseln sich ab mit mit Holz verkleideten Flächen, die eine Textur aufweisen, die auf dem Rhythmus der Bäume und auf den sie schützenden Rohrmatten beruht. Ein Prozess der Suche nach Verbindungen mit dem Kontext, der sich in der Innen- und Außengestaltung widerspiegelt, erzeugt ein Bild des Gebäudes, das Vertrauen erweckt und den Kindern das Gefühl gibt, zu Hause zu sein.

Cette école primaire abrite des installations dédiées à l'enseignement, à la garde d'enfants, aux sports et aux activités de quartier, et remplace une école très réputée du quartier. Le projet évoque l'ancienne école par la conception d'un espace central ouvert qui distribue les utilisateurs et qui se manifeste dans la façade, et par le revêtement extérieur en briques, qui évoque la couleur blanche de l'ancienne école et dont la texture imite les écorces des arbres monumentaux des environs. Les zones blanches alternent avec des zones revêtues de bois, qui présentent une texture basée sur le rythme des arbres et sur les nattes de canne qui les protègent. Un processus de recherche de liens avec le contexte, qui se reflète dans la conception intérieure et extérieure, génère une image du bâtiment qui inspire confiance et fait en sorte que les enfants se sentent chez eux.

Esta escuela primaria alberga instalaciones dedicadas a la enseñanza, los cuidados infantiles, los deportes y las actividades vecinales, y reemplaza a una escuela muy apreciada en el vecindario. El proyecto evoca la vieja escuela mediante el diseño de un espacio central abierto que distribuye a los usuarios y que se manifiesta en la fachada, y a través del revestimiento exterior de ladrillos, que evoca el color blanco de la antigua escuela y cuya textura imita las cortezas de los árboles monumentales del entorno. Las zonas blancas se alternan con zonas revestidas de madera, que muestran una textura basada en el ritmo de los áboles y en las esteras de caña que los protegen. Un proceso de búsqueda de vinculos con el contexto, reflejado en el diseño de interiores y exteriores, genera una imagen del edificio que inspira confianza y hace que los niños se sientan como en casa.

Site plan

1. Protected green area
2. Playground
3. Parking

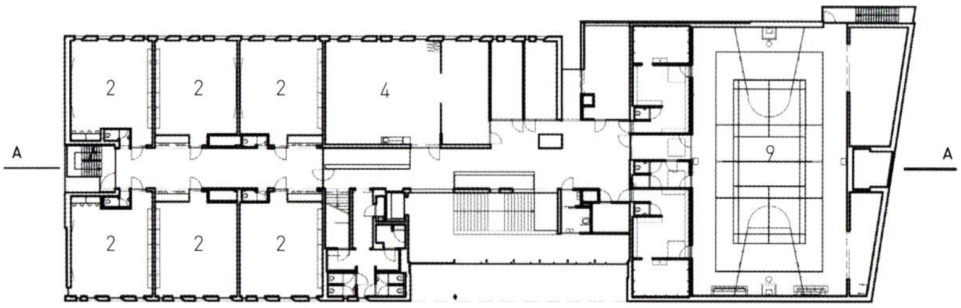

First floor plan

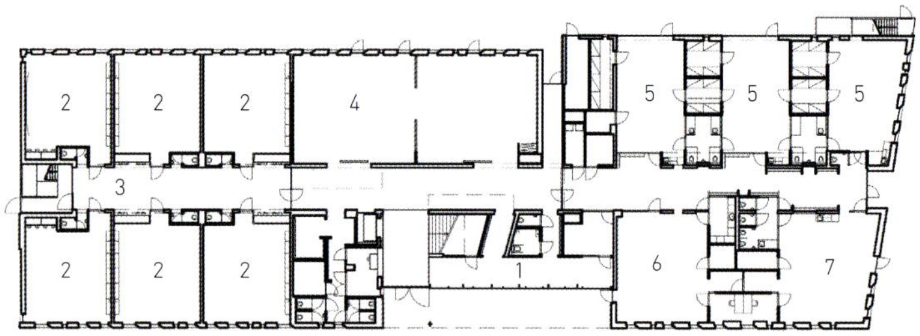

Ground floor plan

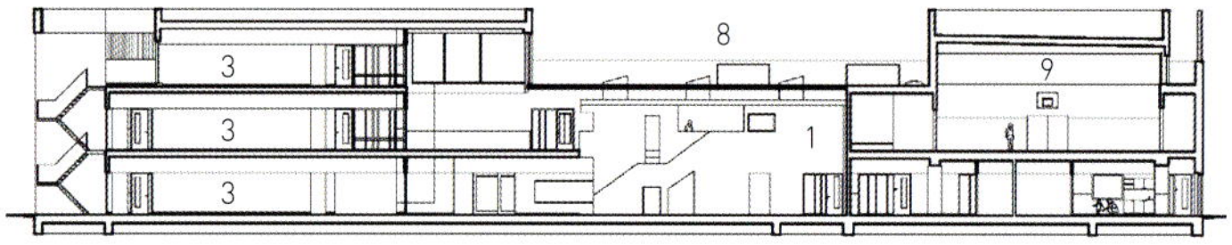

Section A-A

1. Hall
2. Class
3. Digital learning
4. Multifunctional room
5. Day care
6. Extracurricular
7. Kindergarten
8. Roof terrace
9. Gym

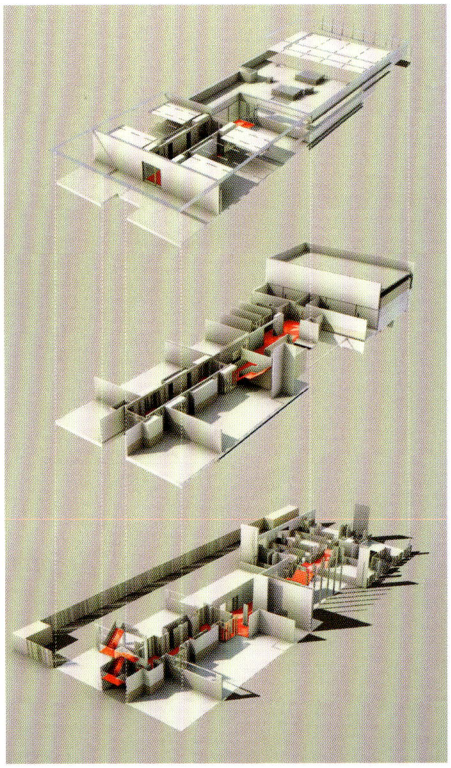

Render

East elevation

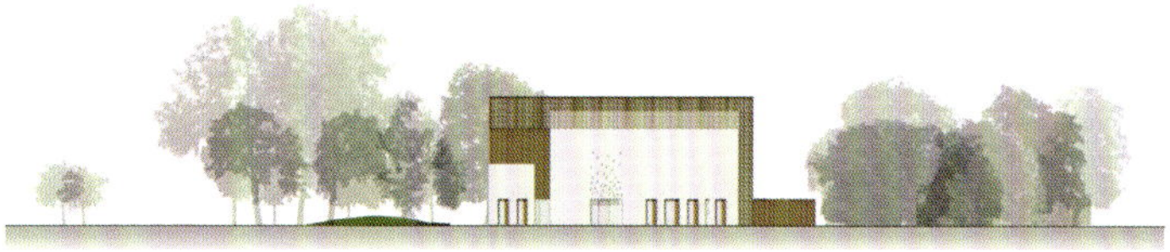

North elevation

South elevation

West elevation

SCHOOL DE BRUG

LOCATION: BOCHOLT, BELGIUM
PHOTOS: © DAAN DIJKMEIJER

The architecture of this school reflects its educational philosophy, in which the children are the central focus and the building is constructed around them. However, in an ambiguous way, this concentric scheme is superimposed on a centrifugal arrangement of the classrooms that generates a compact volume and expresses the children's path towards integration into society. In the centre of the building, a skylight directs natural light into the large, circular, multi-purpose common space that constitutes the heart of the school. The wooden cladding at the entrance and in the central space gives the interior a warm texture. The recycling and sustainability measures implemented, as well as the outdoor green areas, make the building an educational tool that promotes environmental awareness as a fundamental part of the school experience.

Die Architektur dieser Schule spiegelt ihre pädagogische Philosophie wider, bei der die Kinder im Mittelpunkt stehen und das Gebäude um sie herum gebaut ist. Dieses konzentrische Schema überlagert jedoch auf mehrdeutige Weise eine zentrifugale Anordnung der Klassenräume, die ein kompaktes Volumen erzeugt und den Weg der Kinder zur Integration in die Gesellschaft zum Ausdruck bringt. In der Mitte des Gebäudes lenkt ein Oberlicht natürliches Licht in den großen, kreisförmigen Mehrzweck-Gemeinschaftsraum, der das Herz der Schule bildet. Die Holzverkleidung am Eingang und im zentralen Raum verleiht dem Innenraum eine warme Textur. Die umgesetzten Recycling- und Nachhaltigkeitsmaßnahmen sowie die Grünflächen im Freien machen das Gebäude zu einem pädagogischen Instrument, das das Umweltbewusstsein als grundlegenden Teil der Schulerfahrung fördert.

L'architecture de cette école reflète sa philosophie éducative, dans laquelle les enfants sont au centre de l'attention et le bâtiment est construit autour d'eux. Cependant, de manière ambiguë, ce schéma concentrique se superpose à un agencement centrifuge des salles de classe qui génère un volume compact et exprime le cheminement des enfants vers l'intégration dans la société. Au centre du bâtiment, une lucarne dirige la lumière naturelle dans le grand espace commun circulaire et polyvalent qui constitue le cœur de l'école. Le revêtement en bois à l'entrée et dans l'espace central donne à l'intérieur une texture chaude. Les mesures de recyclage et de durabilité mises en œuvre, ainsi que les espaces verts extérieurs, font du bâtiment un outil éducatif qui favorise la sensibilisation à l'environnement en tant que partie fondamentale de l'expérience scolaire.

La arquitectura de esta escuela refleja su filosofía educativa, en la que los niños son el foco central y el edificio se construye alrededor de ellos. Sin embargo, de forma ambigua, a este esquema concéntrico se le superpone una disposición centrífuga de las aulas que genera un volumen compacto y que expresa el camino de los niños hacia la integración en la sociedad. En el centro del edificio, una claraboya conduce la luz natural hacia el gran espacio común multiusos de forma circular que constituye el corazón de la escuela. El revestimiento de madera de la entrada y del espacio central aportan una cálida textura al interior. Las medidas de reciclaje y sostenibilidad implantadas, así como las áreas verdes exteriores, convierten al edificio en una herramienta educativa que fomenta la conciencia medioambiental como parte fundamental de la experiencia de la escuela.

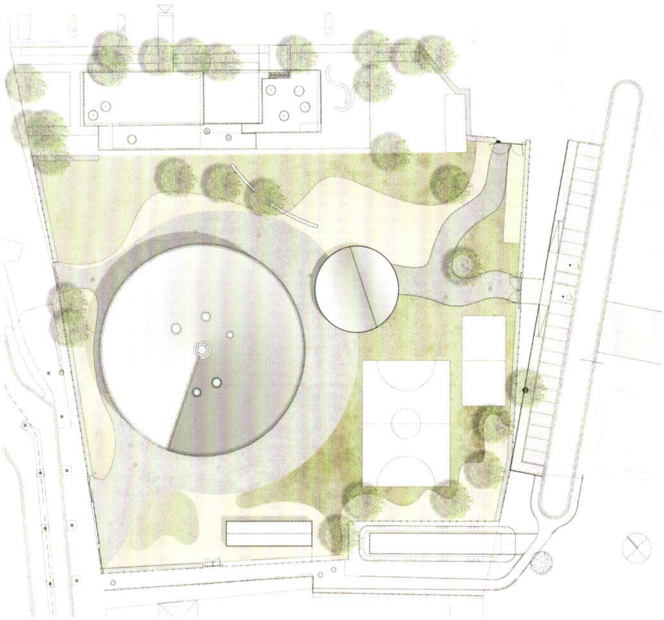

Site plan

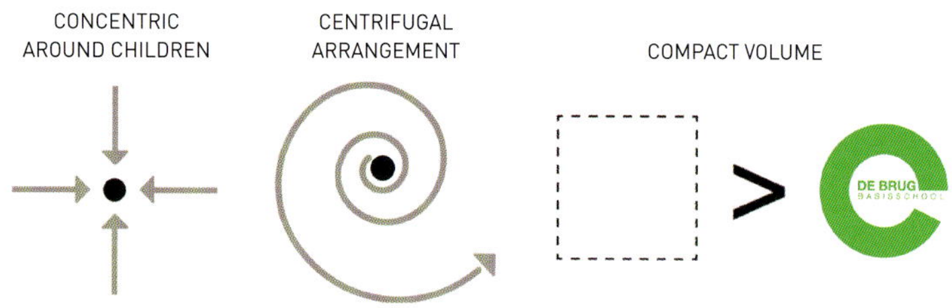

Conceptual diagram

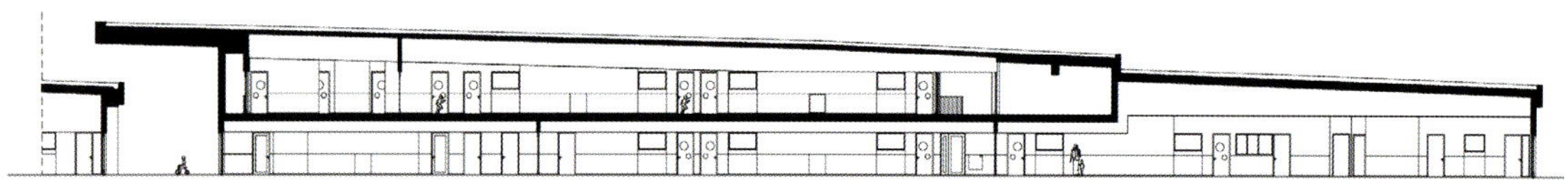

Section

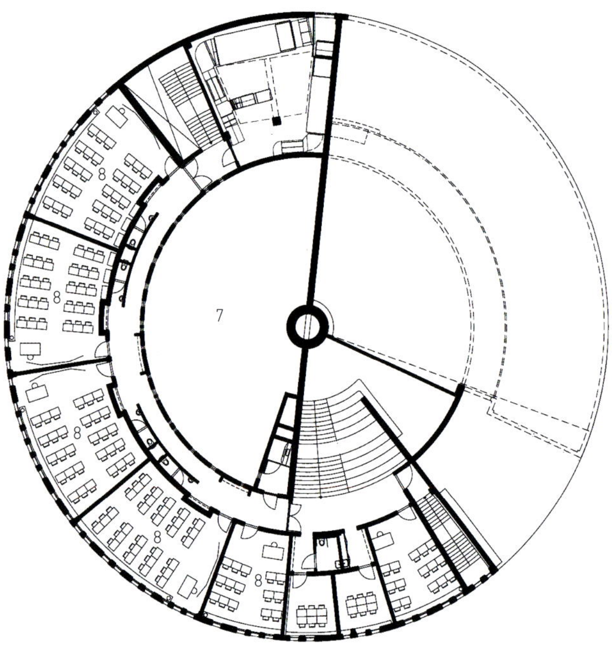

First floor plan

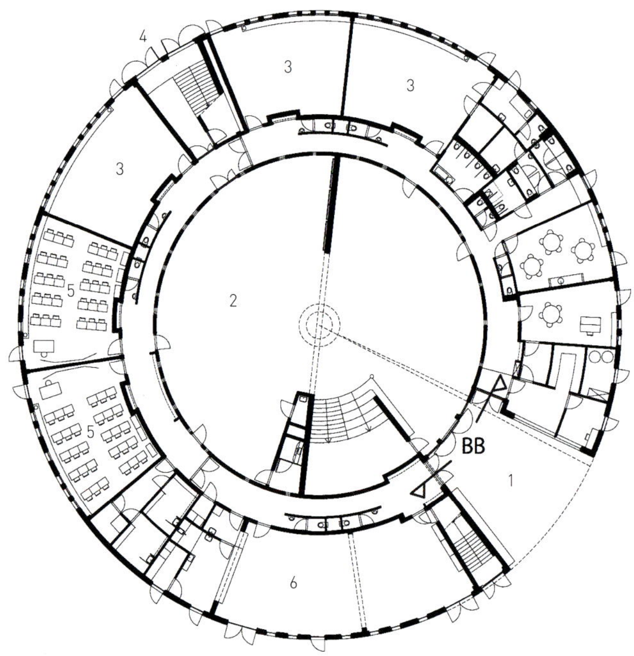

Ground floor plan

1. Entrance
2. Common space
3. Kindergarten
4. Second entrance
5. Classroom
6. Restaurant

v-architekten

// PROJECTS //

1. **BERKERSHEIMER SCHULE**
2. **BLAUE KITA MONHEIM**

www.v-architekten.com

v-architekten

1.

2.

v-architekten was founded in Cologne in 2008 by Tim Denninger, Jan Hertel, Markus Kilian, Diana Reichle and Michael Scholz. Characteristic for our work is an open and curious approach to new projects. We do not regard construction tasks that require a complex examination of the existing building, whether in an urban context or in the building stock, or planning under difficult conditions, such as a tight budget or a tight time frame, as a restriction, but rather as a special challenge. It is precisely these constraints that give rise to simple and clear concepts through precise analysis, which develop their strength from the inner logic of the location and function. Against the background of a holistic approach to each construction task, we design buildings and urban spaces in close cooperation with the owners, specialist planners and future users, which will be successful in the long term, and thus, sustainable.

v-architekten a été fondée à Cologne en 2008 par Tim Denninger, Jan Hertel, Markus Kilian, Diana Reichle et Michael Scholz. Notre travail se caractérise par une approche ouverte et curieuse des nouveaux projets. Nous ne considérons pas comme une restriction les tâches de construction qui nécessitent un examen complexe du bâtiment existant, que ce soit dans un contexte urbain ou dans le parc immobilier, ou une planification dans des conditions difficiles, comme un budget ou un délai serré, mais plutôt comme un défi particulier. Ce sont précisément ces contraintes qui donnent naissance à des concepts simples et clairs par une analyse précise, qui développent leur force à partir de la logique interne de l'emplacement et de la fonction. Dans le cadre d'une approche holistique de chaque tâche de construction, nous concevons des bâtiments et des espaces urbains en étroite collaboration avec les propriétaires, les planificateurs spécialisés et les futurs utilisateurs, qui seront couronnés de succès à long terme, et donc, durables.

v-architekten wurde von Tim Denninger, Jan Hertel, Markus Kilian, Diana Reichle und Michael Scholz 2008 in Köln gegründet. Charakteristisch für unsere Arbeiten ist eine offene und neugierige Herangehensweise an neue Projekte. Bauaufgaben, die eine komplexe Auseinandersetzungen mit dem Bestand erfordern, sei es im städtischen Kontext oder im Gebäudebestand, oder das Planen unter schwierigen Rahmenbedingungen, wie einem knappen Budget oder einem engen Zeitrahmen, sehen wir nicht als Einschränkung, sondern vielmehr als besondere Herausforderung an. Gerade aus diesen Zwängen heraus entstehen durch präzise Analysen einfache und klare Konzepte, die ihre Stärke aus der inneren Logik des Ortes und der Funktion heraus entwickeln. Vor dem Hintergrund einer ganzheitlichen Betrachtungsweise jeder Bauaufgabe entwerfen wir in enger Zusammenarbeit mit den Bauherren, Fachplanern und künftigen Nutzern Gebäude und Stadträume, die langfristig – und damit nachhaltig – Erfolg haben.

v-architekten fue fundada en Colonia en 2008 por Tim Denninger, Jan Hertel, Markus Kilian, Diana Reichle y Michael Scholz. Lo característico de nuestro trabajo es el enfoque abierto y curioso frente a los nuevos proyectos. No consideramos que las tareas de construcción que requieren un examen complejo, ya sea en un contexto urbano, en un proceso de remodelación, o en la planificación en condiciones difíciles, tales como un presupuesto o un plazo de tiempo reducido, sean una restricción, sino más bien un desafío. Son precisamente estas limitaciones las que dan lugar a conceptos simples y claros a través de un análisis preciso; conceptos que desarrollan su fuerza a partir de la lógica interna de la ubicación y la función futura. Con el trasfondo de un enfoque holístico de cada tarea de construcción, diseñamos edificios y espacios urbanos en estrecha colaboración con los propietarios, los especialistas y los futuros usuarios, lo que asegura el éxito a largo plazo y, por tanto, su sostenibilidad.

BERKERSHEIMER SCHULE

LOCATION: **FRANKFURT AM MAIN, GERMANY**
PHOTOS: © **CONSTANTIN MEYER**

The layout of this primary school and its position in the centre of the plot create three outdoor areas that allow for differentiated activities. The main access through the school yard leads to a large double height hall, around which the different areas are organized and which constitutes the heart of the building. This foyer can be used as a meeting area or for large school events, which turns the spacious staircase connecting the two levels into a "seating landscape". The design of the building adopts the passivhaus insulation standards and incorporates various sustainability oriented measures. The new school is attractive and open in its spatial structure and in the design of its façade, developing an architecture that reinforces the concept of inclusion, the main objective of its educational philosophy.

Der Grundriss dieser Grundschule und ihre Lage in der Mitte des Grundstücks schaffen drei Außenbereiche, die differenzierte Aktivitäten ermöglichen. Der Hauptzugang über den Schulhof führt zu einer großen Pausenhalle mit doppelter Höhe, um die herum die verschiedenen Bereiche organisiert sind und die das Herzstück des Gebäudes bildet. Dieses Foyer kann als Versammlungsraum oder für große Schulveranstaltungen genutzt werden, wodurch das großzügige Treppenhaus, das die beiden Ebenen verbindet, zu einer „Sitzlandschaft" wird. Der Entwurf des Gebäudes orientiert sich an den Passivhaus-Dämmstandards und berücksichtigt verschiedene nachhaltigkeitsorientierte Maßnahmen. Die neue Schule ist attraktiv und offen in ihrer räumlichen Struktur und in der Gestaltung ihrer Fassade und entwickelt eine Architektur, die das Konzept der Inklusion, das Hauptziel ihrer pädagogischen Philosophie, verstärkt.

La disposition de cette école primaire et sa position au centre de la parcelle créent trois espaces extérieurs qui permettent des activités différenciées. L'accès principal par la cour de l'école mène à un grand hall à double hauteur, autour duquel s'organisent les différents espaces et qui constitue le cœur du bâtiment. Ce foyer peut être utilisé comme lieu de réunion ou pour de grands événements scolaires, ce qui transforme le spacieux escalier reliant les deux niveaux en un « paysage de sièges ». La conception du bâtiment adopte les normes d'isolation passivhaus et intègre diverses mesures axées sur la durabilité. La nouvelle école est attrayante et ouverte dans sa structure spatiale et dans la conception de sa façade, développant une architecture qui renforce le concept d'inclusion, l'objectif principal de sa philosophie éducative.

El esquema en planta de esta escuela primaria y su posición en el centro de la parcela crean tres zonas al aire libre que permiten actividades diferenciadas. El acceso principal a través del patio escolar conduce a un gran vestíbulo a doble altura, alrededor del cual se organizan las diferentes áreas y que constituye el corazón del edificio. Este vestíbulo puede utilizarse como zona de reuniones o para eventos escolares multitudinarios, que convierten a la espaciosa escalera que conecta los dos niveles en un «paisaje de asientos». El diseño del edificio adopta los estándares de aislamiento *passivhaus* e incorpora diversas medidas orientadas hacia la sostenibilidad. La nueva escuela es atractiva y abierta en su estructura espacial y en el diseño de su fachada, desarrollando una arquitectura que refuerza el concepto de inclusión, principal objetivo de su filosofía educativa.

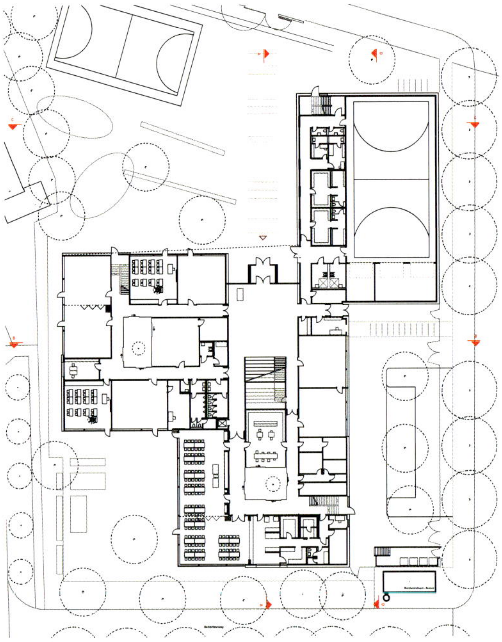

Ground floor plan

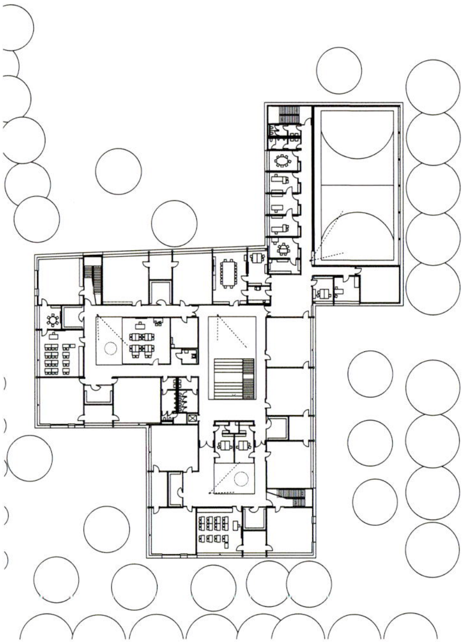

First floor plan

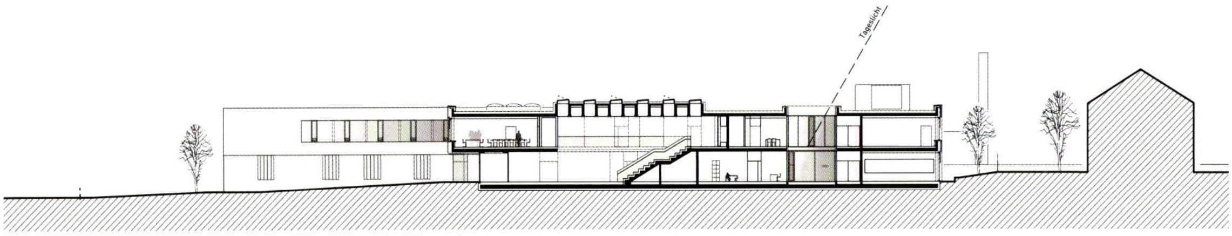

Section

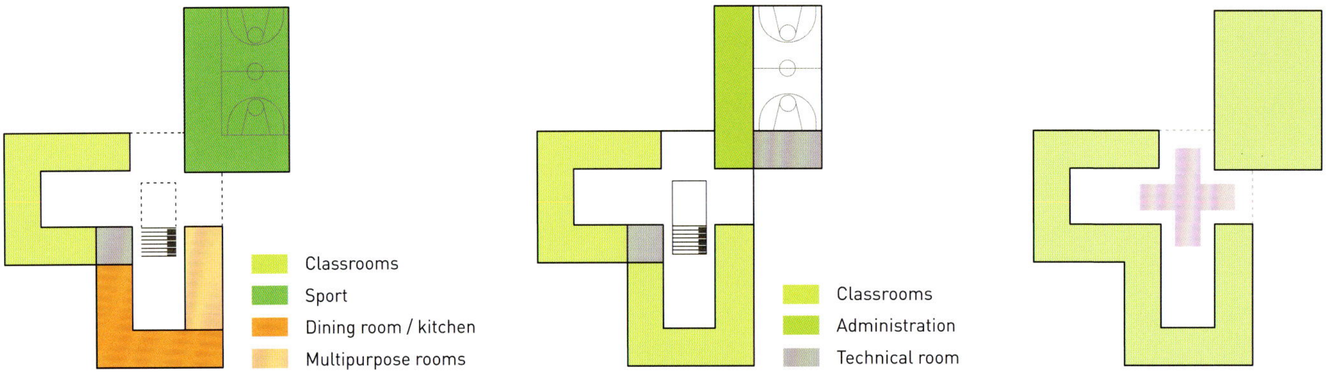

Concept diagrams

BLAUE KITA MONHEIM

LOCATION: **MONHEIM AM RHEIN, GERMANY**
PHOTOS: © **CONSTANTIN MEYER**

The construction of this "blue nursery" is part of a series of urban and social projects aimed at transforming a grey and peripheral area of the city of Monheim am Rhein. Its program is structured into four separate classrooms or "houses" facing the garden to the south, in front of which is a succession of intermediate play areas that also act as the building's longitudinal communication axis. The "houses" are characterised by the different slopes of their roofs and by the assignment of a characteristic colour to each one, which is used in all the interior finishes and which helps the children to identify with their space. The different rooms of the school are sheltered under an irregular folded roof whose striking blue colour extends to the side and to north façades giving coherence to the whole.

Der Bau dieser „blauen Kinderkrippe" ist Teil einer Reihe von städtischen und sozialen Projekten, mit denen ein graues und peripheres Gebiet der Stadt Monheim am Rhein umgestaltet werden soll. Das Programm gliedert sich in vier separate Klassenzimmer oder „Häuser", die nach Süden zum Garten hin ausgerichtet sind und vor denen sich eine Reihe von dazwischen liegenden Spielbereichen befindet, die gleichzeitig die Kommunikationsachse des Gebäudes in Längsrichtung bilden. Die „Häuser" zeichnen sich durch die unterschiedlichen Dachneigungen und die Zuordnung einer charakteristischen Farbe zu jedem einzelnen aus, die in allen Innenausbauten verwendet wird und den Kindern hilft, sich mit ihrem Raum zu identifizieren. Die verschiedenen Räume der Schule befinden sich unter einem unregelmäßig gefalteten Dach, dessen auffällige blaue Farbe sich zu den Seitenfassaden und zur Nordfassade hin erstreckt, um dem Ganzen Kohärenz zu verleihen.

La construction de cette « pépinière bleue » fait partie d'une série de projets urbains et sociaux visant à transformer une zone grise et périphérique de la ville de Monheim am Rhein. Son programme est structuré en quatre salles de classe ou « maisons » séparées qui font face au jardin au sud, devant lequel se trouve une succession d'aires de jeux intermédiaires qui servent également d'axe de communication longitudinal du bâtiment. Les « maisons » se caractérisent par les différentes pentes de leurs toits et par l'attribution à chacune d'elles d'une couleur caractéristique, qui est utilisée dans toutes les finitions intérieures et qui aide les enfants à s'identifier à leur espace. Les différentes salles de l'école sont abritées sous un toit plié irrégulier dont la couleur bleue frappante s'étend aux façades latérales et à la façade nord pour donner une cohérence à l'ensemble.

La construcción de esta «guardería azul» se enmarca dentro de una serie de proyectos urbanos y sociales encaminados a transformar un área gris y periférica de la ciudad de Monheim am Rhein. Su programa se estructura en cuatro aulas separadas o «casas» orientadas hacia el jardín situado al sur, frente a las cuales se sitúa una sucesión de zonas de juego intermedias que actúa también como eje de comunicación longitudinal del edificio. Las «casas» se caracterizan por las diferentes pendientes de sus techos y por la asignación de un color característico a cada una, que es utilizado en todos los acabados interiores y que ayuda a los niños a identificarse con su espacio. Las diferentes estancias de la escuela se refugian bajo una cubierta plegada irregular cuyo llamativo color azul se extiende hacia las fachadas laterales y hacia la fachada norte para dar coherencia al conjunto.

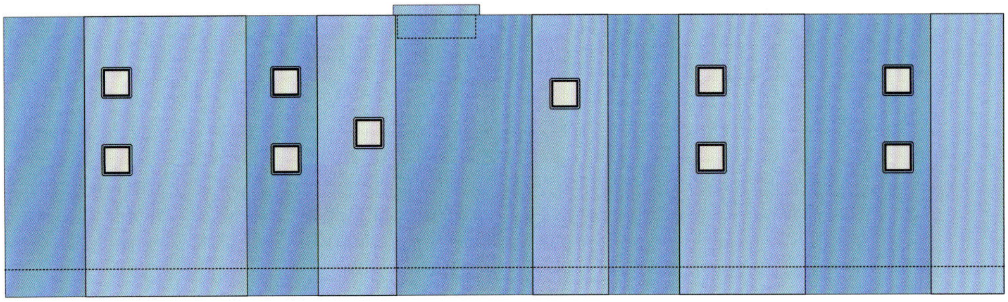

Roof plan

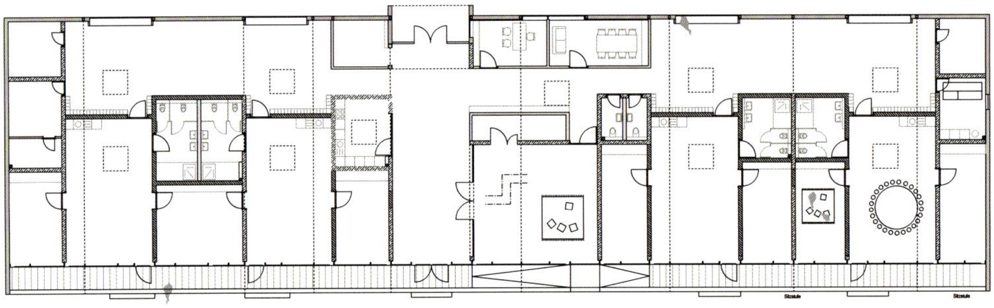

Floor plan

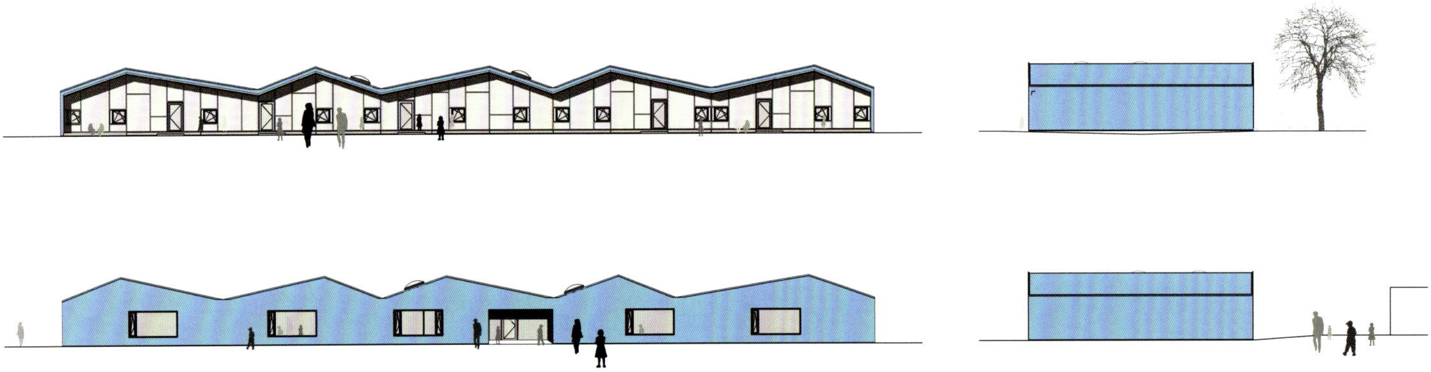

Elevations

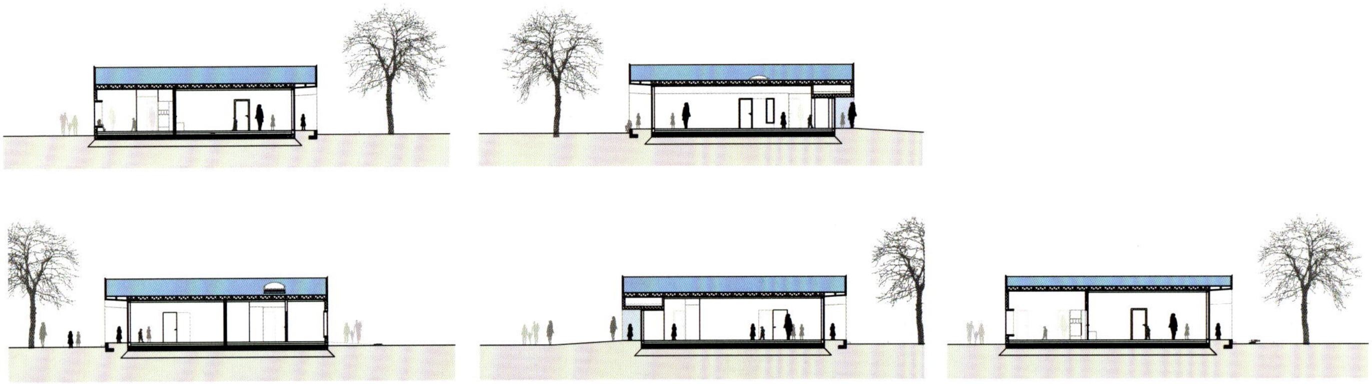

Sections

VMDO Architects

// PROJECTS //

1. BLUESTONE ELEMENTARY SCHOOL
2. BUCKINGHAM COUNTY PRIMARY AND ELEMENTARY SCHOOLS AT THE CARTER G. WOODSON EDUCATION COMPLEX
3. DISCOVERY ELEMENTARY SCHOOL

vmdo.com

VMDO Architects

1.

2.

3.

As an architectural practice founded in 1976 by a University of Virginia professor and his three best students, VMDO's employees are connected by a common belief in the power of design to educate, inspire, and uplift. As such, VMDO has focused the entirety of its practice on designing for educational institutions. As a teaching practice focused on education, VMDO has an unwavering commitment to architecture as a craft. This means not only developing beautiful detailing, but also delivering buildings and campuses that can be easily maintained by their owners, that fluidly adapt to ever-changing needs and desires, and that grow more beautiful over time. VMDO's designs have achieved international and national acclaim from a variety of societies and associations. This collective knowledge-sharing ensures that each of design is more sustainable and innovative than its predecessor, while being tailored to the unique needs and locations of each school community.

Les employés de VMDO (un cabinet d'architecture fondé en 1976 par un professeur de l'université de Virginie et ses trois meilleurs étudiants) sont liés par une croyance commune dans le pouvoir du design pour éduquer et inspirer. En tant que tel, VMDO a concentré toute sa pratique sur le design pour les établissements d'enseignement, et a donc un engagement inébranlable envers l'architecture en tant que métier. Cela signifie non seulement développer de beaux détails, mais aussi livrer des bâtiments et des campus qui peuvent être facilement entretenus par leurs propriétaires, qui s'adaptent en douceur à des besoins et des désirs en constante évolution, et qui deviennent plus beaux avec le temps. Les créations de VMDO ont été acclamées au niveau national et international par diverses sociétés et associations. Cet échange collectif de connaissances garantit que chaque conception est plus durable et plus innovante que la précédente, tout en s'adaptant aux besoins et à l'emplacement uniques de chaque communauté scolaire.

Die Mitarbeiter des VMDO (ein Architekturbüro, das 1976 von einem Professor der University of Virginia und seinen drei besten Studenten gegründet wurde) verbindet der gemeinsame Glaube an die erzieherische und inspirierende Kraft des Designs. Als solches hat VMDO seine gesamte Praxis auf das Design für Bildungseinrichtungen konzentriert und hat daher ein unerschütterliches Engagement für Architektur als Handwerk. Das bedeutet nicht nur die Entwicklung schöner Details, sondern auch die Lieferung von Gebäuden und Campussen, die von ihren Eigentümern leicht gewartet werden können, die sich reibungslos an die sich ständig ändernden Bedürfnisse und Wünsche anpassen und die mit der Zeit immer schöner werden. Die Entwürfe der VMDO sind national und international von verschiedenen Gesellschaften und Verbänden anerkannt worden. Dieser kollektive Wissensaustausch stellt sicher, dass jeder Entwurf nachhaltiger und innovativer ist als sein Vorgänger und sich gleichzeitig an die einzigartigen Bedürfnisse und Standorte jeder Schulgemeinschaft anpasst.

Los empleados de VMDO (estudio de arquitectura fundado en 1976 por un profesor de la Universidad de Virginia y sus tres mejores estudiantes) están conectados por una creencia común en el poder del diseño para educar e inspirar. Como tal, VMDO ha centrado toda su práctica en el diseño para instituciones educativas, y por tanto tiene un compromiso inquebrantable con la arquitectura como oficio. Esto significa no sólo el desarrollo de bellos detalles, sino también la entrega de edificios y campus que puedan ser fácilmente mantenidos por sus propietarios, que se adapten con fluidez a las necesidades y deseos siempre cambiantes, y que se vuelvan más bellos con el paso del tiempo. Los diseños de VMDO han sido aclamados nacional e internacionalmente por diversas sociedades y asociaciones. Este intercambio de conocimientos colectivos garantiza que cada uno de los diseños sea más sostenible e innovador que su predecesor, al tiempo que se adapta a las necesidades y ubicaciones únicas de cada comunidad escolar.

BLUESTONE ELEMENTARY SCHOOL

LOCATION: **HARRISONBURG, VIRGINIA, USA**
PHOTOS: © **ALAN KARCHMER; LINCOLN BARBOUR**

The design of this school was driven by several guiding principles: 1) serving a diverse student body with children from over 60 countries; 2) sensitivity to the local geography and ecology; and 3) creating a net-zero ready building that responds to global climate change concerns. The school emphasizes a variety of spaces and scales for differentiated learning opportunities while creating welcoming communal areas that embody the school's commitment to learning in an inclusive environment. The landscape creates a communal, active, and bio-diverse habitat that supports human and ecosystem health while providing innumerable hands-on learning activities. The school received the 2019 Livable Buildings Award from the University of California, Berkeley, based on user surveys demonstrating high occupant satisfaction, excellent design, and innovative operation strategies.

La conception de cette école a été guidée par plusieurs principes directeurs : 1) servir un corps d'élèves diversifié avec des enfants de plus de 60 pays ; 2) être sensible à la géographie et à l'écologie locales ; et 3) créer un bâtiment prêt pour le net-zéro qui répond aux préoccupations mondiales en matière de changement climatique. L'école met l'accent sur une variété d'espaces et d'échelles pour des possibilités d'apprentissage différenciées tout en créant des espaces communs accueillants qui incarnent l'engagement de l'école à apprendre dans un environnement inclusif. Le paysage crée un habitat commun, actif et biodiversifié qui soutient la santé des humains et des écosystèmes tout en offrant d'innombrables activités d'apprentissage pratique. L'école a reçu le prix 2019 Livable Buildings Award de l'Université de Californie, Berkeley, sur la base d'enquêtes auprès des utilisateurs qui ont démontré une grande satisfaction des occupants, une excellente conception et des stratégies d'exploitation innovantes.

Die Gestaltung dieser Schule wurde von mehreren Leitprinzipien geleitet: 1) Bedienung einer vielfältigen Schülerschaft mit Kindern aus über 60 Ländern; 2) Sensibilität für die lokale Geographie und Ökologie; und 3) Schaffung eines netto-null-fertigen Gebäudes, das den Anliegen des globalen Klimawandels Rechnung trägt. Die Schule legt Wert auf eine Vielfalt von Räumen und Maßstäben für differenzierte Lerngelegenheiten und schafft gleichzeitig einladende Gemeinschaftsbereiche, die das Engagement der Schule für das Lernen in einer integrativen Umgebung verkörpern. Die Landschaft schafft einen gemeinschaftlichen, aktiven und biologisch vielfältigen Lebensraum, der die Gesundheit von Mensch und Ökosystem unterstützt und gleichzeitig unzählige praktische Lernaktivitäten bietet. Die Schule erhielt den Preis für lebenswerte Gebäude 2019 von der University of California, Berkeley, basierend auf Benutzerumfragen, die eine hohe Zufriedenheit der Bewohner, ein ausgezeichnetes Design und innovative Betriebsstrategien belegen.

El diseño de esta escuela fue impulsado por varios principios rectores: uno, servir a un cuerpo estudiantil diverso con niños de más de sesenta países; dos, sensibilidad a la geografía y ecología locales; y tres, crear un edificio listo para la red que responda a las preocupaciones del cambio climático global. La escuela hace hincapié en una variedad de espacios y escalas para las oportunidades de aprendizaje diferenciado, al tiempo que crea zonas comunales acogedoras que encarnan el compromiso de la escuela con el aprendizaje en un entorno inclusivo. El paisaje crea un hábitat comunitario, activo y biodiverso que apoya la salud humana y del ecosistema al tiempo que proporciona innumerables actividades de aprendizaje práctico. La escuela recibió el Premio de Edificios Habitables 2019 de la Universidad de California, Berkeley, basado en encuestas de usuarios que demostraron una alta satisfacción de los ocupantes, un excelente diseño y estrategias de funcionamiento innovadoras.

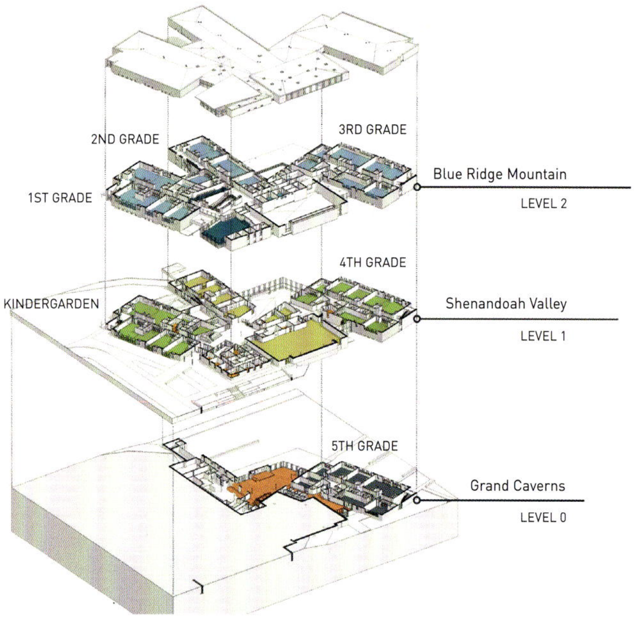

Wayfinding + environmental graphics

LEVEL WAYFINDING MURALS

WonderLab
Nest

BUCKINGHAM COUNTY PRIMARY AND ELEMENTARY SCHOOLS AT THE CARTER G. WOODSON EDUCATION COMPLEX

LOCATION: **BUCKINGHAM COUNTY, VIRGINIA, USA**
PHOTOS: © **ALAN KARCHMER**

In 2009, this school community decided to focus on the future of its youngest students by giving priority to health and design, thus creating a holistic and innovative learning environment. To this end, healthy eating and physical activity design guidelines were followed as an antidote to the childhood obesity epidemic, written in collaboration with public health researchers. This collaboration produced a healthy LEED Gold school that reflects the intimate connections between architecture, health, learning environments and academic success. The existing school campus was redesigned as a sustainable environment that provides diverse opportunities for play, exercise and learning, and that highlights natural ecosystems and local resources to inspire a love of learning and understanding of place.

Im Jahr 2009 beschloss diese Schulgemeinschaft, sich auf die Zukunft ihrer jüngsten Schülerinnen und Schüler zu konzentrieren, indem sie der Gesundheit und dem Design Priorität einräumte und so ein ganzheitliches und innovatives Lernumfeld schuf. Zu diesem Zweck wurden Richtlinien für gesunde Ernährung und körperliche Aktivität als Gegenmittel gegen die Adipositasepidemie bei Kindern befolgt, die in Zusammenarbeit mit Forschern des öffentlichen Gesundheitswesens verfasst wurden. Aus dieser Zusammenarbeit entstand eine gesunde LEED-Goldschule, die die enge Verbindung zwischen Architektur, Gesundheit, Lernumgebungen und akademischem Erfolg widerspiegelt. Der Schulcampus wurde zu einer nachhaltigen Umgebung umgestaltet, die vielfältige Möglichkeiten zum Spielen, Bewegen und Lernen bietet und natürliche Ökosysteme und lokale Ressourcen hervorhebt, um die Liebe zum Lernen und das Verständnis für den Ort zu wecken.

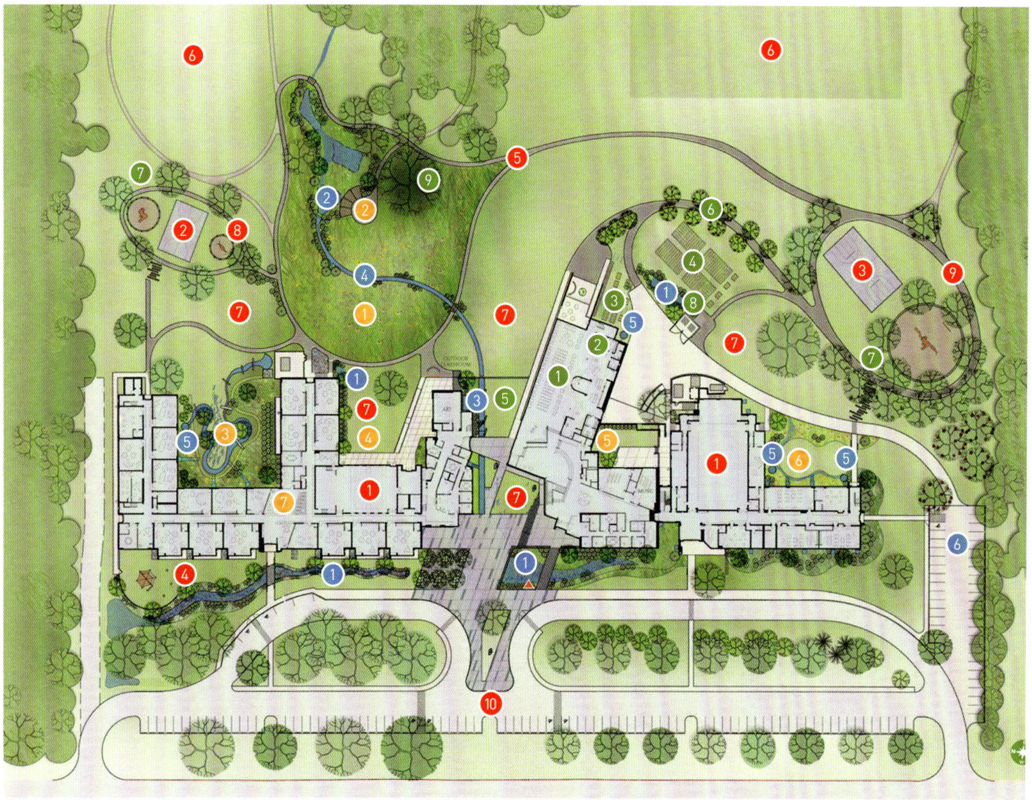

Floor plan

Physical activity zones
1. Gymnasium + fitness rooms
2. K-2 Play terrace + water station
3. 3-5 Play terrace + water station
4. Tot lot natural play area
5. Eco-walks / jogging paths
6. Recreational sport fields
7. Open + free play
8. K-2 exercise loop (4 laps = 1/4 mile)
9. 3-5 exercise loop (5 laps = 1/2 mile)
10. Weekend + off peak bicycle loops

Foodsmart kids zones
1. Dining commons + food lab
2. Teaching kitchen lab
3. Kitchen gardens
4. Edible community gardens
5. Great lawn + grab-n-go berry patch
6. Fruit tree allee
7. Nut tree circle
8. Compost demonstration garden
9. Picnic knoll
10. Outdoor dining + classroom

Eco activity zones
1. Native meadow grasses
2. Frog bog observation deck
3. K-2 science garden
4. Arts terrace + garden courtyard
5. Sonata terrace + garden courtyard
6. Pollinator bee + bug garden
7. Woodland hub

Hydrological systems
1. Bioswales + cleansing biotopes
2. Frog bog wetland
3. Slate channel + waterfall scupper
4. River rock stream
5. Rainwater cistern (1,400 gallons)
6. Pervious parking court

En 2009, cette communauté scolaire a décidé de se concentrer sur l'avenir de ses plus jeunes élèves en donnant la priorité à la santé et au design, créant ainsi un environnement d'apprentissage holistique et innovant. À cette fin, des lignes directrices sur la conception d'une alimentation saine et de l'activité physique ont été suivies comme antidote à l'épidémie d'obésité infantile, rédigées en collaboration avec des chercheurs en santé publique. Cette collaboration a donné naissance à une école LEED Gold saine qui reflète les liens intimes entre l'architecture, la santé, les environnements d'apprentissage et la réussite scolaire. Le campus de l'école a été redessiné pour devenir un environnement durable qui offre diverses possibilités de jeu, d'exercice et d'apprentissage, et qui met en valeur les écosystèmes naturels et les ressources locales pour inspirer un amour de l'apprentissage et de la compréhension du lieu.

En el año 2009, esta comunidad escolar decidió enfocar el futuro de sus alumnos más jóvenes dando prioridad a la salud y al diseño, y crear de esta manera un entorno de aprendizaje holístico e innovador. Para ello se siguieron unas pautas de diseño de alimentación saludable y actividad física como antídoto contra la epidemia de obesidad infantil, redactadas en colaboración con investigadores de salud pública. Esta colaboración produjo una escuela LEED Gold saludable que refleja las conexiones íntimas entre arquitectura, salud, entornos de aprendizaje y éxito académico. El campus de la escuela fue rediseñado como un entorno sostenible que ofrece diversas oportunidades para el juego, el ejercicio y el aprendizaje, y que pone de relieve los ecosistemas naturales y los recursos locales para inspirar el amor por el aprendizaje y la comprensión del lugar.

DISCOVERY ELEMENTARY SCHOOL

LOCATION: **ARLINGTON, VIRGINIA, USA**
PHOTOS: **© ALAN KARCHMER; LINCOLN BARBOUR; DIGITAL IMAGING & DESIGN, INC.**

One of the largest net-zero energy buildings in the world, Discovery Elementary School has been a trailblazer for net-zero energy schools, both in demonstrating performance and engaging students in learning about sustainability. Its design takes advantage of the topography to create differentiated academic areas and separate outdoor play spaces for different levels of education. The result is a building cluster that respects the scale of the surrounding residential neighborhood. Light participates in multiple ways throughout the school, culminating in a rooftop solar lab that allows students to experiment. As its name suggests, Discovery offers hands-on learning opportunities that encourage students to take ownership of their sustainable school and contribute to its carbon-neutral culture.

Die Discovery Elementary School, eines der weltweit größten Netto-Nullenergiegebäude, hat bei der Schaffung von Schulen in derselben Energiekategorie Pionierarbeit geleistet, sowohl bei der Demonstration von Leistung als auch bei der Einbeziehung der Schüler in das Lernen über Nachhaltigkeit. Sein Entwurf nutzt die Topographie, um differenzierte akademische Bereiche und getrennte Außenspielräume für verschiedene Bildungsstufen zu schaffen. Das Ergebnis ist ein Gebäude-Cluster, das die Größenordnung des umliegenden Wohnquartiers respektiert. Das Licht nimmt auf vielfältige Weise in der gesamten Schule teil und gipfelt in einem Solarlabor auf dem Dach, in dem die Schülerinnen und Schüler experimentieren können. Wie der Name schon sagt, bietet Discovery praktische Lernmöglichkeiten, die die Schülerinnen und Schüler ermutigen, die Verantwortung für ihre nachhaltige Schule zu übernehmen und zu ihrer kohlenstoffneutralen Kultur beizutragen.

L'école élémentaire Discovery, l'un des plus grands bâtiments à énergie nette zéro au monde, a été la première à créer des écoles dans la même catégorie d'énergie, à la fois pour démontrer les performances et pour inciter les élèves à s'informer sur la durabilité. Sa conception tire parti de la topographie pour créer des zones académiques différenciées et des espaces de jeu extérieurs distincts pour les différents niveaux d'enseignement. Le résultat est un ensemble de bâtiments qui respecte l'échelle du quartier résidentiel environnant. La lumière participe de multiples façons dans toute l'école, avec en point d'orgue un laboratoire solaire sur le toit qui permet aux élèves de faire des expériences. Comme son nom l'indique, Discovery offre des possibilités d'apprentissage pratique qui encouragent les élèves à s'approprier leur école durable et à contribuer à sa culture de neutralité carbone.

Uno de los edificios de energía neta cero más grandes del mundo, la escuela primaria Discovery ha sido pionera en la creación de escuelas de la misma categoría energética, tanto en la demostración de rendimiento como en la participación de los estudiantes en el aprendizaje de la sostenibilidad. Su diseño aprovecha la topografía para crear zonas académicas diferenciadas y espacios de juego exteriores separados para los diferentes niveles de enseñanza. El resultando es una agrupación de edificios respetuosa con la escala del vecindario residencial circundante. La luz participa de múltiples maneras en toda la escuela, culminando en un laboratorio solar en la azotea que permite experimentar a los estudiantes. Como su nombre indica, Discovery ofrece oportunidades de aprendizaje práctico que animan a los estudiantes a apropiarse de su escuela sostenible y contribuir a su cultura de neutralidad de carbono.

First floor plan

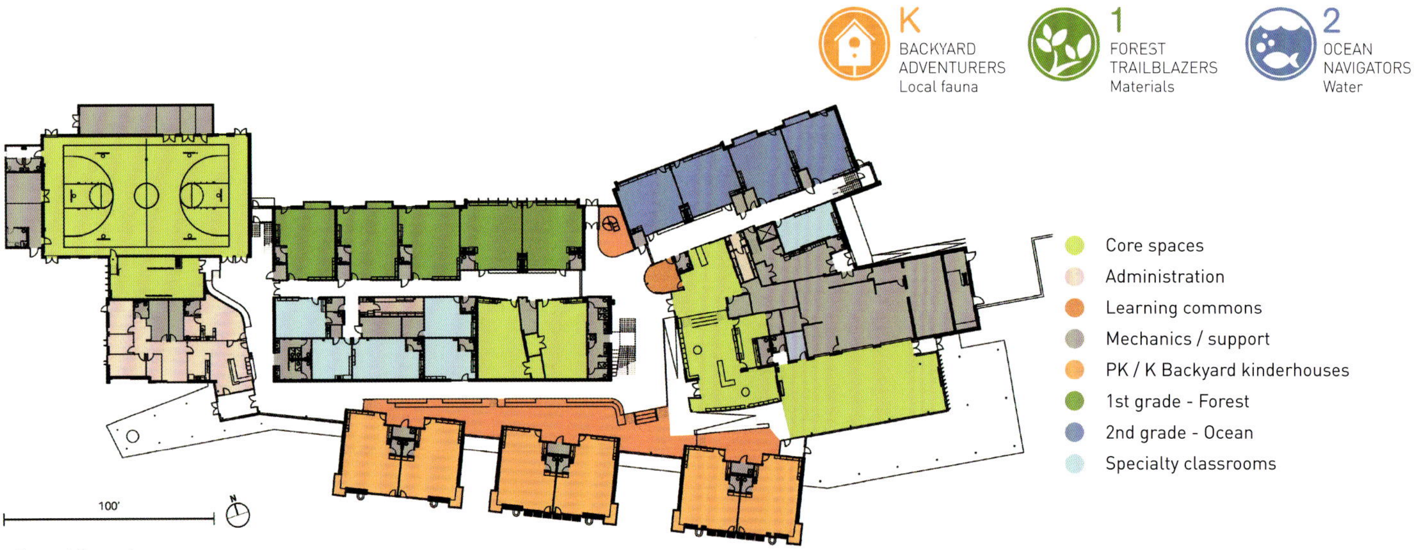

Ground floor plan

Section with Black Line-Solar

WEB
BACKYARD

FOREST

EXIT
OCEAN

GALAXY VOYAGERS

DIRECTORY

1+1>2 ARCHITECTS
MR. HOANG THUC HAO
-Lecturer at National university of civil engineering NUCE
-Winner World Architecture Festival Award 2015
-SIA-Getz Architecure Prize 2016 for emergent architecture in Asia
-Vassilis Sgoutas Prize 2017 by the International Union of Architects

Sentia school
Project Team: Hoang Thuc Hao, Do Minh Duc
Construction period: 2016
Total built area: 3,826 m^2
Awards:
-WAF 2016 shortlist
-Top 5 Spec go green award 2018
-3rd prize National Architecture Award 2019
General contractor: Local contruction team
Suppliers: DULUX, TOTO, Viet Phap Steel Company
Consultants: 1+1>2 Architects

Jungle flower
Project Team: Hoang Thuc Hao, Son Vu
Construction period: 2016
Total built area: 1,413 m^2
Awards:
-The International Architecture Award 2017
-Vietnam Green Architecture 2018
-AMP Architectural Design Award – Educational project 2018
General contractor:
1+1>2 Construction Contractor
Suppliers: 1+1>2 Construction Contractor
Consultants: 1+1>2 Architects
Invested by Phoenix Foundation

Da Hop School
Project Team: Hoang Thuc Hao, Nguyen Duy Thanh (lecturer at NUCE), Tran Hong Nam, Vien Thi Thu
Total built area: 2,200 m^2
General contractor: CCU11
Suppliers: Phuc Tri Trading Construction Invesment Company Limited, DULUX
Consultants: 1+1>2 Architects

ABAU | ANTONIO BLANCO ARCHITECTURE AND URBAN PLANNING
Kindergarten in La Pañoleta
Project Team: Antonio Blanco Montero
Construction period: Nov. 2011-June 2012
Total built area: 1,000 m^2
General contractor: Construcciones Temir
Suppliers:
-Color glass: Vanceva
-Zinc: VM Zinc
Consultants: Sergio Estévez Salazar (structural analysis)

ARCHIKON ARCHITECTS
Vizafogó Kindergarten
Project Team: Csaba Nagy, Károly Pólus, Ágnes Tőrös, Miklós Batta, Gábor Laczkó, Bence Várhidi, Jakab Urbán, Nikoletta Zsidai
Construction period: 2018-2019
Total built area: 1,962 m^2
Awards:
-PIRANESI Award 2020, shortlisted
-HIGHLIGHTS of Hungary 2020, shortlisted
-HUNGARIAN MEDIA Architecture Award 2019, First prize winner
-HUNGARIAN MEDIA Architecture Award 2019, Audience award winner
-HUNGARIAN MEDIA Architecture Award 2019, Building Reconstruction special prize winner
General contractor: PRÍM Építő Kft.
Collaborators:
-Structure: Tibor PINTÉR (Ékiterv Mérnökiroda Kft.)
-HVAC: Zoltán SOR (PHQ Kft.)
-Electricity: István KARÁCSONY (Kartel60 Bt.)
Builder: Municipality of Budapest District XIII

Fairytale Kindergarten
Project Team: Csaba Nagy, Károly Pólus, Ádám Pásztor, Ágnes To˝Rös, Tamás Kiss, Bence Várhidi
Construction period: 2015-2016
Total built area: 2,640 m^2
Awards:
-BIGSEE Architecture Award 2019, winner
-MIES VAN DER ROHE Award 2017, Nominee
-PIRANESI Award 2016, nominee
-RIBA Award 2017, nominee
-HUNGARIAN MEDIA Architecture Award 2016, Jury special prize winner
-HUNGARIAN MEDIA Architecture Award 2016, Audience award winner
-HUNGARIAN MEDIA Architecture Award 2016, Special prize winner for energy efficiency
-EXCELLENCE Award of Budapest Chamber of Architects 2017, winner
-FIABCI Hungary XIX.th Prix d'Excellence Award 2017, winner
-FIABCI Hungary XIX.th Prix d'Excellence Award 2017, Public building category winner
-FIABCI Hungary XIX.th Prix d'Excellence Award 2017, Special prize winner for energy efficiency
-FIABCI WORLD Prix d'Excellence Award 2017, nominee
-ENERGY GLOBE Award 2017, Building Category winner
-PRO ARCHITECTURA Award 2017, nominee
-FAÇADE OF THE YEAR, Baumit 2018, Special prize winner
-LIFE CHALLENGE, Baumit 2018, nominee
General contractor: FK Raszter Építő Zrt.
Collaborators:
-Structure: Tibor PINTÉR (Ékiterv Mérnökiroda Kft.)
-HVAC: Zoltán SOR (PHQ Kft.)
-Electricity: István KARÁCSONY (Kartel60 Bt.)
-Graphics, painting: Tímea FERTH, Zsuzsanna HERLING
-Passiv house expert – Imre MISKOLCZY (Energiaterv Kft.)
Builder: Municipality of Budapest District XIII

ARCHITEKTEN + PARTNER DANNIEN ROLLER
Day Care Center Max-Planck-Campus Tübingen
Project Team: Matthias Roller, Maren Dannien, Simon Kirsch, Claudia Hegelau
Construction period: July 2016-September 2017 (without planning)
Total built area: 603 m^2
Suppliers:
-Landscape Architecture: Stefan Fromm
-Structural engineer: Schneck Schaal Braun Ingeniuergesellschaft Bauen mbH
Owner: Max-Planck-Gesellschaft, Munich

ATELIER 56S
Recreational Center and School in Elven
Project Team: Fanny Landeau, José Prieto
Construction period: 2019
Total built area: 740 m^2
General contractor: Legendre Construction, ACM, DUVAL, ADB
Suppliers: Reckli, Reynaers, Keller, Le Prieuré
Consultants: ECB

Primary School in La Couyère
Project Team: Fanny Landeau, José Prieto, Lise Gaillard
Construction period: 2017
Total built area: 250 m^2
Award: Chilean Architecture biennale, ADC awards 2019
General contractor: COREVA, SER AL FER
Suppliers: Terca, ALU K
Consultants: BECB + La Plage

ATELIER BNK
Yuni Nursery School
Project Team: Tatsuya Goto, Hiroshi Horio, Hideyuki Hatakenaka, Takeshi Murakuni, Yo-shihiro Miura
Construction period: January 2002
Total built area: 868 m^2
Award: Hokkaido Red Brick Architecture Award 2003
General contractor:
-Main contractor: Konoike Construction Corporation, Kawakami Corporation JV
-Electrical Engineering: Ono Corporation
-Mechanical Engineering: Umehara Corporation
Suppliers: Yuni town
Consultants:
-Structural Design: Shichida Structural Design
-Mechanical & Electrical Engineering
-Design: IU Engineering, Nishibu Engineering
-Landscape Design: Atelier BNK

Itoi Elementary School
Project Team: Makoto Kato, Masayuki Yamaki, Takeshi Murakuni, Aoi Akimoto, Ryoko Yamamoto, Yoshihiro Miura
Construction period: October 2007
Total built area: 3,893m^2
Awards:
-Public Building Award, Excellence Prize 2012
-Annual Architectural Design Commendation, Architectural Institute of Japan 2010
General contractor:
-Main Contractor: Tanaka Corporation, Suzuki Corporation, Asahi Corporation JV
-Electrical Engineering: Hasegawa Corporation, Miyatake Corpotarion, Kyoko Corporation JV
-Mechanical Engineering: Fujiya Corporation, Union Corporation JV
Suppliers: Shibetsu city
Consultants:
-Structural Design: Kanebako Structural Engineers
-Mechanical & Electrical Engineering Design: Sogo Consultants
-Furniture Design: Atelier BNK
-Landscape Design: Atelier BNK
-Environmental Adviser: Northern Regional Building Research Institute

Numata Elementary School
Project Team: Makoto Kato, Hideki Suganuma, Mitsutoshi Ikehata, Nana Ikemura, Toshimi Takemura
Construction period: December 2012
Total built area: 4,185 m^2
Awards:
-Selected Architectural Designs of the Architectural Institute of Japan 2015
-Japan Architecture of the Year 2014 selected by the JIA
General contractor:
-Main contractor: Iwata Chizaki Corporation, Koshin Corporation, Makari Corporation JV
-Electrical Engineering: Toko Corporation
-Mechanical Engineering: Ikeda Corporation, Matsuro Jusetsu Corporation, Matsuo Corporation JV
Suppliers: Numata town
Consultants:
-Structural Design: Kanebako Structural Engineers
-Mechanical & Electrical Engineering Design: Sogo Consultants
-Furniture Design: Chiori Design, Conde House
-Landscape Design: Atelier BNK
-Environmental Research: Northern Regional Building Research Institute

BARKER ASSOCIATES ARCHITECTURE OFFICE AND 4 | MATIV DESIGN STUDIO
Maple Street School
Project Team:
-BAAO: Alexandra Barker, Principal and Adrien Allred, Project Architect
-4|Mativ: Priya Patel, founding partner and Esther Beke, partner
-Marvel Architects: Architect of Record
Developer: Hudson Companies
Construction period: 2015-2016
Total built area: 306 m^2 and 93 m^2 exterior
Awards:
-National Society of American Architects Award
-AIA New York Award
-AIA Brooklyn Queens Design Award
General contractor: Bolt Construction
Millworker: Jose Palaguachi
Suppliers:
-Bathroom tile: Dal tile keystones
-Engineered Maple flooring: Kahrs
-Furniture: Community Playthings
-Perforated Aluminum Roof fencing: Mc Nichols hardware
-Roof pavers: Unity
-Maple acoustical ceiling: Decoustics
-Acoustical baffles: Armstrong
-Lighting: I-Light and Delray and Oxygen

Mi Casita
Preschool and Cultural Center
Project Team:
-BAAO: Alexandra Barker, Principal and Christina Ostermier, Project Architect
-4|Mativ: Priya Patel, founding partner and Esther Beke, partner
Construction period: 2018-2019
Total built area: 232 m²
Awards:
-National Society of American Architects Award
-AIA New York Award
General contractor: 360 Interior Concept
Suppliers:
-Bathroom Tile: Dal Tile
-Entry tile: Cle Tile
-Pendant lighting: Seagull
-Bathroom wall tile: Dal Tile
-Custom stainless steel trough sink: Kohler Faucets
Consultants:
Structural Engineer: Avishay Mazor, PE
MEP: Levin Engineering
Expediter: Philip Ferrara
Special Inspections: Ace Inspections

CHALLENGE DESIGN
JIE LEE
Ton Wen Kindergarten
Project Team: Peng Xu, Linheng Tang, Ling Tao, Xiang Ao
Construction period: 6 months
Total built area: 10,800 m²
Award: The 8th Architecture Creation Award of ASSC Winner
Consultants: IPPR (Xiamen) Engineering Design and Research Institute Co., Ltd.
Client: Shimao Group

Park Legend Kindergarten
Project Team: Fang Yan, Suya Lin, Hailian Li, Wubing Feng, Wei Lin, Xiuxian Xu
Construction period: 7 months
Total built area: 5,600 m²
Awards:
-2019 German Design Awards Winner
-2019 Iconic Awards Winner
-2019 American Master Prize Winner
-The 8th Architecture Creation Award of ASSC Nominated
-2019 World Architecture Festival Shortlist
Suppliers: Lidao New Material Manufacture
Consultants: ARCH-AGE DESIGN
Client: Chengdu Nancheng Vanke

COBE
Forfatterhuset Kindergarten
Project Team: Andy Minchev, Caroline Krogh Andersen, Chloé Blain, Christina Matos, Dan Stubbergaard, Eik Bjerregaard, Elin Parry, Gabrielle Ubareviciute, Greta Tiedje, Jens Kert Wagner, Kato Hiroshi, Magnus Meulengracht, Martin Jonsbak Nielsen, Martin Laustsen, Michal Kniaz, Tobias Mürsch.
Construction period: 2013-2014
Total built area. 1,927 m²
Awards:
-Mies van der Rohe Award 2015 Shortlist
-Architizer A+ Award 2015 Finalist
General contractor: Kjær & Lassen
Landscape architect: PK3
Engineer: D.A.I.
Client: City of Copenhagen

Frederiksvej Kindergarten
Project Team: Agnieszka Krasuska, Agnieszka Szczepanska, Claes Nilsson, Christian Sander, Dan Stubbergaard, Davide Pontoni, Eik Bjerregaard, Greta Tiedje, Jens Wagner, Jonas Nordgren, Kato Hiroshi, Rune Boserup.
Construction period: Completed 2015
Total built area: 1,700 m²
Awards: ArchDaily Building of the Year Award 2017
Consultants: Learning spaces
Landscape architects:
Preben Skaarup Lanskab
Engineers:
Søren Jensen Rådgivende Ingeniører
Client: City of Copenhagen
Contractors:
Brdr. Thybo, Caverion, Juul & Nielsen

CONTINIARCHITETTURA
MARCO CONTINI & SARA CHIARI
Primary school in Loiano
Project Team:
-Architects and project managers: Marco Contini & Sara Chiari
-Work direction: Marco Contini
Structures: Schrentewein & Partner s.r.l.
Electrical installations: Giampaolo Vecchi
Mechanical plants: Simone Dalmonte
Construction period: 2017
Total built area: 2,536 m²
Awards:
-School ecosystem, XIX Legambiente report on the quality of school buildings, structures and services, 18 October 2018: 10 innovative and sustainable school buildings
-Archilovers, Best project 2018
-Sustainability award 2019, AESS
General contractor: Ferruccio Maestrami S.R.L
Suppliers:
-Main Materials: wood, concrete, glass

School Complex in Felino
Project Team:
-Architects and project managers: Marco Contini & Sara Chiari
-Work direction: Marco Contini
-Structures: Thomas Schrentewein
-Electrical installations: Giampaolo Vecchi
-Mechanical plants: Massimo Bocchi
Construction period: 2009-2012
Total built area:
-Lot size of School Complex: 19,137 m²
-Primary school: 3,765 m²
Awards:
-First Prize ANCI Environmental and Social Sustainability for the Municipality. Energy efficiency and innovation in construction. Best implementation for energy efficiency in non-residential municipal buildings)
-School ecosystem - XVIII Legambiente report on the quality of school buildings, structures and services - Rome, 17 October 2017: 10 innovative and sustainable school buildings.
General contractor:
A.T.I. Coverall s.r.l e Satrini Elvi, Perugia
Suppliers:
-Main materials: wood, steel, glass

DANIEL VALLE ARCHITECTS
Classroom renovation at the German Foreign School in Seoul
Project Team: Daniel Valle, Jiwon Hur, Sunmin Lee, Irene R Vara, Iago Blanco
Construction period:
June 2016-September 2016
Total built area: 150 m²
General contractor: EAN construction
Consultants: Ju-Sung Engineering, Hangil Engineering

Maebong Daycare Center
Project Team: Daniel Valle, Irene R Vara, Sunmin Lee, Yejun Pee, Sojeong Noh, Javier Chan Porras, Iago Blanco
Construction period:
September 2017-July 2018
Total built area: 800.34 m²
Consultants: Ju-Sung Engineering, Hangil Engineering, Jinwon Structure
Local architect: Zign Partnership

DIETRICH | UNTERTRIFALLER ARCHITEKTEN
Mobile Kindergarten Innsbruck
Project Team: Peter Nussbaumer, Christopher Braun
Construction period: 2018
Total built area: 715 m²
General contractor: Kaufmann Bausysteme, Reuthe
Consultants:
-Statics: Merz Kley Partner, Dornbirn
-Building physics, building services: E-Plus, Egg
-Electrical: Meusburger, Bezau

Unterdorf Elementary School Höchst
Project Team: Peter Nussbaumer, Katharina Reiner
Construction period: 2015-2017
Total built area: 2,530 m²
Awards:
-The Plan Award 2018; Big See Wood Design Award 2018;
-Wood, Design & Building Award 2017 (Canadian Wood Council)
Suppliers:
-Timber construction & façade: Fussenegger Holzbau, Dornbirn
Consultants:
-Site management: gbd, Dornbirn
-Structural engineering timber: Merz Kley Partner, Dornbirn
-Structural engineering concrete: Gehrer, Höchst
-HAVCR: e-plus, Egg
-Electronics: Hecht, Rankweil
-Building physics: Weithas, Lauterach
-Ecology: Spektrum, Dornbirn
-Landscape: Heinrich, Winterthur

Edlach Elementary School Dornbirn
Project Team: Peter Nussbaumer, Anna Norrgard, Christopher Braun
Construction period: 2015-2016
Total built area: 3,770 m²
Award: 2017 National Award for Architecture and Sustainability
Suppliers:
Timber construction & façade:
Fussenegger Holzbau, Dornbirn
Consultants:
Site management: Flatschacher, Hohenems
-Structure: PN Statik Peter Nagy, Dornbirn
-HAVCR: Cukrowicz, Lauterach
-Electronics: Meusburger, Bezau
-Geotechnics: 3P Geotechnik, Bregenz
-Building physics: Weithas, Lauterach
-Ecology: Spektrum, Dornbirn
-Fire protection: K&M Brandschutztechnik, Lochau

EDUARD BALCELLS ARCHITECTURE +URBANISM+LANDSCAPE, IGNASI RIUS, DANIEL TIGGES
El Til·ler School
Project Team: Eduard Balcells, Ignasi Rius, Daniel Tigges, Manuel Romero, Elisabeth Terrisse
Construction period:
October 2017-August 2018
Total built area: 950 m²
Awards:
-Finalist Arquitectura Plus Awards, Selected FAD Prize, Selected
-CAATEB-Catalunya Construcció Awards
General contractor: Maheco
Suppliers: Macusa (wooden façades), Massachs, Hormipresa, Carimbisa, FINSA, Roca, Ducasa, Suberolita

FÖLDES ARCHITECTS
Nursery in Nagykovácsi
Project Team:
Principal architect: László Földes
Architect: Péter Sónicz
Assistants: Dániel Laczó
Johanna Csűri, Katalin Fábry
Construction period: 2015
Total built area: 755 m² btto
Award: Architects Media Price, selected among 10 finalist
Suppliers: European Union
Consultants:
-Structure: Zoltán V.Nagy
-Mechanical: Attila Lucz
-Electric: Judit Balázs
-Garden: Tamás Sándor
-Rehabilitation: Éva Jávor

HIBINOSEKKEI + YOUJI NO SHIRO + KIDS DESIGN LABO
YM Nursery
Architects: Taku Hibino, Shota Suzuki
Project Team: HIBINOSEKKEI + Youji no Shiro + Youji no Shiro
Construction period: Jan. 2017-Feb. 2018
Total built area: total floor area: 1,146 m²
building area: 1,112 m²
Awards:
-2019 Good Design Award
-World Architecture Festival 2019
-13th -KIDS DESIGN AWARD
-A'Design -Award&Competion Iron Award
-2018 The IAI Best Humanistic Care Award
-2018 China Good Design Award
General contractor: HH Social Welfare Corporation
Furniture: KIDS DESIGN LABO

HN Nursery
Architects: Taku Hibino, Kyoko Koshimizu
Project Team: HIBINOSEKKEI + Youji no Shiro + KIDS DESIGN LABO
Construction period: March-December 2017
Total built area:
floor area: 573 m², construction area: 588 m²
Awards:
-The IAI Special Jury Award
-The International Design Media Award
-4th Good Design Award
-12th Kids Design Award
-A+AWARD 2019
General contractor:
UF Social Welfare Corporation
Suppliers: Furniture: KIDS DESIGN LABO

KM Kindergarten and Nursery
Architects: Taku Hibino, Mari Sasaki
Project Team: HIBINOSEKKEI + Youji no Shiro
Construction period:
October 2015-June 2016
Total built area:
surface area: 1,244 m², building area: 799 m²
Awards: 2017 China Good Design Award
-The American Architecture Prize 2017 Good Design Award
-A+AWARD 2017
General contractor: Social Welfare Corporation JF

ISON ARCHITECTS
JEAN SON
Iddeul Kindergarten
Project Team: Seok-Hoon Jung
Construction period: 2014-2015
Total built area: 2,939.79 m²
Awards: KIRA (Korean Institute of Architects) Awards. Best seven of the year 2015
General contractor:
Dasan Construction Group
Suppliers: EAGON Holdings Co Ltd, Union Altech, YOO DUCK Environment, Je-il Geotech, Sejin E&A
Consultants: CNS Engineering, Opus Pearl, Naeill Solution.

KLAB ARCHITECTURE
Public Nursery in Glyfada, Athens
Principal architect:
Konstantinos Labrinopoulos
Project architect: Veronika Vasileiou
Project team: Konstantinos Labrinopoulos, Veronika Vasileiou,Petra Xynidou (intern), Myrto Lantza (intern) Electra Pangalou (intern) Kelly Kaga
Construction period: 2015-2016
Total built area: 400 m²
Award: Nomination for EUMIES Award 2019, Domes 2019
General contractor: Kafestidis
Consultants: Future Constructions

LUCA PERALTA
PERALTA DESIGN & CONSULTING
Kindergarden school
Sandro Pertini
Lead Architect:
Luca Peralta (dott. ing., M.Arch.AA, ARB)
Architecture, Interiors
and Landscape Architecture:
PERALTA - design & consulting, Rome (IT)
Building Engineering:
3TI Progetti Italia, Rome (IT)
MEP and Structure: 3TI Progetti Italia, Rome
PERALTA's Interior and Landscape Design team: M.Lattanzio, D. Nardella, N. Hasanefendic, S. Mezzetti, R. Percacciuolo, S. Costa, G. Vitiello.
PERALTA's Competition and Detail Design team: Gerbino, T. Ricciardi, J. Atoche, M. Colletta, R. Fellenbaum, T. Benedict, L. Nefasto, M. Lattanzio.
PERALTA's Consultants: ing. G.Ricchitelli (site manager), R.Sini and R.Capecci (Landscape), G. Tittobello and E.Marinucci (Renewable energy), A.Denapoli (Geology), L. Cosmai (Fire Safety), A.Simone (Site Survey).
General Contractor: Mannelli Impresa SRL, Monopoli (IT)
Awards:
-Nominated Mies van der Rohe Award 2019, Barcelona (SP)
-Winner BIG SEE Architecture Award 2019, Ljubljana (SI)
-Winner special prize INTERARCH 2018, Sofia (BG)
-Winner Qualità Italia, Rome (IT)

NAF ARCHITECT & DESIGN
Akio NAKASA
Seiwa Kindergarten
Architects: Akio NAKASA(Principal Architect), Makiko SUDA
Location: Machida-City, Tokyo
Construction period: March 2018-July 2019
Total built area: 997.70 m²
General contractor: Minowa Construction
Producer: Yuzen SAITO

small pond
Architects: Akio NAKASA(Principal Architect), Teppei AMANO
Construction period: May 2018-January 2019
Total built area: 747.86 m²
Awards: Good Design Award 2019
General contractor: Shin
Producer: Koryo SAITO

NAYA ARCHITECTS
MANABU NAYA, ARATA NAYA
Showa Early Childhood Education and Care Center, Showa Woman's University
Project Team: Showa Woman's University / Yasushi Moribe (structural engineer) Setsubikeikaku Co.,Ltd (technical engineer) Yoko Ando Design (curtain design) inter. office, AWATSUJI design (signage design) Izumi Okayasu Lighting Design (lighting design)
Taiji Fujimori Atelier (furniture design)
Location: Setagaya-ku,Tokyo, JAPAN
Construction period: August 2015
Total built area: 1,710.96 m²
Awards: 2017 Special Prize, Association for Children's Environment Award
General Contractor: Tokyu Construction

OPUS ARCHITEKTEN BDA / PROF. ANKE MENSING, ANDREAS SEDLER
New Building +e Kita (plus-energy- /solar-building) Marburg
Project Team: Kristin Egermann, Uwe Kühn, Jessica Mazur, Tina Ritter
Construction period: 2013-2015
Total built area: 1,100 m²
Awards:
-2015: BUILD Architecture Award
-2016: ICONIC AWARDS 2016 des Rates für Formgebung – German Design: Council Winner – Kategorie Architecture
-2017: DAM Preis für Architektur in Deutschland – Aufnahme in Architekturführer Deutschland
-Heinze Architekten AWARD 2017 – Winner „Nichtwohnbau"
-2018: Simon-Louis-du-Ry-Plakette Nominations:
-2015: MaterialPREIS 2015, nomination
-2016: DGNB Preis „Nachhaltiges Bauen", one of three finalists
Suppliers:
- Flooring: forbo flooring systems, DisbonCaparol
-Terrace covering: BSW
-Wall coating (inside): Caparol, Disbon Caparol
-Façade: Schüco
-Solar panels: ertex solar
-Sunscreen: Warema, MHZ
-Loose furniture: brunner
-Sanitary ware: Keramag, Duravit, Voit & Partner
-Amatures: Grohe
-Electrical installations: Busch-Jaeger
-Fittings: FSB
Consultants:
-Energy concept: ee concept / Sebastian Fiedler, Martin Zeumer
-Structural engineering: osd – office for structural design / Prof. Klaus Fäth, Frank Brückner
-Mechanical, Electrical, Plumbing (MEP): Plan4Life – Ingenierbüro TGA / Thomas Helbing, Michael Knauer
-Electrical engineering: Schaub & Kühn – Ingebieurbüro Elektrotechnik / Norbert Kühn
-Landscape planner: Köhler Landschaftsarchitekten / Günther Köhler, Markus Papenbrock

PIERRE-ALAIN DUPRAZ
ARCHITECTE ETS FAS
Crèche de Saint-Jean
Principal architect: Lionel Spicher
Collaborateurs: Jürg Hodel, Fernando Lopes, Emmanuel Périnet-Marquet
Construction period: 2004-2006
Total built area: 1,207.69 m²

Ecole enfantine et UAPE
Principal architect: Nicolas Chong, Frederico Vieira
Collaborateurs: Julian Behrens, Maxime Beljansky, Kira Graf, Paolo Marchiori, Pierre Mencacci
Construction period: 2013-2015
Total built area: 1,665.2 m²
Awards: Best Architects 17 Nominations: Arc Award 2016 et Die Besten 2015

SOA ARCHITEKTI
Elementary School Amos for Psáry and Dolní Jircany
Project Team:
Lead architects: Ondřej Píhrt, Štefan Šulek, Ondřej Laciga
Collaborators: Irena Vojtová, Pavel Směták, Tereza Březovská
Construction period:
April 2018-August 2019
Total built area: 9,308 m²
Awards:
Energy-efficient House Award Czech Republic 2019 – jury award winner (category New Passive Buildings)
General contractor: PKS stavby
Interior supplier: DVD Jaroměřice nad Rokytnou
Consultants:
-Construction engineer: Projekt Centrum NOVA
-Energy consultant: Porsenna
-Graphic designer: Barbora Zachovalová
-Gastro engineer: InGastro
Client: Town Psáry

SULKIN ASKENAZI
NIA School Bosques
Project Team:
Jack Sulkin, Gabriel Askenazi, Fernanda Barrera, Ramon Aguilar, Aidee Lorenzo
Construction period: March-November 2019
Total built area: 605 m²
General contractor: Sulkin Askenazi
Suppliers: Tega, Humbertony, ARCA, Crivial, IERI, Hnos. Rodriguez, Visata Tecnología, GTEC, Apolinar Flores, Urban Deco, Maderas Finas, Intercera-mic, Alfombras y Pisos D.F., Marmex, Helvex, American Standard, Mool, Idelika, Formacryl.
Consultants: Arcilla Taller, GTEC.

NIA School Pirules
Project Team: Jack Sulkin, Gabriel Askenazi, Fernanda Barrera, Ramon Aguilar, Aidee Lorenzo
Construction period: under construction
Suppliers: Tega, Humbertony, ARCA, Crivial, IERI, Hnos. Rodriguez, Visata Tecnología, GTEC, Apolinar Flores, Urban Deco, Maderas Finas, Interceramic, Alfombras y Pisos D.F., Marmex, Helvex, American Standard, Mool, Idelika, Formacryl.
Consultants: Cristina Luna

SYNTAX ARCHITECTURE
Hugging the garden
Project Team: DI Martina Barth Sedelmayer, DI Michael Barth, DI Alexander Spauwen
Construction period: 2010
Total built area: 1,600 m²
Awards: wood construction award
General contractor: carpenter: Fahrenberger GmbH, builder: Domweber
Consultants: woschitz group

TALLER VIGA MAESTRA
Escuela Rural Cantino
Project Team: Jaime Gatica Martínez / Taller Viga Maestra
Construction period: 2019-2020
Total built area: 762,10 m²
General contractor: Constructora Pizarro

Jardin Infantil Las Abejitas
Project Team: Jaime Gatica Martínez / Taller Viga Maestra – Álvaro Sanzana Medina /JUNJI
Construction period: 2018-2019
Total built area: 1,313 m²
General contractor: Constructora Sergio Artigas

TEKHNÊ ARCHITECTES ET URBANISTES
Requalification du groupe scolaire Marcellin Berthelot
Project Team: TEKHNE, architecture
-ARBORESCENCE, Design office of the wood structure
–DPI, Design office of the concrete structure
-ASTRIUS, Fluid Design Office
–EEGENIE, QE Design Office
-ACI, Kitchen design office
-CSD INGENIEURS, Design office for soil remediation
-DENIZOU, economist
Construction period: 2017
Total built area (useful surface):
-Extension: 1,662 m²
-Rehabilitation existant: 1,631 m²
Awards:
-1er Prix Régional de la Construction Bois 2019
General contractor: Terrassement SOTERLY

Groupe scolaire maternelle et primaire Simone Veil
Project Team: TEKHNE, architecture
–DPI, Bureau d'études structure béton
-SYLVA CON-SEIL, Bureau d'études structure bois
–ASTRIUS, Bureau d'études fluides
–TRIBU, Bureau d'études Qualité environnementale
-ACI, Bureau d'études cuisine
-CSD INGENIEURS, Bureau d'études dépollution sol
-DENIZOU, economist
Construction period: 2014
Total built area: useful surface 1,783 m²
Awards:
-1st Prix International Green Building award 2015

UARCHITECTS
MISAK TERZIBASIYAN
IKC de Geluksvogel
Project Team:
Misak Terzibasiyan (principal architect)
Construction period: 2015-2017
Total built area: 2,100 m²
Awards:
-Shortlist nomination for the WAF 2017 category school
-Nomination for Reynaers prijs 2017
-Winner of de Victor de Stuersprijs 2017 (Maastricht)
-Winner of American Architecture Prize 2017 in the category education
-Gold Winner of Muse Design Award 2019
-Second Award of the Architecture & Design Award 2019
-Shortlist mention of UK Brick award 2019
General contractor: BMV, Veldhoven
Suppliers: Accoya wood, bricks of façade Beek, MBI, Bolidt
Consultants: ZRi advies, K+ adviesgroep, Castermans Engineers
Client: Mosalira, Maastricht

School 't Hofke
Project Team:
Misak Terzibasiyan (principal architect)
Construction period: 2012-2014
Total built area: 3,300 m²
Awards:
-Shortlist nomination for the WAF 2014 category education and Wood Prize in Singapore.
-Award at IDEA TOPS 2014 in the category education with in Shenzhen (China)
-IDA Design Award: Gold in the Architecture category institutional in Los Angeles (USA)
-Winner of De Dirk Roosenburg prize 2015
-American Architecture Prize, Bronze in the category education 2019
-Rose Gold Winner of Muse Design Award 2019
General contractor: Nieuwenhuizen Daandels Bouw, Uden
Suppliers: Plato wood and bricks of Wienerberger
Consultants:
Structural design: Van de Laar, Eindhoven
HVAC consult: Volantis
Client: SKPO

School de Brug
Architects: UArchitects in cooperation with Lens o ass architecten
Project Team: Misak Terzibasiyan (principal architect)
Construction period: 2016-2019
Total built area: 2,100 m²
Awards:
-2011: 1st Prize, Arch School Awards, School 'de Brug' in Bocholt (Belgium).
General contractor: Democo
Suppliers:
Accoya wood, bricks of façade Beek
Consultants:
-Structural Engineering: Arcadis
-Landscape: UArchitects
-HVAC Consultants: Arcadis
Client: AG Real Estate Co-Production in Development NV
Director of the school de Brug:
Anne-Mie Michielsen

v-architekten
Berkersheimer Schule
Project Team: Tim Denninger, Jan Hertel, Markus Kilian, Diana Reichle, Michael Scholz mit Peter Knörr (Projektleiter), Sebastian Arzet, Lisa Görke, Nathalie Gozdziak, Preslav Krastev, Kasia Osiecka, Charlotte Wermuth
Construction period: 2014-2019
Total built area: 5,400 m²
General contractor: v-architekten
Suppliers: gba – Gottstein Blumenstein Architekten BDA (Bauleitung), Pirlet & Partner Ingenieurgesellschaft mbH (Tragwerksplanung), Alhäuser + König Ingenieurbüro GmbH (Haustechnik), knp.bauphysik GmbH (Brandphysik), Götte Landschaftsarchitekten (Freianlagenplanung)

Blaue Kita Monheim
Project Team: Tim Denninger, Jan Hertel, Markus Kilian, Diana Reichle, Michael Scholz mit Marc Knechtges
Construction period: 2009-2011
Total built area: 877 m²
Award: best architects 2015 Award, BDA Architekturpreis Bergisch-Land (Anerkennung)
General contractor: v-architekten
Suppliers: Stefan Nix-Pauleit (Bauleitung), GrünArt Landschaftsarchitekt (Freianlagenplanung), SGB Spiessbach-Gerhards-Berg (Tragwerksplanung), HPI Himmen (Haustechnik), Sachverständigenbüro Kaufmann (Brandschutz)

VMDO ARCHITECTS
Bluestone Elementary School
Project Team:
Prime Architect: VMDO Architects
Mechanical, Electrical, Plumbing
Engineering: CMTA Engineers
Structural Engineering: Fox & Associates
Civil Engineering: Gay & Neel
Landscape Architecture: JJM Design
Environmental Graphics & Wayfinding: Iconograph
Foodservice Design:
Foodservice Consultants Studio
Geotechnical Engineers:
Froehling & Robertson
Construction period:
March 2016-August 2017
Total built area: 103,703 GSF
Awards:
-2019 Livable Buildings Award Winner, University of California, Berkeley's Center for the Built Environment
-2019 Project of Distinction, Association for Learning Environments
-2019 2nd Place Academic Project, Virginia Energy Efficiency Leadership Awards
-2018 Platinum Design Award, Virginia School Boards Association
-2018 Best Design Award, Virginia Association for Learning Environments
-2018 Outstanding Project, Learning By Design
General contractor: Nielsen Builders

Buckingham County Primary and Elementary Schools at the Carter G. Woodson Education Complex
Project Team:
-Prime Architect: VMDO Architects
-Mechanical, Electrical, and Plumbing Engineering: 2rw Consultants, Inc.
-Structural Engineer: Fox & Associates
-Civil Engineer and Landscape Architect: Waterstreet Studio
-Foodservice Design: EIS, Inc.
-Environmental Graphics & Wayfinding: Iconograph
Construction period:
April 2011-August 2012
Total built area: 135,000 GSF
Awards:
-2018 Tucker Design Award, Natural Stone Institute
-2017 James D. MacConnell Award Finalist, Association for Learning Environments
-2014 Education Facility Design Excellence Award, AIA Committee on Architecture for Education (CAE)
-2014 Education Sector - Design Is... Award, Shaw Contract Group
-2014 Excellence Award (Inaugural Award) Center for Active Design
-2014 Honor Award for Design Excellence In Architecture, AIA Central Virginia
-2014 Innovation Gold Award, Virginia Chapter of the Association for Learning Environments
-2014 Juror's Choice For Outstanding Project of the Year, Greater Virginia Green Building Council
-2013 Award For Excellence in Architecture, AIA Virginia
-2013 Outstanding Project, Learning By Design
-2013 Project Of Distinction / Lee J. Brockway Award, Association for Learning Environments
-2012 Prize for Design Research + Scholarship, AIA Virginia
-2012 Gold Design Award and People's Choice Award, Virginia School Boards Association
-2012 3rd Place in Childhood Obesity Challenge, American Journal of Preventative Medicine
General contractor: Blair Construction

Discovery Elementary School
Project Team:
-Prime Architect: VMDO Architects
-Mechanical, Lighting, Net-Zero Energy Design: CMTA Consulting Engineers
-Power, Plumbing, Fire Protection Engineer: 2rw Consultants, Inc.
-Structural Engineer: Fox & Associates
-Civil Engineer: Bowman Consulting Group
-Foodservice Design: EIS, Inc.
-Environmental Graphics & Wayfinding: Iconograph
-Landscape Architect: Oculus
-Traffic: Toole Design Group
-Cost Estimating: Downey & Scott
-Construction Manager: Heery
-Construction Specifications: SpecGuy
Construction period: March 2014-August 2015
Total built area: 98,000 GSF
Awards:
-2019 Inaugural Net Zero Award, USGBC National Capital Region
-2019 Community Champion Award, USGBC Virginia
-2019 ICF Builder Awards First Place, ICF Builder Magazine
-2018 First Place Academic Project, Virginia Energy Efficiency Leadership Awards
-2018 First Place Technology Award, ASHRAE Region VII
-2017 AIA COTE Top Ten Award Winner, American Institute of Architect's Committee on the Environment (COTE)
-2017 Green Ribbon School, U.S. Department of Education
-2017 Presidential Citation for Sustainability, AIA|DC
-2017 Platinum Design Award, Virginia School Boards Association
-2017 Special Jury Recognition Award, Virginia Chapter of the Association for Learning Environments
-2016 Project of Distinction, Association for Learning Environments
-2016 Honor Award, AIA Central Virginia
Fall 2016 Honorable Mention, Learning By Design
-2015 Award of Excellence, Design Arlington Awards
General contractor: SIGAL Construction